THE
INNER WORLD
OF
CHILDHOOD—

a cornerstone study of child behavior in
a modern, new edition. Here Dr. Wickes,
in her barrier-breaking investigation of
the psychology of children, follows up on
some of the patients she studied so inti-
mately forty years ago.

*"Sensitive ... highly profitable ...
she is mindful that she is informing
us about a human being, and not an
object for scientific dissection."*

Library Journal

*"Her penetrating studies of children have opened
up a new world of understanding. To her, the
child is a 'person' possessing innately the right to
be 'individual' and to experience the world about
him in the light of his own subjective experience ... the child psychologist needs to have at
least in some measure Frances Wickes' sensi-
tivity, wisdom, and love."*

Dr. M. Esther Harding,
Analytical Psychology Club of New York

*"She offers concisely a valuable key to
understanding children and through this
understanding a greater appreciation of
life itself."*

Houston Chronicle

Frances G. Wickes

THE INNER WORLD
OF
CHILDHOOD
A Study in Analytical Psychology

INTRODUCTION BY

Carl G. Jung

A SIGNET BOOK

PUBLISHED BY THE NEW AMERICAN LIBRARY

To the memory of my son
ELIPHALET WICKES
whose flamelike spirit
made clear many things

Revised Edition
Library of Congress Catalog Card Number: 65-27218

This is an authorized reprint of a hardcover edition published
by Appleton-Century, Affiliate of Meredith Press.

SIGNET TRADEMARK REG. U.S. PAT. OFF. AND FOREIGN COUNTRIES
REGISTERED TRADEMARK—MARCA REGISTRADA
HECHO EN CHICAGO, U.S.A.

SIGNET BOOKS are published by
The New American Library, Inc.,
1301 Avenue of the Americas, New York, New York 10019

FIRST PRINTING, JUNE, 1968

PRINTED IN THE UNITED STATES OF AMERICA

PREFACE

In the early years of my studies with children, I was deeply impressed with the fact that in their adjustments, or their failures to adjust, cause and effect seemed so surprisingly disproportionate. Acts extremely disconcerting to the adult suddenly intruded. A question as to motive frequently brought the reply: "I don't know why I did it." If an answer was insisted upon, something so fanciful was produced that the child might be accused of lying.

Often an interview which began with a sympathetic desire to help ended in baffled anger, politely termed righteous indignation, on the part of the adult, and in complete bewilderment, designated obstinacy, on the part of the child.

But did the child know why? Did we with our more adult understanding always know our own motives? I for one was convinced that I did not. I frequently had a suspicion that the adult who was so zealously pursuing the child's inner motive did not understand her own anger at the child's bewilderment. Was she genuinely distressed at the child's situation or emotionally disturbed because she had been made to feel powerless and inadequate? Did she resent being confronted with those power desires within herself which she was unable to control in a baffling situation? Honest answers to these doubts made one feel that so-called adulthood might only provide immunity to the type of question which could always be asked a child, but did not guarantee an understanding of the motives that ruled conduct.

Other questions forced themselves upon me. Why was a

child, usually well poised, suddenly deprived of the power of speech in certain recitations? It was evident that the child derived no more enjoyment from the situation than did the teacher. Why should a child do well one year and badly the next? The innate mentality of the child had not varied so suddenly, nor could the entire burden be laid upon the instructor, for all children were not so affected. What had become of that intelligence and feeling which a year before had shown itself in quick mental grasp and delightful personal response? Where had that force gone, with what was it busying itself? It must be pursuing some activity apart from the situation at hand.

Were the conflicting reports of the school and the home in the case of certain children entirely due to prejudice or over-indulgent love on the part of parent or teacher? In many cases it seemed as if there must be a satisfactory explanation if one could only penetrate deep enough; for when an apparently honest teacher and an equally honest parent were widely divergent in their estimate of a child, one could not dismiss this variance as mere prejudice on either side. The fact that I, a parent, was often at loggerheads with myself as an educator, and also with myself as an individual, forbade me to dismiss these questions as unimportant. Then this unwelcome thought continually intruded: we are teaching children, and none of us seem to have a concept of what a child really is.

It was while I was engrossed in this multitude of questions that my first intuitive perceptions of unconscious motivations came to me. The revelations of the unconscious which were being used in the treatment of adults were as yet little applied in the educational field or in the attempt to understand ill-adapted children; I did not doubt, however, that here lay the answers to many of the questions that had perplexed me.

Then the children themselves began to help me. It was as though they sensed the love that lay back of my sympathy, bewildered as it often was. Shyly, very shyly, they began to open the doors that led to their inner world. They let me step a little way into that land of their own unconscious where fears and unreasoned joyousness, fantasies and intuition, moved and spoke. It was a surprising world, but gradually out of the multiplicity of apparently contradictory elements certain continuities and purposes began to emerge.

As I went farther, two things stood out clearly in this exploration of the kingdom of the unconscious. The first was that the most important element of early normal development was a sense of security in the fundamental relationships of life. The parents' love, understanding, courage, and honesty in facing the problems of life not only were the foundation of the patterns of the later emotional life, but also furnished the environment in which the child could grow normally with his psychic life firmly rooted in the security of wise and understanding love. This led back from the problem of the child to the problem of the parent and often necessitated an analysis of the adult most closely connected with the child's emotional life. Such an analysis could not be undertaken by anyone unless he had himself been analyzed and also possessed a theoretical and technical knowledge of the workings of the unconscious and an understanding that arose from having faced these same problems of love or power within his psyche.

The second was the realization of the thread of purpose that ran through all these manifestations of the unconscious. Stepping into this inner world I found it peopled by fanciful, grotesque, even apparently meaningless characters who were playing their part in the child's drama of self-creation. Often he did not himself know the purpose for which they had been called into being.

The imaginary playmates, who took so important a place for a time and then silently vanished, were not mere amusing bits of childish imagination but were distinctly related to the problem of life with which the child was at that time confronted. They were used to integrate warring elements, to eliminate the undesirable, to furnish a pattern, or to compensate for a failure and to provide an excuse for retreat. Through an understanding of them one could obtain an insight, not only into the particular problem, but also into the temperamental difficulties of the whole psychology of the evolving personality.

There were other denizens of this land. Fears, hates, deceits, sudden masterful emotions walked about here. Many of them were masked figures whose faces could not easily be seen. It was only through love, through sympathy, through understanding, that these shy creatures could be induced to take off their masks and show themselves in their real form. Angers now might reveal themselves as fears, deceit and even theft as creatures motivated by desire to obtain knowledge or love which had been wrongfully withheld; fears, apparently meaningless and disproportionate, became related to a hidden sense of insecurity, a forgotten experience, or could be followed far back to their origin in the collective unconscious.

It is these masked figures who are the real subjects of discussion in the following pages. They appear in dream, in fear, in fantasy, in antisocial rebellions, always in close relation to the special child in whose life drama they find their existence. They also mask potentials that must become realities if the child is to live freely and creatively, as well as with necessary acceptance of his need to adapt to his social environment. A consideration of the importance of the unconscious motive brings the realization that we must take with us two things if we would enter into the inner world of childhood: love, and an understanding which includes both intuitive perception and deep technical knowledge of those forces which rule our conscious and unconscious life. But it is from the children themselves that we learn, and it is from their gifts to us that we grow in understanding.

More than forty years have passed since these children entrusted me with the material out of which this book grew. Confronted, in this my ninetieth year, with the request for a new edition, my somewhat battered and recalcitrant ego asks the question: "Why?" As though in answer, the words of a six-year-old boy flash upon the screen of memory: "I should think every woman would want to live to be a grandmother. Then she would know how it all turned out. And the things she told about would be *real*." And she could bear witness to the things that were true and went on and on into life.

Surely, as years go, I have lived long enough to be, not only a grandmother, but also a great-grandmother: long enough to know that I do not know: long enough to see that life and death are not interested in the finished product that has "turned out" this way or that way; but are concerned with the eternal process of being and becoming; the process of growth, transition, regression, transformation: a process where the unexpected is forever breaking through the pattern of the seemingly established, and at every turn of the river of life new vistas may be opened, enabling the soul to glimpse that country where ultimate mysteries, unknown and unknowable, abide.

We know that we do not know. Yet with the passing of long, long years, if we have really lived and not just gone through the accepted motions of living, we have learned to distinguish, with clearer vision, between those experiences which are transitory and those that are eternal and lead into greater understanding of the timeless realities of the soul. And we reverently discover that both these kinds of experience are necessary; for if the temporary is not met at the place where it first challenges us, it will return and block our pathway on our journey toward the timeless.

Experiences of timeless realities may come to a very young child. Such experiences are recorded in the chapter on imaginary companions and in the discussion of children's dreams. As the child grows older, problems of the outer world press upon him. His ego must grow to meet the demands of greater consciousness and numinous experience may appear to be forgotten by the ego, but it is remembered by the self—that sage who from the beginning lives in the psyche of the child and speaks the defining word in times of peril. Then in the long journey on the spiral of life's pathway, the child, now become the man, may find himself confronted, on this new level, with the unsolved problem that he felt he had left behind in that remote country called childhood. As long as it is unsolved, it may reappear at any turn of the spiral and confront him with its demand. It is then that the long forgotten but still numinous experience comes to the aid of the perplexed traveler and shows him what he must now do if he would be free to continue on his way. Thus the self gives testimony to the Great Realities of the Soul.

And we who are old may, through keeping in touch with these children and thus knowing the development of the inner experience, be able to add our testimony to these histories of spiritual growth. I know that Twinkle and Pitch Black Dark still companion the child now become the man. I know that the dream of good and evil that came to the three-year-old child still works out its miracle of faith in an old, old woman. And in seeing how it all is *not* "worked out" but is continuing in the lives, not only of the children themselves but in the lives of their children, we can add our testimony to the truth that is in every human life and bear witness to our faith in life itself. This faith is communicable, and it is through our lives that we communicate it.

Therefore I am grateful for this request for a new edition, and hope that any material I may add will also be a testimony to the spirit of life that moved in Jung and through him into the life stream of so many people.

The present edition includes the introduction that Dr. Jung wrote for the German translation which he really fathered by choosing both translator and publisher.*

* *Analyse der Kinderseele*, Julius Hoffman Verlag, Stuttgart, 1931.

This new and enlarged introduction, he said, was not only a birthday present to me, but was also a word of thanks in acknowledgment of the material that he had used in his London lectures.* But it is I who owe thanks to him; for any "bread cast upon the waters" of the vast sea of his wisdom came back to me not only generously buttered by his comments but also spread thick with the jam of his penetrating intuition.

Jung had no anima involvement, however remote, with the White Queen of *Alice in Wonderland* fame. His return gift was not a stingy "jam yesterday and jam tomorrow, but never jam today." His jam pot of stored-up wisdom was always on his cupboard shelf, and you were free to help yourself to all that you could digest. This new edition has made liberal use of this honeyed jam of his intuitive perceptions, his wisdom and his love of life.

I am also including in this edition a paper that I wrote for the book which was presented to him on his eightieth birthday, "Three Illustrations of the Power of the Projected Image." He spoke of this chapter with warm appreciation, and was especially interested in the synchronistic happening which was the crux of the experience in the case of the youth three thousand miles away who received the message at the moment it was uttered.

F. G. W.

* Jung: *Collected Works,* vol. 17, Bollingen Series 20, New York, 1953–56.

ACKNOWLEDGMENTS

I wish to acknowledge my great indebtedness to Dr. Jung for the inspiration and illuminations which made possible this book in its present form.

I am grateful also to Margaret and her twin Anna, and to the outcast Daphy of the Kiki House (see Chapter 8, "Imaginary Companions"), for it was Margaret who first introduced me to Dr. Jung. A doctor who was interested in the story of Margaret and her companions was studying with Dr. Jung in the winter of 1922. He asked me to write him about Margaret's progress. In a letter containing a chapter of her history I wrote out of my own ignorance, "I do not know that I envy you your work with Dr. Jung. We have just had a visiting analyst at St. Agatha. He 'raised to full consciousness' the sexual and homosexual fantasies of a child of fourteen. The child, reared in a Puritanical household, was so filled with self-horror that she jumped out of the window and killed herself."

The doctor took the entire letter to Dr. Jung, who commented, "when you answer that letter, tell her that even if she does not want to meet me I want to meet her, for she is intuitively following with children the same pathway I followed long years ago with adults. Tell her to bring her case histories along." Needless to say, the winter of 1923 found me in Zurich, and my hours with Dr. Jung opened the door to a new understanding of life. This understanding, reinforced and reillumined by many subsequent trips to Zurich, I hope is still growing in this my ninetieth year, and for this I am increasingly grateful to Dr. Carl Gustav Jung.

CONTENTS

INTRODUCTION *

What this book provides is not theory, but experience. That is just what gives it its special value for anyone really interested in child psychology. We cannot fully understand the psychology of the child or that of the adult if we regard it as the subjective concern of the individual alone, for almost more important than this is his relation to others. Here, at all events, we can begin with the most easily accessible and, practically speaking, the most important part of the psychic life of the child. Children are so deeply involved in the psychological attitude of their parents that it is no wonder that most of the nervous disturbances in childhood can be traced back to a disturbed psychic atmosphere in the home. This book shows, from a series of remarkable examples, just how disastrous the parental influence can be for the child. Probably no father or mother will be able to read these chapters without realizing the devastating truths of this book. *Exempla docent*—example is the best teacher! Once more this proves to be a well-worn yet pitiless truth. It is not a question of good and

---

* The first three and a half paragraphs originally appeared as an introduction to Frances G. Wickes, *The Inner World of Childhood* (New York, 1927). The book was subsequently translated into German as *Analyse der Kinderseele* (Stuttgart, 1931), and for it Professor Jung expanded his introduction to the present dimensions. It is here translated entirely anew.

Mrs. Wickes worked for many years as a psychologist in schools. She collected numerous case studies, and these were later illuminated for her when she encountered Professor Jung's theories, which she was able to confirm and extend. The most important part of her thesis demonstrates how the unconscious of parents can cause many psychic disorders of childhood.

wise counsels, but solely of deeds, of the actual life of the parents. Nor is it a matter of living in accordance with accepted moral values, for the observance of customs and laws can very easily be a cloak for a lie so subtle that our fellow human beings are unable to detect it. It may help us to escape all criticism, we may even be able to deceive ourselves in the belief of our obvious righteousness. But deep down, below the surface of the average man's conscience, he hears a voice whispering, "There is something not right," no matter how much his rightness is supported by public opinion or by the moral code. Certain instances in this book show very clearly that there exists a terrible law which stands beyond man's morality and his ideas of rightness—a law which cannot be cheated.

Besides the problem of environmental influence, the book also gives due weight to psychic factors which have more to do with the irrational values of the child than with his rational psychology. The latter can be made the object of scientific research, while the spiritual values, the qualities of the soul, elude purely intellectual treatment. It is no good having skeptical ideas about this—nature does not care a pin for our ideas. If we have to deal with the human soul we can meet it on its own ground, and we are bound to do so whenever we are confronted with the real and crushing problems of life.

I am glad the author has not shrunk from opening the door to intellectual criticism. Genuine experience has nothing to fear from objections, whether justified or unjustified, for it always holds the stronger position.

Although this book does not pretend to be "scientific," it is scientific in a higher sense, because it gives a true picture of the difficulties that actually occur in the upbringing of children. It merits the serious attention of everybody who has anything to do with children, either by vocation or from duty. But it will also be of interest to those who, neither for reasons of duty nor from educational inclination, wish to know more about the beginnings of human consciousness. Even though many of the views and experiences set forth in this book have nothing fundamentally new to offer to the doctor and psychological educator, the curious reader will now and then come upon cases which are strange and will give pause to his critical understanding—cases and facts which the author, with her essentially practical turn of mind, does not pursue in all their complexities and theoretical implications. What is the thoughtful reader to make, for instance, of the puzzling but unde-

niable fact of the identity of the psychic state of the child
with the unconscious of the parents? One is dimly aware
here of a region full of incalculable possibilities, a hydra-
headed monster of a problem that is as much the concern
of the biologist and psychologist as the philosopher. For
anyone acquainted with the psychology of primitives there
is an obvious connection between this "identity" and
Lévy-Bruhl's idea of "participation mystique." Strange to
say, there are not a few ethnologists who still kick against
this brilliant idea, for which the unfortunate expression
"mystique" may have to shoulder no small part of the
blame. The word "mystical" has indeed become the abode
of all unclean spirits, although it was not meant like that
originally, but has been debased by sordid usage. There is
nothing "mystical" about identity, any more than there is
anything mystical about the metabolism common to
mother and embryo. Identity derives essentially from the
notorious unconsciousness of the small child. Therein lies
the connection with the primitive, for the primitive is as
unconscious as a child. Unconsciousness means non-dif-
ferentiation. There is as yet no clearly differentiated ego,
only events which may belong to me or to another. It is
sufficient that *somebody* should be affected by them. The
extraordinary infectiousness of emotional reactions then
makes it certain that everybody in the vicinity will involun-
tarily be affected. The weaker ego-consciousness is, the less
it matters who is affected, and the less the individual is able
to guard against it. He could only do that if he could say:
you are excited or angry, but I am not, for I am not you.
The child is in exactly the same position in the family: he
is affected to the same degree and in the same way as the
whole group.

For all lovers of theory, the essential fact behind all this
is that the things which have the most powerful effect
upon children do not come from the conscious state of the
parents but from their unconscious background. For the
ethically minded person who may be a father or mother
this presents an almost frightening problem, because the
things we can manipulate more or less, namely consciousness and its contents, are seen to be ineffectual in comparison with these uncontrollable effects in the background, no
matter how hard we may try. One is afflicted with a feeling of extreme moral uncertainty when one takes these unconscious processes with the seriousness they deserve.
How are we to protect our children from ourselves, if conscious will and conscious effort are of no avail? There can

be no doubt that it is of the utmost value for parents to view their children's symptoms in the light of their own problems and conflicts. It is their duty as parents to do so. Their responsibility in this respect carries with it the obligation to do everything in their power not to lead a life that could harm the children. Generally far too little stress is laid upon how important the conduct of the parents is for the child, because it is not words that count, but deeds. Parents should always be conscious of the fact that they themselves are the principal cause of neurosis in their children.

We must not, however, exaggerate the importance of unconscious effects, even though the mind's love of causes finds dangerous satisfaction in doing precisely this. Nor should we exaggerate the importance of causality in general. Certainly causes exist, but the psyche is not a mechanism that reacts of necessity and in a regular way to a specific stimulus. Here as elsewhere in practical psychology we are constantly coming up against the experience that in a family of several children only one of them will react to the unconscious of the parents with a marked degree of identity, while the others show no such reaction. The specific constitution of the individual plays a part here that is practically decisive. For this reason, the biologically trained psychologist seizes upon the fact of organic heredity and is far more inclined to regard the whole mass of genealogical inheritance as the elucidating factor, rather than the psychic causality of the moment. This standpoint, however satisfying it may be by and large, is unfortunately of little relevance to individual cases because it offers no practical clue to psychological treatment. For it also happens to be true that psychic causality exists between parents and children regardless of all the laws of heredity; in fact, the heredity point of view, although undoubtedly justified, diverts the interest of the educator or therapist away from the practical importance of parental influence to some generalized and more or less fatalistic regard for the dead hand of heredity, from the consequences of which there is no escape.

It would be a very grave omission for parents and educators to ignore psychic causality, just as it would be a fatal mistake to attribute all the blame to this factor alone. In every case both factors have a part to play, without the one excluding the other.

What usually has the strongest psychic effect on the child is the life which the parents (and ancestors too, for we are dealing here with the age-old psychological phenomenon of original sin) have not lived. This statement would be rather too perfunctory and superficial if we did not add by way of qualification: that part of their lives which *might have been* lived had not certain somewhat threadbare excuses prevented the parents from doing so. To put it bluntly, it is that part of life which they have always shirked, probably by means of a pious lie. That sows the most virulent germs.

Our author's exhortation to clear-eyed self-knowledge is therefore altogether appropriate. The nature of the case must then decide how much of the blame really rests with the parents. One should never forget that it is a question of "original sin," a sin against life and not a contravention of man-made morality, and that the parents must therefore be viewed as children of the grandparents. The curse of the House of Atreus is no empty phrase.

Nor should one fall into the error of thinking that the form or intensity of the child's reaction necessarily depends upon the peculiar nature of the parent's problems. Very often these act as a catalyst and produce effects which could be better explained by heredity than by psychic causality.

The causal significance of parental problems for the psyche of the child would be seriously misunderstood if they were always interpreted in an exaggeratedly personal way as moral problems. More often we seem to be dealing with some fate-like ethos beyond the reach of our conscious judgment. Such things as proletarian inclinations in the scions of noble families, outbursts of criminality in the offspring of the respectable or overvirtuous, a paralyzing or impassioned laziness in the children of successful businessmen, are not just bits of life that have been left deliberately unlived, but compensations wrought by fate, functions of a natural ethos which casts down the high and mighty and exalts the humble. Against this neither education nor psychotherapy is of any avail. The most they can do, if reasonably applied, is to encourage the child to fulfill the task imposed upon him by the natural ethos. The guilt of the parents is impersonal, and the child should pay for it no less impersonally.

Parental influence only becomes a moral problem in face of conditions which might have been changed by the parents, but were not, either from gross negligence, slothfulness, neurotic anxiety, or soulless conventionality. In this matter a grave responsibility often rests with the parents. And nature has no use for the plea that one "did not know."

Not knowing acts like guilt.

Frances Wickes's book also raises the following problem in the mind of the thoughtful reader:

The psychology of "identity," which precedes ego-consciousness, indicates what the child is by virtue of his parents. But what he is as an individuality distinct from his parents can hardly be explained by the causal relationship to the parents. We ought rather to say that it is not so much the parents as their ancestors—the grandparents and great-grandparents—who are the true progenitors, and that these explain the individuality of the children far more than the immediate and, so to speak, accidental parents. In the same way the true psychic individuality of the child is something new in respect of the parents and cannot be derived from their psyche. It is a combination of collective factors which are only potentially present in the parental psyche, and are sometimes wholly invisible. Not only the child's body, but his soul, too, proceeds from his ancestry, in so far as it is individually distinct from the collective psyche of mankind.

The child's psyche, prior to the stage of ego-consciousness, is very far from being empty and devoid of content. Scarcely has speech developed when, in next to no time, consciousness is present; and this, with its momentary contents and its memories, exercises an intensive check upon the previous collective contents. That such contents exist in the child who has not yet attained to ego-consciousness is a well-attested fact. The most important evidence in this respect is the dreams of three- and four-year-old children, among which there are some so strikingly mythological and so fraught with meaning that one would take them at once for the dreams of grown-ups, did one not know who the dreamer was. They are the last vestiges of a dwindling collective psyche which dreamingly reiterates the perennial contents of the human soul. From this phase there spring many childish fears and dim, unchildlike premonitions which, rediscovered in later phases of life, form the basis of the belief in reincarnation. But from this sphere also spring those flashes of insight and lucidity which give rise to the proverb: Children and fools speak the truth.

Because of its universal distribution the collective psyche, which is still so close to the small child, perceives not only the background of the parents, but, ranging further afield, the depths of good and evil in the human soul.

The unconscious psyche of the child is truly limitless in extent and of incalculable age. Behind the longing to be a child again, or behind the anxiety dreams of children, there is, with all due respect to the parents, more than the joys of the cradle or a bad upbringing.

Primitive peoples often hold the belief that the soul of the child is the incarnation of an ancestral spirit, for which reason it is dangerous to punish children, lest the ancestral spirit be provoked. This belief is only a more concrete formulation of the views I have outlined above.

The infinity of the child's preconscious soul may disappear with it, or it may be preserved. The remnants of the child-soul in the adult are his best and worst qualities; at all events they are the mysterious *spiritus rector* of our weightiest deeds and of our individual destinies, whether we are conscious of it or not. It is they which make kings or pawns of the insignificant figures who move about on the checkerboard of life, turning some poor devil of a casual father into a ferocious tyrant, or a silly goose of an unwilling mother into a goddess of fate. For behind every individual father there stands the primordial image of the Father, and behind the fleeting personal mother the magical figure of the Magna Mater. These archetypes of the collective psyche, whose power is magnified in immortal works of art and in the fiery tenets of religon, are the dominants that rule the preconscious soul of the child and, when projected upon the human parents, lend them a fascination which often assumes monstrous proportions. From that there arises the false aetiology of neurosis which, in Freud, ossified into a system: the Oedipus complex. And that is also why, in the later life of the neurotic, the images of the parents can be criticized, corrected, and reduced to human dimensions, while yet continuing to work like divine agencies. Did the human father really possess this mysterious power, his sons would soon liquidate him or, even better, would refrain from becoming fathers themselves. For what ethical person could possibly bear so gigantic a responsibility? Far better to leave this sovereign power to the gods, with whom it had always rested before man became "enlightened."

Carl G. Jung

1

THE SCOPE AND METHODS
OF ANALYTICAL PSYCHOLOGY

No matter how simply we may attempt to treat the problems of modern analytical psychology, there are technical terms which must be defined, and a background of historical significance which must be explained, if the reader is to grasp the importance of these new discoveries in the interpretation of the forces of life. The more familiar terms have been defined in many places; yet, since they remain somewhat vague in the lay mind, a brief discussion of them is included here in the belief that it will make the rest of the volume more easily comprehended.

The term the *unconscious* has passed into common parlance. No longer is it a nebulous term denoting something evoked in modern black magic; nevertheless to many it still looms as a shadowy and monstrous ghost. Defined quite simply, the unconscious is that substratum in which exist all the contents of the psyche of which we are unaware at any given moment. It contains all the memories that are not in our immediate field of consciousness. That field is continually shifting. Any of these memories (either the objective memories of our outer life or the subjective memories of our inner life) may at any time come to the surface and become conscious; or those things that are now conscious may drop back into the unconscious. Jung puts it thus:

The conscious consists only of those complexes of ideas that are directly associated with the ego. The psychic factors which possess a certain intensity be-

come attached to the ego; all that do not reach the
necessary intensity, or those that have had it and lost
it again, are below the threshold, subliminal, belonging to the sphere of the unconscious. On account of
its indefinite extent the unconscious might be compared to the sea, with the conscious like an island
towering out of its midst. This comparison, however,
must not be pushed too far; for the relation of the
conscious to the unconscious is in many ways essentially different from that of an island to the sea. It is
not in any sense a stable relationship; it is a ceaseless
welling-up, a constant shifting of content. The unconscious, like the conscious, is never at rest, nor ever at
a standstill; it is something living, and it is in a perpetual state of interaction with the conscious. Conscious
content which has lost its intensity, or actuality, sinks
into the unconscious, and this we call forgetting: conversely out of the unconscious, arise new ideas and
tendencies, which, emerging into the conscious, are
known to us as fancies and impulses. The unconscious
is to a certain extent like a matrix, out of which the
conscious grows gradually from small beginnings—
not coming into the world a finished product.

To readers unfamiliar with analytical literature a brief
historical survey may make the concept clearer.

The present-day knowledge of the unconscious is based,
not upon theory, but upon experience with the workings of
its forces. The first understanding of it came through the
study of cases of hysterical amnesia (forgetting). It was
shown that by means of hypnotism the patient was enabled to recall events, experiences, and emotional urges
which were completely lost to conscious memory. These
experiments of the French school were made the basis of
further investigations by Carl G. Jung of Zurich and Sig-
mund Freud in Vienna, who showed that these forces
were at work in the normal psyche as well as in the pathological cases.

While Jung was at work upon association tests, Freud
was exploring the dream life of his patients, making the
revolutionary discovery that the dream contained in symbolic or cartoon form pictures of the unconscious content
which bore close relation to the immediate problem that
was causing the neurotic illness. By a process of free association (talking freely of all the ideas suggested by the
dream figures) various repressed contents were brought

back to consciousness. In this way the patient could be made aware of unrecognized forces which were at work below the level of consciousness, drawing down the normal energy, or perhaps breaking through to the surface in fears or obsessive thoughts.

Freud was primarily concerned with tracing the root of the neurosis back to the instinctive or infantile level. His conception of the unconscious was that it was the storehouse of the infantile and perverted memories, especially the infantile sexual memories, which had been thrust down from the conscious mind by a system of repression. This material was guarded, he maintained, by a censor, who did not permit it to return to consciousness save through symbols. Since one of the greatest repressions of modern life has been the repression of the sexual, it is not surprising that he found so much infantile sexuality in the unconscious. Though in theory he gave a psychic rather than a literal interpretation to sexuality, including in that term love and the creative impulses, yet his analysis was reductive. The creative, artistic, and religious strivings of man became nothing but an attempt to escape from primitive and infantile sexuality.

At this time Jung and Alfred Adler were both students of Freud. Adler was the first to break away from the exclusively sexual interpretation. He came to consider man's struggles as an expression of the ego instinct, a will to power, "the masculine protest." Neurosis, in this interpretation, rose from undue self-aggrandizement; or from a sense of inferiority roused by the failure of the individual to impress himself upon others, to conquer his environment; or from his powerlessness to achieve a goal which he had accepted but which too often had been chosen for him and was unsuited to the possibilities of his own nature. The ego instinct, which when baffled produces feelings of inferiority, was held by him to be the root instinct.

Jung, however, felt that no single instinct could adequately explain the infinitely varied possibilities of the aims of the human psyche. He found patients whose histories bore out the theories of Freud and others who fell under the category described by Adler. He realized that two men could look upon the same phenomenon and see totally different things and that this showed inherent differences in the psychological processes of the investigators themselves.

He found in the dream material presented to him something more than a representation of the neurotic problem and of the disguised personal repression of the patient. He saw the attempt of the unconscious to present through symbols indications of a new way of life. He studied the material of the unconscious as an archaeologist would explore a buried city. Above ground was the conscious, the ego which the patient presented to the world and to himself. Below this was the layer of forgotten personal memories and experiences. Some of these, as interest in them became less keen, had dropped out of consciousness by a perfectly normal process of forgetting, and if normal associations suggested them, they returned to consciousness without arousing resistance on the part of the patient. Other contents had been pushed down into the unconscious because of painful associations or disturbing qualities which had interfered with the attempted conscious attitude; by deliberately turning the back upon them and refusing to admit them to consciousness, the patient had at last pushed them down into the unconscious. Such are the "repressed memories" upon which Freud built his theories of the unconscious as the repository of the infantile and instinctive, at war with the civilized conscious of modern man.

This is the mechanism employed in neurosis. The patient separates himself from certain disagreeable experiences which have carried with them overweighted feelings, such as those of guilt or shame or inadequacy. He seeks by repressing them to be relieved of their burden, to separate himself from them. If this forgetting is carried to abnormal lengths, there is a resulting split in the personality. Hysterical forgetting, or so-called dual personality, may result; or the patient, finding himself unable to adapt to the demands of life, may take refuge in physical symptoms. The unconscious is not a mere storehouse but a living force; and its power becomes here an added danger, for it exercises a magnetic attraction upon associated content in the conscious, drawing it down and so carrying the process of forgetting beyond conscious control.

Further explorations brought to light another type of material which could not be the product of the patient's personal experience. Here lie buried cosmic symbols, archetypal images carrying with them intuitions of spiritual or mystic meaning. In pathological cases where the whole attention is withdrawn from the world of outer reality, these images take an objective or personal form. They become ghosts, demons, voices of the gods. They have to the patient all the compelling power which gods and devils have to the primitive. They are objectifications of elemental hates, fears, or religious ecstasies—embodiments of racial experience. The patient loses his identity; he becomes a puppet ruled by blind forces which he mistakes for mysterious fate or for God. Here lies one of the lures of insanity. It permits us to lay upon this mysterious fate the burden of our own responsibility; it furnishes a retreat which we feel to be an adequate excuse for our own inability to adapt to life.

This is the abnormal aspect. In normal life we find persons who are creatively in touch with these underlying treasures of the unconscious. In them images of compelling beauty or terror, symbols of the spiritual experiences through which man has developed, mythological and cosmic images rise to the conscious and become the material of the poet, the artist, or the spiritual prophet. The images, in their chaotic state, lie in all of us; genius gives them form and new living values. The process which is at work when a little child, denied sex knowledge, weaves a fantasy of swallowing a flower seed to get a baby (an old myth of impregnation) is the same that produces the stupendous images of fate in *Oedipus Rex*.

Jung has termed this lower layer the *collective unconscious*. It is our inheritance from ancestral and racial psychic life. He also says that it "consists of the inherited potentialities of human imagination." In this broader view we see the unconscious, not simply as a repository for repressions or for forgotten or subliminal impressions, but as a great creative force, a stream of energy underlying all our psychic life, an energy which is undifferentiated, containing both good and evil, quickening either to death or to life, the manifestation of its force being dependent upon the orientation of the individual through whom it flows.

An intelligent study of the collective unconscious is necessary for those who would deal with the problems arising in the inner life of the child, but we are to use this knowledge only for understanding, never in the direct analysis of the child. His task is the integration of the conscious.

At first, ego-consciousness has little or no continuity. It is like a flickering light that comes and goes. A real sense of an existing conscious personality may be very slow in developing; it involves memory of acts and experiences, and the power to relate them to each other and to oneself. As ego-consciousness develops, events or emotions of significance are no longer merely experienced and forgotten. They become part of the stream of memory.

Memory, as the reanimation of experience, carries with

it a certain critical quality; it enables the ego, through the comparison of experiences, to establish its relationship to events and its responsibility toward them. The ego, therefore, directs (or should direct) conscious choice. It experiences, selects, weighs, evaluates. It develops through each consciously accepted experience. To establish its continuity is a primal necessity.

By many people this continuity is never attained; life just happens to them. It all *seems* to come from outside. They fall into one situation and out of that into another, often a similar one. They are victims of circumstances, or they are varying personalities reacting differently to each change of circumstance or to each change of mood in accordance with the fragment of personality that assumes temporary control. Therefore, they never really experience their life; they never ask, "Why did this come to me? What does it mean? What is its value or its peril? What in me made it take this form? What is its connection with my particular life? What, in short, is the *me* who has this experience, and what is my connection with this event that has happened?"

We must, however, understand those images which well up from deep levels and appreciate their value in cultural expression and also in the collective attitudes of society. Primitives live largely in the collective unconscious; hence their legion of gods and demons and their absorption in magic. Children, too, are near this inner world; hence their abundant fantasy power and their easy belief in mythological beings. Credulity is a normal attitude of childhood. More will be said of this in later chapters.

Another way in which the collective unconscious constantly influences our conscious life is through collective ideas which owe their life to racial imprints. Whether we like it or not, we cannot escape the pressure of psychic evolution. No matter how independently we seem to think, we cannot blot out the impressions made by generations of Christianity, or the extraverted attitudes produced by our Western scientific thought as against the mystic withdrawal of the East. We see the result of varying racial heritage in the diverse symbols produced during analysis from the collective unconscious of individuals of different races. This diversity of racial inheritance affects not only the form of the material produced, but also the attitude of the patient toward that material. All this is true of feeling as well as of thinking. Certain collective attitudes toward feeling are inherited as a result of gradually deepened brain imprints, so that special feeling reactions which are contrary to the accepted collective attitude cannot come through into the conscious.

In our conscious adaptation we have many thoughts which are merely the echoes of the collective thinking of the society in which we live. Only a few have become our own through a process of winnowing and choosing; fewer still are our own from true inner conviction. But it is these few that make our individuality.

Out of the world of collective images certain ones have arisen which have a compelling influence upon mankind. The image of the Jehovah God, the all-powerful Father, is one of these. This image has changed with man's growth in knowledge and understanding, for man has continued to make God in his own image, that is, the image of the father which rises from his unconscious. This concept of the tribal father, with his power of life or death over his children and his subjection of the mother, is seen by Freud as a menacing figure, yet one whose overthrowal is the origin of creative activity in man. It is the struggle of the son to "overthrow the father and possess the mother" which he sees as the central problem of mankind. It is this that he has termed the *Oedipus complex*. From the original slaying of the father by the son rose the sense of guilt, and from the possession of the mother rose incestuous infantile longings. In female psychology the process is reversed, the daughter longing for the death of the mother in order that she may possess the father. In Freud's case the father problem is evident in his refusal to recognize the findings of those who have been his followers. Psychologically he is the tribal father, and this problem of his own is projected into all of his findings. He sees the desire for the mother as an actual though unconscious sexual desire, which, because of the ancient incest barrier, is pushed down into the unconscious and finds its expression in infantile regressive acts. If the growing youth cannot break from the mother and find his love-life outside the family, then there is an infantile retreat and neurosis ensues.

Jung conceived of the problem symbolically. To him the desire of the child for the mother is the expression of the longing to remain a child, that is, to remain unconscious of himself and of the demands of adult life. Because the mother protects and guards the child, taking upon herself the responsibility for his well-being, she represents to him the happy irresponsible state before the awakening of consciousness and individual responsibility—the Garden of

Eden. In this aspect she is "the terrible mother" who would swallow his awakening individuality and keep him always a child, dependent upon her. This is one side of the mother image; the other side is the mother as the giver of life.

The problem of development is "that we may have life, and have it more abundantly." Psychologically, man seeks to return to the mother for a renewal of life, a rebirth into a higher attitude. He explores the unconscious, not that he may remain in a state of infantile unconsciousness, but that he may understand the forces that lie within himself and from contact with them may obtain a new way of life, a spiritual rebirth. As Antaeus, in his battle, touched the mother earth and each time received double strength, so man goes back to this eternal mother for renewal of his life in greater consciousness. If Jung has himself turned to mysticism, it is not, as some of his critics have stated, to become lost in the labyrinth, but in order to find in that storehouse of spiritual experience those living symbols which have been the pillar of cloud by day and of fire by night and have guided the race in the path of progress.

The image that is formed by a combination of the inner individual image and contact with the actual parent (or other person with whom relationship is formed) is termed in analytical psychology the *imago*. The problem of imago will be discussed in greater detail in the chapter on adolescence.

The difference between the imago and the actual object shows the tendency of the mind to project upon others certain things which are a part of our own psychological processes. When we find within ourselves fears, weaknesses, angers, or other disturbing qualities, we may rid ourselves of their burden by fastening them upon someone outside ourselves. Often in adults whose conscious attitude is one of extreme rectitude and outward charity, there are wellings up of unacknowledged hatred and resentment. Since it would be too disturbing to admit these to consciousness and have to reckon with them as related to the ego, someone outside is used as a peg on which to hang the garment which we cannot wear openly. If we accepted these things as a part of ourselves, we should have to say, "In spite of my conscious attitude of love, I have many bitternesses and resentments toward life which I will not face." We therefore attach these hatreds to some other person. Frequently I have had patients say to me, "If you could actually know how detestable a person he is, you would understand that it must be he who has upset my life, rather than anything within myself."

In the child, projection is one of the earliest forms of thought. He projects his own attitudes into things animate and inanimate. He endows inanimate things with personality, and his projection becomes universal. If he bumps himself, it is on a "bad" table; if he is angry, it is Mother who is bad. The primitive uses this form of projection in his chiringas and his idols. Wherever hatred, or any unreasoning overemotion, is vented in abnormal proportion on an object *so that the subject cannot seem to escape from the object,* we may feel sure that the overweight of emotion is a projection.

Another form of infantile adaptation is identification. Identification is an unconscious process in which the attitudes of another are taken over as if they were one's own. It differs from imitation in that imitation is a conscious process, in which we choose certain things that seem admirable, and strive to make them our own by this means. Imitation may also become an unconscious process. The gesture, the manner of the beloved object may become so habitual that the imitator is completely unaware that these expressions are not originally his own. There is a primary state of identity between the child and the parents, in which the child *is* a part of the parent. From this identity he emerges as he becomes individually conscious. If the process of individual growth becomes arrested and the child remains too long in that primary identity, a process of true identification takes place. Then the growing child takes over unconsciously the thought and feeling processes of a parent and accepts them as his own way of life. Frequently this identification is so prolonged as to block the development of the individual way. Then the emotional attitudes that fail to mature drop down into the unconscious and arise later to find their expression in infantile acts which are surprisingly at variance with the accepted conscious attitude. This will be illustrated later in the development of definite cases.

The process of growth necessitates the separation of the individual from these parental identifications, also from identification with collective ideas and accepted formulas. It requires the acceptance of the individual way, the highest *ought* of the personality. Such an aim necessitates the recognition of the whole man, the needs of his inner being and the demands of his outer adaptation.

While the life energy (the *libido*) is being turned toward

subjective inner values, the process is termed *introversion*. When that same energy flows out in interest in objects, it is called *extraversion*. According to the predominance of one or the other of these two processes, a man is termed an *introvert* or an *extravert*. The balance between these two currents is one of the problems of individuation which is the goal of analysis.

Introversion must be guided so that it may not become morbid introspection, which shuts the person away from the world of human activity and human relationships, but rather a process making for greater understanding of these and leading at last to a realization of the god within. Extraversion must be controlled so that men may not become lost in the multiplicity of things, but may be able to meet squarely the responsibilities of adaptation to the world. Neither of these two forms of psychic activity may be emphasized at the expense of the other if man is to develop as a whole. Any attempt to stimulate the growth of one side while suppressing the other must result in frustration.

The man who has spent his life acceding to every demand of outer adaptation may awake to a sense of emptiness and futility.

The dream and the fantasy which follow show the result of pushing either of these adaptations to the extreme. The first is a dream of an overextraverted woman:

"I had cut myself up and was passing myself around on a large and handsome platter. At first there seemed nothing unusual about it, but suddenly I became terrified and tried to pull away the platter and escape, but I could not move or speak. Then a monstrous woman, I think a Negress, appeared and began throwing the people away. She was quite dreadful but I was not afraid of her and felt she might help me. Then I woke, saying, 'I must blow my nose.'" Blowing her nose was a clearing of the instinctive intuition so that she could smell out situations.

A small boy developed sullen moods; he failed at school; he would not adapt to the community interests of the home. When pressed, he often gave way to violent fits of temper. There were three boys and as he was the middle one he always shared a room with one of his brothers, who were alike in boisterous temperament, whereas he was the only one who desired quiet. One day he explained a fantasy of his:

"I have my land. It is an island in the middle of a lake-river. The bank of the lake is very winding and there are towns on it, but the boats have to zigzag back and forth to get to them and everywhere they pass my island they see high rocks, so they cannot land. There is only one way to get there. Back of two towns and between them there is a wood. It is very dark and mysterious. There are big rocks there, and they all look alike but one of them lifts up and back of it is a door, and back of the door is a tunnel, and you can go through that tunnel and under the lake and come out in the middle of the island where the trees are thick around a little quiet place. That's where I go to think. [Then, scornfully,] *They* don't know about it. *They* don't know who I am." This fantasy had become a retreat from every proper demand of outer life. In working this out he came to some realization of the times when he ought to leave the island, a rudimentary understanding of the balance of adaptation and inner withdrawal.

He drew a picture of the island, the curving bank of the lake and the course of the boats. This map really was in accord with the old eastern drawings of the inner center of the psyche. His deep distrust made him cut himself off from all communication, because he had found no one who valued his desire for withdrawal into himself.

Introversion unbalanced by proper contacts with the objective world may lead into a land of shadows where the realities of human life appear monstrous and menacing.

Development toward maturity and individuation implies an increase of consciousness. If psychological adulthood is to be obtained, it must be through a greater understanding and control of the inner forces. There are certain abstract concepts necessary to our understanding which cannot be defined as we define concrete things. Such elusive terms as truth, beauty, God, freedom have a definite significance. This is true of certain psychological terms, such as *psychological adulthood*.

To be psychologically adult one must have found an individual way of life as distinguished from a mere identification with collective standards. This does not mean a rebellion against the collective, for true individuation accepts the responsibility of the individual as part of the social order. This adulthood implies a conscious control not only of the intellectual functions but of the emotional life. It involves an acceptance of the self and of the task which life is presenting. It is not a crystallized or completed form but is a continuously evolving condition.

What has all this to do with our dealing with children? There we are confronted with problems quite different from those which we must meet in the analysis of an adult patient. Growth in consciousness in the adult involves self-scrutiny and careful examination of buried content which must often be brought slowly and painfully to light. The same process which in an adult develops a higher, liberating form of consciousness may develop in the child only a morbid self-consciousness or drive him into a world of fantasy which cuts him off from reality. We must ourselves have the knowledge of the perils which he may meet. We must know our own inner life if we would know the child.

No one would embark upon a journey without a vision of the destination, and one ought not to attempt to meet the problems of child development without a knowledge of the goal of that development. There is no way in which we can understand the problems of the child's unconscious except to have met and faced those problems in ourselves. The first requisite for one who wishes to work with ill-adapted children is a searching personal analysis. Only the free individual who has found his own way of life can help others to freedom.

In the meeting of any two persons the smallest point of contact is the conscious or known part; all the rest is in the unconscious unknown. Unless we understand the thing which the difficult, neurotic child may stir in our own unconscious, we cannot deal with him justly; nor can we estimate our influence over him unless we realize that all that we are is going to make up that influence. Besides this, we must be able to meet the problems of the parents, which often lead deep down into the unconscious life.

2

INFLUENCE OF PARENTAL DIFFICULTIES UPON THE UNCONSCIOUS OF THE CHILD

In our early contacts with the little child we must bear in mind two things. The first is that our goal is to help in the creation of a free individual, one who has found a way of life of his own and who is in conscious contact with the inner world as well as with the world without, who is not a puppet pulled by wires reaching up from the non-understood world of the unconscious, nor the limits of whose being are collective social ideas. Second, we must realize that psychologically, as well as physically, he is the result of racial development. The greater part of his life lies in the unconscious. He is a potential, bearing all the possibilities for good or evil, but all these possibilities lie embryonic in the unconscious from which he is developing.

We must think of life as developing from within as well as from without. The old psychology laid all the emphasis upon the growth through outer contacts. Sensation, reflexes, habit formation were the important phenomena. While it is quite true that these outer contacts are necessary and that without them we should be unable to develop out of a mere animal state of being, yet they are only one side of the picture; the other side is our growth in deeper life through making conscious those forces which lie buried within us all. A compendium of child psychology would present both sides of the picture; here we deal with only one: the inner side.

At first the child has an infinitesimal conscious. The states of consciousness are fleeting impressions attached to no central or ego sense. There is no continuity of memory.

Slowly these fragments begin to integrate and a sense of self develops. The child begins to think of himself as something separate from his surroundings. The "I" emerges; a personal life slowly takes form. At first the child is in a condition of identity with his surroundings and with the psyche of the parent. Even as the "I" emerges, the unconscious is still held in that close identification.

We recognize the physical and economic dependence of the child upon the father and mother. We do not attach sufficient importance to the psychic bond which in early childhood often amounts to a condition of identity of the unconscious of the child with the unconscious of the parent. Through this identification the disturbing forces that lie below the level of conscious adult life are intuited by the unconscious of the child and give rise in their milder forms to vague fears, apprehensive fantasies, and disturbing dreams. In the more tragic instances dissociation from reality or antisocial acts result.

Until birth the child's body is actually part of the mother's. It is not until the umbilical cord is cut that this connection is severed and the child becomes a separate physical entity. The psychic cord still remains. Much more slowly does the child achieve a separate personality, one which is not linked with that of the parent. This does not mean that the child is psychologically a mere repetition of the parent; each one bears within himself the germ of his own individuality. We see in the same family children born of the same parents, submitted to the same environment, who nevertheless show from a very early age completely different type reactions. In spite of these marked differences in type each child is, in his own way, strongly affected in development or retardation of growth by the attitude of the parent and by the unconscious influences of those in the home.

Frequently in the analysis of an adult, where infantile conditions have continued over too long a period, we find an overemphasis of a normal reaction. This helps us to understand the underlying principle of psychological identification. It is possible for the unconscious life of one person to be so completely fed from the unconscious of another that it is as though the soul of the one so fed remained like an infant in the mother's womb, drawing sustenance through the psychic umbilical cord. If this is suddenly snapped, it is as disastrous to the newborn individuality as the premature severing of the physical cord. When the unconscious is suddenly deprived of its food there may ensue a feeling of being utterly lost and cut off from life, an abnormal and hopeless type of grief.

A man of fifty had, from his earliest childhood, maintained such an identification with his mother. He had attained eminence in his profession, and his intellectual life was highly evolved, yet in his emotions and feelings he was still an infant dependent upon the mother for nourishment. He could go nowhere without her. Her influence reached into all his acts. When she died quite suddenly, he was like an unborn infant cut off from his sources of life. Since individuality depends upon psychological development, not upon years, the psychological cord had in this case been prematurely cut. It was severed before he was ready for a life of his own. He became a prey to irrational terrors. While engaged in his work, he would all at once seem lost in a great void, his whole self dissolved in abysmal blackness. The terror ensuing was utterly engulfing and primeval. It was as though he had no self to oppose to this horrible force. He was swallowed up by it.

When he described this terror to me I was reminded of a story which a patient had told me of an experience of her childhood. When hardly more than a baby she had lost her mother in a holiday crowd. She said, "I have never felt any fear like it. I can feel the blind terror of it yet. I could not seem to see or hear, or to know where I was going. I was swallowed up in it. It was the most awful helplessness that I have ever known." The man's terror was like that of this lost child.

From the study of such a case we see not only the mysterious strength of these inner forces, but also the danger that arises when an infantile adaptation is continued past its proper time, and the burden of taking up adult life, whether of feeling or thinking, is not accepted. It is right that the little child should have this close identity with the parent. It is in this identity that he finds security in his first contacts with the outside world, and that his inner world is brought into connection with reality thinking. It is these contacts that make the difference between the development of the civilized child and the primitive.

The greater part of the psychic life of the child lies in the unconscious, as does the life of the primitive. With the primitive these unconscious forces remain the ruling ones; for the collective society in which he develops is ruled by elemental fear and superstition, and love and hate, and in instinctive participation in the forces of na-

ture. Fantasy thinking in his world is the reality, and the
events of life are explained by magic and by myth. The
child, like the primitive, is primarily a creature of sensation and intuition. Thought and feeling develop slowly. (I
do not speak here of the first instinctive emotions but of
feeling as a judging function.) Through sensation he
comes into contact with the outer world of objects;
through intuition he becomes aware of the inner forces at
work in himself and in those about him. In his own inner
world lie embryonic the fantasy-building powers of the
collective unconscious. From them he often weaves for
himself strange explanations of the newly discovered
world.

In our ignorance of the underlying spiritual truth of
many of these fantasy explanations we may laugh at these
fantasies. By so doing we cut ourselves off from one of the
most vital sources of relationship with the child. Quite
rightly he does not expose his inner life to ridicule, and
the result of our amusement is that while the child continues to fantasy, he takes the greatest care that these creatures of his imagination shall never again be exposed to
our rude treatment. This attitude on our part is frequently
because we have ourselves grown callous and indifferent to
the spiritual symbols which are contained in the early
myth and fairy tale. When we are cognizant of these inner
values we can accept the fantasy for what it really is, a
self-made fairy tale, and give the child the true explanation without doing violence to the inner processes. In accepting the irrational side of the child, we have also
strengthened the relationship. We all know how glad we
are to find a person to whom we can tell our inmost
thoughts, certain of a sympathetic understanding even
though that understanding may be used to show us where
we have gone far astray. It is important that we be sufficiently in touch with our own unconscious to respect and
understand the workings of the unconscious of the child.
We must keep this door of communication open between
us so that his fantasy may not be used as a retreat from
reality and a barrier between him and ourselves. The primitive is at the mercy of his unconscious, but the civilized
child receives his education through an integration of the
conscious and unconscious forces, drawing up the latter
and subjecting them to contact with the cultural valuations
of our adult world.

Much of our world means but little to a child; our conscious morality, our laws of right and wrong, have no spe-

cial value for him. Even the words which we speak carry different meanings. It is our own reality that is always and ultimately the test of the value of our contacts with the child; and it is this which is recognized by his unconscious. It is the sum total of our personality which we give to the child. It is out of that sum total that we react to an emergency, and it is to that intuited sum total that the child reacts when he is desirous of pleasing us, or of bringing to us the strange creatures that he finds within himself. This is true, however, only when we can establish a genuine relationship which is free from the attitudes and prejudices carried over from some previous relationship.

In analysis we speak of projections. That, in its simplest form, means that we read into the situation or into the other person something that really exists in ourselves, or which we have found to be true in a previous relationship. We find, therefore, what we expect to find. A child carries over to his teacher certain attitudes which have developed in his life with his parents. If the parents have been evasive and have broken promises or met situations equivocally, the child expects a similar attitude on the part of the teacher. What appears as a fundamental lack of trust in the child is really a projection of parental attributes upon the teacher.

The younger the child, the less directly do we deal with the unconscious elements that give rise to his fears and maladjustments, and the more do we look to the unconscious of the adults who surround him; for all that lies behind the conscious life goes to make up the sum total of personality, the sum total of character, the impression that is given, and the influence brought to bear on others. We all know how the silence of one person can bear in it hostility or malignity, or how that of another can convey restfulness and peace.

Children gather from us the atmosphere of all that we most carefully ignore in ourselves. If our conscious goodness is founded on fear and repression, the atmosphere that we impart must be one of fear, restraint, or insincerity. If such destructive undercurrents are intuited by the child, he may resent the commands which seem reasonable; then resistance is raised and the spirit of rebellion against authority is engendered. If, on the other hand, our attitude is a conscious acceptance of our own highest law, and a readiness to face the ever-present forces within ourselves which may become manifest in evil as well as in good, then by that very attitude we stimulate a growth to-

ward life and courage. The child then reacts to the motive
which rules us, as well as to our spoken word.

Few of us realize how much our goodness is an acceptance of public conscience, and traditional faith, instead of
an individual acceptance of our own highest ought and a
conscious struggle for growth. Therefore, if we are afraid
to face a thing in ourselves, and if, instead, we repress it,
it is bound to avenge itself by filling us with resentments
and bitterness toward those who have more courage. This
is felt by the child, and erects a barrier which his confidence cannot pass. His unconscious recognizes behind the
conscious attitude this destructive element from which his
inner life must hide.

We must remember that it is not the existence of the
problem itself, but our own attitude toward it that gives it
power for good and evil, whether in our own lives or in
our children's. Out of poverty may come determination,
undaunted courage, and cheerfulness; or degradation,
meanness, sodden resignation, and spiritual apathy. Out of
riches may come selfishness, sensuousness, gratification,
materialism; or opportunity, service, culture. In either case
it is not necessary that the bank account be known by the
child in order that he may be profoundly influenced by the
attitude toward money and the general atmosphere of the
home.

It is the same with moral and psychological problems.
The child need not, usually should not, know the actual
problem, for often it is one that taxes all our adult understanding to the utmost, and its knowledge would impose
far too heavy a burden upon the childish mind. But we
should face the problem fairly ourselves, we should drag it
out into the light of our consciousness and attempt to relate it fearlessly to the conduct of our own lives. The child
then intuits the strength, courage, and honesty that come
from a real attempt at understanding, instead of that lurk-
ing fear, cowardice, and doubt that come from shutting
the skeleton in the closet and always knowing that it is
there. Have you ever entered a room where the atmosphere is surcharged with hostility and suspicion though
outwardly it is filled with courteous, friendly people? You
sense these uninvited guests that are crowding all about. It
is this sort of thing which the child intuits—the fears we
will not face, the unwelcome forces within ourselves which
we pretend to solve by repression instead of through understanding. It is this distinction that is often so hard for
parents to grasp. When you tell them that the child is

suffering from the weight of their own unsolved problem they reply, "But surely you would not have us tell the child about it, he is too little." Of course he is. Why should he carry the burden that thus far has proved too hard for them? But while they refuse to face it consciously and it remains, unsolved but operative, in their own unconscious life, they are placing on him a heavier burden, that of vague fear and mistrust of life which his own unconscious intuits from theirs. Many of us are so factually minded that we realize the importance of the objective experience, but are quite blind to the intensity and force of those intuitive experiences, which come when the child feels all that lies below the surface, though he is unable consciously to formulate these feelings even to himself.

It becomes apparent therefore that when we are dealing with the neurotic difficulties of children it behooves us to examine the unconscious life of the parent, for when his difficulties are cleared the troubles of the child often vanish of themselves.

An analysis of several cases which bear out the theory of identification will perhaps prove more enlightening than further discussion of the theory itself. These are all histories of definite findings and they have not only the theoretic value but the pragmatic one. They worked out in results. In each one the unsolved problem of the parent was intuited by the unconscious of the child. These intuitions started disturbing undercurrents, which in their turn worked themselves out in unsocial acts, or resulted in neurotic conditions of anxiety, terror, extreme dependence, or unbalanced emotional conditions. In all of these cases it was the parent who needed analysis and who had to be brought to an understanding of his own unconscious repressions. In each instance the outer life was apparently well adjusted. The needs of the children were not consciously neglected. All the questions of proper environment, and physical or educational care had received conscientious attention. Also in many cases there was not only love, but even an overemphasis of love; and a strong attachment existed between the child and the parent. Yet in each case we see how the child is handicapped in normal adjustment by things of which he was supposed to be entirely unconscious.

The first case illustrates the keenness with which the actual problem of the parent may be intuited, and the way in which the unconscious of the child accepts the responsibility for its solution. The child in question was a little nine-year-old girl who had a strong father identification. Their relationship was very real. This increased the difficulty, for the strength of the bond of love and sympathy, not only in the conscious but also in the unconscious, militates to reinforce the neurosis should one arise through a parental problem. The father had suffered a severe nervous breakdown. He was unable to take up work or to return to normal relations in the outside world. His whole self was in a condition of retreat, his attitude toward life was one of defense. The child was nervous, underweight, and subject to night terrors. One night she woke screaming and trembling. She told the following dream:

"I was Thetis and Arthur was my son, Achilles, and he would not fight. There was a great battle and he ought to fight. So I got two shields and I gave him one and I made him go out, and I went with him and we had to fight. I was afraid but I had to make him fight."

This battle clearly is not her own but her father's. In this dream the child lives out for her father the solution that he is seeking in his own unconscious where he has never really accepted his neurosis as a way of life. She becomes, in a manner, the personification of his conscience, his moral sense. She shows him the way that he must take. In the dream she assumes the role of mother and in that capacity she sees it her duty to drive the son out into the world, to force him once more into the battle of life. She is afraid, yet her love makes her fight with him spiritually and psychologically through her identification.

Apparently this child was shielded from every harm, and had everything that money and love could provide. Actually she was bearing a burden far too heavy, and it was a burden that could be lifted in only one way— through the acceptance by the father himself of the problem of his own adaptation to life. Neither an increase of love on the father's part nor a rude attempt to break the bond in the unconscious would avail anything. There was no way out except to face the actual problem. To analyze such a dream with a child would result in greater confusion and disaster. It would add to the unconscious apprehension a conscious fear. One could not say to this child, "It is really your father who is afraid and who is not facing life. You are only afraid because he is." That would be to fasten the burden still more firmly upon the child. When the father did take up the problem of his own infantile attitude, the child's night terrors ceased. She began to sleep peacefully, to gain in weight and to make a normal adaptation as soon as the father took up courageously his own psychological burdens.

The second case is that of another little girl who was suffering from night terrors, sudden fears, nervous hesitations, and inability to concentrate on her schoolwork. She had received a careful physical examination, and the report showed the existence of no difficulty beyond the indefinite one of being slightly under par. On the surface there appeared to be nothing to disturb this child's life.

The father was a professional man who was meeting with rather more than the ordinary amount of success; the mother an attractive, somewhat oversolicitous woman who was apparently devoted to the child, and who spent a good deal of time with her. The young woman who had charge of her during certain hours of the day was kindly, sympathetic, and patient. There were apparently no special difficulties, material or otherwise. The child, however, gave one the impression of having a continuous sense of insecurity. Usually she was in retreat from persons and surroundings, apart from the situation; but at times she would show a clinging, almost bewildered dependence upon the adult in whose charge she found herself. At home she was described as being "quite a little mother." She liked to run errands for her father and to do small things for his comfort. He, on his side, lavished far more affection on her than on any of his other children. He was delighted and amused at her motherly attention and made a great baby of her.

She seemed always uneasy at parting from either parent, especially the mother, showing almost as much dread as though she might not find them on her return. She was reticent about her night terrors, but as her dreams came to light, they were of sinking in a sea, falling suddenly, being lost and not able to get back. There was nothing definite in the dreams which would give any clue to the situation, beyond emphasizing the abnormal sense of insecurity. As soon as her unconscious took charge in sleep, it showed how small was her sense of safety. This, taken in connection with her unreasonable and unreasoned fear of losing her father and mother whenever she was separated from them in an ordinary way, pointed to some extreme instability in the family relationship quite apart from the individual relationship of the parents to her.

Except in the case of extreme indulgence it is not normal that a child should have such fears when the parents leave home or when he is starting for school or play. The business in hand is too alluring and the sense of the home too secure to demand any anxious thought. Since nothing abnormal in the child seemed to warrant such a condition it seemed reasonable to suppose that there was here an intuition of some hidden danger, for those undercurrents which may sweep away the established foundations are often sensed by the unconscious of the child.

The mother had been brought up in a home where the father's authority had been negligible and his children had missed any positive relation with him. This daughter had tried to find the missing authority in an early marriage with a man who was of an opposite type—a positive, authoritative, dominant male. But here she had only exchanged one difficulty for another, for she was still the child. Her husband in his psychological development had never passed beyond the tribal attitudes. To him the man was still the patriarch, the absolute ruler of the home. The wife at best was a sort of favorite child who was dependent upon him for even her thought life. Not strong enough to combat this, she had taken refuge in living for her children. Such a substituted life will not satisfy. More and more she was conscious of tides of hatred and resentment which made her at times do most unexpected things.

Some time before the birth of this child she had formed a friendship with an old acquaintance of her brother's. It was a mere embryonic thing which might or might not have developed into something real. The husband became jealous and forbade her seeing him, and succeeded in fastening on her a sense of guilt, so that the man became to her a symbol of sinful possibilities within herself. To expiate this she gave herself with more slavish devotion to her children, enveloping them in an unwise love, trying to shield them from the consequences of any mistakes that they might make. Her real guilt was, of course, in abandoning her own individuality, in denying her real values as a human being. This she had been doing for years; this incident served only to crystallize the situation. She shut the door on the possibility of love with all its responsibilities and, suffering the punishment of the murderer, she found herself now given over to fears, to suspicions, and to hatreds that were quite out of keeping with the conscious attitude of Christian self-sacrifice. She began to take a strange delight in helping the children to outwit their father, telling herself that she was running risks for their good. Especially she hugged her sense of guilt, for it gave her an excuse for entertaining ideas of suicide which were becoming more and more fascinating to her as a means of escape.

Is it remarkable that, with such evil undercurrents, the child could feel no sense of security? All the children suffered in various ways; but this one, *receiving the most love,* suffered most, for her unconscious was thereby brought into closer relation to that of her parents.

Facts like these are more revealing than any deduction that we can make. Here again was a child with every material want supplied, and with the love of both parents, yet she was breaking under a burden heavier than neglect. The father, who believed himself to be a model parent, insisted that the children should find their lives only through him. The mother struggled frantically to find her life only through them. Neither parent was working out his own salvation or respecting the potentials of personality of the child. In either case the child was used as something to fulfill the parent. The failure shows that we cannot live our lives by proxy, and illustrates the truth that each one of us must find the way to individual success, instead of handing the unfulfilled task on to the children.

As a result of the fact that neither parent had a real individuality, the child had no sense of security in relationship. It was as though there were no actual parents. The man, who prided himself on his masculinity, was a mere expression of old images from the collective unconscious. He had no individual self, but was a mere identification with this old pattern. The woman, having refused the responsibility for her own life, tried to find her justification in a "self-sacrifice" in which the real sacrifice was the child. The normal process of identity with the parent, which gives an early security from which the child as an individual slowly emerges, was denied this child. This was because the parents were themselves unreal; they were mere shadows of the unconscious. The father was too satisfied with his own adaption to see any such need of change. He set up the image of the Jehovah God, and worshiped it in himself. The mother, more able to see her need, did work out some individuality and in so doing greatly helped the child.

That the first interview was to be made as brief as possible was evident from the moment that the mother entered the room. She had brought the child herself only because the physician who had asked me to take the case had told her that she must do so. The child was "nervous," listless, was doing badly in her schoolwork, and had night terrors.

There was "nothing really the matter." If I would "just
talk to her and stop her from being so silly." They had
tried tonics; "oh, everything had been done for her always."
During this conversation the child had sat obediently in a
big chair in an adjoining room, quietly occupied with a big
book. She could not be left with me that day; it would not
"be convenient." I arranged that she be brought the next
day by the person who was with her most (who proved to
be the nurse) and left for an hour or two.

The next day they arrived on the moment of the appointment. The nurse was a large, dominating type of
woman, of the order usually described as competent.
Under one arm she carried a satisfied, arrogant little Pom-
eranian. The child seemed almost effaced from the land-
scape. It took only a few moments to see that she was in
terror of the woman. At the end of the hour, when the
nurse returned, the child immediately shrank back into
self-effacing shadows.

I sent for the mother, who again tucked the interview
into an odd moment. I told her that the first difficulty was
to be found in the relationship with the nurse, of whom
the child was evidently in great fear. "I know," she answered with some irritation, "that she can't get along with
Elizabeth, but you see, we have never had anyone who
was so good to the dog."

The mother was in love with the dog! An infantile
woman, petted, spoiled, utterly selfish, but fond of attention and caresses, she had failed to make any real relationship with her husband, who had tired of her eternal baby
ways. The baby, at first viewed as a doll, was soon an an-
noying disturbance. Human love required adult attitudes
and the acceptance of adult responsibilities. It was too
hard. Sexuality was "horrid" but it was "nice" to be petted.
Failing in all real love relations, she had made the dog the
surrogate. Sometimes she did not see the child for two or
three days. She was at school before the mother waked,
and the mother was out when she came back. The dog
was brought in with the breakfast tray and was "too cunning." She saw him the first thing every morning.

The woman had no desire to grow up. She preferred to
treat the serious things in the situation as fantastic nonsense. Had it not been for the father, a materialistic businessman, but a man accustomed to put things through, the
nurse would undoubtedly have remained with the little girl,
and nothing could have been done. He, however, insisted
on a change, and a placid, motherly woman was provided.

She furnished a background of serenity and security. The child made a mother-transference to her and that transference, combined with the help that I could give to her, did much toward restoring nervous poise. The physical symptoms disappeared and she was able to take her place in school.

It was at best only a substitute and could not take the place of the love tie which was the child's normal right. Her fantasies about her "beautiful mother" showed how deep was the longing for reality. At its best the tie with the nurse could not fill the needed place. It could not grow into a true relationship later. It would probably be a broken one, not one evolved into an adult comradeship. Unless she had very wise handling at the period of psychological puberty, she would unconsciously be ever seeking the things which she had missed as a child.

The mother, turning from her task in life, could not fail to be caught in the futility of the trivialities which she chose. Her loss was even more tragic than that of the child. Sometimes, with this infantile type of parent, the child will be made to fill the position of pet animal. A mother will caress and fondle him with overemotional physical demonstration when in the mood, but push him off with indifference or unconcealed annoyance when he becomes tiresome, when her own mood has changed. This is not only baffling to the child, destroying all his sense of security and continuity in the life of feeling, but it arouses also tempestuous emotions which, unsatisfied, can only feed themselves in fantasy or auto-erotic practices.

Lack of love and understanding between parents is most disastrous to the child, whether it works out in this spasmodic demonstration or in the attempt of either parent to make the child compensate for the love that is missing. It is a common practice of unhappily mated couples to take it out on the child, using him as a vehicle to drain off the extra emotionalism, which is frequently of an unconscious and primitive type. This emotion may be pent-up hatred or love, but it does not really belong to the child. It is a mere effort at self-satisfaction of the parental need. Since it is, therefore, insincere at root, it cannot be productive of reality. Whenever we make a relationship with the child on any basis but that of his own individuality, we violate something in his soul.

When these overintense feelings are turned back upon the child, he feels a hopeless sense of inadequacy. What has he done that the love that seemed so surely his is his no longer? Some crime, unconscious perhaps, must have been committed by him. A man who has been made the puppet of his mother's undeveloped emotions may fear ever to make a relationship with a woman, or, having made one, may seek the continual reassurance of exaggerated tenderness and maternal demonstration from his wife, or from a mistress on whom he can vent the tempestuous primitive demonstration or from whom he can feel he continually receives it.

If the parent refuses to grow up and to accept his problem, the only way in which the child can grow up and be freed from these compelling forces in the unconscious is to see the parent as he is, and to break from the bond. In this case the parent must lose the child before he can become himself. It is an irrevocable loss, for no new and finer comradeship takes the place of the outgrown one. Such parents are usually loud in their protests against the ingratitude of the children and their lack of natural feeling. They lay to cruel fate the thing which they have brought upon themselves.

Another example of the results of the unhappy marriage is shown in the following case. A boy was deceitful, willful, and frequently cruel to other children. He was doing badly in school and was reported as seeming to have "sufficient mental ability but little moral sense." Early in the interview he gave indications of being a child with strong emotional nature but with very little conscious affection and no stable relationships. Since it was necessary to have some legitimate approach for the first interviews where the task was to gain his interest and trust, we first took up the difficult problems of the schoolwork. I was soon convinced that the difficulties were not all of his own making.

The first interviews with the mother, who really tried to be frank with me, brought out the fact that from his early infancy she had felt an instinctive repulsion toward him, and that though she had never let this affect her attitude, and had been all the more scrupulous in doing her full duty, there were times when she "could hardly bear to have him near her." Of course the question which immediately rose in my mind, but which it was too early to ask her, was what was the thing in herself which she feared and hated, which his presence brought to the surface. Often we hate in others the thing which we fear in ourselves; or we hate because the other person raises to our consciousness some fault or inadequacy which we would prefer to have remain unconscious, and therefore without power to disturb our self-complacency.

It soon became evident that the boy had no trust nor conscious standards of integrity, because he had never had a relationship in which he had felt these to be the ruling factors. The first task was the analysis of the mother. As she was a nervous invalid she was anxious for help on her own account and was willing to work upon her own difficulties. It was a long process, and there is not space here to give more than a brief outline of the situation.

The parents had been engaged when very young. During the engagement the man had found that his real love belonged to another woman, but the woman to whom he was engaged had refused to give him up. As she first stated it, she "had loved him so much that she was willing to forgive him for being unfaithful and to trust him just the same." Incomprehensible as it seems, she had really convinced herself that this was her real attitude and that she was ruled by worthy motives. That love which demands the sacrifice of another's happiness is not love but intensive selfishness was an idea which she fought bitterly, for it meant the sweeping away of all her defenses. Her invalidism was a power struggle to hold the thing that she had obtained under false pretenses. Knowing that she had not her husband's love, she took refuge in hysterical weakness in order to demand his attention. He feared to make any demands for liberty because any worry or disappointment immediately made her illness much worse. She asserted that time had proved her right in holding to the engagement, for he was so devoted to her now that all her friends spoke of it. Yet ever there appeared her distrust of him, which was inevitable. She could never really forget that she had stolen her position, and that therefore it must always be insecure. The boy looked very like the father and she had concentrated upon him the unconscious animosity which she had always had for the man who had loved another woman better than herself. She had never really forgiven him in spite of her conscious attitude of devotion, nor had she ever outgrown her distrust of him.

The father had sought the ever-present help of the American man who finds the problem of relationship too involved—business. In supplying lavishly every material need of the family, he had tried to compensate for the greater values which he could not give. He was one of the people sacrificed to our collective social conscience which lauds the barren and useless sacrifice instead of helping the individual to work out the highest human values in himself and for others. In his early perplexity the young man had gone to an old clergyman who had told him that true happiness could be found only in sacrificing desire for honor and that he ought to keep his word. He therefore sacrificed, not only himself, but the woman who really loved him, and had spent most of his life in helping to keep a selfish woman in a state of childish dependence and infantile power.

This is another illustration of the danger of substituting the collective social standard and generalized thinking for an individual attack on our own difficulty. The yielding of the strong to the weak is of value only when that yielding helps to make the weak stronger, not when it increases the weakness, and cripples the one who might be strong. Sacrifice is a law of life and growth, but it must be the sacrifice of the lower to the higher, otherwise death of the spirit is the result. There was, of course, an element of unrecognized cowardice in the man, for it had seemed to him less ruthless to sacrifice the woman who would not make a fuss rather than the one who would. Of the real measure of the pain inflicted he found it easier to remain unconscious. His refuge in business had been clearly a compensation for his failures in other departments of life. He had begun gradually to accept the general estimate of his value, his income tax, and to stifle as selfish and unworthy all finer aspirations. His conscious justification for such a course was that he was acting for the good of the family in supplying lavishly all their material needs. The unconscious but compelling motive was a desire to evade the realities of the situation.

In his conversations with the boy, which were not many nor intimate, he had tried to talk with him about right and high ideals. None of this had ever made any impression; the thing that the boy really got was an admiration of his father's business ability and a desire to get things himself. This was inevitable. Children pay little attention to what we say, they intuit what we are. If the parent's yardstick is material values, all the preaching of other standards of measurement is wasted breath. The child realizes that it is the material yardstick by which he will in the end be measured; and whether he tries to attain to the parental standards or not depends on whether he wishes to be like the parent or as different as possible. In either case the reaction is to the parental attitude and not to the spoken words of admonition. The boy had quite a clear conception of the lack of any real relationship between the father and mother, and was very cold-blooded in his attitude toward affection, although both the father and the mother had tried "to keep everything but expressions of affection from him."

The boy here lived out in acts of cruelty to other children the unexpressed hostility of his mother, and in his evasiveness and dishonest acts expressed the deceitfulness of the father who had built his life upon unreality. The father was absorbed in his material success, the mother in her own buried animosities; the care for the child's needs was prompted by a conscious attitude of duty. This child was caught in the evil currents at work in the unconscious of the parents and gave them life through his own wrong acts. This was a case where the bond of love was not sufficiently strong and the reactions were quite different from those of the child described in the first case. Yet each child was living out the parental unconscious, the one in overanxiety and emotional instability, the other in antisocial acts.

One must in a case like this be slow to blame, especially in such instances as that of the father. It was a pathetic case of one who, in trying honestly to "save his soul," by the collective standards which were the best he knew, had lost it. In failing to work out his individual problem he had fastened it upon the unconscious of his child.

Each of us must bear the burden of individual choice, and of the struggle for individual consciousness. The thing that really helped the boy was a gradual change in the attitude of the father and mother, and an attempt on their part to work out a relationship based on reality, though love in the deeper sense was not possible. In becoming conscious of all her buried feelings toward the father, the mother no longer projected these hostilities upon the child. She was able to see him apart from the father and to give him a real affection and interest and to acknowledge her responsibilities.

This strange animosity of a mother for a child is by no means rare. Frequently the solution attempted is to be overzealous in regard to every conscious demand for the child's welfare or oversolicitous in protestations of affection. Under these conditions the psychic life of the child invariably suffers almost, if not quite, as much as when the child is frankly neglected. There is no real solution in such cases but for the father and mother to look within themselves for the cause. Often the child is a reminder of

something which we wish forgotten; but there is no real
solution in forgetting or repressing. The thing which is,
must be faced, understood, and related to life before we
can escape from its power.

Children who lack real love and understanding frequently lie and steal through the desire to obtain something which they have not worked out in their unconscious, through acts of cunning and deception. Children
who are victims of the parental unconscious are frequently
bad-tempered and unreliable. There is unfortunately no society for the prevention of cruelty to children when that
cruelty is inflicted by the unconscious of the adult who
holds the power over the young life.

In *Rosmersholm* Ibsen gives a picture of the somber
tragedy of a woman caught in the darker forces of the unconscious. She is drawn, step by step, into the attitude of a
compelling fate and in this role pushes a weaker nature
into suicide.

There are tragedies of like nature enacted upon children
though we are too blind to see them. A young girl whose
inferior mentality and physical weakness stood in the way
of her mother's social ambition was pushed slowly but inevitably into insanity by the power of the mother's unconscious. Contrary to the advice of physician and psychologist, the mother insisted upon being with the child and
tried continually to force her into positions that were too
difficult. She seemed invariably to do and say the thing
that roused all that was undesirable in the child, until at
last the emotional storms, the sense of inferiority, and bewildered resentments destroyed the already unstable nervous balance. When it became necessary to send her from
the home, the mother "bowed to the will of God" and
went on her ambitious way, quite unconscious of the motives that underlay her expressed determination to "do her
full duty by the child."

We are all at times at the mercy of unknown forces
within ourselves. We must therefore look carefully at the
nature of the underlying motive if we feel any dislike or
resentment toward a child. It is possible that this child
stands between us and something which we desire or
rouses things in our unconscious which we fear to face.
Instead of trying to forget the antagonistic feeling we must
examine it with the greatest care and remain conscious of
its existence when we are dealing with the child. Our
whole attitude toward childish traits and individual children must be highly conscious and lovingly understanding.

The mechanism of projection is repeatedly employed in cases where the parents have resentments toward each other. The things which they repress in their conscious relations are vented upon the children. Often one child who in some physical aspect or mental characteristic resembles the hated parent will receive the full brunt of this projected hatred while the others go scot-free. The parent reacts toward the child as though he actually were the other parent. Since the love situation is repressed, the unconscious assumes control, and the emotions so displayed are of a primitive emotional type. Such a child, to whom normal love is denied, will often become deceitful, cheating and stealing to obtain praise and approval. As a great hunger will drive one to take food, so this craving in the unconscious drives its possessor to get love. Overdeveloped sexuality, or sexual distortions in the form of homosexuality or masturbation, often result. I am not dealing in generalities. Every reaction mentioned here has been found to exist in particular cases.

Often projections of hatred are made when people of different racial inheritance have married without having realized the obstacles which they may have to meet in their own very real differences of creed or ancestral unconscious, or in the attitudes of society toward their social adjustment. Sometimes these parental projections may arise from anxiety or fears which have their root in the early life of the parent.

An anxious mother came to consult me about her son. He was failing in school and his reports were growing more and more unsatisfactory. At the time when he had begun to be most bewildered about his work, one of the wholesale intelligence tests had been given at the school. It was evidently given by a rule-of-thumb psychologist who amassed statistics instead of studying individuals, as apparently no account was taken of possible emotional or neurotic reactions. The boy had a rating far below normal. This was written on a report and accompanied by comment as to his marks to the effect "doing as well as he can with his grade of mentality." The card, not enclosed in an envelope, was given him to take home. Of course his failures became more marked. A remark of the mother's was most significant. "When I got that report I knew it was no use. It was true, *he just couldn't succeed*." Evidently the mother's fear had antedated the report.

The boy was a fine, manly-looking young fellow, yet in the presence of his mother his reactions were those of a much younger child. There was a dependence which showed in his manner with her and in an anxiety when she left; there was also much love in his attitude. Evidently the mother-child bond had not been broken.

In his talk with me he showed lack of initiative, and an acceptance of himself as an inevitable failure. He was very sorry about it and anxious to do everything in his power, but he did not believe that would be very much. He was very suggestible and after a while, when his enthusiasms awoke, he was eager to enter a well-known preparatory school. "But do you think they would ever take me?" he asked. After rapport was established I introduced a few intelligence tests to see which way his mind liked to work best, but with no thought of examination. He was slow but did not fail. Association tests showed fear complexes.

From all this my intuitions were that the situation was one rooted in the mother-son relationship and that my real task lay with the mother. We worked back slowly through her fears until we came to the underlying cause. She had an only brother to whom she had been greatly attached. This boy, who had evidently been the mother's favorite, had failed completely in his masculine adaptation. Whenever he found a situation too hard, the mother decided that he was ill. He learned to take advantage of every slight cold and indisposition. He never finished school, he was "not strong enough" to try for college, and business soon became too hard. He finally drifted into the position often occupied by a favorite daughter, a comfort to his mother and a help and companion in the home. With this role his mother's unconscious desires were satisfied. Consciously she was deeply solicitous about getting him well so he could take a position, yet she invariably pulled him back by her anxieties.

The sister had been closely identified with him. She felt his failure deeply and had tried to take over on herself the burden of living out his life. For a time she attempted a masculine adaptation, but when she married her feelings of responsibility were replaced by anxieties. She feared that if she ever had a son he too would be a failure. When her daughters were born she had not feared and had been happy in them, but when her newborn son was first shown her, she had thought, "He is a boy, he will fail." Deep down in her unconscious she felt the sense of an impending fate. To compensate for this she bent every conscious energy toward making him succeed, but all her efforts were surcharged with anxiety. The boy, who could not know that in her mind he was completely identified with an uncle whom he had never seen, felt her anxiety and accepted it as something for which he must in some way be responsible. He was staggering under the burden of his uncle's ghost, which was sitting as firmly astride him as ever the Old Man of the Sea sat upon the shoulders of Sinbad the Sailor, and who, like the Old Man, was choking out the potentials that were really his.

When all this was raised into the mother's conscious, she was able to see that not only was the boy a separate entity, but that in reality he was an opposite type from her brother. She could see, also, that even in her brother's case the failure was not so much due to lack of potentials as it was to the mother's desire to keep him with her, as her child. This unconscious desire had been instrumental in making her nourish every weakness. The fate, which she had considered inevitable, was only her own tendency to repair this mistake of her mother's.*

I have known many cases where children were forced to bear the sins of their ancestors, not because of inheritance but because these ghosts were fastened to them by the processes of projection and identification. Sometimes the anxiety lest a child follow in the father's footsteps will produce an obsessive fear of the act which will result in a compulsion to perform it. We must exercise the greatest care in our use of a child's unconscious material, especially the dream material, lest we draw him into problems that are not suited to his understanding, or put him in contact with forces too overpowering for the unconscious. Yet we cannot overestimate the value of this material in giving us a key to neurotic disturbances which might seem to be caused by some obscure physical malady or congenital mental deficiency.

A striking case which I had a long time ago was used by Jung in his London lectures on children.† I include it here with his permission—his words were, "It is your case. You loaned it to me. I return it with a few comments." With his cooperation, I am quoting directly from his pages the case and conclusions as I gave them to him and his own comments, which add so greatly to their value.

* A case which showed striking similarity to this is given in Chapter 3, "Three Illustrations of the Power of the Projected Image." I include both cases, as they show such projection is not a unique phenomenon.

† Jung: *Collected Works*, vol. 17, Bollingen Series 20, New York, 1953–56.

The case concerns a little girl about nine years old. She ran a low temperature for three months and was unable to attend school. She had no other special symptoms except loss of appetite and languor. The physician could find no cause for the condition. Both the father and mother were sure that they had the child's full confidence and that she was not worried or unhappy in any way. The mother finally admitted that she and the father were not happy together; but she said they never discussed their difficulties before the child, who was completely unconscious of them. The mother wished for divorce, but could not make up her mind to the changes involved. It remained an open question between the parents. In the meantime they made no effort to adjust any of the difficulties that caused their unhappiness. Each had an unduly proprietorial emotional attachment to the child who, in turn, had a strong father-complex. She often slept in his room in a small bed close to his and came into his bed in the morning. She gave the following dreams.

"I went with Father to see Grandmother. Grandmother was in a boat, a big one. She wanted me to kiss her and wanted to put her arms round me, but I was afraid of her. Father said, 'Why, I want to kiss Grandmother.' I did not want him to. I was afraid that something would happen to him. Then the boat went off, and I couldn't find anybody, and I was frightened."

Several times she dreamed of the grandmother. Once she was all mouth, wide open. "I dreamed of a big snake. It came out from under my bed and played with me." She often spoke of the snake dream, and had one or two others which were similar. The grandmother dream she told with reluctance and then confessed that she was afraid whenever her father went away that he would not come back. She had guessed the parents' whole situation, and said that she knew her mother did not like her father; but she did not want to talk about it because it "would make them feel bad." Her father went away on business trips and then she was always afraid he would leave them. She also had noticed that her mother was happier then.

The mother came to see that she was not saving the child but only making her ill by leaving the situation unsolved. The parents had either to attack their difficulties with each other and endeavor to work out a real adjustment, or decide to separate. They chose the latter course, and explained the situation to the child. The mother had been sure that a separation would make the child ill, but instead her health improved just as soon as the real situation was brought into the open. She was told that she would not be separated from either parent, but would have two homes, and, though the divided time seems a poor arrangement for any child, her relief at no longer being a prey to her vague fears and intuitions was so great that she returned to normal health and to a real enjoyment of her school and play.

Jung comments as follows:

A case like this is often a great puzzle to the general practitioner. He seeks in vain an organic cause for the trouble and he does not know that he should look further—for no medical textbook would admit the possibility that trouble between father and mother can be made responsible for a child's low temperature. To the analyst, however, such cases are by no means unknown or strange. The child is so much a part of the psychic atmosphere of the parents that secret and unsolved trouble between them can influence the child's health profoundly. The *"participation mystique,"* that is, the primitive unconscious identity of the child with its parents, causes the child to feel the conflicts of the parents, and to suffer from them as if they were its own troubles. It is hardly ever the open conflict or the manifest difficulty that has the poisonous effect; it is almost always a disharmony repressed and neglected by the parents. The real first cause of such a neurotic disturbance is, without exception, the unconscious. It is the things vaguely felt by the child, the oppressive atmosphere of apprehension and self-consciousness, that slowly pervade the child's mind like a poisonous vapor and destroy the security of the conscious adaptation.

What this child seemed to feel most was her father's unconscious. When a man has no real relationship with his wife, then naturally he seeks another love object. If the man is not conscious of this seeking, or if he represses fantasies of that kind, then the

libido on the one side regresses to the memory image
of the mother and on the other side it invariably
seeks the daughter, if there is one. This is what one
would call unconscious incest. You cannot hold a
man responsible for that, as it is an entirely automatic process; but he should be held responsible for
being unconscious. It is morally wrong for him to
neglect his love problem. Unfortunately, it is almost a
collective ideal to be as negligent and unconscious of
love matters as possible. Behind the mask of respecta-
bility and decency the power of neglected love poisons the children. Of course you cannot blame the average man, as he receives no guidance in solving the
great problem of love from current ideals and conventions. These, unfortunately, are all in favor of negligence and repression.

The dream of the grandmother shows how the father's unconscious processes are penetrating the
child's unconscious. He wishes to kiss his mother, and
the child feels forced in the dream to kiss her. The
latter, being "all mouth, wide open" suggests swallowing. Obviously the child is in danger of being swallowed by her father's regressive libido. That is why
she dreams of a snake; for the snake, since of old,
has been the symbol of danger: of being caught in
coils, or swallowed, or poisoned. You will understand
such dreams better if you note what I have written
about serpent-symbolism in my *Psychology of the
Unconscious*.

The case also shows how apt children are to see
very much more than the parents would suspect. It is
of course quite impossible that parents should have
no complexes at all: that would be superhuman. But
they should deal with them consciously, they should
not evade their troubles to avoid painful discussions,
and so repress them. The love problem is part of
mankind's heavy toll of suffering, and nobody should
be ashamed that he must pay his tributes. It is a thousand times better in every respect for parents frankly
to discuss their problems instead of leaving their complexes to fester in the unconscious.

In such cases, what possible good could come from
telling a child about incestuous fantasies and father-
fixations? Such a procedure would make the child believe that it was all the fault of her own immoral,
non-moral, or at least foolish nature, and would heap

a burden of responsibility on her which was in reality her father's. She suffers, not because she has unconscious incestuous tendencies, but because her father has them. She is a victim of the wrong atmosphere in the home, and her trouble disappears as soon as her parents settle theirs.

In another case a child who was having difficulties of adaptation naïvely told the following dream, which seemed to have made a deep and disturbing impression. "My father and mother were living on opposite sides of a river. It was a very big river but every day I had to row across and cook my father's meals. Then I rowed back and I did not see my father again until the next day." In this dream the child was living out the mother's problem. The father and mother were living virtually separated lives so far as real relationship was concerned, but the mother neglected none of the duties of the home: she "rowed over every day and cooked the meals," no matter if the river which separated them "was a big river." The duty side of the situation was attended to, but with that the relationship ceased. "I did not see my father again until the next day." This dream, like all other dreams, could not be interpreted except in the light of the conscious of those persons involved. It is only through the cooperation of the parents and their honesty in taking up the problem suggested by the dream that we can obtain any light that will give us much help in solving the child's difficulty. Even with this understanding we can do pitifully little; the help must come through the courage of the parent. We can be of use only in applying our knowledge of the processes of the unconscious to show where the difficulty lies and then leave the responsibility to the person to whom it belongs.

Besides the problem which belongs to the parent and is for his own solution, the actual relationship between the parent and the child must be given consideration. Since the happiness and success and value of our lives depend so much upon our attitude toward relationships and our power to form true and wise ones, it is necessary to look well to the pattern on which the first are formed. In our psychic life, as well as in our intellectual, we cannot safely skip steps. In classroom work we know too well that if a child has had no grounding in the fundamentals of primary arithmetic he cannot do the work of the advanced grades with any certainty. So it is with relationships. If a child has not the experience and development, the sense of

security and trust that are the outgrowth of the proper
parent-child relation, he will be unable to cope with the
greater demands of adult relationships. But he should not
remain in these relationships too long, any more than he
should repeat grades. The relationship of the parent and
child should be continuously progressive. Its aim should be
the liberation of the child as an individual, so that he may
follow his own path whether or not that path is the one
that we would have chosen for him. He should be united
to us only by the bonds of comradeship and understanding. In the larger sense we can choose nothing for our
children. We can try to choose our own path clearly and
then use our clearness of vision to help the child upon his
own way.

THREE ILLUSTRATIONS OF THE POWER OF THE PROJECTED IMAGE

The enormous, even sinister, influence of the unsolved parental problem upon the unconscious of the child is vividly illustrated in this paper which I wrote for the book presented to Jung on his eightieth birthday.

"Everything unconscious is projected." * Hence the history of the development of consciousness is also a history of the release of psychic energy from the power of the projected image. While one remains in a state of unconsciousness life is a play of images that have their origin in the psyche and move from there to take possession of the outer world. Through this shifting of the subjective and objective man sees, not the reality of the object, but the mysterious quality of the image which has been projected upon it. Since the image is endowed with the magic of the unknown, the unconscious, element, it can exert a magnetic power of attraction or repulsion which appears to be a quality of the object itself.

In this way the tension of the opposites which exists within the psyche (the love-hate, fear-trust, affirmation or negation of experience) is seen as a struggle with factors of the outer world that seek dominion over the still infantile and fragmented ego. The outer world is filled with personifications of one's own loves, fears, desires, hates, and the

* Jung: *Two Essays on Analytical Psychology* (p. 195).

inner world is impoverished through a loss of creative possibility; for if the energy that escapes in projection could be retained within the psyche and used in the acceptance and assimilation of the shadow content, a new integration could take place, a newly created attitude could come into being, also an increased power of differentiation between inner and outer realities would be achieved.

Only by becoming related to the subjective factors can one become related to the object, for not until projection is withdrawn can relationship emerge from the shadow of the projected image into the light of consciousness where subject and object can face each other as separate personalities each existing in his own right.

Also all that has once been conscious and is repressed into the unconscious seeks its escape in the form of projection. Since the process of transformation is always at work in the unconscious and, as strange metamorphoses take place in the shadow land of the buried or forgotten affect, the image that reemerges often seems to bear no resemblance or relation to the "dead" emotion that was interred. Both the creator of the image and its victim are unaware of the real nature of the ruling emotion which is projected, and the encounter with the image seems a new experience with a newly discovered object.

The projected image has an uncanny way of discovering the vulnerable spot, the unlocked door, in the psyche of its chosen victim, and through this door it effects an entrance. Jung says: "Even the worst projection is at least hung upon a hook, perhaps a very small one, but still a hook offered by the other person." * Without this hook the projection would fall harmlessly to the ground.

It is the secret, often the unknown because unconscious, desire that offers this "hook" or that opens the door to the inner citadel of the psyche. If the man who resents the projection that has been thrust upon him would turn the mirror of vision upon himself he would discover the creature within his psyche who welcomes the intruder. He did not lock the door because this secret element wanted the projection to get in. It is this inner entity with whom he must deal if he would find the reality of his relation to himself, also to the object, for "we are betrayed by that which lives within."

The emotionally undeveloped man who is unconsciously looking for a mother will discover, or will be discovered

---

* Jung: *Contributions to Analytical Psychology* (p. 52).

by, the woman who is seeking a permanent child, one who will not grow up and leave her. He who hates his own life will find an image of hate confronting him in an outer object. He who fears commitment and would shirk responsibility will encounter a tyrant ready to enter in and take over his life.

The more unconscious a person is, and the more he lives through identification and *participation mystique,* the greater is the power of the projection for, like the child, he has not yet emerged from the collective unconscious and images that arise from these deeper levels have primeval strength and can evoke all the power of the archetype. This gives the image its uncanny and overwhelming power. The witch, the demon magician, the vengeful god may become constellated in a relationship which would, if considered in its human reality, be quite harmless. Jung speaks of the devilish effect that can arise between two people neither of whom is in any way a devil but who simply have a mutual antipathy on which projection may be hung.

The projected image is a clever contriver of disguises; disguises that conceal its true nature from its creator as well as from the object it seeks out. It can clothe domination in the guise of selfless love, it can conceal hate with the mask of anxious concern, it can creep into the unconscious as guilt and emerge as fear that dogs the footsteps of its victim, or as hate that casts its shadow upon another life.

One of the favorite disguises of the projected image is the mask of so-called love. Any unconscious emotion can assume this mask. Jung says: "Where love reigns there is no will-to-power and where will-to-power is paramount love is lacking. The one is the shadow of the other." * Yet it is this shadow that often appears wearing the mask of love. Not until we have perceived and dealt with the shadow side of our own emotional involvement can we begin to understand the true nature of love that has a respect for the innate difference in, and the freedom of, another personality.

Love's shadow, will-to-power, often appears as overanxious solicitude which takes the form of making over, protecting (really limiting) the beloved object. There is an effort to prune, manipulate or enclose growth, lest the wrong thing develop in the psyche of the one so loved. Or buried guilt creeps out as fear which weaves a web of anx-

* Jung: *Two Essays on Analytical Psychology* (p. 52).

ious love in which the object may be caught. Also the need
to be loved opens the door to the projection and the wish
to be "as you desire me" welcomes domination and distorts
the personality; fearing to lose love one loses the self. Or if
one loves only the projected image, this creature of one's
own creation, any assertion of the reality appears as betrayal—a proof that the beloved is unworthy of the love be-
stowed. This interplay of the shadows of love enters into
every unconscious relationship, parent-child, anima-ani-
mus, savior and disciple. The field of projection is limitless,
touching every aspect of life. In this brief paper I am
choosing three examples taken from the also vast field of
mother-child relationship which illustrate the power of the
projected image to darken the lives of both.

The ego of the child is still too unformed to be able to
set up barriers against the invasion of forces that move in
the unconscious of the adult to whom he is still bound in
an identification which is only broken as his ego attains a
degree of conscious integration which permits personal
freedom of choice. He is also so near to the region of the
collective unconscious that the image of the parent is a
blending of personal and archetypal which gives to the parental image a mythological power as of a god.

The most loved child may be the one most endangered
by the projection of the parent's problem because the emotional tie is strongest between the unconscious of the loved
child and the parent and so has all the strength of primal
identification.

When through fear of taking up her own life, the mother
refuses to face her own problem, it can infect the unconscious of the child. This is especially true when the problem lies in the field of Eros for it is in this field of relatedness that woman's life must be primarily lived. If she
evades this she falls into the power of the unconscious animus and love loses its clear differentiating power which
would free it from the grip of the dark mother forces that
seek dominion over herself and the child. The images of
fear then appear to have their origin in the child's own
psyche. Only when the mother raises the problem to consciousness and accepts it as her own can the child be freed
from the shadow of the projected image.

The first example illustrates how the child's unconscious
may be infected by the fears which the mother refuses to
recognize as her own because they relate to a love problem
which she has evaded and "forgotten." The contagion in

this case was so great that the images of fear appeared to have their origin in the child's own psyche.

The mother came to consult me about her eight-year-old daughter, her "most loved" child, who had become the victim of irrational fears. At night, even though a friendly night light burned in the hall and she knew that the family were at home, she would wake in panic at the slightest sound. A cat's footfall on the piazza roof was a burglar stealing in with intent to rob or even murder; a small crackling sound flamed into conviction that the house was on fire, it would burn down. Recently the fears had moved into the daytime. She was afraid to go to school, she would forget her lessons, the children would laugh at her, she would be disgraced. "She is really very bright," the mother said, "in some ways the brightest of the children. She has an uncanny way of producing the right answers, and she says the most amazingly true things about people—sometimes it is quite embarrassing. I think the real fear of school is riding in the car. We live in the country quite a distance from the school and all the children ride, but she is so afraid of an accident that she anticipates disaster at every turn of the wheel. I want to ask if I may send the car to bring you to see her? We do not ask her to come to town any more. It is such a strain for her."

I asked how they had handled these fears.

"You can't reason with her. If you try to show her how silly the fears are she says, 'But people *do* get killed in automobiles. I see it all the time in the papers. Houses *do* burn down.' Of course you cannot deny that they do sometimes, and all the hundreds of times they do not make no impression upon her."

It was evident that the child was an intuitive, one of those people to whom facts, statistics, and the law of probabilities are nonexistent as argument, for only the intuited potential has validity. Since good and evil exist in every situation either element can be perceived as ruling factor of the coming event. If the intuition is oriented by fear and insecurity or by destructive emotion, the negative possibility is the one immediately sensed and becomes the dominant of the coming event. Therefore no matter how sensible and patient and reasonable the argument may be, intuition dodges behind statistics and probabilities and seizes upon the possible element of danger, magnifying it until it becomes the almost inevitable certainty. Trust and love are the only arguments that have a convincing power which is beyond the rational and which triumphs, also irrationally, over such fear.

What was the X, the unknown yet existing problem that had undermined her sense of security and had made her live in a state of continuous apprehension? There must be some basically dangerous element apprehended by her unconscious, which had worked an evil magic that now manifested itself in these irrational fears. What was the unknown X and to whom did it really belong? Was it a will-to-power working in the unconscious of the child herself which used her superior function in autocratic power over the parents, or was it an unacknowledged problem of an adult who had power over the child's emotional life?

The home had every appearance of normal, healthy country living, also an atmosphere of culture, a little on the sensible well-bred side perhaps, but this only to the critical eye. The other two children were healthy little animals interested in their sports and pets and daily events.

The child's creative imagination had been starved by a diet of oversterilized facts and an unnourishing ersatz brand of optimism given in an effort to curb the destructive fantasies. Of course this had only made them search more persistently for food. Therefore with her I went straight into the enemy territory where forbidden fruit flourished —the land of myth and fairy tale, where frogs turned into princes, witches worked their good or evil spells and a cat might turn out to be the Robber Kitten or a Puss in Boots. She went with me eagerly into this country and talked of "the people who live inside your head." Also some of the energy of her fantasy went into stories of her own, but the basic fears were untouched—the outer world was still a place where danger lurked. As soon as darkness fell, or a new situation presented itself, there were the fears, real and waiting. Then, as we became friends, the deep secret fears showed themselves. She would be sent away to school and never come back; the family would move away in the night and she would be left with strangers, etc. etc. The inner fears all showed her deep insecurity in that domain of love which should be the child's natural emotional home. A truly loved child is not apt to be the victim of such fears. From whom did they come?

The mother's solicitude became more obvious as we talked of the child's problem. In fact it became so fraught with anxiety as to become suspect. Could it be that she was defending the child against something dangerous in herself?

At last "for the sake of the child" she began to talk of

herself and of her marriage and her relations with her husband. It was all so as-it-should-be, even the problems were well-bred. Then, lured by an attractive dream, she started analysis, cautiously at first, trying not to venture more than ankle-deep in the dangerous waters of the unconscious, but before long one of those banal little dreams that seem so harmless appeared. Association led her back to the summer before this youngest child was born and the "forgotten" rose and confronted her—an inexplicable fascination which a man much older than herself "had exerted over her." He had "roused terrible feelings in her." He had tempted her to run away with him and she had almost yielded to the temptation, but the realization that she was in the early weeks of pregnancy and that this child must be born under the father's roof had saved her from "this terrible act of sin." So nothing had happened, and yet everything had happened, for she had caught a glimpse of a strange creature who lived inside herself and she was afraid, and because she was afraid she set strict watch on her every impulse lest it should arouse this creature again and it would devour her respectable life.

She was afraid, desperately afraid of herself. She tried to project this fear upon the man—it was his evil fascination that she feared; so she refused ever to see him again. This should have freed her but it did not. She was beset by alien desires. She was tormented by fear, at times she hated the unborn child who had "saved her from herself." The child became the image of the savior but also of the one who had deprived her of the life for which she passionately longed.

After the child's birth she tried to forget the whole experience. She thrust the disturbing emotions back into the unconscious and bade them sleep. Unfortunately her intuition had also come alive and acted in her present life. She saw flaws in this nice conventional life that had hitherto satisfied her, also she saw flaws in this nice conventional man that she had "loved" and married. She tried the expedient of not looking, and went back to the activities of her conventional life and to the security of church and home and of everything-as-it-should-be.

But the buried fears lived a projected life in this child who, she felt in her unconscious, had saved and deprived her. She had herself known how the small crackling could burst into the destructive flame, she too had feared the robber who in her life could steal the jewel of her conscious virtue. In outer objective form the child lived out her mother's inner symbols of fear.

As the analysis proceeded and images rose from the unconscious she began to face the problem of the fear within herself—a fear that if she accepted her own reality and in turn demanded certain realities in her marriage relationship the whole carefully constructed structure might collapse.

The steps of her analysis do not belong here but the fact that when she raised her own fears to consciousness and accepted them and began to deal with their influence upon herself, the child began almost immediately to be freed of the burden which had been projected upon her. She would speak with amusement of the time when she thought the people who were "walking about in her head" were trying to get in the window, and refer to her former self as that silly girl who wouldn't ride in an automobile. None of the fears were dealt with directly; they vanished with the dawning of a new day.

When the mother faced her own Eros problem she could also face the ambivalence of her love for this child. She could now see the child objectively, and separate her from the subjective elements of her own emotional life. In this way her love for the child was no longer darkened by the shadow of the projected image but could function in conscious understanding. It was this security of love that acted with the magic of good medicine, that changed the orientation of the child's intuition so that it had the healthy normal interest in the new, and the anticipation of the potential of good, which is the birthright of the normally loved child.

The child never knew the mother's problem. It did not belong to her. When the mother accepted it as her own the child's intuition could begin to free itself from the spider web of fear in which it had been caught. Also as the mother became able to accept the child's reality apart from the projection, she was able to give true and deserving love instead of the anxious, guilty emotion that she had misnamed love. In this new security the child's own feeling could function normally and her intuition, her superior function, was not the autocratic and negative ruler of her life.

The mother's evasion of her love problem was the creator of the projected image that had lived its shadow life in the child's unconscious.

Guilt and fear of life were creators of the image which was projected upon this second child. The image in the mother's unconscious had such authority that it snuffed out the flame of the child's own being.

Many, very many years ago, when in the world of educators the Stanford-Binet tests outranked the Bible as the infallible word of God, I was asked if I would recommend a special school for a defective nine-year-old boy. He had been given the intelligence test in his own school and later the school's diagnosis had been confirmed through his again being tested, this time at the psychological clinic of a university. In both tests he was classified as a low-grade defective—almost a borderline moron. The diagnosis confirmed the school's verdict that he was unable to function in any school for normal children. Both the school and the doctor in charge felt that the problem was now clear, a good school for defective children must be found. The doctor asked if I could recommend one.

I replied that I could not select a school until I had not only seen and talked with the parents but had also studied the child and had been given time to make friends with him and to estimate his needs through knowledge of his own personality, a knowledge that could only come when he felt at ease and secure. Since the child "had always been surrounded by love," this request was considered unnecessary but was reluctantly conceded. The parents came to see me first.

The father was making the best of it in a direct, reasonable, masculine way. He wished to do everything to meet the inevitable by supplying whatever was right for the child no matter what it cost. He did not speak of his own disappointment nor of the failure of his hopes for his only son except indirectly as he talked of the child's babyhood, the years before the inevitable had become the proven. But when I said that I believed the intelligence tests did not infallibly reveal the innate potential of intelligence, but only showed the amount of intelligence available to the child at the time of testing, nor did they show the emotional blocks that might make innate intelligence temporarily unavailable, he eagerly grasped at this new hope and I knew I should have a chance to establish relations with the boy. Also whatever evil magic might be at work here, it did not come from the father's unconscious.

The mother's attitude was one of fatalistic despair. She dared not hope, dared not postpone decision lest it might be "all too late." The right school now was the answer, but

she would not override her husband's decision. I knew that
if the problem could be solved I would have many encounters with the denizens of her unconscious though I
had no intuitive preknowledge of their nature.

Then the boy came. His mother brought him and, at my
request, left him alone with me. There were two small
aquariums in the room, one filled with incessantly hungry
tadpoles. I suggested his feeding them and his conversation
with and about the largest tadpole seemed to me normal,
but any direct question roused fear and confusion. If a direct answer was demanded he cast about for any random
word, or he stared at me dumbly. Evidently direct questions were to be avoided. The interview could have been
classified as uneventful so far as diagnosis was concerned,
but he wanted to come again.

I made an appointment with the mother for the following day. Again I was met by a fatalistic attitude. To her
the present situation was only the working out of the already known, something that could not have been otherwise. There was deep grief, despairing love, but one felt
everything moved in a world of shadows where there was
no living reality.

The mother's preknowledge of doom was suspect. Why
had she "always known this had to happen"? From what
unsolved problem of the past had this ghost of presenti-
ment arisen? Whence did it derive its authority? What ancient image dominated her unconscious? Casting questions
about in the waters of the past as a fisherman casts his fly,
I asked about her family—a sister? a brother? Here a
fear-fish rose and swallowed the bait. "I had a brother,"
she said, and the shadow of the projected image darkened
her face. "He was like M. He was a sweet baby but he did
not grow up. He died when he was fifteen. I was glad. I
did love him once but I was ashamed of him. The children
laughed at him, and they looked at me as if I was different
too. I wouldn't let him play with me. But God always pun-
ishes you for such things, my mother told me he would,
but I laughed at her. And she wouldn't send my brother
away where he could be cared for properly, to some place
where he could be happy. No one could make her, not
even the doctor. Instead she made me feel it was my fault
because I did not really love him, because I neglected him.
Then after he died I was afraid, afraid of my own wicked-
ness because I was glad he was dead. I was sorry too, because I kept remembering what a sweet baby he had been,
and I kept loving that baby. I meant never to marry be-

cause I might have a child, it might be a boy, it might be like him. But I fell in love and took a chance. I had no right to because I *knew*.

"When I found I was pregnant I prayed to God every night that the baby would be a girl. When they told me it was a boy I turned my face away and wept. I could not bear to look at him. When I did look at him, I saw he was like my brother and I *knew*."

To be able to tell this secret to another person lifted a burden of lonely guilt. She could begin to talk of it as part of her own experience. She could hope for a way of deliverance. She could envision a possibility of understanding it. She started analysis which revealed a tragic play of images. She had been unconscious of their domination of her whole life pattern.

The presiding image of fear was Jehovah, the God of vengeful justice. He was created in the image of her mother's animus which was the force that had ruled her childhood. This God would contrive to punish her by making her do, in humiliation and penitence, the thing that she had wickedly refused—just as her mother made her eat, at a future meal, food she had refused at a former one, and even arranged at times that this food would appear when there were visitors so that she would be shamed before them. "In the end you'll be made to do it when you won't like it so well." This was what God was waiting to do to her. He would manipulate her life so she would be forced to do the thing that she had tried to escape. The obvious way would be to make her repeat in the life of her child the experience she had refused to face with her brother. "You can't get away from it," she said. "Sometime you have to face it—it is always there waiting for you." But she did not realize that the thing waiting to be faced was within herself, her own guilt over denying love that she had been ashamed to let live openly.

The shadow of the projected image had darkened her marriage, for her love for her husband was seen as the weakness that had betrayed her—a weakness that had drawn him into the circle of fate presided over by this spying, waiting, God of vengeance. Through loving him, she had brought punishment upon him also. "He was so proud of having a son. It nearly killed me when I knew what would come of it all."

Her analysis was a long one dealing with many tangled threads of her Eros problem—the love and hate for her mother—the Terrible Mother from whom she had never

dared free herself; her "guilty" love for her husband that
had brought about this fulfillment of her doom; the buried
sense of power that had imposed on him the acceptance of
this image which she had projected upon his son. The
working out of her own victim psychology that had made
her unconsciously seek retributive punishment in order to
atone and so remove the sense of guilt at having evaded
the problem of love with her brother. It was as though a
power in her unconscious had forced her to evoke the
image of her brother and to project it upon her son to
prove to herself that she could go through with it—could
pull it off. He was not only her just punishment but also
the victim of her urge for self-justification and of a twisted
and distorted desire for redemption. She offered him as a
sacrifice to the terrible father God even as Abraham had
offered Isaac, but her vengeful God had provided no ram
as a substitute.

There was another element involved in her determination to send him away "where he would be happy," for by
the act she was unconsciously achieving a triumph over
her mother who refused this sacrifice. "Where will-to-
power reigns love is lacking." In all this fatal drama her
unconscious will-to-power had made her see herself as
playing the central role. All the other actors—even God
himself—were only supporting images who acted the parts
to which she had assigned them.

As she withdrew the projections and took over her own
problems she became able to see both her husband and her
child as realities existing in themselves and became able to
love them with growing understanding, but that took a
long, long time.

The liberation of the child began as soon as she accepted the problem as her own and turned her anxiety
upon herself. He did not know that this ghost-uncle who
cast the shadow on his life had ever existed, nor did he
ever need to know. The atmosphere about him cleared. He
no longer breathed the poison gas of his mother's projected passion for sacrifice.

In a new school where it was considered normal for a
child to grow at his own pace and where a time for con-
valescence from a psychological illness was also considered
to be normal, he began to function without fear. His innate intelligence became liberated long before his mother
finished her intricate analysis. Yet it was when she started
on her way that he could start on his.

Nearly thirty years after my first meeting with this boy

I found in a New York paper the picture of Dr. M. X.—recently appointed departmental head in one of our leading hospitals. The unusual name arrested my attention. There was something vaguely familiar in the face. It was, as subsequent inquiry proved, the "defective" child whom I had seen so many years ago.

The third illustration deals with the perils of the selfless life, also with the hook of infantile irresponsibility that reaches out toward the selfless one. The clue to the play of unconscious images is found in the words of the selfless mother concerning her relation to her only child, her son —"I cannot live my own life unless *he is safe."*

She had never lived her own life because it had never seemed to have importance for her. From early childhood she "really had not cared" about herself. "It did not seem worthwhile." Remaining unconscious of the demand of life for a central integration, a self-choosing, without which there can be no real relatedness to experience, she had drifted from act to act, from situation to situation, reacting sometimes to the momentary demand of her own desires or the temporary activations of libido that arose from her own very truly creative potentials, but more often she yielded to the demands which were made upon her by others. Even her marriage had not been dictated by her own emotional urges or sense of personal values, but by the impetuous and passionate demands of a man who had projected his soul-image upon her. He asserted that she *must* marry him—so she did.

He was brilliant, unstable, without self-determination. He was a prey to the sudden impulses that arose within him, and was swayed by every wind that blew through him. His unconscious saw in her, not only an object of his own desires, but also a means of escape from his own over-possessive mother who had ruled his emotional life and from the will of his father that had dominated his masculine libido in a form of patriarchal castration that had thwarted his creativity and had driven him toward a goal not his own. This father had early determined upon the son's future career and had "made a place" for him in his own world—a world for which the youth was temperamentally unsuited and in which he failed. The young man assumed no responsibility for this failure. He maintained that it was his father's fault because he had not been allowed to choose for himself.

In marriage he demanded this freedom from his young

wife. Not only must she carry his feeling for him but also she must accept his vagrant impulses as though they were conscious responsible choice, and devote herself to carrying them out. The wife accepted his ultimatum that he must choose for himself, even as she accepted his animal projections, and she tried to live out his present choices for him and bring them through to fulfillment through her own efforts. This only delivered him, more and more, over to his own unconscious. The marriage broke in disaster, as might have been expected. This occurred when the only child, a son, was an infant. All the mother's libido now became involved in the life of the child. "For his sake" she returned to a safe, conventional environment and took up a pattern of life that was in no way her own, and where nothing of her own would interfere with the dedication of her life to his. Here in this "safe" environment, encircled by her protective love, he was to choose for himself.

The boy was temperamentally like his father. He had the same intuitive brilliance, the same low threshold which made him near to both the perils and the riches of the unconscious. She feared every manifestation of these innate potentials for she was convinced that they had brought disaster to the father.

Both she and the boy were now caught in the ambivalence of the attitudes that governed her anxious love. On the one hand she was convinced that the primary cause of her husband's failure was that he had been forced into a life that was not his own choice, on the other hand she was equally convinced that the potentials of his own personality were dangerous and destructive and were the cause of his disaster. She was too afraid of life to see that potentials are the raw materials of personality which may be used creatively or destructively, depending upon the central attitude of the one who uses them. Her fear saw only their peril and she projected these fears upon the boy. In this way her unconscious delivered him over to the shadow-side of his own potentials, and to the power of her negative image of his father.

She was caught "between the devil and the deep blue sea." He must choose for himself—he must be saved from himself. The old rhyme comes to mind:

> *"Mother, may I go out to swim?"*
> *"Yes, my darling daughter:*
> *Hang your clothes on a hickory limb*
> *And don't go near the water."*

So his adventures into the waters of life must be guarded from any encounter with the waves of chosen experience.

Then she rationalized the problem of the contradiction. He must choose as soon as he was mature enough to choose with discretion—in the meantime he must be kept safe from his own perilous potentials through "giving him every opportunity"—provided the opportunity met with her preconceived idea of what was best for him.

So she built a nice protective wall about a pasture of well-selected clover. Here he could safely choose which clover head looked most tempting. The trouble was he didn't like clover and he objected to the wall. He tried to find a way out but since he had breathed in the poison of self-distrust he was frustrated by his own doubts and fears. At last he took the only way he saw open to him. He leaped the wall. He ran away.

Despair seized upon the mother. He had gone and he had taken with him her only reason for living. She was tempted to suicide but the small hope that he might return and still need her was the thread that held her to life. She could not choose even death for herself. Life and death were both conditioned by his possible need.

She had already made some tentative attempts at analysis but the ruling conviction that her own life did not matter made her associate all dream images with his problem. No suggestions that the images related to her own life "clicked." Yet in her despair she returned to analysis, for the transference now represented her only remaining emotional tie; yet she also clung to the hope that she might become more able to enter into his life should he return.

At first the analysis followed the old pattern, but as the dream sequence developed and dealt more and more with the symbols of transformation, she saw them as arising within her own psyche and having relation to her individual need and to her life as a woman. She stopped struggling to make them mean what she intended them to mean. She let them act upon her.

Summer came and she was leaving town. It was her last hour of analysis before fall. As the hour drew toward a close, there came to her, like the breaking of a new dawn, a consciousness of her own separate life, a gift originally given, an individual potential which was hers to live, whatever might happen in the life of another. She said: "I am going to take up my own life and learn to live it even if I never see him again. My sorrow will go with me always but it will be my own life that I shall live." It was the end of the hour. The clock struck twelve.

Three days later she received a letter. Its date was the day of her decision. It read: "Dear Mother, I am sitting on a hillside three thousand miles away. Just now I heard the clock strike nine and suddenly I felt that a fear that had been with me always was gone. I am coming home."

The striking of twelve had occurred simultaneously with the striking of nine in the faraway village. It was at the moment of her decision that the fear of her enveloping love fell from him. There had existed between them an identification so close that it was not broken by separation nor by the thousands of miles between them. Only when, by conscious act of choice, she broke the threads that bound her life to his, could he feel released from his fear of her.

Yet no one can accomplish the inner release of another person. Freedom can be offered but it must also be accepted in order for it to "take." The task of living is an individual one. Her acceptance of responsibility for her own life did not automatically bring about his acceptance of his.

Until now her desire to live his life for him, so as to protect him from the shadow image which she had projected upon him, had furnished ample excuse for his evasion of responsibility, but when this was withdrawn he had nowhere to go except inside himself. He must now find the creature in his own psyche who had made the projection welcome. This did not suit him at all. One is often surprised at the indignation of the victim at being set free. The luxury of resentment is removed and there is no one to carry the blame for one's own mistakes.

His act of rebellion had been only a narcissistic flight from the mother. He did not overcome the mother, he simply ran away from her because of his negative involvement. After his return he continued to run away, not from the personal mother but from the demands of Great Mother Life, demands that he should accept his freedom and his responsibilities and grow up. His fear was now the fear of Life and he demanded from the Great Mother the sympathy and indulgence that his human mother had hitherto given him.

His life now became a series of episodes rather than one of conscious choice. After each unsuccessful attempt he returned for help to the mother who now struggled to give him true freedom of choice. She was aware of the damage that he had suffered from the projection that had darkened his childhood and accepted the responsibilities of the new relationship without carrying for him the burden of his still vagrant choices. Her love, freed from fear, could function in discrimination and clarity but this he was not yet able to accept.

Then he had a dream—a nightmare. He was in his childhood home. A sinister figure was pursuing him. He fled in terror and, as he fled, he knew the pursuer to be his father. The dream became a panoramic rehearsal of his whole life, even as, in times of great danger, all of life may be reviewed in an instant of time. In the dream he fled from place to place—home, school, college, work—and still the father followed after, chasing him from every situation where he had tried to find a hiding place from his own masculinity.

He then saw that he had been caught by the shadow image of the father which had once been projected upon him and now had power over him because of his infantile and regressive attitude. It was this shadow that he must now turn and face, for it had possession of his own potentials. This shadow he must now overcome and so win for himself the positive values of his own personality. Only so could he deal with the traitor in himself who had opened the door to the projection of the negative father image. Only so could he overcome the mother, his own infantile desires, and wrest from the shadow his own masculine authority.

It is a long journey from identification and projection to clear and conscious relationship. Before this can be accomplished the magnetic power of the projection must be broken by each of the persons involved through bringing the unconscious elements into the light of consciousness.

Perhaps the greatest defense against projection is a reverence for life and a respect for the value and the dignity of the human personality.

4

EARLY RELATIONSHIPS

From the time of its conception the child is moving toward the attainment of an individual life. As in the womb his body is being prepared for an individual and separate existence, so during the necessary identifications of infancy his psyche is being prepared for separate and individual life. At each tiny step forward he is beset by two great currents which from his birth to his death he must meet whenever he is confronted with a new situation: the surge toward the new, and the pull backward toward the safety of the old.

The first adaptations of a baby seem to us so simple that we do not realize that great forces are at work from the beginning. Progress and regression, rebirth and death are present from the earliest days, and are shown in the little acts of the little child as well as in the larger acts of the larger adult. The problem of life is always how to meet the demands which life makes upon us at any given time. From this point of view our sense of values changes. We no longer see the events of childhood as over small or over great; we see all phases of life as of equal importance.

This attitude of equal reverence toward every stage of growth makes us look beneath the outer expression to the inner unfolding. Since we can see so short a way into that inner life, we become patient in the presence of slow growth, and fearful of manipulating or dictating. We learn to think of a child as a tree planted beside the rivers of water, that brings forth its fruit in its season. We wait for that deep relationship which is our only way of discovering the real depths of a child's nature; of another human being we can have only that part which is revealed to us in love. The more we combine love with understanding the more truly do we know our children.

A normal nature must progress. It must develop like a plant toward its own form of maturity. If a bud loses its power of unfolding we recognize that it is blighted and that this is an unnatural condition. If a child fails to progress from an infantile adaptation to one better suited to a later period of growth we must realize that some blighting influence is at work. Nor can the life force of an individual be arrested and remain static. Life must move, either forward or backward; if the set of the libido is not progressive it becomes regressive.

There is a form of regression that is normal, existing in every normal human being. Whenever a new situation is to be met, there is a strong compulsion toward retreat to the old and easier way, as well as an impulsion toward the newly demanded development. This is a wise provision of nature; it gives balance and caution. Its normal use is to provide a temporary response from which is gathered impetus for a new advance. In this way we retreat to gather strength, to gain the forward push of life. When the compulsion toward retreat becomes the dominant force we have an individual whose life current is turned in the wrong direction. One of the most potent causes of this wrong use of the retreat is fear, which holds the individual in a temporary paralysis and may cause a split in the personality. While one part desires to grow up, the other desires to remain a child, in the safe shelter of the familiar.

In a child, and even in later periods of development, this attitude often finds expression in infantile regressive acts which earlier in life were normal adaptations. To the infant the most interesting things in the world are himself and what goes into him. The mouth is the first organ of sensation, food the most important object, sucking the most important occupation. Undisturbed by countersensations of pain, he will placidly suck and sleep and suck again. Touch, sight, and hearing all contribute to this pleasure-pain world of sensation. Objects are felt at first subjectively; the outside world exists as a part of his sensation and for his comfort. Then he discovers his toes and his fingers; his body becomes his natural toy. For the infant auto-erotism is a normal adaptation; it is one of the stages through which each must pass. It is not a mysterious evil to be mentioned only in whispers. It is not even harmful unless dwelt in too long.

A child who has normally passed beyond auto-erotic acts may be thrown back into them by an abnormal urge toward retreat. It may take any of the forms belonging to that earlier stage of development, for instance, finger-sucking, or bed-wetting. Then we must be careful not to attach importance to the symptom rather than to the disease. When we find a child remaining in, or returning to, such infantile acts, we should try to investigate his fantasy life, or in some way to find out from what he is retreating, instead of taking coercive measures to stop the act itself. The direction of the force must be changed, or when shut off from one expression it will find its outlet in some other regressive form. The new outlet may be an increased fantasy thinking, more detrimental though not as apparent from the outside, but leading to unaccountable failures or acts of obstinacy, and to separation from reality.

In his laboratory work with adult patients, Jung became convinced that the fundamental problem of a neurosis was not to be found in the disturbing experiences that lay in the early life of the patient but was rather concerned with the present, and was shown in a failure to meet some duty or task which life now presented. The obstacle which was considered too great might lie in some outer circumstance, or it might arise from some inner necessity. In either case there was need for a new attitude toward life, for a different conception of the self and of human relationships. Failure to make the new adaptation produced conflict and a desire for retreat, which resulted in a sense of defeat. To overcome this the patient took refuge in a more infantile form of life, or in a neurotic illness which furnished him with an excuse which he could present, not only to others but even to his own unconscious, for his failure to accept life. The real problem in the analysis became: from what present duty is the patient retreating.

It is true that to understand a neurosis it must be traced back to its very beginning. It is not enough to cut off the top of a weed; the roots must be dug up. It is necessary to go back through a painstaking analysis in order to discover innate tendencies, and to find out what, in the early years, drove them down into the unconscious or gave them an abnormal strength. Often a shock, either real or in fantasy, is found to be the starting point of a neurosis. Nevertheless, the crucial problem continues to be the present attitude.

When we study children, no matter how young, we see that this principle holds good also with them. It is when the task is too hard that there is a tendency to slip back into an easier way, a more babyish adaptation. In order to avoid the feelings of inferiority that this would give, the problem is pushed down into the unconscious, and much of the life energy (the libido) is withdrawn from use in the conscious life and becomes busy with regressive fantasies, or finds expression in infantile acts whose meaning is not understood by the actor himself. Jung found that in the dreams of adult patients there was a tendency to go back to the images of the past, not only to those of the personal past, but also to those inheritances from primitive life, the archetypes and symbols of the myth.

We find a similar process at work in the daydreams of children. They go back to the fantasy form of thinking and repeat certain well-known patterns: the Cinderella fantasy, the neglected and misunderstood little girl who is discovered by her fairy godmother and who has every wish immediately fulfilled and all her virtues accepted; the giant killer who removes with magical ease those "larger ones" who threaten his path, and instantly becomes himself the hero. In a certain type of child there is an outbreak of childish and unreasonable acts, or a return to some outgrown childish habit that gives a sense of babyhood and security. In the unconscious of each of us lies an image of childhood as a protected, carefree time, a period when life makes no difficult demands. This picture may be absolutely untrue in any individual case, yet it remains in the unconscious of each one of us and may operate regressively.

A child was brought to me for thumb-sucking. The parents had tried punishment, reward, tying up the thumbs, in the attempt to cure the isolated symptom. The child was naturally bright, but she had lived the most of her life in fantasy. She was fond of curling up in an attitude that resembled that of a child in the womb; then she would tuck her thumb into her mouth, and drift off into a world of daydreams. Here all was elaborate self-aggrandizement. She wove fairy stories of lovely princesses to whom all things came as if by magic; she indulged in bombastic lies. The stories were evidently an expression of her unconscious wish to obtain everything without effort, an attempt to cover up a feeling of inferiority that intruded in spite of the dreams. We chose one of her own make-believe figures upon whom we could project the lies and the boastings.

This person could, we agreed, do things that were not permissible to people in our real world. In so separating herself from the undesirable, she began to emerge as a distinct personality. We continued the fairy tales, differentiating them from child stories of real life. When we drained off the unreal by attaching it to the fantasy figure, the residue made up a very babyish little girl who was not willing to do her job of growing up like ordinary little girls.

When the fantasy identification was broken, she began to be herself and to take up her own little responsibilities. The new attitude was accepted, and the thumb-sucking stopped automatically. The story-making continued, but in the form of story-writing which required directed thought. In this way the imagination was not depreciated but given a new value. Such identifications are not limited to childish experience. There are many persons who go through life living on fantasy identifications, or else identifications with money or reputation or family prestige, which save them from facing the reality of their own individual worth.

A four-year-old boy wet his bed every night. He knew that it was a babyish thing to do. He was ashamed of it, and wished to stop it, but the accident continued to occur regularly. He had a strong mother-fixation and a will to power. His mother would get up every night and change his clothes and his bedding, and this was gratifying to his unconscious power demands. Running counter to these infantile desires were others of a more progressive kind, which made him want to grow up and be a man like his father. He and his father talked of things that they would do together. One day his father suggested an excursion for the next day but wondered if the small son was old enough. It was decided that he had better stay at home with his mother. That night he said, "No rubber sheet for me. I am too old for it. I am never going to wet the bed again." The mother had keen intuitions. She expressed no doubt, but removed the sheet. The next morning the bed was dry. The new adaptation had been made through the acceptance of the desire to grow up as the ruling motive. The new trend of the libido ruled the child even in his sleep. The next day the boy took the proposed excursion with his father, and entered upon a new relationship.

The infantile act was never repeated. Consciously he had tried to stop this act before, but it was not until the conscious willing and the unconscious desire were both directed toward the same end that the desired result was accomplished. Had the mother argued or insisted upon leaving the sheet, the child might have been thrown back upon his old attitude through distrust of his powers to meet the new, and, dropping back into his old fantasies, would have continued the act when his unconscious took control during sleep. We must be quick to accept new and more adult attitudes, and to give the child every opportunity to act upon them. There is always an inner distrust to be met and overcome, and if we add to that our own distrust we make the new impossible.

Bed-wetting is always a regressive act, though it may arise from various causes. Sometimes it is an expression of regressive sexuality. A child punished for masturbation, or one who has acquired a strong sense of guilt which has focused his attention on the act instead of helping him to outgrow it, will substitute bed-wetting. He receives from this an unconscious satisfaction, but is relieved of the sense of guilt since the act takes place when he is asleep and therefore not to be considered responsible. In such cases it is necessary to let him talk out his fantasies, and to answer any questions that may arise.

In Freudian analysis great emphasis has been laid upon the infant's interest in excretion as the first act of creation from the self. Personally, in my work with many hundred children, I have found that this interest occupies a negligible place unless it has been linked up with some regressive neurosis, a thwarted sexual curiosity, or an interest stimulated by the attitude of the parent or the nurse. A little child once asked, "Why do people speak of God and the toilet in the same tone of voice?" We can all recognize that hushed and mysterious tone which mothers who are inculcating a false and overemphasized sense of modesty use in mentioning any simple bodily function. Such an emphasis inevitably carries with it an undue awakening of interest, as does the repeated attention, if the child receives praise for the act. "Good baby"; "Now be a good baby for mother." All such encouragement arouses a feeling of personal accomplishment in connection with what should be a casual act of the toilet. We are slow in realizing that if we take natural processes naturally the child will probably do so.

Reading too much primitive psychology into the child also results in an overemphasis of these interests. In primitive tribes we find scatological rites used as symbolic of creation and the use of the inner powers. Such symbolism is still existent in the collective unconscious, and appears in dreams during adult analysis, especially in persons whose whole sexual interest has been repressed from conscious life, or whose introversions have been unproductive of creative reality. These fantasies from the collective may be reanimated in a child during a period of regression. If they have been connected with guilt or mystery, they assume an undue amount of interest. They must then be talked out and put in their proper place. I have found usually that a simple explanation of the elimination of waste material, with the analogy of all kinds of refuse, which have about them no mystery, but simply are not objects of interest, together with a feeling of complete freedom in talking of the fantasies, disposes of undue interest. In extreme cases the use of modeling materials (creation from primitive elements) helps to make reality use of the fantasy.

All sorts of adult reactions have been traced to this function, usually in a highly fanciful manner. Obstinacy, greed, liberality, creativeness, are all traced back to habits of excretion. I have found that an obstinate child is apt to be obstinate in this act also, and that sometimes where curiosity is dammed up there is a resulting constipation. With one introverted child, the question, "What do you really want most to know?" brought out a flood of repressed curiosity, after which constipation was automatically relieved. This child had as great difficulty in submitting her fantasies to reality thinking as her outer acts to any adult control. Whenever her fantasy thinking and her curiosity became locked, there was a recurrence of constipation. Even in her fantasy life she showed marked power attitudes. It was always, "Now you be what I pretend."

As the child's kingdom increases through contact with reality the small monarch is attacked by opposing forces from without as well as by rebellious subjects from within. In his attempts to hold his own in this strange new world that confronts him, he begins to have a feeling of self and of his own power. This sense of power may be used in meeting successfully the small experiences of his life, or it may be used, as in the case just quoted, in fantasy or in rebellion against reality and the parental, or other, authority.

If a child fails to make his adaptation to new situations, he may be seized by wild furies of self-assertion. By these rages he tries to obtain for himself the thing which he cannot get in any other way, and tries also to compensate for his sense of defeat. These seizures often appear to be quite out of proportion to the size of the objective stimulant. A child who will renounce a really desired object with great docility will be filled with anger and self-assertion over some very trivial incident. Frequently this self-assertion is mixed with wild boastings and imperious demands. At times a child seems to have a histrionic sense of himself as an actor, and lashes himself up to the part. At other times he seems at the mercy of the passion. Rages such as these are not really evoked by the outer stimulus; they are caused by a reaction in the unconscious. A small thing raises the sense of inferiority, and this passion is a form of retreat.

When a child is unwilling to attack his real problem or task, he may compensate for his defeat by infantile power adaptations: childish demands upon the mother, cruelty to a smaller child or animal, or a sickness used to command attention. Some foolish parents reinforce this infantile use of power by the way they allow children to behave toward servants.

One child was brought to me for treatment because of nervousness and sleeplessness. She had been taken out of school where she was failing, and allowed to play with smaller children whom she ruled. Her arrogant manner with her nurse was immediately noticeable. It developed that this woman was required to minister to her whims when she was wakeful. The child kept herself awake in order to enjoy her sense of power by making the woman read to her, rub her, and do little errands in the night. "That's what she's paid for," she remarked with a malicious little air of satisfaction. This false superiority relieved her from any shame at not attacking her real problems at school and in play with other children. If such power manifestations can be directed constructively, to power over the self and the task, they become as helpful as they were previously destructive. We are likely to confuse force and its use. It is not power that is to be feared, but the childish use of power—will-to-power instead of power over her own shadow qualities.

A regressive tendency resulting from failure does not always seek compensation in power. It may result in a withdrawal of forces. We speak of habit ordinarily as connected with behavior or thought; we take too little account of its deep emotional content. The habit of failure may have its start in early failures which were beyond the control of the child; then it may become deep-seated. Circumstances overpowering in their weight, conditions imposed by an unwise authority, demands in themselves reasonable but unsuited to the powers of a particular child, any one of these may be the initial cause of failure. The failure brings with it discouragement and lack of self-confidence. Now when a similar situation is to be met there are two sets of factors to overcome: those that lie in the outer difficulties, and those that lie in the resistance roused in the individual by the previous failure.

Let us consider for a moment those failures that have their origin in apparently inevitable circumstances. A child is ill. He must be guarded from strain and exposure. He cannot compete with his fellows on equal terms. His work is intermittent, and his play restricted. When he can enter into competition with others he finds himself severely handicapped, or he may perhaps be able to compete for a time and then, just at the critical moment when the harvest time has come, he is again ill and must stand aside. An examination for which he has been preparing finds him back in bed; a play for which he has been rehearsing comes off when he has a return of illness; he enters a swimming contest and his strength gives out just before he reaches the goal, though on another day when he was in good physical condition he out-distanced this day's record. In such an event there are several things which may happen. The child may become embittered and decide that he is the victim of circumstance. The worry and the expectation of illness may make him more liable to collapse at the critical moment. Each failure increases the nervous tension, and each increase of nervous tension increases the probability of failure; it becomes a vicious circle. He decides that just because he is *he,* things are bound to go wrong. I have seen children who at an early age had acquired pessimistic, or even fatalistic, views of life which endangered their future success.

Another type of child retreats into an infantile attitude toward responsibility. He expects things to be made up to him; he wants special indulgences as compensations. He begins to enjoy poor health. Anyone familiar with adult analysis knows that type of person who always returns to the handicaps of childhood, not alone as an excuse, but even as a reasonable cause, for failure in middle age. He cannot see that success is not a matter of circumstance, but of power to meet circumstance. He is sure that he could easily have met the problem of the other person; but because of the peculiar nature of his own problem, and the unfortunate early circumstances that attended his life, his failure is not at all his own responsibility.

In dealing with situations where early failures have been caused by illness, we must keep several things in mind. The thought must be directed to general gain and growth; no emphasis must be placed upon possible failures along the way. Although life does continually present to us contests, it is not primarily concerned with special occasions, but with general growth. A child may be ill for a long period, but he is not even then necessarily delicate for life. I once heard an old country doctor say, "It's not so hard to cure a child as it is to convince the mother that he is really well." On another occasion, when the anxious mother of an only child said, "Doctor, what shall I do for him, he is so delicate?" he replied, "Madam, have eight more. Then you wouldn't have a chance to remember every illness he has had since he was a month old, and he would have a chance to grow up."

Give the child abundant help and sympathy in all real misfortunes. Try to see that he is not placed in circumstances that are too hard for him; then do not continue this help and sympathy too long. Seize every opportunity to emphasize his return to health. Offer as many legitimate opportunities for success as possible. When a child has this feeling that circumstances are against him and that it is of no use to try, the parent has a temptation to do the thing which only reinforces this attitude: to sympathize, and to make his path too easy. Unfortunately the world will not accept parental judgments. It does not ask, How good is your excuse? but, How real is your value? The child must learn to consider adverse circumstances as something to spur him to greater effort.

A boy had repeated illnesses and physical misfortunes. His difficulties began with an almost fatal illness in early infancy, one which left permanent traces. An operation, unskillfully performed, left him with an infection which caused repeated illness and great pain. He had heard the doctor blamed, and himself referred to as the victim of circumstance. He had a fine spirit and wonderful courage, yet as though dictated by malicious fate, illnesses continued to come at times when they robbed him of much-desired pleasures, or of the fruits of real effort. His fine courage began to be undermined by a feeling that it was useless to try, that fate was against him.

The great event of his summer was a boys' tennis tournament. A return of his old illness put him to bed for a

few days, but before the important date he was pronounced well enough to play again. As he started out to
practice he met a friend who told him that the tournament
had been put forward a week, the lists had closed the
night before, and the first match was in progress. Without
a word he came back and started upstairs to his room. As
his mother started to offer sympathy he said, "It's just my
luck again. Something always happens." Suddenly she saw
that this was a crisis, the fine courage was dimmed by a
look of defeat. "I am ashamed of you," she said. "Are you
going to meet life lying down? Go out and get what you
want, even if it is hard."

"You are unjust," he said, and his face was white.
"Could I help being ill? What can I do about it?"

"That is your job," she answered. "Find your way." He
was silent a moment, and then went out.

Several hours passed. Lunch time came and went, and
still no boy. She sat fearful of what she might have done,
struggling not to cry; for she knew that whether he failed
or succeeded in this special thing he would have found a
new independence, and would never be her little boy
again. There was the even more serious danger that if he
failed his sense of defeat might be deepened. In the middle
of the afternoon he appeared.

"Can I have some lunch?" he asked. "I have to get
down to the club and play my first round."

No explanation was offered nor asked, but the lunch
was immediately forthcoming. On the last day of the tournament he came home with a cup. As he put it on the
table he said, "I am going to keep that to remember that
you aren't beaten till you think you are."

The same danger of the habit of failure holds good in
school. It is possible to establish standards which stimulate
the powers of every child without overtaxing any. This
can be done only through the real standards of the teacher
himself. The true competition is the competition of the
child with his own self. The record which he ought to beat
is that of his own past work. This is possible even in
schools where a rigid marking system is still in vogue.

Children have a deep love of justice and fair play. If
they are properly directed they will espouse the cause of a
child who has not been long at school, or who has been ill,
or who finds difficulty with some special subject. I have
frequently heard children praise a paper of low grading
which showed improvement, and criticize one of much
higher quality which fell below former standards. The

child with the better paper accepted the criticism as just. The acceptance of this standard does not make the child satisfied with poor work, but rather accelerates his progress, for each gain which is recorded spurs to greater effort. It removes the sense of injustice which comes from seeing someone else praised for the thing that is easily obtained while his own greater effort passes unnoticed. Then, when he slips below his newly gained record, he accepts criticism as deserved.

The inner attitude of the teacher is the determining factor. If she cares more for the scholastic record of the class as a credit to herself than she cares for the development of the individual child, she may preach tolerance in vain. The children will be ruled by her unspoken desires which they unconsciously intuit.

No child should be allowed to fail continuously either at school or at home. This is one of those apparently simple truths whose acceptance brings us face to face with a most difficult problem, one which may involve us in a long and painstaking investigation of both the child and the environment. It is like saying that no child should be allowed to continue with an insidious form of tuberculosis or blood poisoning. In the case of the physical illness we recognize our responsibility and spare neither time nor expense to effect a cure, but we are only just beginning to recognize that these psychic poisons may be even more malignant. They call for a most careful investigation of the environmental, emotional, and neurotic factors.

Failures, whether intellectual or emotional, are not always due to innate disability. The undercurrents set in motion between the unconscious of the teacher and that of the child account for many inadequacies. A child will find great difficulty in following a person whom he cannot love and respect, even though he may make a conscious effort to do so, for all the forces of the unconscious work against him. These forces rise up to guard the child from the person distrusted. They assume the form of vaguely understood rebellions, of intense dislike for certain tasks or subjects that are considered too hard, or of antipathies to persons or qualities. Where there is love and trust there are no such barriers. The conscious and unconscious work together and are enlisted on the side of the parent or the teacher. This clears the way for the acceptance of ideas of right, and for the understanding of principles.

Because of certain unavoidable home conditions a very young boy was sent to boarding school. He was reported insubordinate in manner rather than actually disobedient. In particular he seemed unwilling to accept the word of those in charge. A careful investigation convinced the mother that the head master was not a man to be trusted. In answer to the boy's own question, "Do you like the head master yourself?" she replied, "I am sorry to say that I do not, but I may be wrong. Your job is to do your best while you are here, and we will see what can be done."

The boy was sent to another school, and this time the basis of choice was the character of the head master rather than curriculum or location. On one occasion when the mother visited the school, the head master said, "Your boy paid me a fine compliment the other day. I was telling him something that I thought it best for him to do. It was not required, but I advised it. He said, 'All right, sir,' but I felt that he was not convinced in his own mind. When I asked, 'Are you doing this because you agree with me?' he answered, 'No, I don't really agree with you.' I said, 'Why do you do it then? You know that I don't require it.' He looked embarrassed, and finally burst out: 'You see, sir, I've got such a lot of belief in you that I'd rather do the thing you say, and take my chances on seeing a few years from now why you feel that way.' "

There was never any question of insubordination or disrespect in that school, although the boy's new attitude had not been discussed. When he became conscious of the fundamental sincerity that underlay this relationship, the matter of his own way in the minor questions of daily conduct did not seem to him of vital importance. He knew instinctively that in any matter of principle he could, as long as he was himself sincere and honest, discuss his own point of view; and he was glad to give loyal support to the man who inspired his respect.

The fact that he refused allegiance to the unworthy authority was, instead of being an indication of insubordination, encouraging proof of an indestructible fiber of idealism. Children who give love too easily accept many second-rate ideals. Often the child who seems least docile is the one who, if understandingly treated, will develop the greatest individual values. It is because of my knowledge of many cases like this that I say to parents: "Look over all the curriculums and locations that you wish; but base your final choice upon the character of the head master or head mistress, for it is upon that character that the whole morale of the school is built."

Young people have an intuitive knowledge which, besides guarding them from unworthy allegiances, keeps them from discussing their personal problems with people who have no understanding. In one school where the head mistress had a conscious desire for truth, and a very real and broad sympathy with certain types of scholarly mistakes and failures, a girl came to me with sex problems. Earlier in the year, when she had been in difficulties of a scholastic nature, she had received from the head mistress great kindness and a real desire to help. I asked casually, "Why did you not talk this over with Miss X? She is always sympathetic."

"Oh, yes, she is a dear, and awfully kind, but you see she would not understand a thing about it. She would just think it was awfully queer."

That was exactly what would have happened. When the same problem had come to Miss X she had not solved it, but had tried, by repressing it, to become unconscious of its existence. Whenever we thrust problems away from our conscious consideration, we limit our powers of understanding.

If we could once firmly grasp the fact that the child reacts far more to our inner attitudes and to the undercurrents which are set in motion between his unconscious and our own, we should be relieved of the burden of our insincerities and the task of playing a part. We should not have to pretend to virtues that are not ours, nor to perfections far beyond our reach. We could give to the child our own ideals and hero concepts, quite frankly admitting them to be ideals, not actual achievements. We would then be fellow wayfarers on the pathway of life, both on a voyage of discovery; we in possession of a few more charts of the country because of more experience and consciousness, but they with a longer road before, stretching out, we hope, to a larger land. The child must have a god, a hero. He projects the need upon the parent or the teacher. If the adult is not worthy of his love, the child follows a false god.

Just as we must, in sincerity, admit our own imperfections in our relationship with the child, so we must accept the imperfect thing from him if it is the expression of his best effort. In every case the value of the production is in proportion to its release of creative power. When there is a sincere attempt at expressing one's best, our first duty is to see the value and accept it. Then we may criticize, as a help toward better expression in the future. A pretty picture made under too constant direction is of no value in comparison with one which is a full expression of a child's creative power. The adult ideas which so greatly improve the quality of the product may easily destroy the child's individual expression. To regard too highly the finished product is to value material, beyond creative, growth.

If we are offered an unlovely thing because of a lack of desire to give, we should then reject it as unworthy, but here the rejection is directed toward the spirit behind the act. To criticize a loving act because it is awkwardly expressed is to turn back upon itself the awakening of love, and to destroy the spirit for the letter. Manners are not inculcated by such untimely criticism. Only a sense of baffled love is awakened. Receive love reverently, no matter how crude its expression, and emphasize form and manner at a time less weighted with dynamic force.

Understanding, too, must be allowed to come in its own time. When we tell a thing prematurely we destroy a possible individual creation, and substitute for living process a dead form. There is no comparison between the force of the thing which a child is helped to tell himself and the thing which is told him. This premature telling may rouse a wholly natural resentment, or, if the attitude be acquiescent acceptance, the initiative so vital to progress is destroyed. The patterns which we substitute may or may not be good; since they are accepted ones we assume that they are better than the ones for which the child is struggling. We are really prompted by egoism. We like the feeling that we have done the thing well or expressed it well ourselves. Some people have this attitude so strongly entrenched in their unconscious that they will find satisfaction in proving their superiority over even a very little child. The child is, by this treatment, only the more firmly entrenched in his infantile adaptation.

Love properly used is a tremendous asset. When the child feels back of the personal love the parents' adherence to the higher guiding principle and the desire to help him to be true to that higher law, all the forces of loyalty and truth are enlisted on the side of obedience. There is, however, great danger in the personal appeal as a basis for obedience or sacrifice. It is a temptation to both teacher and parent to use the child's love as a means of achieving their end. "Do this because you love Mother" is a most common appeal. A very exaggerated case that was brought to my notice is an illustration of this tendency.

A child was discovered cheating, and there was reason to believe that it was not the first time. While the instructor was trying to obtain the child's confidence the mother appeared. "Why did you do it?" she asked. The child burst into tears and said reproachfully to the teacher, "Mother said she would be so happy if I had good marks! I did it to please Mother." And the mother, instead of being appalled at the havoc she had wrought, said triumphantly as she drew the child to her, "I knew that she couldn't really have been naughty. You surely won't punish her now that you understand that she did it only because she loves her mother. You won't do it again, darling, will you, now that you know that Mother never wants you to do such a thing even for good marks? You will do what Mother wants because you love her." In spite of all the teacher's effort the child departed with a misty sense of misunderstood virtue on her side, and of injustice on the part of the teacher. Though this is an extreme case, I regret to say that it is by no means an uncommon one.

In an extraverted child, that is in one who finds his chief relationships in the outer world of things and people, this type of appeal makes the whole motivation of life a personal one. It cripples the power of giving loyal support to an abstract ideal or to an impersonal cause. It is the "my family whether their demands are just or not, my country right or wrong" attitude. The demands of truth are secondary to the demands of the beloved object. Not only may the wider demands of life be disregarded, but great violence may be done to the individual relationship, for the desire to please is greater than the desire to be true to one's self.

With the introverted child, that is the child whose inner world is the greater reality, the effect is different, but may be no less disastrous. Living in his own inner world, he is more afraid of the outside object. His first reaction is to retreat into himself. In such an appeal he senses the will-to-power that lies back of it, for in this case love means: love me, obey me, be what I desire. The child feels this in his conscious or in his unconscious and, afraid of conflict, he compromises. He may try to conciliate by giving lip service and outer obedience. He may be acquiescent, polite, and respectful, but it is the politeness of the primitive who gives gifts to the totem animal to appease his wrath. The effect of this outward conformity is to make him guard his inner life the more closely, and to create a tendency to deceit. Sometimes he feels a scorn for the person whom he deceives; as in the case of the boy who told me that when he found that his mother had, on a special oc-

casion, used him to help her out of a difficulty by means
of a social lie, he had decided never to believe her again,
and had stuck to his decision. This scorn separates the
child who is greatly in need of making human relationships from any possibility of doing so. If, instead, the child
yields to temptation and does the forbidden thing, he may
resort to lying and deceit rather than face the wrath of the
adult. The scorn is then turned on himself, and helps to
build up feelings of inferiority at his own sin.

A young girl who found great difficulty in making contacts with life, and who was so overburdened with a sense
of inferiority that it caused an impediment in her speech,
told me that as a child she had worshiped her father. He
was "a man of authority" who took pride in ruling his
own family through appeals to loyalty. On one occasion
the little girl followed her own way rather than his. When
questioned her fear was so great that she lied. The lie was
believed, and the incident was forgotten by the father; the
child could not forget it. It became an appalling sin to her.
She dared not confess for fear of losing her father's love,
and she felt that she had no right to his love since she had
betrayed it. Whenever he said such things as, "I can always trust my little girl because she loves me," she was
thrown into an inner panic. About this time she began to
stammer, and this was mimicked and ridiculed by her two
brothers. Her father tried to break her of it by making her
stand in front of him and slowly repeat the words that she
had failed to say quickly. When she could not do this, he
made her feel that she was again failing as a loving daughter. When at adolescence she came to me for stammering,
her sense of inferiority was so great that it was difficult for
her to have any realization of herself as an individual.

The child was extremely sensitive, and in her tendency
to retreat within herself had already the germs of a neurosis, but had the father placed the emphasis upon loyalty
to principle and given her help in the understanding of the
inner laws of right, she would not have become so separated from life. Since she could not face her sense of spiritual wrong, she developed stammering, and when she came
to me she was outwardly quite convinced that that was the
barrier which prevented a normal adaptation.

Her fear and her sense of inadequacy in relationships
were her real problems. Her confidence in my friendliness
had to be established; the feeling that she was accepted by
someone who knew all the things that she had feared to
tell was the first great step in her cure. A new and truer

relationship was built up with the father who, fortunately, was willing to take over his share of the responsibility. The stammering was proved, as is usually the case, to be incidental; lack of relationship was the real illness.

In connection with this question of love or will-to-power on the parent's part comes the deep question of obedience, or free choice and self-government. In our present fear of destroying the individuality of the child we are apt to forget that this individuality is a very embryonic thing. A child is growing *toward* an individuality, as he is growing toward control and understanding. It is through independent choice and decision that strength is gained, but it is a form of strength that must come slowly. As decision makes for strength, so obedience makes for rest and calm.

A child has a right to the restfulness that comes from habits of obedience, provided that it is not an arbitrary assertion of parental authority. The younger the child the more these habits of obedience are needed as a background. They are learned most simply in the early regime of the nursery. They bind the parent as well as the child, for they cannot be a matter of whim or of parental convenience; a rule cannot be enforced today and broken tomorrow; its carrying out cannot be at the mercy of teasing or tantrum weeping. Obedience must be kept in its place as the background, not the ultimate end of discipline. The goal is the development of choice which is based on understanding, and we must be ready to seize every legitimate opportunity to allow the child to exercise that sort of choice. Moral questions are the most difficult in the world and we cannot expect a little child to be able to answer them too early.

We must be constantly investigating our own attitudes. We have no more right to a personal will-to-power attitude with our child than in any other human relation. Often the question of obedience is a mere conflict of wills, and the victory is to the one who can hold out the longest. One mother who had a very willful little daughter said to me, "I don't believe in insisting upon arbitrary obedience. I always argue every question out with her, but she knows that she has to give in in the end, and she always does." The child did give in, but never until there had been an emotional storm, which was not only exhausting, but which she grew actually to enjoy, and which laid the foundation for that type of emotional reaction in which the emotion takes complete control of the person and becomes a kind of orgy.

This desire for emotional excitement may be present in either the child or the parent. It is used to work off pent-up energy which should find its outlet in some positive value. The time to develop the moral attitude of the child is when he is quiet, not in the midst of a storm of anger or obstinacy. The trouble is that at quiet times we are not inclined to bother about him. Any arbitrary display of this form of power on our part awakens the answering demon in the child. It is surprising how many forms this special evil spirit can assume. Bed-wetting which demands the mother's care, night terrors that can be used as an excuse to call the mother, and many other such perplexing habits are power manifestations of the unconscious.

A little girl who had a jealous desire for her mother's love, and resented the measure of it that was given to the little brother, found that she could interest her mother in her dreams. These became night terrors, and every night she woke in terror and had to come to her mother's bed. The mother realized what was happening, and moved up to another floor to sleep. The first two nights were filled with intense suffering for both mother and daughter, but after that the night terrors ceased. One cannot safely treat night terrors in this way unless a clear understanding of the child's problem indicates this cause.

A form of love quite as devastating as the one manifested in power is that injudicious, self-sacrificing love that would shield a child from every hardship, that would make no demand. Whether this sacrifice is made to the petty whim of the child or to some real or fancied superiority, it is inevitably dangerous. In the former case the child is shielded in his weakness; he is the spoiled child who can never grow up. The constant protection from every hardship opens the way for the retreat neurosis of later years. If the child is of an emotional nature, the parent frequently finds satisfaction in his expressions of love; there is a personal gratification from its display. If the sacrifice is made because of some superiority of attainment, or because of unusual mental ability, there is danger that the child will become arrogant and overbearing in his demands. Since the family life has had to give way to the development of his talent, he begins to feel himself outside the family life. Personal ambition becomes dominant at the expense of interests held in common. All sense of proportion is lost. If people stand in the way such a child expects them to be sacrificed. True feeling values are submerged.

An unusually brilliant boy was made the idol of the family. Every sacrifice was made that he might have the greatest advantages of travel and education. During his university career the father failed in business, but the family went to live in a small boarding house and cut every expense, so that nothing should interfere with his career. He started out brilliantly, but he could not ride roughshod over the world. He would brook no interference, and when he began to get into difficulties he developed strange paranoiac fantasies of being the favorite son of God, and privileged, in that role, to hold the opinions of others in contempt. His dreams were grandiose affairs or power manifestations. All the tendencies toward self-aggrandizement, which should have been tempered and held in check by true feeling values and a proper share in the family responsibilities, had been allowed to run riot, and when the actual break with life came they were too deep-seated to be overcome. We see the same thing occurring in a much less marked degree in the life of almost every "favorite child."

Where the child feels a need of a closer relationship than really exists with the parent he may build up an idea of the father or mother and place this creature of the imagination between himself and the actual parent. This fantasy parent, or parent image, is the imago (defined in the introductory chapter). This imago is often used by the unconscious to compensate for some lack, or it may be built up in order to furnish an excuse for the child's own failure in adaptation. Once given life this imago may gain strength with amazing rapidity, gathering traits of injustice or of extreme love as the child projects his own fantasies upon the image. Since one of the most difficult tasks in life is to see other persons as they really are it is not strange that children often confuse their fantasy figures with reality. For this reason the image of a dead, or absent, parent may have a powerful influence on the life of a child through the strength of his own inner world.

Such an image developed in the case of a little girl who had a very insecure relationship with her mother and whose father had deserted the family while she was still a baby. She was a child of slow thoughts and deeply buried feelings. As she was always being contrasted with a younger brother who was quite brilliant she developed a great sense of inferiority and a self-pity because she was "unloved." In order to compensate for this she invented a father figure who could stand between her and the necessity for overcoming her difficulties. This father was also frightfully misunderstood by her mother. He was a tender loving parent who had left home because of her mother's unkindness. She was his favorite child and when he came back he would show everyone, especially the little brother, how he loved her and how good she was. So real did this figure become to her that whenever she was criticized she made no attempt to change but retreated to this compensating idea of the loving father. This also gave her added reason for indulging in feelings of resentment toward her mother.

In such a case the cure is best brought about through supplanting the image by a positive and valued relationship. The mother's second marriage to a man who was sympathetic and understanding caused a sudden transference of affection and the fantasy dissolved before the power of the reality. This new father demanded real values. To obtain his approval she had to relinquish her fantasies as evasion of her own realities. Such a happy solution is not always possible but some real relationship must be found to take the place of the fantasy; sometimes the child can be shown the differences between the image of the person and that person himself.

The imago is not always built from the personal unconscious to meet the special desire, or in answer to a special fear or distrust but may also be influenced by images from the collective. Certain ideas, or ideals, are deep-rooted in our inherited psychology. Upon the father are often projected the old ideas of authority that were prevalent in the Jehovah worship and embodied in the patriarchal government when the father had power of life and death over the sons and daughters. This idea has given way ostensibly to the loving father of the New Testament, yet its traces are not obliterated. The mother figure, symbolizing both life and retreat to the protected time of childhood, carries with it such a weight of associated ideas and collective feeling values that the very words bear a significance that may not properly attach to the individual. We must always take into account the importance of these inner images in considering existing relationships.

The use of the imago is not confined to the parent-child relationships. It is especially carried over into the love patterns of later years. The adolescent boy has deep in his unconscious ideals of the virgin mother, symbol of purity and spirituality; and of the temptress, the other side of the accepted woman-symbol. These conceptions become interwoven with the mother imago as the child develops. No choices which have so great a determining power upon the choices of later life can spring full-fledged into being. We see a change in attitude which forces its way into dynamic activity and we think of it as a sudden thing; but it is a piling-up in the unconscious which has been a slow process, and which now breaks through in a tremendous conscious change. It is like the forces of a volcano which work constantly far below the surface and do not suddenly begin to exist at the time of eruption.

We must realize, therefore, the importance of each step. That *now* is the accepted time is true in the life of the little child and of the adult. Every step is real and important. We live from the beginning; infancy is real life, not preparation for life. It is necessary for the little child to walk without the mother's hand, to dress himself at the proper time, to meet and establish relations with other children, to feel the reality of the love life of the home, not simply as preparation for life but as actual experience in life. This makes life a real and growing thing, unfolding from the beginning. The independence and love of later years have then a deeper reality and a surer foundation.

5

ADOLESCENCE

Though the growth of the life force is a continuous process, yet there are certain marked stages when this force is quickened to meet the new demands of life. There is no stage in the development of a flower when growth suddenly begins, but there comes a time in the unfolding of the bud when a new process seems to have sprung into being. The period of adolescence may be likened to this. Tremendous changes, both physical and psychological, are taking place. The independence which should have been developing slowly through the normal contacts of childhood begins to unfold into individuality. Now the old parent-child relation must give way to a new form of comradeship. Here as perhaps in no other period of our life with our children we must face the truth that "he that loseth his life shall find it." To keep our children we must let the old relation go and leave them free to find their own life. It is only so that we can have living love from them which will develop into true comradeship as they take up adulthood.

As his psychic independence becomes established and his individuality grows, the child begins to look outside the home for contacts with life. Under the urge of awakening forces which he cannot understand he may chafe at even the simplest home direction, scorn home ideals, and do misdirected independent things that fill his parents with bewildered indignation. They become impatient with these evidences of a growth in independence. If they fail to recognize them as a primal necessity they deplore the vagar-

ies that are only his trial and error method of finding himself. Instead, they ought to realize that their task is not to
counteract these forces but to seek for wise ways of setting
the child free.

This freedom involves freedom of the parent. No parent
who has not established his own individual life interests
can be sufficiently separate from the child to face this new
relationship; in addition to this he must have attained psychological adulthood, or the child may leave him behind
and seek elsewhere for advisers. Psychological adulthood
is by no means a universal attainment. It is because of the
tremendous importance of this individual way—the finding
of the self with which to meet the world—that the rites of
adolescence have held so important a place in the religious
and the social life of all early civilizations. Values which
have persisted through ages must have some intrinsic
meaning. It is illuminating to see how, stripped of all the
varieties of form, creed, and social custom, the essential
thing has retained its importance through long periods of
time.

That the problem of the adolescent has always been
considered of vital importance is shown by the initiation
rites of primitive peoples and of earlier civilizations. These
permitted no evasion of the point at issue. The young man
was to put away childish things and to enter into the life
of the tribe. Through these ceremonies he died as a child
and was reborn as a man. He even received a new name.
This new name derived its significance from the fact that
it was earned either by an act of prowess or through a
spiritual experience occurring during the period of isolation which was part of the rite. The name was therefore
peculiarly his and carried with it a sense both of obligation
and of privilege. The severity of the test and its inevitability (for it was as inevitable as birth or death) were
great aids to the youth in attaining his normal independence. Nor could the father or mother hold him back. He
belonged to the larger life of the tribe and that larger life
claimed him. Now our civilization interposes many barriers and offers many ways of escape. Home ties are both
stronger and weaker, tribal demands are gone, replaced
largely by individual ambition, the issue is a more personal
one. The youth is much more at the mercy of the ties,
both conscious and unconscious, which have been built up
between him and his parents.

The other vital issue was the establishment of the heterosexual relation which once followed close upon the at-

tainment of his manhood. This is now postponed by the demands of modern civilization which necessarily erect barriers in the way of its taking a normal place in life, while offering many opportunities for its indulgence as a compromise but not as a vitally accepted issue.

All this adds to the struggle of modern youth. He must take measures to free himself. He must settle for himself the problem of his own sexuality. The very advantages which we heap upon him keep him longer in a state of dependence. This dependence may become an irksome affair. Here again he finds himself bewildered. Consciously he is grateful for the opportunities which may include college, a professional training, long apprenticeship; unconsciously he feels the urge to prove himself, to know that he is a man. Scholastic things, in which he may take a genuine interest, fail to satisfy. If he falls below in these he may be told that at his age his father had been helping to support the family for several years, and that it is therefore reasonable to expect him at least to keep up in his classes. Bewildered by the urge for manhood he may go out to prove his independence in foolish ways. These very acts, foolish though they may be, are indications of a healthy desire and are better than a willingness to remain a child.

It is here that the growing boy or girl needs understanding, not criticism. True understanding does not preclude criticism of the special act under discussion provided there is an acceptance of the problem of the actor and real sympathy with him. The youth must be led to a realization of the fact that the problem of the modern world is his problem also, that in order to share in the fruits of this complicated civilization he must also share in its increased responsibilities, one of which is the lengthening of the period of preparation. In primitive times the hunt, and the warpath were universal professions for the boy, and the home industries for the girl. Now we have the added problem of choice and of long preparation. We cannot disregard this element; the trouble is that we have often allowed it to usurp the whole field. College entrance examinations, intellectual training, social conventions have crowded out the other issues which are, after all, the essential ones.

Then, too, may arise the confusion between his own way, the way of his generation, and the way of his father's; the family traditions and the life in the outside world. Whether these varying claims can be reconciled so that the good of each can be accepted, depends largely upon the understanding of the parents and the confidence which they have established with the child.

In questions of psychological adjustment we find that we must now deal with the child's individual psychology as well as that of the parent or adults who surround him. Let us consider these two sides.

From the point of view of the parent the present problem is to set the child free from the parental bonds, even from those that are caused by too great affection. So long as the youth is held in parental indentifications, whether through infantile love or resentment, he cannot become a personality in his own right. By giving up the outgrown relationship we make possible the growth of a new and deeper comradeship which can properly endure through life. This is an evolving process and cannot be accomplished by any sudden change. From the first we must remember that our children do not belong to us. They belong to themselves and to life. We are only the instruments of life through which they come. The path of life is forward. As we have broken from the ways of the older generation so they must break from our ways and follow new paths. Ways that have been progressive to us may be regressive to them, and the path of regression is always the death of the spirit.

Growth comes through individual experience and the understanding of experience. This must be gained by each one for himself. We do not try to save our children from the labor of education and expect to pass on to them our intellectual attainments, so saving them the process of study; yet we are impatient if they cannot accept the results of our experiences instead of gaining them for themselves. We are reluctant to see that any deeper understanding of the meaning of life can be obtained only by the individual acceptance of joy and pain and that each must gain this through his own efforts. Our experiences can be of value to our child only in so far as we can use the understanding which we have gained from them to give him wider opportunities and a deeper sympathy when he brings us his problems of living.

It is at the period of adolescence that the normal child becomes most eager for experience. In order to choose, in this world of new experience, he must have some standard of value and some place where the unknown can be weighed and appraised. This is furnished him by the home and by his relation with his parents. Since choice is so largely determined by the strength of the forces that rise

up from the unconscious, all the unconscious elements of
the relationship are now of greatest importance. These
often run counter to the accepted conscious attitude. At
this period of awakening sexuality and dawning love life
there is a tremendous quickening of the unconscious. Fantasy, idealism, physical sensation, outer experience and
inner change, all crowd upon the growing youth. The child
becomes conscious of fantasies and sometimes of dreams
accompanying the psychological change. Girls are apt to
accept fantasy while the boy wishes to live out in masculine assertion the thing that seems to threaten him with
sentimentality. Sometimes the urge to assert his own way
is so strong that he looks for any way but that of his parents.

What are some of the difficulties which may undermine
the desired relationship?

Unless the parent is able, from the beginning, to see the
child as a separate entity there is danger that love will become a clutching force using the child to satisfy personal
need or ambition. This may happen when the parent is
disappointed in other human relations and, pouring out all
the pent-up emotion on the child, also feeds himself upon
the child's love.

Another devastating form that parental love may take is
to place the child under a burden of gratitude and of a
sense of duty because of values received. In certain tribes
of northwestern America it was the custom of the great
man of the tribe to use his wealth in holding a feast at
which his riches were given away. This feast was given
primarily to the rival and seems to show the simple and
beautiful generosity of the primitive in so carrying out the
Christian doctrine of "Love your enemies." When, however, we look a little more closely we find that, by tribal
custom, the rival was shorn of all prestige unless he could
return double for all the gifts that he had received. In reality these gifts frequently placed upon him an obligation
which he could not meet and rendered him the bondsman.
The underlying motive of the donor was to establish tribal
supremacy. In this same way some parents who believe
that they are making unselfish sacrifices for their children
are, deep down in their unconscious, acting out the power
impulses of these tribal chiefs upon the ones whom they
believe that they love best.

Many young persons are kept in a state of infantile dependence through being constantly reminded of early obligations. "When you think of all that your mother and I

have done for you and of all the sacrifices that we have made for your education it would seem as though you might feel that you owed us some duty." Such an attitude on the part of the parent fosters in the child either a spirit of unreasoned rebellion or an undue dependence which leads him to sacrifice his own life in order that he may compensate to the parents for all that they have given him.

When conscious duty and self-sacrifice are substituted for the free interchange of love and comradeship deep resentment is often piled up in the unconscious. This resentment may break out in unexplained acts of insubordination and in sudden unreasonable self-assertions, or the self-sacrificing attitude may be manifest in all the parental relations but it may be compensated for by a growing resentment toward the injustice of life itself. In either case there is no way of freeing either a child or an adult except by bringing these resentments up into the conscious and facing them. We cannot drink of a spring that is choked with debris, nor can we make deep personal relations nor find the greater impersonal forces of life if our contacts are choked by resentments which fill the unconscious.

Often patients who complained bitterly of circumstances, but who insisted on stressing their deep love for their parents, have, under the force of the emotional release caused by uncovering some hidden reaction, broken forth into tirades of hatred against these beloved parents —tirades that astonished no one so much as themselves. Bewildering as this experience is it often brings with it a release from buried resentments and a power to face the reality of the situation.

If in such cases the parent refuses to face his share of the responsibility then the youth has no choice but to go his own way and to find his help elsewhere. One is reluctant to help dissolve the relationship of parent and child, but it is better that the child should see the personal failings of the parent and insist upon his own independence and make true relationships, than that he should continue in outer acquiescence and inner rebellion against life.

Two examples may make my point clearer.

A young girl of sixteen began to show signs of nervous irritability. She was falling behind in her schoolwork but refused to change her course or accept any alteration of program which might delay her college entrance. Her mother was greatly distressed. She said that they had always had a very close and happy companionship until within the last few months but that now the girl seemed to have no happiness in her home and would accept no advice about her schoolwork. She was determined to make college at seventeen.

There had been an older sister who had died a few years before. This older girl had been unusually brilliant in her schoolwork. The mother had always loved the younger child best because of her loving nature and had cherished a belief that she also would prove brilliant. She was, however, anxious to do anything which would be for the child's good.

It was difficult to get beyond the polite outer adaptation of the girl herself, but when her confidence was gained she began to talk of the home situation. She loved her father and mother with almost abnormal intensity and felt that she must make up to them for all that they had lost through the sister's death. The sister would have gone to college at seventeen and so she was sure that her mother would be disappointed if she did not. She felt that they were doing everything for her and she must make them as proud as they would have been had the sister lived.

Underneath she was a mass of unconscious resentments toward them for asking her to live out her sister's life. These resentments she projected upon her teachers who, she said, were unfair to her and did not explain things. She blamed the school for not understanding her, and life in general for not having made her clever. She spoke of the possibility of boarding school but feared the separation for her mother. A change of attitude on the part of both the parents and the child was necessary. The parents were very understanding when the situation was uncovered.

The main task was for the mother to face the demands which her own unconscious had made upon the child by projecting upon her such a devouring love and looking to her to compensate for the loss of the older child. She had to detach this excess of love from the child and to take up a personal life into which she could put some of the libido which was now devouring the daughter. In her own consciousness she separated her feeling for this child from the love which she had given to the older sister. The child then felt that in taking her own place in the family she was doing all that was desired of her. When this was actually accomplished the girl showed a great release at being able to be herself and go her own way. She repeated the grade with a varied curriculum, one more adapted to her abilities. Her obstinacy vanished, her happiness and charm returned, and incidentally her schoolwork improved remarkably. Her relationship to her parents was happy and normal.

In the following case where the parent would not change her own attitude the result was very different. A young boy had always been guarded by an overadoring mother. She lavished attentions upon him, she chose his studies and his amusements, she was careful to see that he had only "nice" companions. For a time the boy seemed lamentably ready to be "nice" himself. It looked as though he might be a mother's darling. Fortunately at adolescence more healthy tendencies showed themselves. He began to find friends far outside the selected circle. Then there began to be difficulties at school. Here too he resented authority. His mother wept and suggested boarding school as a dire threat, one which she had no intention of carrying out. Just about this time the boy came under the influence of an extremely manly master who realized the difficulties. Every effort was made to make the mother see what she was doing, but she was sure that she was a loving and unappreciated mother and that the boy would thank her some day. Then the boy adopted the idea of the boarding school as a welcome escape. With the aid of the master he passed some competitive examinations and won a scholarship at a preparatory school. After much persuasion the mother let him try it. He went with the intention of never really coming back home, that is, never coming back to the mother-son relation which home represented, and he succeeded in doing so in essentials. He broke the real relation with his mother, never giving her confidence or asking advice. He spent vacations more and more with his friends. By the break he found himself, but his mother lost him in reality forever.

Love of the parent, no matter how real, cannot be properly used as a motive for determining individual conduct. The growing boy or girl is trying to find standards of right and wrong that shall be his own; demands that he shall decide because of love for parents can do nothing but hamper him. If he has the security which comes from understanding and trust we will voluntarily talk over his problems, but he must be encouraged to make his own decisions. Even in the realm of social relationships the old custom of accepting without question the family circle of friends cannot and should not be expected to hold. Nevertheless these relationships are too important to be left to chance. This is the time when normal heterosexual attitudes must be established. Parents ought to be far more

worried over the absence of friendships with the opposite
sex than over their appearance even with some problem
attached. It is better that the child should make mistakes
than that he should be held back from whatever contacts
come to him naturally. Here again the home may become
a clearing house. If he feels no prejudice or desire on the
part of the parents to dictate his choices he will normally
bring his new friends to the home. Against this background he is pretty apt to judge for himself of their real
value to him. Such a free acceptance will do far more to
reveal to him the undesirable than will anger or opposition.

Earlier in the chapter reference is made to the parent
who has not himself passed beyond psychological adolescence. One cannot expect a development of adult reactions
from a child who sees a parent given over to the pleasure
of the moment, the selfish whim given false emphasis perhaps by some social tag, the pursuit of emotional excitement under the guise of love. A childish father or mother
demanding love and respect as a right implicit in parenthood can expect little from an independent clear-seeing
youth. Temper, tears, rights of possession, demands for
obedience because of authority—these are infantile, not
adult, reactions; and the young person feels rightly that he
has passed beyond such childish demands. It is only if we
have lived deeply and truly in adult experiences that we
can claim the right to advise those who are just entering
upon such experiences.

The father who is still a child looking to his wife for
motherly care, or who has never thought for himself nor
acted from individual conviction, or who treats his children, especially his daughters, as emotional toys, can be of
no real help when the child is reaching out for greater
psychological maturity.

There is also that eternally adolescent type of mother
who not only keeps young for her children but who tries
to keep her children young for herself. Since she cannot
meet the increasing responsibilities of maturity she tries to
prolong her own youth beyond its rightful time. The
daughter is still kept the little girl; the son perhaps begins
to assume the place of the youthful lover. She demands
from him the small gallantries and attentions which he
would normally give to a young girl. Since one can never
cheat oneself with these substitutions without revenge
from the unconscious, she is more and more apt to become dissatisfied, becoming in truth the "devouring

mother." Such conditions usually arise when the parent has failed in her own connections with life and its responsibilities.

If we have passed through certain periods of life without the experiences and the understanding of experience which should be a part of normal development, the unsatisfied element in us is always reaching back to supply the lack. Many people pass through what should be the great experiences of life without any realization of their depth of meaning. This is equivalent to having missed the experience. We are then unwilling to face the fact that we must acknowledge this loss and accept only the things which are now rightfully ours, without trying to filch from the young lives around us.

We see this problem exemplified in the unsatisfied teacher who is using relationships with adolescent pupils to stimulate the sense of youth, as well as in the mother described above. When the unconscious of parent or teacher makes too strong a demand it may dwarf proper forms of relationship and lead to homosexual tendencies or to narcissism, a form of love that cannot pass beyond the self. Both of these manifestations are types of arrested development of the proper love life. They may be the results of infantile parent life.

As individual life has emerged from patriarchal and tribal conditions, the son and the daughter have had to meet special psychological problems. These have left their imprint upon all succeeding generations.

In order to establish his own way of life the boy must overcome the authority of the father wherever it holds him in the position of a child. If the father is overstern, overinsistent upon the exercises of authority, the son may fear to break from the submissive role into which he is thrust, and may accept the inferior position of the grown-up child. In this case he develops into a man who is afraid to assert himself, who is happier in a post that does not call for independent action, who works best under direction. Often he rebels at this and feels that the world is unjust. He sees other men advanced to positions that should have been his, and is quite unconscious of the forces within himself which make him always shrink back at the decisive moment when the better man steps forward. In his conscious he is demanding responsibility but something in the unconscious is forever pulling him back at the moment of advance. It is also impossible for him to take the part of a man in his relationship with women.

· In a boy of different temperament this same overstern father may induce an attitude of rebellion. This boy breaks from control too early, he defies rule, he overthrows authority, he becomes the iconoclast who overthrows idols simply because they are symbols of accepted authority, not necessarily because he has found a better form by which to live. He is in our common parlance "agin the gov'ment," but his rebellion is a childish and unreasoned affair. He is often aggressive in his demands for positions of authority and for his rights. Since his independence is based on revolt and not on development it is an unstable thing and may be overthrown by childish emotional attitudes which surge up unexpectedly from the unconscious.

If, instead of breaking with this overaggressive father, his attitude is one of love and admiration, he may voluntarily accept the position of childish inferiority. In this case he never becomes psychologically adult but continues in adolescent hero worship. He believes his father to be a godlike person to whose every demand he must yield. Such a man will always be a follower. If the actual father relationship is broken by death or other circumstance he immediately seeks to replace it by finding someone else to assume authority over his life.

If, on the other hand, he identifies with his father pattern and tries to repeat these attitudes in his own life, he may himself become a petty ruler over those who are dependent upon him. Such a boy is often cruel to animals and bullying to younger children, and later on becomes a tyrant in his own home. He finds in the Old Testament Jehovah his highest expression of God. If he has been the indulged favorite son of a father who is otherwise stern and autocratic he may in afterlife carry his father-identifications over into paranoiac feelings of self-aggrandizement and consider himself an especially favored child of God. He may even develop a feeling of God-Almightiness which leads him to a disregard of proper human relationships and responsibilities.

In contrast to this a father who is weak and too ready to yield, and who has been unable to take up his own responsibilities, may inspire only contempt in his son. Then the adolescent problem of freeing himself becomes too easy, and his contemptuous attitude is carried over toward all the struggles of life. This is a dangerous postponement of his problem for he meets it later when he has to reckon with the collective authority of society in the adult world.

A weak and acquiescent son having a similar identification with a father of this type may gravitate toward failure, even as his father has done. He is inclined to present his father-identification as an excuse for his own failure to meet life.

The problem of "overcoming the mother," that is, of breaking the infantile ties which bind to the mother is one which must be met by each individual. The forms in which the problem is presented vary with temperamental differences and the types of relationship established with the actual mother. The early ties with the mother are normally those of love and dependence, since it is she who ministers to childish necessities. She becomes therefore the symbol for retreat and negation of life as well as for necessary and strengthening love.

Whenever life becomes too hard or the conscious takes on an overemphasized masculinity in the adaptation to the demands of necessity, there rises up from the unconscious a flood of instinctive desire for infantile satisfaction. This instinctive desire is voiced, not only in the great myths and epics, but even in the sentimental appeal of some popular songs. Such bits of sentimentality as "Make me a child again just for tonight" find their audience because they touch something which lies buried in the unconscious of each of us. The deep serene love of a mother for a child establishes a sense of security. Such love furnishes later a place of rest from which one may go out to a stronger acceptance of life. This is quite different from the infantile retreat which is used to avoid life.

The boy who has been bound by too close a tie to the mother remains emotionally a child, although intellectually he may make adult adaptations. If the bond with the real mother persists he feels no need of other women and does not marry. Then perhaps he finds himself, at middle age, emotionally adrift in the world and, through the infantile urges of his unconscious, is at the mercy of any "good woman" who will mother him. Often the woman may be far from good even according to accepted conventional standards, but this identification of her with his mother image surrounds her with a halo. If he marries and finds that his wife does not, in reality, resemble his mother but possesses an independent personality of her own, he is resentful and either tries to make her over or else repudiates the relationship.

Normal relationship with the mother is a necessity; without it there may result an equally infantile attitude. The youth feels emotionally unsatisfied; he has been deprived of something which is a real need. He too may marry to find a mother, not a comrade, and then may complain bitterly at not being understood and loved enough. Or, beset by feelings of inferiority because of the failure of the early love relation, he may fear to make any contacts with women, believing that it would be impossible for one to love him. Here again we may be confronted with a split in the personality. An intellectual boy or a brilliant, apparently self-sufficient girl are both surprisingly lacking in stable emotional response. As they develop they seem able to manage all sorts of professional or social problems except where their own emotions are involved. This happens because the feelings have not been trained through the experiences of establishing the relationships needed in childhood.

Where the mother is the stronger parent and dominates the household she represents not only love but authority. This makes it more difficult for the son to break away from her and establish his independent manhood. Added to love is now the fear of the power of woman, a fear which has persisted throughout the ages. Man dreads instinctively the sway of emotions which keep him a child. Since in most men feeling is less differentiated than thinking they fear the surges of emotion which may deliver them over to the power of the unconscious. The way in which the boy reacts depends again upon his own type. He may acquiesce, and in the acquiescence lose his own masculine attitude, or he may break the bond, at great expense to his deeper feelings. He then consistently undervalues women, thinking in that way to destroy their power.

In one such case a boy saw his father and older brother both yielding to the rule of the mother. He determined that he would not allow his manhood to be swallowed up. He was about twelve when he came to that decision and he acted upon the first opportunity for direct disobedience. Then to his mother's astonishment he told her that he was a man and never again would he obey her, and that if she insisted he would leave home. Arguments and threats were of no avail and finally, for the first time in the boy's experience, she resorted to the woman's weapon of tears. This nearly broke his resolution. He went out of the house, and for several hours walked the streets fighting to keep himself to his determination. He won his freedom from the actual mother and by so doing took the decisive step in establishing his manhood. This was far better than continued submission, yet he could not entirely free himself from unfortunate results. This mother image was too deeply stamped upon his unconscious and he was never able to make a satisfactory relationship with a woman. He demanded from her extravagantly feminine attitudes of submission and at the same time felt safer with women who had almost masculine professional success. He could not live without women, neither could he feel safe in his relationship with any special one. Therefore though he was in many ways a successful man the problem of his love life remained unsolved.

A boy who is weak and yielding may, under these same circumstances, live more and more in the feminine side of his unconscious, and later on find his satisfactions in homosexual relations in which he plays the woman. These may be psychological feminine adaptations in deeply rooted friendships, or actual homosexual practices. He may seek a repetition of the mother type and marry a dominant masculine woman, thereby duplicating his father's history of feminine acquiescence.

If a man is ruled by the feminine side of his nature which rises up from the unconscious floods of nonunderstood emotion this feminine quality is infantile and undirected. Therefore, in a man who takes over a woman's role these qualities are manifest in their primitive and unevolved form; they are womanish, not even womanly.

In the same way a woman ruled by the masculine elements of her unconscious is apt to be a prey to will-to-power and possessiveness. In either case the positive values of these traits are lost because they take on a primitive and regressive form.

As with the boy so it is with the girl. The first love relationship is with the mother, for it is she who satisfies early needs, and to whom the child turns for comfort in the first encounters with life. The mother is in many ways the psychic pattern for the girl. If her love relations are happy and well-adjusted her daughter will take over that inner attitude which she expresses in a hundred unconscious ways. If she is filled with suspicion, with unreasonable or unsatisfied desires, the girl finds her own love path beset with doubts and possessive impulses. A young girl's unconscious attitude toward men is very frequently the working out of her mother's matrimonial problem.

Sometimes a mother regards the father as merely the source of supply for the family, and feels no necessity for bearing her share of responsibility. If the daughter identifies with her in a partisan type of affection she will have exaggerated ideas of woman's possessive rights in marriage. If, on the other hand, she repudiates her mother's attitude she may fly to the extreme of independence and may herself take on a masculine adaptation. She may take the father's part against the mother, perhaps mothering him herself, in which case she continues this mother attitude in her adult relationships with men. Or if the mother is suspicious of the father's relations with women the girl frequently takes over this suspicion and has a deep distrust of men.

A true comradeship with the mother furnishes not only the pattern for the daughter's marriage relation but also for her friendships with women; upon it too are built up her understanding and acceptance of a woman's part in life.

As a normal basis for her own love life the girl must have a real and satisfactory relationship with her father. The first element of this is the mother's own influence upon the unconscious of the child, especially where there is strong love between them. The father's own attitude furnishes a pattern of what she desires or repudiates in men. If he is too fond, and lavishes upon the child the love that should normally go into his marriage relation, there is danger that the daughter will find herself unable to break that bond. She then goes through life looking for someone who will be as good to her as her father was, someone who will continue for her this father image. She may find all that she wants in the father and fail to marry, or if she does marry she will expect her husband to treat her as a beloved daughter rather than as a wife or comrade.

A young girl came to me because of a nervous condition which followed the breaking of her engagement. When the time for marriage approached she had been seized with apprehension and had waked in the night sick and trembling. She felt sure that she was not strong enough to marry. In the first interview she used the words: "If only he were more like my father I don't think I would be so afraid."

Here was the key to the situation. She was her father's favorite. Even as a child she had gone to him with all her small troubles. The words which she used in describing their present relation were significant. "He always comes in and kisses me every night just as he did when I was a little girl, and he is always doing lovely little things to surprise me." She was frightened for fear her love for her fiancé might be only sexual attraction since she was conscious of such desires when with him. This, to her mind, precluded the idea that she might fear the marriage relation. Instead she had decided that her unconscious was trying to tell her that her love was mere sexuality and wrong. Her dreams showed this fear to be made up of two elements: the fear of sexuality, not because it was wrong but because it symbolized an adult relationship the responsibility of which she was unwilling to accept; and, deeper than this, a feeling of guilt that her sexuality should be given to any man but her father. This was deeply buried in her unconscious and in uncovering it many childish attitudes toward life were revealed and had to be faced and also many things involved in the family situation. The father had never worked out his own marriage relation and in many ways was a disappointed man. He had looked to his daughter to compensate to him for all that he had missed in his own love life and had remained unconscious of all the undercurrents in his affection by persistently regarding her as a child. So strong were these ties in the unconscious that she felt her marriage to be a betrayal of her father. In accepting her marriage she had to put away childish things as represented by these early attitudes, and accept her life as a woman. Viewed in this way her acceptance of sexuality was not a concession to the lower nature of either herself or her lover but a step forward, a part of her initiation into life and rebirth from infantility into adulthood with its responsibilities.

Another and quite different result which may occur when the father is too devoted to the daughter is that she may have an intuition of the danger of his overinsistent demands, both conscious and unconscious, and repudiate him. In this case she is without the foundation of trust and love which is necessary for her love life. She is frequently suspicious of men and of their demands upon her. She senses sexual motives where none really exist, or if they do exist she refuses to see their normal aspect in adult life.

Indifference and neglect on the part of the father may be as disastrous or even more disastrous. Here again the results will vary in accordance with the temperament of the child. If she loves the father and builds up an image of a hero which she substitutes for the reality, feelings of inferiority develop. She feels the humiliation of his neglect. The unsatisfied desires for the normal father love which should come to every child make her go about looking for a father surrogate on whom she can expend this devotion and who will give her the fatherly affection that she has missed. She may marry a man who represents to her this father image, perhaps a much older man, one to whom she can be the beloved daughter that she has been in fantasy. This desire is often an unconscious one. Consciously she has accepted a husband and cannot understand, if the man makes adult demands, why fate has permitted her to be so misled as to the true character of the man to whom she is bound. This destroys the possibility of really adult relationships.

A girl of another type may feel only hate and resentment toward such a neglectful father. If she is independent or aggressive she will not submit to an authority for which she has no respect. Lacking the proper discipline which is a part of development, her self-assertion is often that of a rebellious child. When this is so her consciously aggressive self is offset in the unconscious by infantile desires for submission. She too is looking for a father, but as she lacks the security of the proper feeling values she has not a true standard on which to base her choice, she cannot judge of men and is not discriminating as to what a man should really be. Her love relations may therefore be decided by compulsive forces from the unconscious which seek submission and by authority apart from conscious choice. She may therefore become involved in disastrous situations which seem to her the working of blind fate.

More and more we are realizing that this blind fate is born from the womb of the unconscious. Even as a child must be born of the meeting of the male and female elements so fate is born of a meeting of the outer experience and the inner force. It is only when something within ourselves goes to meet the circumstance that our fate can be born. This is the thing which the adolescent must face if he is to find himself. The responsibility cannot be turned back upon the parent unless the youth wishes to remain a child himself.

Our parents were themselves born of human parents and not of the gods. They, too, had to face the handicaps of their environment and of their psychic inheritance. They had to meet the mistakes and prejudices of their own age. The mistakes which are now blamed upon them were not all of their own making. Each generation must face the duty of becoming conscious and of achieving individual existence.

Up to now as we have met difficulties of adjustment the problem has been to help the parent or teacher to greater understanding so that this may be used to help the child, but with the adolescent our method of attack becomes more direct. We must help him to free himself from the thing within which keeps him in bondage. He must become more fully conscious, and must choose his own way.

The attitude of the parent and the type of relationship which he has established with the child is now only one side of the picture. The adolescent takes over his own life and responsibilities whenever he faces the thing within himself which is holding him in infantile bonds. Anyone who has worked with ill-adapted children and chronologically, but not psychologically, adult neurotics, knows how eagerly they seize upon the analytic method as a means of going back into the past in order to find an excuse for present failure. This leads nowhere. There is only one constructive reason that we can have for going back into the past to discover the places where we first went astray and the influences which were then at work. That is that we may gain an understanding which will enable us to separate ourselves from those influences where they are still operative and that we may look squarely at the thing in ourselves which is handicapping us.

The youth must face for himself the age-old problem of initiation into life, of the rebirth into manhood. It is all the more mysterious and bewildering because it is no longer a clearly defined ordeal leading out into a new and universally accepted way. The two fundamental issues are no longer simply defined; the life of the tribe has begun to broaden out into world relationships, the heterosexual life into the complicated relationships of modern society. The wise men of the old tribe expounded a law for each step of the way. The wise men of today no longer feel assurance of a predestined path, and the voice of authority speaks in many tongues. What wonder that modern youth is confused! Out of the confusion we must try to choose the things which have persisted because they are essential.

First is the necessity for the youth to face infantile attitudes in himself. Here, as Jung has shown in the *Psychology of the Unconscious*, is the conflict of the hero, as perennial as life itself. The "terrible mother" of ancient myth is the regressive pull of the unconscious that draws men back to safer, more childish paths. This is the theme running through ancient myth and religion. The dragon must be slain, the hero must descend into the dark caverns of mother earth to destroy the monster, the night journey under the sea must be undertaken. Jonah must live three days in the belly of the whale, the god must face the terrors of the underworld.

The simple meaning of all this is that the *thing within oneself,* the primitive and childish force of which we prefer to remain unconscious, must be met and acknowledged before we can grow up. The youth must go down into the womb of the unconscious (the terrible mother) and there destroy his own childish adaptations and his parental dependency, and emerge with an independent and adult attitude which is his own achievement.

It is always difficult to make the young person who is smarting under a sense of injustice in the domination of his parents see that the really vital thing in the situation is his own desire to remain an infant, his fear of facing the world and of making his own relationships. He does not readily recognize that difficulties of environment, however great, are of minor importance compared with his own conscious determination in winning his way to manhood.

Quite frequently at this time the real inner conflict will be shown by dreams of amazing clearness. A young boy who complained bitterly of the dominating influence of his mother and of the fact that he was never allowed to have his own way, was in reality a very child in his desires. The "own way" for which he clamored was the infantile way of the spoiled child. Persistently he laid the blame upon his mother and upon her influence over his father and all the others of the household. He had the following dream.

"I was trying to mount my horse; the animal kicked around and acted very strangely, but I could not see any reason why he should behave so nor why I could not get on. Then I looked down and saw that *I had put on one of my mother's skirts.*"

Here the wording of the dream was very significant. *"I* had put on." He was evidently responsible himself for his own predicament. The horse was his libido which was "behaving queerly" so that he could not mount and go his own way. The reason was that he was still identified with his mother, a situation plainly shown by his having put on her skirt. His associations showed that he was playing off his mother against his father. While constantly resenting her rule of the home he used her frequently to obtain things from his father. His position, therefore, was that of hiding behind his mother's skirts, though in his conscious attitude he was assuming the role of rebellion against all authority, especially hers.

Again in dreams there may be a clear connection with

the symbolic figure of the "terrible mother," the regressive
infantile attitude that threatens the newly awakened individuality. Here the symbol takes on gigantic proportions
or the form of a mythical dragon or other beast. In one
case a girl who was having great difficulty in overcoming
her sense of inferiority and making her own connections
with life dreamed: "I was on horseback. We were going
hunting. I did not know much about hunting, and I knew
that I did not. Then a very large massive woman appeared
at my side. She was huge, like some great giantess. She
began telling me the proper way to do everything, to rise
in the saddle, to sit for the canter, and every little detail
about all of it. All of a sudden I knew that I must get
away from her, and the horse and I went on. Then the
horse turned around toward me with the most amused
expression and began to talk to me. He really was awfully
nice and funny. Then he said to me: 'That woman is
awful. She saps all your vitality.'"

The horse was to her very definitely a part of herself
and the woman who was so gigantic seemed like a figure
out of an old myth—not at all her real mother and yet
"some way brought the thought of mother." Here again
the horse was the libido symbol, her own energy, her own
way of adapting to life. The woman was the power of the
conventional attitudes toward life which in her conscious
she had repudiated, but to which she was really bound by
fear and by all the compulsions of her childish dependence. She had blamed her parents for having insisted upon
her accepting their ways of thinking and acting, and their
religious beliefs and customs, yet now she had to see that
deeper than that was her own fear of independence.

She had no standards of her own by which she dared to
live; whenever she acted according to her own newly acquired values she was overwhelmed by a sense of guilt for
which she could find no conscious reason. She had the
same fear of being found out and punished that she used
to have when as a child she had disobeyed a parental command. In consequence she had so far only substituted the
conventional attitude, the safety of the control of old beliefs for the childish safety of parental control. She had
also, in spite of this fear, a delightful sense of humor
which was constantly at war with her overweighted sense
of responsibility and guilt. Innocent and altogether rightful
acts of pleasure would bring questionings as to her moral
responsibility, her duty as a daughter, her possible selfishness. The horse in the dream had exactly her sense of

humor, and in an amusing and whimsical way told her to be herself, a rather joyous young person without so much morbid self-searching. In the associations with the hunt was contained much pertinent material which bore upon other phases of her analysis, but which I have not space to give here.

Another very striking dream, one of even deeper and more terrifying significance, was that of a young girl who had with great struggle started upon her own life of independent thought and action. Her mother and father were both intellectual, rather ambitious people, and her two brothers, both older than herself, were of the hustling American businessman type. She had been the "little daughter," a sort of sentimental toy for the household, one to be indulged and petted. This position, apparently so satisfactory to all concerned at home, broke down before the onslaught of reality when she tried to take her place in the school world or to assume any real responsibility. She had gone through the earlier years without any brilliant record, yet fairly successfully, but now when the time came for her to make a more adult adaptation she was quite unequal to the demands. Of course her failures were never her own fault, she was "misunderstood," "people expected too much of her." She had a good deal of artistic ability for which she had been praised, but since she had never submitted to any real training her things were lacking in technique, they were only possibilities.

After she began to face things, there came a time when she began to place the blame upon her parents for not having trained her. She started out upon her new path with some confidence, which threatened to break at the first real difficulty. Then she dreamed the following dream: "I was on a boat in a darling little harbor. There were green meadows all about and the sun was shining on them. We sailed out. The mouth of the harbor was just a little narrow opening. As we started to sail through I saw the ocean with the waves breaking. The wind was blowing and it seemed quite wonderful. All of a sudden I was terrified. There was just the great ocean outside, and the boat was so little. I felt I must get back before we went out. I jumped and landed on the shore; but as I ran back I felt as though the grass were clutching me, and I saw that the land was trying to suck me in. It had all turned to quicksand. I woke shaking with fright. It was a horrible dream."

Here was her problem most vividly portrayed. She had

embarked upon the sea of life, but she was afraid to face
the perils of the journey and longed to return to the safety
of the pleasant meadows of childhood. When she tried to
get back she found that the pleasant land was no longer
safe. If she turned back the old childish regressive attitudes would "suck her down." It would be spiritual death,
the overpowering of her own libido. There were perils in
the outward journey, but greater ones in being swallowed
back into the old dependence and infantile life.

The narrow mouth of the harbor is here again the rebirth symbol which is employed by the unconscious in so
many varying forms to signify the mouth of the womb
through which the newborn child must pass in order to
obtain life. So the new self must be born by passing
through the narrow way and out into the larger life, which
means coming forth from the safety of the mother. This
type of rebirth must take place whenever the old way is
outgrown and must be abandoned for a higher path of development.

The unconscious does not always give us pictures which
are as vivid and simple as these. Often the dream symbolism seems absurd and grotesque, and utterly without
meaning, and we must give long thought to discovering
the value of the symbols. This value can be found only in
connection with the knowledge which we have of the conscious life and of the problem which is imminent, and
without whose solution no step ahead can be taken.

A young woman who had no belief in her own power
of meeting the world had returned home after an unsuccessful attempt at independence. Though she felt a childish need for security, she resented her dependent position.
Yet she was too distrustful of her abilities to make another
attempt at living on her own.

She dreamed that she was back in her family's old summer estate where much of her childhood had been passed.
This estate was on the coast, and in the dream she was
standing in a familiar rocky cove. The rocks seemed more
menacing than she had ever known them to be, the waves
were dashing about her, the tide was rising. She must venture out upon the turbulent water. Boats were tossing
about, some disappearing under the waves. Then she saw a
curious little pink craft bobbing about, but not capsizing.
A voice told her that this was the only boat which she
could trust to take her safely, that she need not fear if she
would embark in this. She looked closely and saw that it
was a beetleware tooth mug.

The setting of this dream—the rocky coast, the stormy sea, the ships setting sail—was one which might have been related to the situation of any person who realized the necessity for taking up his independent life. But here it had a distinctly personal reference. The summer estate was associated in her mind with childhood pleasure and complete lack of responsibility; and also, at this time, with financial security. Nonetheless, the beetleware tooth mug was the only symbol which could not have been made to bear a general interpretation. It was peculiarly personal.

The young woman was asked if she had any association with this pink mug, and replied, "I have one in my own room." She was then asked why, of all the objects in her own room, should the dream choose this particular one. She was at first puzzled. Then she suddenly realized that this was the only thing in the room which she had bought with her own money.

Her own intuition now furnished the answer and she said, "It looks as though I would have to pay my own way." It was then suggested that money is often a symbol of one's own energy, one's psychic capital. In other words, if she was to take this voyage, set out on her own journey, find her own way, she must depend upon her own abilities, however small they might appear to her.

This young woman's conscious idea was that she had no resources within herself that she could trust. She underestimated her abilities because they were not talents, she distrusted her feelings and intuitions because she overvalued the intellect and was not intellectual. Her conscious mind was full of fear of life and of what would happen to her if she tried to be independent. So the apparently trivial symbol had an important meaning to her at this particular time. It said, "You can trust the thing that really belongs to you." The unconscious gave her a deeply needed assurance that her own resources could really be depended upon. Since she was consciously so full of fear and was so overdistrustful of herself she needed this compensatory picture from the unconscious; she needed to see the aspects of her situation that her fears had excluded from her conscious consideration.

For the dream has a compensatory and balancing quality. If the whole conscious attention is concentrated upon one aspect of a problem, the excluded and conflicting aspect becomes active in the unconscious, and the dream, portraying what is going on in the unconscious, reveals the other side which we need to remember in order to evaluate ourselves properly and to see the complete picture. It says, "This, too, is true." It is as though when the conscious is concentrated upon one aspect the unconscious said, "But this is the way things appear down here—you forget about this."

The dream, therefore, gives us a true picture, but often its truth is only comparative, the truth about one aspect which needs to be brought to our attention. Even when the dream startles us by its vivid, pertinent comment we cannot rely on this as the voice of infallible wisdom. We must connect it with our conscious attitude and our outer situation at the time. For we are full of contradictory elements: we can love and hate, fear and trust, desire and reject, and we must remember that both sides are present when we are in a tight place. Only by a comparison of the "affect" of the dream—that is, the degree of emotion aroused by it—with our own conscious attitude can we see that other aspect, and then choose for ourselves the side we will accept, always remembering the other side with which we must reckon. So the dream is continually reminding us of the part which our conscious is forgetting. It does not speak with any absolute authority; it simply gives a true picture of *a* situation which exists in the unconscious. It speaks truth; but not, as some persons believe, *the* truth. It shows the other side.

6

THE ACCEPTANCE
OF CONSCIOUSNESS

When the essential problems of adolescence have been faced the questions become those of adult analysis and therefore have no real place in this volume, yet the subject of rebirth is one which is so vital in the new psychology that it seems to call for a greater emphasis than can be given in the discussion of adolescence as an initiation into life.

In all the great religions we find this concept strongly emphasized, but we have been accustomed to think of it as a single occurrence. William James speaks of the once-born men and of the twice-born: "the once-born whose world is a sort of rectilinear or one-story affair, whose accounts are kept in one denomination, whose parts have just the values they appear to have, and of which a simple algebraic sum of pluses and minuses will give the total worth." Their world values are static or else move only in accordance with conventionally accepted laws. The twice-born are those whom this simple acceptance of the apparent cannot satisfy. They follow a changing and evolving truth, they look for the things which are unseen. It is true that into such lives may come a sudden change of concept which alters the entire orientation, yet in addition to this sudden and unique experience there is a continuous process of renewal of life and release of energy. There is a constant interplay of the forces of retreat and advance. As soon as life demands a greater degree of consciousness there comes the temptation to retreat, the desire not to ac-

cept the new understanding which must of necessity bring
with it a greater responsibility.

Even very little children feel this urge. Sometimes they
voice this desire to remain unconscious so clearly that certain ones will try to go to bed when they feel that they are
asked to do something too hard (an expression of the desire for sleep and forgetting, the pull of death). Death desires are strong even in children, though usually they are
masked even to the one who feels their urge. Nevertheless
we all have this desire to remain unconscious—unconscious of the suffering and evil in the world about us, of
which it is easier to remain ignorant; unconscious of the
changing demands of society which would force upon us
the consideration of new problems; unconscious of the
things which would necessitate new adjustments of personal relationships; and most of all unconscious of the undercurrents of our own psychology, of the inferior thing in
ourselves which, raised to consciousness, would necessitate
a new valuation of ourselves and a new conception of our
responsibility. Unconsciousness of all these things relieves
us of the burden of growth; but even as the urge of death
is toward unconsciousness the urge of life is toward a
fuller consciousness. Whenever we accept this dynamic
urge of life there is a rebirth of the spirit.

Viewed in this way man is not merely twice-born but
continuously reborn. Whenever life makes a demand that
calls for a new attitude there must be the death of the old
and the birth of the new. St. Paul, having caught a vision
of the transformation of the self through the dynamic release of a new inner attitude, says, "I die daily." There are
special spiritual crises when this rebirth seems to trans-
form the entire personality. There has been a piling up in
the unconscious which finds a release in a new spiritual
concept. The child of the spirit has been growing in the
dark womb of the eternal mother. In this way the hero is
born, the man breaks the bond with the regressive element
and takes over the responsibility for his life of higher individuation in so far as it is expressed in this new attitude.
This is a continuously recurring process. Soon the new self
finds new and greater obstacles to overcome and again a
rebirth must take place. The hero concept might be likened to a symbolic potential and is a universal attempt of
the unconscious to objectify this energy whose release carries the individual forward.

In this continuous life process of rebirth sacrifice assumes a new and greater significance. It is a sacrifice of

the lower self to the higher. It is not a repudiation of the self but a fuller acceptance of all its possibilities. This is the theme which runs through all spiritual concept, even the old myths. So Odin hung nine days over the great void, "a sacrifice of myself unto myself" in order that he might obtain the vision of understanding.

The sacrifice that is made in order to deny the self is barren and makes for death instead of life. It is of the nature of repression. The substitution of duty for a living creative love has drained all the meaning from the precept, "Bear ye one another's burdens." The law of Christ was a law of joyous giving and receiving in human relationships. Here we see the danger of letting a living word crystallize into a Mosaic law. Every sacrifice must be new-born of a fresh and creative impulse. Wherever one sacrifices life for another through a desire for self-righteousness or for sterile duty there are piled up conscious virtue and buried resentment which leave one with a sense of loss and futility instead of a revivifying feeling of attainment. Where the sacrifice is consciously accepted because of a realization of new values, deeper relationship, greater consciousness, fuller life, the result is a release of energy. Fullness of life, not denial of life is our goal. "He came to bring life and to bring it more abundantly."

A conscious self-denial for its own sake helps us to identify with an attitude of goodness which is a form of spiritual selfishness, quite different from the growth which comes from a true feeling reaction. Such a giving away of life gives a false sense of personal achievement.

The true self-sacrifice is the one that sacrifices the hidden thing in the self which would work harm to ourselves and to others. It is an effort to become more and more conscious of all the forces in the unconscious, of the unworthy personal motives that work underground, as well as the inherited forces, so that our lives shall become more and more full of understanding and really conscious choice. In this way we too "descend into hell," the depth of the unconscious where lie all those things that would destroy our conscious attitude and which we most fear to face and acknowledge. From such a descent can come a new life if the new understanding is accepted by the individual.

This new life carries on the vital thing which has been born from the old. It often appears in dreams as a child, thus adopting the symbol of the religious concept and giving it form in the rebirth of the individual. Jung, in his dream analysis, call this child the *puer aeternus*, the ever-living child. In dreams this child often takes on characteristics which symbolize the special need of the individual and which give a clue to the new adaptation needed in order to further his integration.

This eternal child is born of the old. There is a present tendency to throw over all that is old and to assume an attitude of unthinking disbelief. With the loss of the old forms of faith many have lost faith in the vitality of spiritual truths. In casting out the husks we have cast out the kernel. We therefore have no living thing to give to our children. Where disbelief is only easy rationalization it does not hold emotionally, and fears and doubts rise from the unconscious. We then fear to set a child free from our outgrown beliefs for fear the devil might exist and catch him. Many mothers who really believe nothing themselves pass on as literal truths Old Testament truths instead of finding their deep symbolism as shown in all the living spiritual myths. We therefore give husks because we have not time to search for the living kernel.

In spiritual education as in all other types our first task is with ourselves. If we have no inner faith we have nothing to give. If we try to play safe and offer as true a thing in which we do not ourselves believe, the child gets, not faith, but insincerity. If, however, we have found our individual expression of truth to be still living in the old form, then in giving that we still give sincerity, provided we are willing to let the child, as he develops, find his own inner values.

Our greatest task is to have the courage to face the thing that rises within us, whether it take the form of doubt which must be thought out, or the knowledge of the unacceptable thing in ourselves with which we must reckon. In this way only can be found the acceptance of greater consciousness. The *puer aeternus* has also a shadow side in which the man identifies with the ever-living child. The man so identified seeks to be the hero without the struggle—the young Balder the Beautiful who, unslain, lives on.

7

PSYCHOLOGICAL TYPES

There is perhaps nothing more dangerous in our dealings with our fellowmen than a too literal interpretation of a time-honored maxim. The golden rule is no exception to this. "Do unto others as you would that they should do unto you" is not written for the literally minded man who would impress his own psychology upon the world and who would salvage the needy in accordance with his own requirements. His interpretation of his rule into terms of living reality and human relationship is fraught with danger and confusion. The virtuous and conscientious but nonunderstanding man bent upon giving to his neighbor the thing which would be most desirable to himself is often not only met by what seems to him base ingratitude but also is confronted by a confusing situation in which much evil has undoubtedly come out of what seemed to him very apparent good. To find the spirit of the maxim it must read: Do unto others as you would have them do unto you, *if you were they*. To realize this as the meaning adds to the burden of conscious fair play and generosity the greater burden of psychological understanding; for how can we follow this rule, so interpreted, without an understanding of what our brother really is and of how he differs from us fundamentally and will continue to differ until the end of time?

When we start upon this pathway of understanding our problem becomes increasingly difficult. We find the old way of judging a man by his acts will no longer hold. What motives lies behind the act? Even with little children we find these varying motives necessitating highly different judgments. Two children steal. One may greatly desire the object, the other may have no sense of the thing as valuable in itself but only that it may be used to work out some problem upon which his mind is fixed. Two children lie. One may wish to obtain some definite thing desired, the other may be presenting to us a fantasy which has to him a very definite value and a reality greater than one which is merely objective.

As we pursue these motives we no longer feel pleasantly sure of our power "to make the punishment fit the crime." Pooh Bah is puzzled. What, after all, is the crime? Does it consist in the manifestation which we see or does it lie in something deeper? Are we so sure that after all it is a crime?

As we pursue these motives deeper and deeper toward the source of their being we become aware that there are persons, even little children, who react in accordance with inner laws which differ greatly from our own. First we may become lost in the maze of differences, then slowly we begin to see certain typical similarities emerging. We become conscious of certain typical reactions which may form a basis for classification. We begin to expect certain responses from certain kinds of people. If we are honest in our desire for greater psychological comprehension we cannot dismiss any of these differing types as merely persons whose actions we cannot understand. Our duty is understanding, in so far as this is humanly possible, and then acceptance of the fundamental differences which, in many instances, will inevitably make the approach to life different from our own. Easy judgment and complacent self-justification vanish before this new demand of the duty of psychological comprehension of the other person. Until we reach this attitude the child is at the mercy of the psychology of the particular adult with whom he comes in contact. His actions are not interpreted in accordance with the laws of his own being but with the so-called reasonable expectations of the adult in whose charge he may find himself.

In his many years of analytical research Jung discovered that however great were the individual differences of his patients they might be classified in one of two groups which he termed the extraverted and the introverted types. This classification was based upon the natural flow of the interest. In the case of the extravert the flow of the interest was toward the outer world, the world of objects. In the introvert there was "the movement of the interest away from the object toward the subject and his own psychological processes."

In the light of this discovery my own attempts at classification became illuminated and in his discussion of the problem of types I found the key to various problems which I had been intuitively perceiving in my studies of children. Though many of the cases quoted in this chapter were worked out before my studies with Dr. Jung, yet they are now reviewed and the conclusions clarified in the light of my work with him. In all instances I have followed the general line of his classification. My own contribution in this chapter consists in the application of his findings in adult practice to the consideration of child problems. The great difficulty in trying to state this problem in clear terms is that it gives it an unwarranted appearance of simplicity. It is often a matter of long study to determine the type of any individual. The more knowledge one has of the forces which may influence or distort natural reactions the slower he is to make hasty classifications.

The classification introvert and extravert is made upon the basis of the general attitude. One can, however, draw no hard and fast lines, for in every individual both attitudes are to be found. There is a flow of interest toward the outer world, the objective world of persons and things; and also toward the inner world, the world of subjective realities and inner values. Sometimes these interests are so nearly balanced as to make classification extremely difficult. Then, too, children react to environment, especially psychic environment.

As has been shown in the discussion of identification a child may react to a parent or teacher as though he were the person with whom he identifies. The closer the bond between the parent and child the more the child is molded not only by the conscious but also by the unconscious demands of the parent, reacting in many ways as he is expected to react instead of in accordance with his individual type. Such a confusion produces a sense of unreality and makes the integration of the personality a difficult task. There are, however, characteristic reactions by which we may distinguish the child of marked introversion or extraversion.

It is the opening day of school. In the lower grades many or all of the children are newcomers. With what varying attitudes they arrive! Here is a child friendly, eager, intensely interested in the new surroundings. To him each object, including the teacher and other children, is a source of quickly awakened curiosity. The outer world has no terrors. It is something to be seized upon and investigated. Or the attitude may be one of aggressive capture, still it is one of acceptance; the interest still moves toward the object. These are manifestly extraverted reactions.

Next comes a child who is obviously shrinking back from this new world. We feel at once that he is withdrawn and apart from his surroundings. The outside world is something to be approached with infinite caution. He may be unfriendly, taciturn, suspicious, repelling sympathy. In this case he too frequently meets with little understanding in his struggles to overcome the fear which each new object awakens. On the other hand he may have an air of detached friendliness. He may even smile at you, a winning smile yet withal remote as of one who looks from a castle window at a world which is quite presumably pleasant but which nevertheless must not come too near. You feel instinctively that this child is worth the winning but know that he cannot be too quickly won. Both these latter children are introverted. They live in their own world apart. The object must be kept at a safe distance, or if accepted must be carried off to the inner world and its value determined by subjective reactions.

Here, as at every other step, we must be careful not to pigeonhole a child too readily. The shrinking child may be an extravert but the overindulged mother's darling who is too much of a baby to venture out from behind the mother's petticoats, or he may be a child with a normally extraverted attitude who has been driven back inside himself by feelings of inferiority roused by older children or overcritical parental control. The child who meets us with apparent ease may be overtrained in social adaptation, which has resulted in an attempt to reverse his normal introverted adaptation. Our understanding of typical reactions gives us a basis on which to proceed with a sympathetic acceptance of reactions which differ from our own, but the knowledge of the intricacies of the problem holds us back from too hasty a classification.

An apparently trivial incident helps to reveal the mechanism which is at work in a typically introverted child. A class of little children were each trying to finish a piece of work so that it might be taken home before the approaching holidays. The teacher was going about helping with a suggestion here or a touch there. One child had worked hard and had come to a difficulty which was apparently causing needless childish woe. With a deft touch the teacher set the thing straight and returned it for finishing. Instead of the gratitude which she expected there was a burst of uncontrollable grief. "It isn't mine any longer," the child sobbed. "I wanted to give Mother my work."

The fact that the object as it might now be completed was in itself an acceptable gift could not be grasped by the child. She could not forgive the teacher for having robbed her of what to her was the real offering. To this child the important thing was her own inner values. Through conquering the object she conquered her own sense of inferiority. The object had no reality to her except as it represented her own conquest over material. It was this inner value which she desired to offer to the mother; the something which she had herself achieved. The introvert fears the object as possessing a superior power. It is only through its conquest that he can destroy his sense of inferiority in its presence.

The child seated at the same table, who had received a similar helping touch with gratitude, was not more loving, nor was she less sincere nor sensitive. She had an entirely different orientation. To her the object was valued. She desired to give her mother an acceptable material gift, not an inner value. Such a child might presumably say, "Isn't it pretty, Mother? Miss X did that little place. Isn't it pretty? Won't you like it on your bureau?" Or she may never mention the helping touch, not because she wishes to receive thanks for something which she has not done, but because that part is to her too unimportant to remember. She is intent on the object which is to give pleasure.

It is not possible to know whether we are building up or destroying the inner thing without knowing what it is that the child is really doing and where his true values are placed. We cannot judge by the emotional reaction (the affect) of the degree of control which the child possesses, nor of the real depth of the thought or feeling involved, for the widely varying reactions to the same stimuli are determined by the strength of the inner forces set in motion.

Courage or cowardice also can be judged only by the inner resistance overcome, not by our estimate of the outer circumstance which is to be met. A child to whom the fantasy world is vivid and whose imagination creates realities may fear to go upstairs in the dark but may face a dentist or endure physical injury without a quiver. Another child who finds reality in the tangible and who is keenly alive to sensation stimuli will venture into a place of very possible danger without a tremor of fear but be almost hysterical over having a splinter extracted. In either case our estimate of the courage of each child must be based upon an understanding of the measure of his difficulty rather than upon our own orientation to life and the thing which it seems to us reasonable to fear.

The same laws hold good in judging the sudden emotional act. The child given to sudden bursts of anger is not always the most ill-tempered or resentful child. He may be prone to sudden waves of emotion rising from the unconscious, or he may be a timid child overcome by gusts of tempestuous terror and his angers an effort at self-assertion. There may be more real hate lying behind the eyes of the quiet brooding introvert, than exists in the extravert who suddenly performs the harmful act.

In the extraverted child we find a quick response, an easier and more spontaneous adaptation to changing environment. He is ready to enter into group activities, to accept ideas of others, to make many friends, to direct and control an outer situation. He is a good deal in evidence, sometimes even preferring ridicule to neglect. He is apt to side with the majority and to react in accordance with public opinion. He is frequently resourceful and aggressive.

The reactions of the introvert are usually slower. He must take the thing into himself, familiarize himself with it, and submit it to his inner valuations before he can pronounce upon it. This must always be borne in mind when passing judgment upon his mental processes. For instance the time response in the popular use of the intelligence tests may be indicative of type rather than ability. In questions of choice the introverted child may know the accepted value as well as does the extraverted one who gives the prompt reply, but doubts as to the values *to him* fill his mind. It becomes more important to him to find out what he really thinks or feels about it than it is to score on the examination. He may therefore pursue a train of inner reactions and fail to complete his work. In all respects the introverted child is apt to develop more slowly and to hold back from current circulation the things which are developing. It is for this reason that he is often considered slow and stupid as a small child in comparison with the extravert who contributes his values as he goes along.

The introverted child is frequently stubborn, not so much from willfulness as from the necessity of his being which demands that he shall accept nothing until its value becomes apparent to him. Stubbornness is not in itself a problem of introversion. It may, in either type, be an assertion of the ego, a will-to-power, but it is a trait which will be frequently attributed to the introverted child, because he holds back his response until he has solved the problem from within himself.

Since our Western civilization is essentially extraverted we are in danger of undervaluing the introverted child. He needs more reassurance in his contacts with life. There are certain essential differences which must be accepted by each before there can be a true understanding. The extravert views the withdrawal of the introvert as infantile retreat and morbid introspection. The introvert sees in the extravert an opportunist, one lost in the material values and the affairs of the moment, with no inner light to guide. We must remain conscious of these essential differences in orientation or else we shall expect from every man the response which we ourselves would give.

The fundamental attitude is not determined by birth or outer circumstance. It is apparently innate. In the same family we find children who show marked differences in type. We see the same distinctions manifest if we enter a public school in the poorest district or in the most select private school. It lies deeper than position or education. Two children may have the same love or lack of love, the same advantages or disadvantages, yet one springs forward to meet the world either in friendship or in aggression; the other springs forward serenely or fearfully as the case may be. The form of the introversion or extraversion may be modified or the individual stabilized by a balance of reactions but the fundamental tendency remains a matter of temperament. It is most important to keep this in mind in our treatment of children. We cannot and should not expect the same adaptation from these two fundamentally different types, nor can our reactions to them be uninfluenced by our general attitude. It therefore becomes most important that the adult, whether parent or teacher, should not only recognize these types in children but should also have an understanding of his own type in order that he may overcome personal bias and be able, in a clear-sighted way, to help develop the weak adaptation without doing violence to the natural one.

I have known schools where it was possible to predict the success or failure of a child of pronounced type as he advanced from grade to grade and teacher to teacher. In one class he would be spoken of as a boy with an interesting mind and showing promise of great ability; in the next as impractical, dreamy, inaccurate. Or the reverse type of boy would be first depreciated as too ready, lacking in imagination and originality, and in the next grade praised as a fine, accurate, responsive, careful pupil. These verdicts were primarily based upon the type attitude of the teacher and upon the form of work which she valued. The same is true of parents. They feel rapport with the child whom they can understand.

A great peril lies in the attempt to reverse the type attitude. This leads us to a consideration of some of the forms of projection which parents and teachers make upon children. This danger is the more insidious because it frequently masquerades under the name of love and unselfishness. Ungratified ambition, personal pride, thwarted love, all these seek an outlet. If they are repressed instead of raised to conscious understanding in the life of the individual they may seek a means of expression by proxy, through some other life which can be controlled. Since the child is unfortunately nearest at hand and most unprotected, compensation is often sought through him. All unconsciously the power devil is at work and the desire to shape and control another life takes possession. The desire for fulfillment is one of the strongest life urges and should find its expression in each life, but where it is frustrated it may seek satisfaction through other lives. Such cases as the following are by no means unusual.

In the first instance the father was an introvert whose introversion had been sacrificed to economic pressure which had grown continually greater as he had been called upon to satisfy the ever-increasing demands of a large family. More and more the quiet hours of what were to him real living, apart from the outer demands, were snatched from him. Unable to face the situation and to control it so as to preserve his individual integrity he took refuge in compensatory ideas of sacrifice and determined to give to his children the thing which he had missed. More and more he looked back upon his years in a quiet little classical university as the only ones of real satisfaction. As soon as his boy was born he began to plan his career. The boy was to have a classical education with plenty of philosophical studies. He was not to be hurried. He was to have plenty of opportunities for quiet thought. Unfortunately for these plans the boy turned out to be a rollicking extravert whose only interest was in popular

scientific experiments. Clashes of will began early since the
boy would not see what was, in his father's eyes, "his own
best good." When it came to a question of college, hostilities became open. The boy wished technical school, the father insisted upon a small college where the classics were
venerated and the laboratories were by no means modern.
The father won and the boy left home in a state of rebellion vowing that he would get something that he wanted if
only "to spite the old man." What he got was a fine crop
of wild oats, a most unsavory reputation, frequent flunk
marks and finally, by means of much tutoring, just enough
standing in his studies to make graduation possible. He refused the opening that his father chose for him. Finally, as
a last resort, he was permitted to enter the technical
school. He completed the four years' work in three and
graduated with honors. But the worst of the difficulty
could not be undone. The hostility against his father, the
determination to have his own way, the rebellion against
authority, and the ideas of self-aggrandizement that came
from his proving to his own satisfaction that his father
was wrong and he right, produced an overbearing and
aggressive personality which rode roughshod over all who
came his way. Also the habits formed in college persisted,
a character originally open and lovable became perverted
and a life which might have attained to real individual
value was largely wasted.

Another case was of a girl of the introverted feeling
type. The mother was an extravert of the aggressive type
so often to be found in the group of successful American
business women who have identified with their profession.
Before her marriage she had filled rather an important po-
siton. She had conducted her affairs (so multitudinous as
to be bewildering) with an energy and an ability which
were unquestioned. She had been, both in her own eyes
and in the eyes of her particular world, a most useful and
worthy person. She always acted in accordance with consciously accepted standards. Since these standards included
a tenet that a woman's life is incomplete without children
she annexed a quiet little businessman whose inherited fortune seemed to promise security. She continued her
professional activities until shortly before the birth of her
first child when she withdrew from professional life.

Still following a consciously accepted formula she took
up her duties as a mother. She cared for the child entirely
herself, but fortunately the arrival of a boy and another
girl somewhat diverted the stream of her passionate atten-

tion. The first child, however, remained the object of her greatest devotion. This child was a shy little thing, deep of feeling and slow of mind. Her attachment to her mother was passionate. Later analysis showed the existence of a strong secret bond between herself and her father. This was suppressed because a sense of loyalty to her mother made her take over in her unconscious the mother's attitude of ill-concealed contempt. This of course nullified any positive support which she might have found in her relationship with him.

The school which the mother selected for her was one of high scholastic standards. At first all went well but as she grew older the mother's demands continually increased the pressure that was being put upon her. She must make various school organizations, she must have a part in the school plays, she must have many friends among the popular girls. All this time the lessons were growing harder and harder and now called for a degree of reasoning and thought that were beyond her power, especially when she was so strained to make an extraverted adaptation which accorded with her mother's accepted way of life. Then the mother began going over and over lessons with her but this only added to her sense of inferiority and resulted in greater mental confusion. Hopelessly low marks brought from the mother only a challenge to life. "She shall not fail. I will not have it happen."

The special work was attacked with new vigor and an appeal to the sensitive feelings added to reinforce the compulsion. In this way bewilderment of feeling, through an accepted but not understood burden of emotional guilt, was added to the bewilderment of thought. Then came complete failure. The child was heartbroken. The mother said with tears, "I love her more than anything. I have given up everything for her. Why should this come to me?" In the last sentence the unconscious spoke. It was not "Show me what I have done that brought this on her," but, "Why should this have come to me?" The mask of love dropped from the face of power.

The child's own unconscious came to the rescue and neurotic physical symptoms developed. Illness was something which the mother's pride could accept. She could be brought to see the need of complete change of environment and more out-of-door life. In a simple boarding school where there was more living than mere learning the girl was allowed to make her connections quietly. She has begun to readjust to life but it will be long before her self-confidence can be reestablished. Unfortunately in a case like this where the mother would not, or could not, see her own fault, it is only a temporary compromise and the chains are only loosened, not unbound. The only way out is to help the child to see clearly and to face the situation courageously. Then she may free herself, but at the great cost of sacrificing the mother relationship.

I have here chosen two extreme, but by no means unique, cases. In many instances of maladjustment the parent is truly striving for the child's welfare and is himself bewildered by differences which he cannot understand. Where love and courage are stronger than unconscious love of power the problem is far simpler than in the cases here given, for the parent is willing to accept the child when he can obtain help in understanding him, and will leave him free to follow his own path. Nowhere is it more true than in these parent-child relations that "perfect love casteth out fear." If a father and mother have this higher form of love they can face not only fundamental differences in type but even mental deficiencies and still say "I will do the best for my child and help him to be useful and happy in accordance with his own nature no matter what my ambitions for him may have been." I have known many cases in which, in addition to difficulties, real deficiencies had been revealed, yet the unselfish and understanding attitude of the parent safeguarded the integrity of the child and made possible a happy life in spite of serious handicaps.

No farmer could claim to be scientific who would plant without testing the nature of the soil because he feared that he might find it to be less fertile or otherwise different from what he had hoped. He would realize the stupidity of choosing ignorantly at the time of planting and putting the blame of a poor crop on Providence. Yet many parents feel that it would be disloyal to face the real abilities or natures of their children. Understanding is our duty, and the acceptance of the thing that is, then we can help other things to grow.

The classifications extravert and introvert are based upon the general attitude of the individual in his approach to life. Each type has its distinct place and value, provided a balance is maintained. The extravert spending himself freely in relationships and holding himself in continual contact with the world of things and people must learn that we can give only from our wealth, not from our poverty; and realize that without an inner development there may be nothing worth the giving or building, for the outer life may become a mass of disconnected fragments. The introvert, withdrawing constantly into himself, must learn completion through relationships and outer achievement. He must understand that possession without use is also barren and that use in its broader sense involves the connection of the inner and the outer.

With these attitude types defined we still find ourselves confronted by marked differences between persons of the same general type. This makes a further classification necessary. This classification Jung has made upon the basis of the predominating psychological function, defining function as "a certain form of psychic activity that remains theoretically the same under varying circumstances." The basic functions he finds to be thinking, feeling, sensation, and intuition. All of these functions are present to some extent in every individual but as one or the other prevails in the natural adaptation, the individual may be classified as belonging to that function type. Each one of these function types may be introverted or extraverted according to his relation to the object. The method of using the special function is determined by his extraversion or introversion but the predominance of any of these functions may exist in either type.

As we approach a greater understanding of the child, and of the function type to which he belongs, we are enabled to perceive more clearly his natural strength and weakness. We do not expect certain things to be easy for him because they are for us. At the same time we realize the necessity for helping him to build up his weaker side. In this age of specialization there is a tendency to accept a single differentiated function in lieu of an individual. Our task becomes greater than establishing either a person who can make happy home relationships or one who can attain scholastic honors. We cannot focus our attention upon a special achievement. We must use the superior function to best advantage without sacrificing to it the rest of the individuality.

If the function which is left undeveloped in conscious use merely atrophied the results of the wrong treatment of children would not be so appalling, but every function continues its life either in the conscious or the unconscious. Repressed thinking becomes infantile, regressive, crude. Repressed feeling may emerge as compulsive infantile mood or emotion. The whole carefully evolved structure of the conscious life may be overthrown by the sudden emergence of the infantile repressed function.

Of these four functions two, thinking and feeling, are rational. That is, they proceed in accordance with laws of judgment. There are established values by which their conclusions may be weighed. Our popular conception of feeling is of a mixture of mood and emotion. These are products of the unconscious and not to be confused with true feeling.

The other two functions, intuition and sensation, are irrational. That is, their conclusions lie outside the realm of reason. They seem *of themselves* conclusive. They give one a sense of *a priori* knowledge. Rational types are apt to confuse the irrational with the unreasonable. Because of this there exist, between the rational and irrational types, wide breaches of understanding.

Usually it is the thinking type of child who shows to best advantage in the school, for school is primarily the place of intellectual development and thinking is the intellectual form of adaptation to reality. True thinking develops slowly, especially in the case of the introvert. His value therefore may not be recognized in the earlier grades. Glibness, quickness, and a gift of memory must not be confused with thinking since they are often the masks which hide the lack of true thought. Memory is an attribute of even the untutored primitive mind. The memory of the primitive is often marvelous but the reasoning power practically nil.

Stories are told by explorers which illustrate the remarkable power of the primitive to remember. A man who could not count above six apparently counted a large flock of sheep every night, telling whether any were missing. It was found that he remembered each sheep. Children in mission schools often appear to advance rapidly at the beginning because of this power of retention but they soon reach their norm. This is an element which is often to be found in a situation where parents are disappointed in the school's estimate of the child, or the teachers of higher grades find the judgment of earlier ones reversed. Many precocious children reported as repeating nursery rhymes at a remarkably early age, or performing other memory feats, show little real mental ability when confronted by tasks that demand thought.

Power of judgment, reasoning faculty, and deliberation are all marks of the thinking type. We must be careful not to confound hesitation with stupidity since inability to give ready response may come from a high type of inhibition. The child may be forming judgments, assimilating a new idea, or weighing both sides of a question. The child of the extraverted thinking type will the more readily conform to accepted lines of thought. His thinking is more concrete and objective. It frequently seems to have a greater reality value. He accepts the ideas and logical concepts of others more readily. He is therefore more responsive to ideas presented. The introverted thinking child must withdraw with the idea. He takes the thought down into himself. He is intensive rather than extensive. Sometimes his thinking has a bizarre quality owing to its contacts with the sources of the collective unconscious within himself. His conclusions may sometimes appear to be drawn from material other than that under discussion. It is necessary then to have a nice discrimination as to the real quality of the thought produced before dismissing it as an instance of inattention.

Trivial incidents sometimes clarify such a discussion. When children are off guard we often catch little unwary thoughts that show the reasoning or judging faculty. A small boy of four asked: "Why does the world go round when I rub my eyes?" "It does not," was the answer. "It is in your own eyes." A pause, then: "Libby, you rub *your* eyes and let me see if the world goes round."

A small boy of seven, on being taken to the natural history museum, stood for a long time before the skeletons of some prehistoric monsters and then said in a dreamy voice: "Just think, thousands of years before there were men there were things like this, and thousands of years after there aren't any men I suppose there will be other things. How God must laugh when we fuss!" This second youngster was having trouble in school because he could not remember number combinations or give quick answers. It was not till he was much further advanced that his powers of thought began to show in his ordinary work; then he easily outdistanced boys who had responded more readily to the memory demands of the earlier grades and who had shown quicker social adaptations.

As the thinking child develops there is a natural tendency on the part of both the parent and the teacher to exploit the talent. It is such a pleasure to find a little mind that responds readily and eagerly that the ambitious teacher cannot but be gratified at such a proof of her good work, and the fond parent cannot but be proud of the success. It therefore comes to pass that all the stress is laid upon strengthening the function that is already strongest. Often in the home undue sacrifices will be made for the brilliant child. At all costs opportunities must be provided for higher education and even the duties of relationship set aside lest they should interfere with a career. What wonder that this child grows selfish and overbearing and in the increasing sense of intellectual superiority loses the sense of human values? But superiority which is based on the repression of the rest of the normal functions has an insecure foundation.

A child overstimulated intellectually may become possessed by irrational moods, emotional outbursts, childish regressions. This is not because he is overstrained as is so often supposed but because the repressed feelings are growing in the unconscious and when they break through have an unnatural and obsessive character.

A little girl who was unusually brilliant was promoted rapidly. All the effort of both teachers and parents was used to give her greater opportunities intellectually. She was not urged ahead nor subjected to undue pressure. Her own desires were for harder and harder work and she was never so happy as when studying. Yet she began to show sadistic tendencies, she became subject to sudden irrational angers and tempestuous moods, she sucked her fingers, and bit her nails. Physically she was in perfect condition and her mother could not understand why she should be so nervous. It was not nerves but the suppression of all her functions except her thinking. Her own ambition made her turn all her conscious energy into this one channel and the despised functions took their revenge.

In this case all the opportunities provided should have been on the human relationship side and the attention given to bring up the feelings. The thinking would develop sufficiently in ordinary environment. In adult life we frequently see brilliant thinkers who are betrayed by most childish feelings that they do not understand themselves. They find themselves caught in unsuitable entanglements, or suddenly giving way to compulsive emotions quite out of keeping with conscious choice, or even prey to strange primitive urges.

On the other hand we may expect too much spontaneous feeling from the thinking type. We have a naïve idea that anyone can feel if he wants to. But to the sensation, intuitive, or thinking types true feeling may be a matter of genuine achievement. It may be as difficult for the thinking child to feel as for the feeling child to think.

Seeing the ready interchange of affection between others this thinking child may stand on his small intellectual mountain like a wistful little Moses looking down on a promised land which he thinks he may not enter. His struggle does not lie simply in the difficulty of expressing his feelings but also in actually experiencing them. A woman of the thinking type once said to me, "Feeling is so much harder to get than thinking. You can say to any-one, 'Come and think it out with me,' but if you say, 'Come and feel it out,' they think you are crazy."

If, therefore, a child shows innate mental ability let us try to see that he does not develop along this line only. Give him plenty of opportunities for feeling relationships. Above all do not judge the quality of his feeling by the form in which it is clothed. If feeling is not a natural ad-aptation its early manifestations may be crudely expressed. One of the cruelest little incidents which I have ever known of this sort was the result of such misunderstand-ing.

A small girl of introverted thinking type lived a life quite apart from the other children and was very reserved even with her mother. The mother became anxious when she saw that this was making her different from other chil-dren and tried, on the advice of a psychologist, to help the child to free expression of feeling. Unfortunately the mother confused social adaptability with feeling and much of her emphasis was on manners, not feeling. The small girl began to respond to the mother's expressions of affec-tion with real love. She saved some money which was given her for a toy and bought something that she had heard her mother say she wanted. On the way home with her nurse she stopped to play in the park and arrived home disheveled. Her mother had a guest. She burst in, ran straight to the mother, and throwing her gift in her lap cried, "Take that." The mother saw the mussed clothes, was mortified by the abrupt manner, and sent the child from the room. Later when she went upstairs to talk to the child about the affair and incidentally to thank her for the gift the child would have nothing to do with her. She had again taken refuge in her books and refused to come out. The mother in relating the incident said, "I was only trying so hard to make her show nice feelings and have pretty manners!"

The appreciation of feeling and the recognition of the feeling type is made more difficult by the very hazy ideas that are prevalent as to what feeling really is. Any reaction

which carries with it an overweight of emotion we have
been wont to characterize as feeling. True feeling is a rational function governed by laws of relationship values
which we have determined in part for ourselves but which
have in part been determined for us by our social evolution. Moods and tempestuous emotions which we have frequently accepted as indications of feeling are only the undifferentiated material out of which feeling may be built,
but which in their undifferentiated form are unconscious
products. Real feeling is a consciously accepted value. We
also confuse demonstration, which may be an expression
of feeling or which may be only a sensation manifestation,
with the function itself. We cannot accept this demonstration in lieu of feeling, though demonstration without feeling need not necessarily imply hypocrisy. It may be true in
so far as it goes but remain unconnected with real feeling.

We all know people whose feelings we instinctively
trust. We are confident that in an emotional situation they
will react in accordance with certain fundamental laws
which govern their human contacts. On the other hand
others cannot be depended upon. They are at the mercy of
the sudden emotion. They may react in hatred or tempestuous love or may fail to react at all. In case of sudden
storms they explain their behavior by saying, "It was not
really I who did it. I was carried outside of myself." They
disavow the affect and seek to separate themselves from it.
This is because they have been swept away by forces from
the unconscious, and realize that their reactions were not
true feelings for which they wish to be held accountable in
their more conscious moments. When a person of the feeling type tries to make an adaptation to life through another function while repressing the feelings he is apt to be
more at the mercy of the unconscious mood than another
type. The feeling type must possess his feelings or be in
danger of being possessed by them.

The child who functions through feeling usually shows
to best advantage in the home; he makes contacts quickly
in the social relations of the school unless a feeling of inferiority has been roused by emphasis upon difficulty in
thinking. A child slow of thought may be sound of feeling.
It is this distinction between head ability and heart ability
that is one cause of the difference in judgment which so
often makes the teacher and the parent at loggerheads
with each other.

I recall one little nine-year-old girl who was the despair
of her teachers because of her stupidity, and the pride of

her mother because of her cleverness, and both were right. The child was quick to perceive the needs of others and could take unusual responsibilities in the home. At one time on the occasion of her mother's illness she managed the household with an ability far beyond her years. She was the adjuster of small difficulties, the one to be depended on for services apparently small in themselves but important in the happiness of the home. Where her thinking was in the service of her sound little feelings she functioned very well, but there was no feeling interest bound up in her attitude toward arithmetic or other subjects on the school curriculum, and the thought processes involved there lay quite in another realm.

A way had to be found to connect feeling and thinking. Her true strength must be accepted but the weak function must be developed. She was given more opportunities to perform small services in the school, she was drawn into group work and dramatic and play activities so that she no longer felt outside the life of the schoolroom. School was no longer a world from which to escape. With the freeing of her libido more of her energy could go into the work of the class. A great deal of attention was given to helping her to think and slowly her powers along this line developed.

A public-school teacher told me of a boy whose lack of attention, boredom, and general stupidity had exhausted the patience of several teachers. At last one decided to go to the mother and "read the riot act." The case in her mind was clear and judgment day had arrived. "I have come," she began, "to talk with you about Mikey." The mother's eyes lighted. "I've thought many a time I'd like to do that with you. It's a wonderful boy he is. Isn't he?" Clearly something had miscarried. The teacher murmured something unintelligible and waited the cue. "There's no other boy of eleven could do as he does. From morning to night he's busy and when he is not helping me about the house he's doing chores for the neighbors or working for the grocer on the corner and every cent he brings home to me. I'm glad his teacher has a proud feeling for him for he's burdened beyond his years being the man of the house since his father died."

What were the school gradings to her? She had never paid any attention to them. Mikey was her champion. The teacher who had come to blame remained to praise and not till a most amicable understanding was established were the needs of helping Mikey "to get a better chance"

through his schoolwork suggested. Then the cooperation
was enthusiastic. Mikey had a right to the best.

Clearly Mikey had to learn to think. School had its
value but this value could not be accepted by him except
through an understood channel. The approach must be
made through the feelings. A connection made between
the feeling and the thinking values had to be established so
that the forces of the unconscious should no longer be enlisted on the side of resistance. Mikey's worth, both so-
cially and in his own eyes, lay in his character of helper
and provider.

A long sympathetic talk as to how this could be better
accomplished (also a few references to his fine mother
which brought a glow to Mikey's face) gave him a new
light on the possible importance of school and a very different attitude toward that cumberer of the soil known as
"teacher." Then followed a discussion of the kind of place
that Mikey would want later and the advantages that
would accrue to the family. Evidently before such a position could be obtained something would have to be sacrificed to the gods of the school. Arithmetic and reading
now began to assume a definite value as means to a
worth-while end. It was a discouraging fact but Mikey accepted it courageously and attacked the schoolwork with a
mind less distracted because he knew that the home problems could be discussed with a sympathtic friend. I cannot add that Mikey became a thinker. He remained slow
and plodding but he did get a scheme of values in which
thinking had its place. He learned to use his inferior function and to give it a value in his conscious. In this way his
superior function, feeling, was enlisted in behalf of his inferior thinking.

When feeling is repressed and thrust back into the unconscious we may have an apparent reversal of type. Love
repressed can emerge as unreasonable hate. The feeling
becomes unconscious, undifferentiated emotion and the
emotion piles up on the wrong side. If this repressed feeling breaks forth the child may do cruel things and be
characterized as "an unfeeling little brute," when it is
really the normal strength of his feelings that makes it impossible for him to escape into thinking or one of the
other functions. The child who sees another child receiving love and praise for an easy intellectual achievement
which to him is unattainable, who must struggle for logical
thought, who has no intuitions to carry him over the difficult places, whose wealth of feeling is ignored or not de-

sired, develops a sense of inferiority and impotence which may find vent in rage and acts of cruelty. If these surges of emotion are also repressed and a conscious attitude of submission is accepted there are often dreams in which all these repressions find expression.

One such child became very nervous. Nearly every night she cried out in terror. She awoke trembling, often bathed in perspiration. At first she could not be induced to talk of the dreams but at last confessed that they were frequently of murders, usually ones that she had committed herself. She would cut up her mother or playmates so that "the blood ran all over."

It was found that this child was continually criticized for intellectual failure and her affectionate advances were met by such replies as, "Then show that you love me by doing better." Too gentle to take active revenge, and even unconscious of all the bitterness that she was repressing, the outraged feelings seized upon the dream as the channel through which to find their expression. This could not be accomplished without playing havoc with the sensitive organism of the little patient, who need never have been a patient had she been understood and sympathetically treated.

The problem of feeling leads us back into one of the greatest questions of life: What is our attitude toward human relations and on what do we form our estimate of their value? Are we willing to leave these things to chance, or to "fate," as we are accustomed to call the forces of the unconscious?

One of the most difficult types of child to handle justly is the intuitive. He is a child whose rational processes of thought and feeling lie largely in the unconscious. He appears to reach his conclusions by a process of "hitting the high spots." He frequently seems to grasp the situation by a sort of magic contact and so gives back the desired response, but how he arrived at his conclusions is a mystery even to himself. He just "knows it is so." Sometimes, because he cannot retrace his steps and supply the missing logic, he is accused of willful guessing in an attempt to assume knowledge which is not his, but this is as unfair an estimate of him as to accept his answer as a proof of his powers of logical thought. He has arrived at his conclusions by a process which is quite legitimately his, but the working out of this process lies mostly in the unconscious. His first training in thinking must be to help him make conscious the steps by which he has arrived at his conclusion.

It is the irrational element in this child that is so baffling. His friendships seem often to be mere "crushes" happening for no reason, for the emotional reactions are based on those same intuitional flashes that govern the intellectual processes. Hence, in what seems a sudden revelation, rapport may be established and the whole emotional self goes out to the new relationship. Later a countercurrent in the unconscious may as suddenly break the bond and the intuitive is himself baffled as to the cause of the sudden reversal of feeling. It is gone—that is all he knows. That perceptive sense which enables him to grasp the special element of the person or the situation makes for ready sympathy and understanding and if bulwarked by genuine feeling and thought is an inestimable advantage. When unrelated to more stable qualities it turns into a form of identification with the person or thing so that the intuitive seems to have no real nature of his own but to change with every wind that blows. When motivated by negative feeling and malice there is an impish quality which enables him to put his finger on the sore spot, or to do the thing which will most effectively upset the situation. The power to see behind the scenes now becomes a sort of goblin prying.

The extraverted intuitive shines in the world of action. This is the child who, when a visitor comes, chooses the right moment for some small attention; who disarms criticism by a caress or a word of insight aptly chosen; or who meets you with a disarming bit of humor when you would be most severe. In the schoolroom every dramatic opening is seized. Reading may become a histrionic feat without much attention being paid to the actual words; those which are too difficult are conveniently displaced or swallowed by a bit of intonation. In English there is a clever turn of thought or a bit of fantasy but construction is dismissed as dry bones. Usually much more work is planned than completed, for the intuitive deals in possibilities. It is in this that he finds both his strength and weakness, for he senses the potential, he feels the thing that is about to be.

If, in order to give stability and balance, this child is so handled as to reinforce the functions which are weaker in him, all this natural intuitive wealth becomes of value. The trouble in dealing with a child of this type is that, like the Irishman's flea, as soon as you catch him he isn't there —he has neatly hopped on to the next situation. This child may be the joy or despair of a parent or teacher. He requires infinite patience and a very judicious use of praise and blame. Praise must be given for directed effort. Whereas his values are to be accepted, the thing too easily achieved must be passed over lightly. There must be a continuous demand for stable values of thought and feeling. Demonstration cannot be accepted instead of obedience and effort, cleverness instead of judgment and reasoning. The child must be made to feel that his little circumlocutions of thought and act are clear as daylight, that you see behind the scenes even better than he does and can meet him at his little game while teaching him a better. Also, since it is the new possibility that always lures, he must be trained to finish the task begun even where it takes painstaking effort, instead of abandoning it for the beckoning ideal beyond.

The intuitive introvert is most at home in the world of inner vision. In action he retreats, finding his reality in inner images. He is keen to sense hidden inner qualities of a situation. Often he produces imaginative creations of great beauty but usually he is unable to relate these to life. This is one of the children who is apt suddenly to drift off into daydreams. He is accused of inattention, for the outer world of fact fades. A small household task, a spelling lesson, simply is not. One word may have called up an image much more real and compelling than the text on any page could be. When this happens the child literally does not hear what you are saying.

This type may develop into the unprofitable visionary or the genius. The lines from Rupert Brooke must have been written of such a one:

But there's wisdom in women, of more than they have known,
And thoughts go blowing through them, are wiser than their own.

The task here is to help such a person to connect the vision with life, or to test the truth that comes "of itself" by submitting it to reality. To the rationally minded the mental processes of the intuitive appear to work backward. His conclusions are reached before his premises. This is not because the steps which connect the two have been omitted but because those steps are taken by the unconscious. This gift of the intuitive must not be depreciated. Without intuition there would be no vision of future possibilities. Many

scientists catch a sudden glimpse of a possibility in material
or theory of life. There is a certainty that in this thing so
perceived is the real solution of the problem. Then the
theory must be tested and the theorist must rearrive at the
result by proved steps. Sometimes ideas or solutions present
themselves with such an appearance of certainty that they
appear to come from the outside. The person will wonder
if they are really his own or if he has been told of them or
has read them.

Where the intuitive falls prey to his intuitions and believes them to be true of necessity, they can work damage.
He must, however, have faith in the value of this faculty
and believe this *a priori* knowledge to be worth acceptance
as working theory. In the things of the spirit the intuitive
perceives the symbols of the collective unconscious. These
when interpreted into terms of living values are vital spiritual experiences, but their mere occurrence does not mean
higher spiritual development.

It is extremely difficult to diagnose a child of this type
for he is not to be confused with the child who drifts off
into daydreams from a desire to escape reality. To the
trained observer there are little signs along the way; the
type of material presented if he can be induced to reveal
the inner things, little expressions of face and speech. With
a child of this type we must again follow our rule of accepting the value of the thing that is, and linking it up with
the thing which we desire to produce. If we deny this value
we rouse either antagonism to ourselves or feelings of inferiority and confusion in the child.

A little girl was failing in her work because of inattention. Observing the child carefully I saw the sudden light
that came in her eyes before the look of abstraction. When
we were alone I said to her, "What was the lovely thing
that you saw when the others were having arithmetic? It
seemed as though it must be very beautiful." She told me
of an image roused by a word in a problem. We talked of
the land that lay behind our foreheads and of the wonderful things that were to be found there, *and that was our
only subject that first day*. We pointed no morals, we dwelt
upon no dangers. The entire visit was given over to accepting the thing which was valuable to the child and in the
child.

She came again, and this time without criticism, we
spoke of the schoolroom difficulties. With her realities appreciated, she was ready to discuss her difficulties and failures. From this we arrived at a comparison of values. She

felt quite convinced that she was asked to give her attention to things quite stupid and valueless. She loved a garden but could see that if everyone spent all of life in a garden regular life could not go on. It was not because the garden was not worth while, but because other things were also to be considered. Her dreams were of value but not when they pushed into the place belonging to other things which were also valuable.

To tell this child that these images were silly and something to be ashamed of would have been not only to rouse her antagonism but also to state an untruth. Through accepting the thing which was hers she could be led to reciprocate by accepting things valued by others. She was not asked to give up her reality but to keep it from devouring all else; and, as time went on, to make use of her intuitive wealth.

In dealing with this type we must try to connect the rational function with the irrational, to reinforce the fleeting loveliness. As the intuitive grows older, if his light is not smothered under a pile of objective reality, this imaginative power may produce fantasies colored by imagination or expressed in deeply mystical images of terror or beauty. It is one of the most delicate tasks to lead such a child to an appreciation of the importance of the everyday task with its underlying note of drudgery without closing the doors on the other world where his fantasy takes flight.

Sensation is the first means of contact with the outside world. It is the basic material from which thought and feeling are molded. It is the function by which we perceive concrete reality. Jung defines it as "that psychological function which transmits a physical stimulus to perception." It is not, therefore, a mere physical reaction but a perceptive one. In children as well as in primitives we find sensation and intuition strongly dominant.

The primitive lives in his sensations and intuitions, the latter taking on a magical character as their strength increases, the former furnishing him with a sense of material reality. To the primitive there is the very real world which he sees, hears, and feels and which must be met in solving the problems of food and other daily needs; and there is that other strange, but no less real, world full of unknown forces whose magic working he sees in every accident or lucky happening.

The child moves in a somewhat similar world, but since the sensations and intuitions of the child are constantly brought into contact with the thought and feeling of the adult world which surrounds him, they become more speedily modified. Then, too, he has within himself, through heredity, the potentials of those psychic changes which have taken place in the development of the race and which are as much his heritage as the physical changes. He has influences both from without and from within which at an early period bring his sensations and intuitions under the influence of reason and of feeling judgment. These latter functions, however, develop more slowly.

We find many persons who continue to approach life mainly through these sensations of concrete reality. Such persons belong to the sensation type. These sensations may be developed to a fine point of discrimination as in the artist or musician or the discriminating lover of beauty, or they may remain in a more undifferentiated form. The sensation type may have other functions highly developed but his approach to life is primarily through sensation. When typically extraverted these are often persons to whom life is not so much a picture canvas to be understood and its meaning and details evaluated, as a cinema whose object is to crowd as many impressions as possible into a single film. Through this attitude they grow to live in the variety and vividness of the sensation rather than in the depth and meaning of the experience.

To a child so oriented the busy atmosphere of one of our large cities seems the very breath of life, but it is really the most insidious poison. I remember once watching a class of small children putting on their things to go home. One eight-year-old ran to another asking her if she could come to lunch and to play in the park. A consultation with the mother showed no free day for nearly two weeks. Movies, dancing-class, music, a children's party, filled the time.

The poor child with only the street for a playground has no more leisure, for here sensations crowd. Even the popular and very useful play-class has the danger of swallowing all the child's time in group activity so that the needed leisure and quiet is crowded out. During adolescence this whirl of sensation-activity frequently increases at the very time when it is most important that there should be less strain and more time to adjust to the new demands of life. This is the time when we should give our children more understanding and less chaotic sensation stimuli. This over-stimulation during adolescence is especially dangerous for the sensation type as it pushes him over into the extreme of the function which needs most control and guidance.

In the introverted child sensation-adaptation is not so

easily detected because the strength of the reaction is to an inner perception. The object is still the necessary stimulus but the perception is so modified by the inner attitude that frequently it seems to have lost all connection with the actual object perceived. To such a type the object becomes an image of beauty or terror or of symbolic suggestion. A child of this type touched a green silk curtain; as she did so a look of joy came into her face and she said, "How lovely the sea is!" Another child of this introverted sensation type told me that when she touched feathers she saw lovely ladies bending over her. A contact with harsh surfaces produced terror. Certain tones made her perceive flowers and others, especially strident bass notes, called into being ugly little black men.

A woman who all her life had found her world bewilderingly unlike the world in which other people appeared to live told me that one of the most vividly remembered experiences of her childhood was encountering the images of terror evoked by the whistle of a particular steamboat. It is hard for most people of a different type to imagine a world in which hearing a compelling tone becomes a never-to-be-forgotten experience. As a child she loved a special walk which led from her home to the harbor but she would go shuddering for fear that this special boat, which went back and forth to a near-by town, might approach and whistle. She tried to walk at times when this boat would not be coming into the harbor. If she miscalculated and was caught by the sound she was encompassed about by such forces of terror that she would run blindly for the shelter of home. She feared to see anyone angry, not because she felt afraid of what they might do but because of the sense impression that came from the ugly expression which anger impressed on the face and which roused these inner images. These children need the reassurance of relationship. As a keenly sensitive dog shrinks close to his master when first confronted by the noise and confusion of a city street, so these children shrink back to the protection of a love that remains secure in these changing images of the outer world. If such a child feels alone or inferior he is terribly delivered over to the power of the object.

We see how far these images may lie from the world of tangible reality in the case of a child who was seized with sudden terror at the sight of some flowers on my table which were nodding in the breeze. "I see a queer little man waving himself at me. I don't like him." Or a woman who said, "I have that vase there for when I look at it I see the

Holy Grail, though I know it is not in the least like the form in which the vessel is depicted." Though in certain cases this adaptation seems akin to synesthesia (a condition in which a stimulus to one sense gives rise to a subjective sensation different from the one expected and referable to some other sense, for instance a sound producing a sense of color, or a color producing a definite taste), this introverted sensation-adaptation differs in that it deals with the subjective image and is closely linked with fantasy.

The world is a bewildering place to such a child. More or less distinctly he begins to perceive that the things which are so compelling to him have little or no power over others. This makes him feel separate, different, and frequently inferior. We must try to understand what is happening inside a child so oriented to the object. If we realize that this irrational effect is not a personal idiosyncrasy caused by some whim or queerness, but is a reaction which is in accordance with certain laws of the child's own being—in fact, a type reaction—we shall have sympathy even though these manifestations may be so far from our orientation that we cannot understand sufficiently to put ourselves in his place. To such a child some form of sensation expression is a necessity. It draws away from the magic power of the object. To be able to produce in music the sounds which seem so wizard-like in their power to evoke images, to paint or model the thing which causes these strange inner reactions, places the object outside the self where it can be handled as a reality divested of its mysterious compulsion. Such products retain subjective elements which enhance their beauty, and which through their expression in the material are raised to consciousness and so add to the individual's understanding of himself. In such a sculptor as Meštrović these innner images break through the conventional form and give a suggestion of the soul, struggling to find expression in the medium of stone. Little children of this type produce pictures, which, no matter how crude, serve the same purpose.

When we have done our best to make a clear and simple statement of the intricate problem of types we are confronted by the fact that in some ways we have only complicated the whole matter; for we have given an appearance of simplicity to a thing which never can be simple. People are not clearly defined function types with predetermined reactions. They are highly complicated organisms with all the functions operative either in the conscious or the unconscious. It takes great skill to determine with any degree of accuracy which are unconscious manifestations and which are evidences of conscious adaptation. Frequently an identification with a parent will make a child take over a type attitude which is not his own. This borrowed attitude may be so thoroughly entrenched as completely to deceive the ordinary observer and to make it a difficult problem for even the trained psychologist to discover the real self. This chapter is not offered as a basis for diagnosis. The problem is too complicated to be solved in any such easy fashion. Its aim is to broaden the sympathy and understanding of those who work with children, so that they shall have a greater respect for the child's own way of life and less temerity in the demands of adaptation that they make upon him.

8

IMAGINARY COMPANIONS

Mrs. Comphret lived on the cellar stairs. She was short and plump and comfortable, and she was always smiling. She wore a little black bonnet tied in a neat bow under her chin. It had a jet ornament that stood up in front and tinkled as she walked or nodded. Sometimes she sat out on the cellar door in the sun and smiled. When the days were warm the cellar doors were opened and my sister and I played on the cellar stairs with Mrs. Comphret. She did not talk much but was just comfortable and smiling and slow and quiet. We liked to feel her there. I never went to school or anywhere without stopping to talk to Mrs. Comphret, or if we were in a great hurry at least we whispered good-bye.

Aida Paida was quite different. She was grown up too—that very uncertain grown-up age which means any stage of antiquity to children—probably about thirty. Aida Paida did not stay at home as Mrs. Comphret did, but went with us on all our walks. On the other side of the road, quite far from the house, was a big basswood tree. The branches came down nearly to the ground so as to make a big green room, and the twisted roots made furniture. We could not go over to the basswood tree without permission, but sometimes on bright afternoons we were allowed to have parties there. Aida Paida always came with us. She sat on a big gnarled root and we served her with mud pies. Going to the basswood tree was an adventure, but we always felt quite safe with Aida Paida. She went to walk with us too. There was always a little circle of security about Aida Paida and we moved in it with her. Things that might have got us never could. Aida Paida never did anything to them, but they never could get at us. She made them keep their distance.

One day a neighbor died. There was a funeral, a "finneral" we children called it. We were very much impressed with the solemnity and hush. It was not very real to us except as an impressive bit of drama, but in that way it seemed very mysterious and important. Then one day Mrs. Comphret died and had a "finneral." It was strange to have her go but she never came back. I knew she never would.

Aida Paida stayed a little longer and then just faded away. I cannot remember how she went but I am sure that she did not die. She just receded and at last vanished completely.

Whimsical, quaintly charming as this fantasy is, we find that it has a deeper meaning. When we come to study its reason for being, its relation to the actual life of this particular child, we find that it was called into existence because of a psychological need.

This child felt the lack of certain things in her relationship with her mother. The mother was, like Mrs. Comphret, a small woman, but there was no plump restfulness, no quiet smile. Instead she was alert, quick, dominating. The next thing to be done must be done at once. It did not matter where the development of an important game might be, it was time right now to go out, or to wash one's hands, or to put one's things away. Something was building in the child's world, perhaps was nearing completion. It was intensely, absorbingly important, but it must be swept away, demolished, because "we were going down to the store," or "supper was ready." Her mother's voice was quick, charged with nervous energy, immensely disturbing. It broke in upon play or fantasy with irritating persistency. She always intended to be very fond of her mother but before she quite accomplished it the voice would break in upon something very important and then she would be angry and very far away.

She "adored" her father. He was slow and quiet. If they were going anywhere he would come in ahead of time and say, "We'll be going in half an hour. You might begin to get washed up in fifteen minutes or so." Or, "Ten minutes more to bedtime." With Mother everything had to be done in a hurry, toys picked up anyhow and all at once. The child, too, was high-strung. Her mother's jangling nerves set hers jangling to the same discords. Her father's quiet soothed her. He was a farmer and she loved to tramp the fields after him, wearing boy's shoes, passionately pretending that she was a boy. But after all she was also very much of a girl and loved girl's things. She liked dancing school and liked to be admired by boys. Very early she had a special boy whom she liked to consider quite her own. As she grew older the intense love for her father increased. She and her mother made conscious attempts at establishing a relationship, but they could never reach across those intangible barriers.

Mrs. Comphret was the personification of the things she had wanted in a mother and had not found. Gradually, as the relationship with her father had grown more satisfying, that need had grown less insistent. Mrs. Comphret, quiet, restful, slow, and smiling, died and had her "finneral."

Aida Paida was a less important figure. She faintly resembled a little aunt who sometimes came to visit them. She took them for parties under the basswood tree, parties with real cookies instead of mud pies. In her absence Aida Paida took her place as guardian. She was a holiday sort of person but not so necessary as Mrs. Comphret. When she could tramp the fields with her father or go farther away with her sister, Aida Paida faded away. She, too, became unnecessary when the father filled her place.

Consciously the child missed nothing, since her father filled the place of both father and mother in her affections. But a single relationship should not be called upon to carry a double significance. It thereby becomes overweighted. The ties in the unconscious become too hard to break. This young woman said that she had never married because she had never found a man to compare with her father. She had many men friends but none who would understand her as he had done. If Mrs. Comphret's place could have been filled by her mother through a change in the mother-daughter relationship, there would not have been such an excess of emotion carried over to the father. It would then have been possible for her to accept the normal adult love relationship in its proper time.

We can no more blame the mother for not grasping the significance of the fantasy than for not understanding the not-yet-invented radio. Twenty years ago one would have laughed at the idea of attaching psychological importance to such a bit of fantasy. The mother was not neglectful. She was busy attending to the needs of the household as she saw them. It was unfortunate that she and this little daughter "got on each other's nerves." It did not happen with the other, more placid child. Unfortunately their likeness, instead of making for greater understanding, accentuated the difficulties of each. If the meaning of Mrs. Comphret (who was a well-known person to the mother) could have been made plain it might have kept her from always being so "careful and troubled about many things"; and instead she might have found time for that quiet in which relationships, like other fruits of the spirit, can grow.

Often this fantasy self or dual personality is projected into some toy or other object. Girls frequently make use of dolls for this purpose. As in the following case, a little drama may be staged where the puppet actors represent different sides of the child's own nature, or of her fantasy self.

She was a slow, overgrown, clumsy child. Her body and her emotions were both too big for her. Because the quick expression of thought was as difficult for her as graceful bodily movement she was supposed to be stupid. It never occurred to anyone that the overgrown, pent-up emotions got in the way of her thought expression as her too-big self got in the way of her bodily control.

She did not play much with other children but she had a large family of dolls on whom she lavished her devotion. They had varying personalities and two were singled out for the star roles. One was a small, blue-eyed, golden-haired, wax doll; the other a rag doll, large and stolid. Many were the triumphs, both social and intellectual, of the golden-haired beauty. She lived a brilliant, dazzling life. The rag doll was regarded with scorn for the most part. She was slow and stupid. The beauty always surpassed her in her lessons when they played school. Yet every now and then the blue-eyed darling would commit some sin for which she had to be punished with great severity. This generally took the form of a violent beating. Then the rag doll would be taken to the child's bosom and loved and praised, and overwhelmed with floods of maternal tenderness.

The intensity of the emotion shown in this play was so far removed from the child's ordinary quiet, controlled self that the mother was puzzled and asked advice.

A guarded exploration into the fantasy life of the child revealed a similarity in underlying idea. Her favorite story was of Thumbelina, the tiny blue-eyed girl born in the tulip. She used to act this story when she was alone. Usually she was Thumbelina, though sometimes Thumbelina came as an imaginary companion to see her, and they had long conversations. The child hated the stories of big, clumsy people who were undone by the cleverness of little ones. There was an element of personal resentment in the feeling that she expressed about these tales. Then, as she began to talk more freely, there were references to her own clumsiness, mixtures of self-scorn and resentment. Once when asked if she would like to sit and rock in a tulip, she replied, "It would look nice when I sat in it, wouldn't it?"

The meaning of the doll-play now became evident, as did the cause for the intense display of emotion. The despised rag doll was herself as she believed people really regarded her, and as she really believed herself to be. The tiny doll was her fantasy self, the fairy princess whom she wished to be. Through this princess doll she lived her other life. In her identification with her she experienced the triumphs and joys that she thought would be hers if she were only little and graceful and fair. Through her she obtained release from the too difficult world of reality. But sometimes when this real world pressed too hard (when, for instance, her brother greeted her with, "Hello, Clumsy!" or she felt awkward in a group of strangers) she became too painfully aware of the difference between her actual and her fantasy self. Then, in a flood of self-pity, she took vengeance upon the child of her dreams and gathered the rejected self into her arms. The fantasy self now ceased to be a sufficient refuge from her own insistent inner ego which felt so baffled by life. These dolls served a very real purpose in draining off the emotion which otherwise might have been the basis of a neurosis. Yet there was a danger that there might be a split between these two personalities, and the mother was wise in investigating the cause of these waves of savage emotion though they were vented only on a doll.

The sudden anger roused by a trivial incident is not really anger at, or because of, the incident; it is an anger roused by the power of the inner forces set in play by that incident. It is those inner forces which we must explore. Certain forms of emotion which have been exploited in literature are accepted. The touch of the hand of the beloved is supposed to arouse intense emotion. The shudder of the victim when the villain taps him lightly upon the shoulder is not expected to be in proportion to the physical sensation aroused by the severity of the tap. But why, we ask, should a little girl be seized with a paroxysm of almost hysterical anger because a blue-eyed doll slips down, and in so doing knocks an old doll from her place on the sofa? If, however, we understand that the rag doll represents her despised self and that her identification with that self has just been made painfully apparent by some awkward act for which she was rebuked, we are no longer surprised at the savage revenge taken upon the desired fantasy self. It does not show some "strain of innate cruelty" as the mother feared, but a natural outbreak of pent-up emotions.

Understanding this, the mother was able to enter into the child's play, and to show an appreciation of the virtues of the rejected rag doll. Things which the child undervalued in herself were praised in the rag doll. Little glittering attractions which she had passionately overestimated and which she had worked out in the successes of the blue-eyed other self could be put in their place by a deft revaluation. Above all she could revalue the child herself and make this new understanding the guide in establishing a more sympathetic relationship. Here again is a place where we cannot directly analyze the situation with so young a child, for it would lead to greater self-consciousness; but through the child's own vehicle, play, which made use of these little marionette personalities to project her own unlived feelings and to eliminate the undesired, one could build up a new sense of values, break down the disintegrating sense of inferiority, and help the child to integrate with her own individuality which she had identified with the despised rag doll.

To pursue the retreat of the fantasy still further I would mention a case of extreme introversion where this same fantasy self was encased within the child herself. It was the same "other self" which in one child finds expression through the imaginary playmate and which in this last instance is projected into the doll. In the next case the withdrawal is so complete that the imaginary playmate remains within the self. I will quote the words of the young woman who told me of this inner life.

"I am larger than most girls of my age. I love beauty. I especially admire small girls with golden curls and deep blue eyes. I like to dream that there is such a person inside me, and that I am just a shell, and that some day all this outer appearance of me will drop off and I shall appear like the lovely princesses in fairy tales, ravishingly beautiful, and lovable and gracious."

This inner self assumed a definite individuality. It pursued its own life. It compensated for the failures of the outer self. In the next reminiscence is shown the attempt of the child to win recognition on her own merits through the outer self which others saw. The pitiful rebuff drove her further back to the companionship of the inner self who she hoped was one day to become manifest.

"My father used to seem kind and sweet and worth knowing, much gentler and more patient than my mother, but infinitely remote. I wondered if he did not like me because I never had as much to say as my sister did. Most people among our relatives and friends thought me silent and hard to get acquainted with and I wanted dreadfully to have them like me. One day I was all washed and dressed in a perfectly new dress. It was Sunday and I found Father sitting reading in the living room. I went up to him and told him how clean I was and asked him if I couldn't sit in his lap, and if he didn't think that he could love me."

The father allowed her to climb up but did not even seem aware of the act. He went on reading and after a little the child slipped down and wandered away. She had made her best attempt to be received as her real self. She was "all washed and clean" and had put on a "perfectly new dress." She felt sure that if she was ever to be received on her own merits it would be now. Had the father accepted her then she would have felt reconciled to herself as she really was, but being repulsed she retreated farther into herself, there to compensate with fantasy. She remained throughout her girlhood and early womanhood unable to face the task of accepting herself. Whenever a relationship became of value and importance to her she retreated at the first sign of difficulty. She projected upon others her own attitudes toward herself and so was always expecting to be repulsed. She was beautiful and immediately attractive to people but she had no sense of stability in human relations. Especially was this so in her relations with men. She erected barriers which effectually cut them off. "Men never love women who are as big as I am," she said.

But to return to the early inner companions. As desires for more contacts grew the inner world became more populated. "Eating is funny business. I wonder where all the food goes, and what it does. Maybe there is another world inside me with cities and people and everything the way I see it outside. Or perhaps there is a ring of happy dancing children waiting down there to be fed when I am fed, but almost too happy and gay to care for such things as eating and sleeping and all the things that I love to do."

The gay happy children grew very real to her. She saw them dancing about in a ring. She herself was continually weighed down by a sense of duty and the need of being good and helpful, but these dancing children had no cause to be troubled by such things. She liked to feed them when she ate. They were also "playmates" but buried deep within herself. Through them she experienced some of that light-hearted joy which she felt she must not try to have herself because she was "different." The children helped her to separate herself more and more from life. Fantasy as compensation began to cast its spell. When she felt that these inner children were not enough and that she herself must have something, she did not go out to life but created another fantasy world in which she gave herself a place.

"When I was a little girl in the fourth grade I used, after not too happy days, to look forward with eagerness to the time when I went to bed, when I could lie unmolested by other people and weave fantasies. At first I dreamed that I was a lovely young woman in Holland, with a beautifully kept house and gardens and dairy, and spotless clothes and a pretty crisp cap." (Again we have the being very clean, spotless, which she had hoped would appeal to the father and win an expression of his love.)

"Then as I grew older I was fascinated with the power of teachers over boys in school. One very sweet-faced teacher entered my waking dreams. I'd see her standing with a boy who had been naughty whom she had to punish. The fact of her striking him seemed an evidence of deeper tenderness. I dwelt upon her putting her arms around him, and her power over him after she had punished him. Later I had a masterful, rather masculine teacher and I fantasied about situations involving myself and her."

Punishment took an important place in her fantasies as the split between the two selves grew greater.

Her sister made friends easily, and this increased the sense of inferiority which her own isolation gave her and made her take refuge in lessons where she could easily assert a superiority. The thinking self (which was not real for she was a feeling type) took control of the outer life, a very dutiful, clean, spotless, useful life. The inner play-mate, the blue-eyed feeling self, was driven further and further back into the unconscious. Where a function is not allowed to develop through use it remains infantile, it drops back into the unconscious and there retreats to more and more primitive levels. Since change is the law of life, where there is not progress there will be regression. The feeling self living only in the inner world of fantasy went back to the world of the collective unconscious. Strange unreasoning emotions took possession of her, obsessive thoughts rose up apparently of themselves, perversions which our civilization has outgrown but which still retain their power pursued her. Now the retreat was cut off. The fantasy life, too, became peopled with forces of terror and she took refuge in a neurosis.

I do not mean that any such clear form of the difficulty lay open to inspection. To follow the thread of such a fan-tasy leads us through a labyrinth more twisted than that of Crete, and the silken thread by which we would find our way out is often tangled and broken. The original fantasy of the blue-eyed inner self did not persist unchanged but took on many forms. Nevertheless it was this fantasy self which marked the first split in the personality—the separa-tion between the thinking self and the self of feeling and relationships.

Here we may trace the analogy between this type of fantasy and the old fairy tale. The Frog Prince must be taken in the maiden's lap in his form of ugly frog. Beauty must kiss the Beast while he is yet a beast, and recognize the love and kindliness that has shone through his beastly outer self. It is only when we feel ourselves accepted as we really are, our whole selves with both the good and evil, that we can find true release of our feeling selves. Through feeling ourselves acceptable to one whom we love we can also accept ourselves. If the child's father had accepted her as she really was and shown his love, if she had been conscious of his love for her, she would not have needed this inner self as a refuge from reality.

Of course I do not mean that this single act of the fa-ther had in itself so far-reaching an effect. It was destruc-tive because typical of the entire attitude. If there had been confidence and friendship between them a single act of absent-minded coldness would have had no such disas-trous effect. As a crystallization of all that the child had dimly perceived in the situation, it impressed her, little as she was, with a sense of finality.

Contrast this with the imaginary playmates of a happy, much loved child. She was friendly as a puppy and had the puppy's confidence in the friendship of the world. She did not go to school until she was over seven, and before then had not many flesh and blood children with whom to play. This did not trouble her, for the garden was full of children. She would call to them from her window when she was dressing in the morning. She would run out to say good morning before breakfast, and whenever she was alone would invent games with them or tell them stories. They had parties and dances. Fairies lived under the big syringa bush. "The children" did not go there except when the fairies gave permission. Mr. Migglesby lived in the pear tree. He was little and wore brown clothes and had bright, beady, black eyes like a robin. He was great friends with all the creatures and people who could fly. He told stories about them and scolded the baby birds when they were naughty. Mr. Migglesby had one alarming quality. He walked into strange places. The child used to creep into a low branch of the pear tree to read. There were certain books that belonged to the pear tree. *Revelations* was one. Mr. Migglesby got mixed up with the strange beasts and with angels with flaming swords. He was suspected of having conversations with cherubim. At such times Mr. Migglesby was not like a robin but was full of almost unpleasant mystery. Usually, though, he was friendly and amusing. There were a great many other people in the garden too. In winter many of them moved into the house. Two children lived back of the parlor sofa. Mr. Migglesby never came in. He preferred the pear tree even if it snowed. Sometimes so many children came into the house that grown people (who never could see very well) had to be careful where they sat down, or they might sit on one. When the child went to school these playmates gradually disappeared, or perhaps came back only on rainy days. Even when they were most present they never interfered with the other joyous affairs of daily living, and when real children took their places they came less and less often.

Another child of much the same type had two children who were always near by. She had only to stretch out her hands, and immediately one of these children would seize each one and they would all three run or dance together. She called them by name, she talked to them. They were as real as any people. But here again there was no separa-

tion from life and as their places were more and more filled
by actual children they vanished away. With both these
children, however, there remained a quality of imagination
which greatly enriched life. Though they apparently vanished I know that in one instance at least they lived again
and again in adolescent fantasy and adult dream.

This projection of the imaginary playmate may take
many forms; the form corresponds to, and is indicative of,
the type of child.

An adopted child of extreme sensation type found her
means of satisfaction through sensory excitement, especially through the sense of touch. She was greatly moved
by caresses and physical demonstration. Her imaginary
playmate was the tail of an old fur piece. Whenever she
felt neglected or slighted she would bring out this bit of
fur, and while making it stroke her, would hold long,
whispered conversations with it. In this play the fur
showed its love for her by its soft contacts. Sometimes one
caught such sentences as, "You love me, Dear One. Don't
you? Of course you love me." The sensation of satisfaction
from this physical contact was manifestly that of self-love.
It was akin to the auto-erotic manifestations of masturbation and self-caresses. Here, however, they received an
added gratification through projection. By endowing the
fur with personality she could enact a little drama in
which she received attention from someone outside of herself. From this person she could receive approbation without the trouble of winning it through real effort.

When she had been criticized or had failed in her
school adjustments, she would take this fur, or a similar
soft "playmate," to bed with her. From the expression on
her face when talking to it I believe that she used it in
masturbation or to stimulate masturbation and fantasy at
night. I know that several times she took it with her to
the bathroom. This occasionally happened at school, and
from the expression on her face on return I feel sure it
was used in this type of fantasy. She would steal her hand
into her desk caressing it and at that time she had a curious detached smile: not the smile of a happy friendly
child ready for human contacts, but the smile of one who
has withdrawn to a secret world.

As is frequently the case with adopted children she felt
a sense of insecurity in her emotional life which showed
itself in outbursts of jealousy. When walking with her father and mother she did not wish to have them talk of any
things which did not directly include her. If a conversation

on an adult topic started she would dart between them seizing a hand of each. Then if the conversation continued she would toss away their hands and seize something to caress and whisper to. If they were in the country she would perhaps take a smooth stone and stroke her cheek or press a sharp one into her hand. This might be followed by a "black mood" when she would be contrary, forgetful, or even directly disobedient. The substitute had not really satisfied, and the pent-up emotion found its outlet in these negative reactions which attracted attention to herself and gave her a gratification even though the attention took the form of punishment. Spanking, or any form of physical punishment, is to be especially avoided with children of this type since it is often a sensation gratification. It is this type of child who is frequently described as "spoiling for a spanking"; and who will work up scenes until the desired spanking has been administered and then find release in the stimulation of the physical sensation and the resulting emotional storm. After this there is a calm reaction which appears as "goodness." The child is usually unconscious of what she is doing and does not understand what is driving her to acts which she knows will bring the punishment, and her tears are quite genuine. I have, however, known children who were quite conscious of these urges. One little girl, daughter of a pious New England pastor, quite openly described to other little children how good it felt to be spanked and how she did one specially forbidden thing because then she was always spanked with a hairbrush and it "felt so good all over and even way in your stomach." Another child, a boy who had abounding muscular energy and a highly energetic mother, described to a group of children the sensations in his genitals when his mother, following the good old custom of energetic mothers, turned him over her knee and used the palm of her capable hand with an effect quite as satisfactory as the hairbrush. Both the pious pastor, who feared physical gratification as traffic with the devil, and the overworked mother, who was afraid her son might get beyond her control, would have been surprised and horrified at knowing the actual results of their fears lest they "spare the rod and spoil the child." Such children are commonly known as masochist or children who take pleasure in having pain inflicted upon them.

But to return to our special case. It was harder to establish a sense of ordinary values than is usual, for failures and disapprobation drove her to seek comfort with her

playmate and her fantasies. The games with "Dear One"
furnished a retreat. When she did begin to make contacts
with children her fantasy life showed in an unusual curiosity as to their visits to the toilet and in whispered "secrets"
which had to do with bits of sex information gathered
through underground channels. This was not at all surprising, for self-gratified sensation links up with such fantasies. Also this knowledge gave her a certain power which
she could not obtain through legitimate accomplishment.
Her love of color and sound and beauty was not sufficiently differentiated to make her willing to make real
effort in order to accomplish something in her music or
her painting. The easy way of achievement through fantasy had too great a lure.

Here then was the problem, to use the knowledge obtained from the interpretation of the playmate in a constructive way. The child was not abnormal or perverted,
terms which we use so freely to cover our lack of skill.
She was simply a difficult child swayed by forces which
she could not understand. The key to the difficulties lay
in the understanding of this inner life. The child could not
be left too much alone. She needed human contacts, not
just offered for her refusal but made attractive so that they
would be desired. She must have socialized standards and
directed desires so that she would be willing to work for
real achievement and the approbation of real people for
whom she cared. Since her fantasy was a retreat and not a
creative thing, she must find a substitute in something
which made use of her sensation function in a positive
way.

The fact that her normal approach was through sensation must not be disregarded nor undervalued. With our absurd horror of the physical, so deep-rooted in our sex fears,
we are apt to consider the sensation type as inferior. But
even the city of the New Jerusalem (the inner kingdom of
the spirit) has four walls and in each wall three gates and
there is no one gate selected by which alone the elect may
enter. The important thing is that we may enter in, and
possess the city, instead of remaining at the gateway. This
child's approach to life, to human relationships, to feeling
and thinking would normally be through sensation, but it
must be a trained and differentiated sensation.

Through modeling and painting and music she could be
drawn to a sense of creation. This had to be done by
group work where she had a sense of values through
group criticism. She was made a member of a play class

where she found group activities in which her little world of fantasy compensation had no value. It is generally a pity to fill a child's day so full that there is no time for games or thoughts of their own devising, but in such a case the more filled the better, provided there is a real purpose back of the activity. Difficult situations should not be handled just before bedtime nor should the child of this type go to bed with feelings of inferiority uppermost, for these feelings will be appeased by fantasy and masturbation, and it is quite natural that this should be so.

Most important of all is the establishing of a real feeling relationship, both for her schoolwork and for her general development. Children, like most grown-up people, are not greatly influenced by high-minded abstract ideas of duty. They do the things that seem normal and pleasant and interesting. Dull forms of effort are illuminated by human interests to which they are attached. This child loved attention and was given to violent attachments. These interests could be used. With such a child a caress must never be accepted as a substitute for an act of real feeling, neither must it be treated as something shameful. It must be accepted as something valuable when, and only when, it is offered in connection with some positive feeling act. Careless work or disobedience cannot be expiated with caresses. A nice balance must be kept so that physical expression shall neither be rebuffed nor allowed to exist in and for itself. In the more abstract forms it must be directed into creative channels.

Of a very different type is this boy who also chose an inanimate object as an imaginary companion. Here was objectified a side of himself, the ease-loving, sensation self that he dimly felt must be conquered if his other self was to develop. I give his own reminiscence.

THE DRESSER

It wasn't ugly. No, that would have made the whole matter commonplace and drab (one always hears of people detesting ugly furniture) and I wouldn't have paid any more attention to it than my white iron bedstead. The fact that it was really the nicest thing in the room, that it was carved almost beautifully, that it ostentatiously exhibited in its every line that self-satisfaction of knowing that it *was* nice—these were the things I loathed.

Let me explain. You spoke of imaginary companions as beings whom one created to fill a need, to whom one turned as to a friend in time of trouble. Unfortunately you forgot to say anything about those who had no need to fill, those poor souls who had everything necessary to fulfill ambitions, who railed and wept and stormed against a well-to-do, middle-class life. I had friends, why create another? I had dreams, why force them into the shape of a definite fancy? I had food, and clothes, and books. The whole world wished me well and tried to help me. Why burden myself with more well-meaning friends?

Sometimes I wish I had been born to a poverty-stricken life, to a hard unsympathetic family, to a childhood full of misery and pain. There would have been so much more incentive to get somewhere, to do something. There would be that aura of romance and glory attached to "lifting myself by my own boot-straps."

It was in these moods that I talked to the dresser. Talked, did I say? Nay, rather stormed, scolded, wept, and beat at it with puny fists. There was no *talk* in our communion!

There was one night I remember about seven or eight years ago. I had been scolded for some minor infraction upon household custom and as usual had retired to my room to sulk and muse darkly upon the hard life that was mine. There it stood, hideously smug and complacent, silent but firmly reproving me for being a naughty little boy. How I hated it! How I fought, and argued with it! Hour after hour, far into the night! I talked, trying to show my side, and, if possible, grasp the other. And hour after hour it stood there just as silently as ever but in a firm manner telling me, "Now you're all excited, dear. Go to sleep and tomorrow you'll feel much different."

"I will not go to sleep. I will not! Oh, you're good, aren't you? You great, big fat smarty! You and papa and mamma, and—Oh, I hate you."

"Now please, Leo, go to sleep like a good boy—"

And so on. Of course I fell asleep at last—from exhaustion. It was my own pounding at life and life, as yet, was the stronger.

Two and a half years ago, just before I ran away, the dresser was discarded. Since I've come back I've missed it. There, at least, was something real to fight —life now is so much harder to battle, for it has no symbol to grasp. It eludes one, and leads one on like a will-o'-the-wisp until one sinks in the marshes. In time, I could have overcome the dresser—it is well-nigh impossible to overcome that which has no substance.

On May 18, 19—I suddenly betook myself to Philadelphia, found a job the following day, grew homesick the next and wrote home. On May 22nd, my brother-in-law came down and brought me home, meek and penitent.

Your other queries are not so easy to answer. As I've told you, the more introspective I get, the less I know about myself. I'm sure I'm the last person in the world who can say whether I dislike ease and comfort. There are times when I think it is the greatest deterrent to my career, and other times when it becomes the most necessary factor in my life. The whole matter is so inextricably woven into the pattern of my existence that I could explain very little to you without writing reams upon reams of senseless paper. In a general way, though, I think I can say that the idea of ease and comfort as commonly accepted does not make for what I want to be.

It's all very indefinite and indistinct, you see.

The last paragraph means this: that the dresser was an emblem of life, much as a flag, in battle, was an emblem of a nation. Conquer the emblem and you have conquered the nation. But since the dresser was thrown out, I can fight life only in the vaguest of abstracts—and I'll never know if I've won or lost.

We now come to one of my most interesting cases, a part of which has been quoted elsewhere by Jung.

At seven years of age, Margaret was confronted by the world of outer reality and found it too hard. Up to that time the world had been made up of a very loving father and mother, a pet or two, here and there a much younger child, and a whole world of people, unseen by other eyes, who came and went, danced, sang, played, or rendered homage as her imagination dictated. Now, suddenly, like a cloud that swallows up the sun, had come school that ate chunks out of the day which had always been exclusively hers and that paid no attention to her realities.

There had been a reason for her finding her life in this other world and for the special protection with which she had been surrounded. An operation in very early infancy had left a train of physical handicaps and a nervous instability that made some of the simple things, like dressing and waiting on herself and performing small tasks for others, things to be postponed because of the undue nervous strain entailed. There was a lack of muscular coordination. Progress had to be one step at a time. She had the same difficulty in handwork; writing and drawing were very hard. Compensating for this was a vivid imagination that sometimes stimulated her to undue excitement. When interested in fantasy she would spoil nearly completed papers by scrawling "funnies" over them. Overeffort brought inevitable reaction.

Confronted with such a situation what could be expected except that love would become a shielding and protecting power? Also, inevitably, the child became aware of this protection. It invested her with a sense of satisfaction and power which normally comes from accomplishment. A child will try over and over to walk and when in spite of many falls he can trot about, seems to know no weariness in his own exertions. When normal advance is checked and the child has to have things done for him which he would usually do for himself the sense of power becomes diverted and he finds his satisfaction in ruling others and accepting their attentions. So with this child certain physical disabilities were continued because they made it possible for her to dominate her parents. She was herself unaware of the fact that she clung to certain symptoms because they gave her a means of demanding attention, and it was not until she was thrown with other children who quite frankly regarded these things as inferiorities that she suddenly became aware of them as real limitations. Now came a split between the motivation of the conscious and the unconscious selves. Consciously she wanted to do as the others did and she pitied herself for the inabilities; unconsciously she clung to the weapons that gave her her power. After struggles to adjust in this new world she would retreat into the old attitude of helplessness and fantasy, and at these times certain difficulties in walking and using her hands became exaggerated. Real playmates were not amenable to direction and besides they were lacking in interest; therefore the imaginary ones took on added luster. As quickly as possible she returned to the land of make-believe.

After a time at school it became evident that she needed special psychological help and she began working certain hours under this type of direction. Reading was the normal approach to the mental discipline of formal training, for her natural approach was through the world of imagination. For the sake of stories, carefully selected because of their imaginative appeal, she learned to read and, once started, made rapid progress, though great care had to be taken not to permit overexertion. In other studies, though, progress was still slow and there were continued resistances.

One day she announced: "I have a twin. Her name is Anna. She is just like me except that she always wears beautiful clothes and never wears glasses." (Glasses meant to her weak eyes that kept her from poring over the books that she now loved.) "If Anna were here, I should like to work better."

"I should like to have Anna too," was the answer. "Suppose you invite her."

Margaret went out of the room and returned with Anna who was at once provided with a chair and table and instructed by Margaret as to the work to be done. In order to show Anna she began to write. After this Anna was always there. First Margaret would write and then Anna. It was interesting to note that if she became discouraged and wished to show temper or obstinacy she always slipped out of Anna's seat and had her outbursts in her own character of Margaret.

One day everything went wrong and at last she burst out, "I shall never learn to write and it is all my mother's fault! I am left-handed and she never told my first teacher. I had to try to write with my right hand and now I shall grow up and never write at all, all because of my mother."

The psychologist told her of another child who was left-handed and whose mother had made the same mistake. Margaret said eagerly, "So he can never write?"

"Of course he does," said the psychologist, "he writes stories and all sorts of things. It was just harder for him, that is all. He generally writes with his left hand now. You may write with your left hand if you wish."

Margaret replied, "But I like my right hand best."

"Oh, then it does not seem to be Mother's fault. I wonder whose fault it is?"

The child would only answer, "I don't know." Thereupon it was suggested, "You might ask Anna."

She left the room, and after a while she returned saying, "Anna says it is my own fault and I had better go to work," and she immediately did so.

Now began a new phase of her development. Before

this she would not discuss her own responsibilities, but now she would go out of the room, and talk it over with Anna, and bring back the result. Sometimes she would return with every sign of rebellion, but she would always tell the truth as to what Anna's dictates were and she would go out again to remonstrate, but Anna insisted, "Margaret, it is your fault. You've got to try."

Shortly after this there was an outbreak of emotion in which she called Anna her darling who could not love her, and then breaking from Anna's stern rule she spoiled all her work with "sillies" and would talk only nonsense. Anna was banished for a short time, but after a day or two Margaret said, "Anna is quite lonely, I think it is time she came back." Anna returned but she had lost none of her firmness of character.

About this time another person made her appearance. She was a blind child and had to be helped in every way. She also could not hear very well and could not be asked to do any work. Anna, the inexorable, decided that she could not be at school, but she was always waiting just outside. During this time Margaret told the following dream: "I went to see Miss X (her gymnasium teacher who gave her special arm and foot exercises that she did not enjoy) and another teacher met us at the door and said, 'You can't come in, children, Miss X is very ill.' We went in and Miss X was in a bathrobe with big buttons. She said she would be sick a long time. It seemed very nice." Since in her conscious she was trying so hard to live up to Anna's requirements her unconscious was, in a dream, showing her a way out which would not be her own fault. Soon after this she produced what I believe was a fantasy, though she called it a "dream story."

"What do you suppose happened? Why, I was blind and Father and Mother and everybody were so sad and unhappy and so sorry that they had been bad to me and they did everything that I wanted."

She went on to explain the advantages of being blind because then no one would think you ought to do things that you did not want. I explained how the blind learned to read, and the next day I brought a lovely bit of work done by a blind child. She was deeply impressed for she saw that a handicap meant that you must work the harder, and she was too honest to deny a thing that she really understood. Now the blind child came less frequently but when she did she was treated with great tenderness.

All this time Anna was with us though there were signs

that Margaret was growing restive under her dictatorship. One day she had an outburst of anger against her mother. She stormed into the room crying, "Mother is horrid, horrid, horrid!"

"Who is horrid?" she was asked.

"Mother," she replied.

"You might ask Anna," I suggested.

There was a long pause, then she said, "Pooh! I guess I know as much as Anna! I'm horrid. I'll go tell Mother."

She did this and then returned quietly to work. She had now accepted Anna as a projected part of herself and had taken another definite step forward. But we progressed as did the famous frog in the well, three feet up and slip back two. Progressions are followed by regressions which sometimes seem to carry us even further back for they take us into deeper layers of the unconscious. Some days later she stopped in the middle of a lesson and burst forth, "I hardly ate any breakfast, I did not eat any lunch. I shall not eat any supper. Tonight I am going to die. Yes, that is what I shall do. I shall die in about the middle of the night." After working again for some time she looked off into space and said, "How they will weep!"

About ten days later she was unable to do any work. She could not remember familiar words. She was confused, said $2-2=6$ and nearly wept. Then I said, "What do you really want to think about today?"

"Nothing."

"Are you trying to work?"

"It doesn't seem so."

"Would you like me to tell you about the work or something else?"

She turned her back. "I don't want anything."

After a time she turned again but, seeing me looking, quickly turned her back. Then I got up and walked to the window. After some time I said quietly, "Well, what is it?"

She came running to me, her face was pale and her eyes glared. "I want to see someone die. I want to watch them do it. I *want to!*"

"Do you want to die?"

"No, but I want to see someone else. I must."

I said, "I have seen people die."

"Tell me."

"One person whom I saw die went to sleep and then just stopped breathing."

"What happened afterward?"

"Nothing that we could see. The spirit went away."

"What was the place like where it went?"

"We don't know, only God knows that."

"If she had done bad things would God want to hurt her?"

"I don't think God ever wants to hurt us. We hurt ourselves when we won't do right."

She sat thinking, then softly to herself: "I pray to God and so does Anna." Then she was still, I think, ten minutes or more. "Were you very near her when she died?"

"I was right beside her holding her hand."

Silence again, then a deep sigh as though she were pulling herself up from a depth. "Then you know." After a moment she said, "I'll read now."

All through the hour she worked with a concentration that was unusual. How slow we should be to pass judgment. It is only by knowing the inner life of the individual child, as we cannot know it except through a sympathetic relationship, that we can arrive at the motivation of a single act. Here was every evidence of obstinacy and naughtiness yet the cause of it was the interest with which she was pursuing a speculation which has absorbed the minds of philosophers. Of course, in this child, the idea had also a personal fascination in that her problem just now was the desire of the unconscious to retreat from the too difficult task, but there was no trivial naughtiness.

The idea of death now wove itself into her fantasies. She told a story of a misunderstood little girl and of her beautiful deathbed surrounded by weeping friends and family. All the time the reality of living was making stronger and stronger claims. Real children were assuming more and more importance, real achievement was becoming more and more worth while. It is a great mistake to try to separate such a child from her world of imagination for it is a world of untold wealth and resource if only it is not used as an escape. Both worlds were growing more real to her. One day after hours of hard work she said to her mother, "I want to hurry home today. I want to think."

"What are you going to think about?" her mother asked.

"Oh, all my people, the real people."

When at home she climbed into a chair and sat perfectly still for nearly two hours, after which she climbed down entirely satisfied and went back to the world of outer realities.

During this time of her struggles to integrate with Anna

another playmate appeared during her hours at home. This was Daphy who lived in the Kiki House. The Kiki House was a little old wooden house which the child passed on her way to the park. It was a house that belonged to the past generations, the only wooden house in that part of the city. It appealed to the child's imagination and immediately she began to people it. Whether or not her unconscious recognized it as belonging to the past would be impossible to say but it is an interesting coincidence that she chose this as the home of her regressive self. Daphy would not grow up, would not "be good." She was the other side of the unconscious, the dark side, as Anna was the bright, the progressive side. Daphy never appeared at school or during her hours of special work. There the task was growing up, accepting the new attitude. But when the old psychological habits reasserted themselves at home (a place of relaxation and babyhood) Daphy was greatly in evidence. With her changing standards it was no longer possible to accept this very infantile person as herself so Daphy took over the burden, and the undesirable self was projected upon her. It was Daphy who made all the naughty suggestions. It was Daphy who could not dress herself or tie her shoes or keep her temper. When Daphy became quite unbearable and something obviously had to be done with her, she was put in the Kiki House and not allowed to come out.

Since Margaret herself never mentioned Daphy during her hours of work it would have been a great mistake to have discussed her or to have opened the doors for her appearance at these times. She might then have been seized upon as a possible way of escape from the difficult task which those hours represented. Whatever might have been gained in psychological insight or theoretical knowledge of such problems would have been more than offset by the loss to this special child. This was one of the places where the workings of the unconscious must be respected. It must never be forgotten that the child is a mysteriously developing individuality, not a laboratory case.

All this time Anna continued to occupy an important place though she no longer assumed the role of dictator. Margaret was directing her own affairs. She had joined a play class and found the necessary adjustments none too easy. One day when there had been storms she was sent home. She wept bitterly, but insisted that she was weeping for a farm where she had been the summer before and for a very much younger child with whom she had played. She told me of this most dramatically and said, "You should have seen me weep."

The next day she brought this dream: "I was in K playing with H (the farm and the little girl). We were in the woods. I filled my wheelbarrow with leaves. Then I ran right over H and killed her dead. Just think, I killed her! squashed and dead!" A long pause; then a wicked gleam appeared in her eye. "Some day soon I think I'll run over the twin and squash her dead."

She was taken back into the play class and began to adjust with the children. The twin vanished. She had "killed her dead."

I cannot leave the description of this struggle with the adjustment of the two worlds without quoting the following bit of doggerel verse, which she made at the time of one of her failures. She thought about how good she had been yesterday and how beautiful she was going to be tomorrow.

> *It's easy enough to be happy*
> *When your house is full of good things*
> *But if you want to fly*
> *You'd better not try,*
> *Unless you've a pair of wings.*

But to return to Anna and her psychological importance. Because of early illness a certain amount of overdependence had been a necessity. It had been necessary to give her more help and sheltering than is the case with a perfectly well child. Since this care was motivated by a deep love and sympathy, the tendency was toward overprotection and the child found in it a refuge from all the things that were too hard. In these special circumstances it is difficult to know just when this care should be withdrawn.

If the way is made too hard discouragement and feelings of inferiority will arise which are more destructive than the results of protection. The child who has too much love stands a better chance than the child who has too little, but in either case there is a difficult time of adjustment to the ordinary life and to its responsibilities. When Margaret stepped out of this safe little world in which she had lived and was confronted with a world where she was not the object of special devotion, she was bewildered. Power had come to her through her weaknesses, so naturally she took refuge in them. All the infantile part of herself hung back from making the struggle necessary for this new adaptation. But deep down within, down in the unconscious, two selves were struggling: this regressive self and the progressive growing self. Since in her outer adaptation she was allied with the infantile self, the other self became projected into the figure of Anna. She was innately honest, therefore she could not reject Anna. In such a case a split arises such as takes place in pathological cases of dual personality. The two selves confront each other. Now the problem which must be faced is whether these two selves will continue upon ever-diverging paths, or whether they shall become merged in a single individual. In the former case the regressive self continues to exercise childish power and retreat while the other self pursues a purely compensatory life in the fantasy world; in the latter case the progressive self becomes integrated in the individual, and through its acceptance a unification takes place. Here is a test of the honesty of the individual. Margaret was not able to face all these new demands when they were first presented, but when she retreated from her task she knew that she was making the wrong choice. Anna was called into being and she accepted from this other self the truth that she could not admit from the outside. Each time that she went the same road as Anna the division grew less, until finally she "knew as well as Anna." Then Anna became unnecessary, outgrown; the very continuance of her life now became a regression and Anna was "killed and dead."

With a child so attuned to the inner world of the unconscious it is interesting to note how the dreams also present the problem. Space here is too limited to give the dream progression, but the two dreams quoted show the close connection between dream and fantasy. In the dream of Miss X is shown the strong desire to have the responsibility taken from her. Miss X, who represents the work she does not like, is ill, and "it seemed very nice." Later when she fails in her play class and her relationships with children her own age, the much littler girl returns as the symbol of the easy regressive way; but now she has really accepted the other path so she triumphantly runs over this other self and "squashes" her. Anna, now having become integrated in her own individuality, also becomes part of her outgrown past and so she kills her and takes up her own responsibilities in her real self as Margaret.

I do not mean that with the death of Anna the fantasy life ceased. It continued in varying forms, sometimes as creative imaginations, sometimes as compensation, and sometimes projections of things that needed to be rejected from the developing self. It would be a great loss if this fantasy life should cease, for it contains the living creative element, all the more living because of its growing power to reject the outworn symbol and to accept a new one better suited to the present need.

In contrast to this I would give the imaginary playmate (the projected fantasy self) of a child whose task was apparently not so hard but who chose the divided path and who developed a definite split between the real and the fantasy self. This second child was an intuitive extravert. She skipped along the road of life lightly taking the high spots. She was pretty, rather precocious, but without depth or power of sustained effort. She, too, received too much rather than too little love, but it was an unwise and over-admiring love, not one evoked by the special need of the child. Very early she had learned the power of creating an effect. With an air of lovely unconcern she could stray out of an organized line quite upsetting the usual order and looking sweetly unconscious of such remarks as, "Isn't she cunning!" Or she could rush into a room breaking in on whatever was in progress and focusing all the attention upon herself.

The first days at school brought no sense of difficulty but rather a feeling of new worlds unrolled for triumphant conquest. But when conquest began to involve real effort this new world lost its charm. Taking time to finish a piece of work neatly, relinquishing the center of the stage to others, trying to sound out a word instead of making it up, all these things required hard work, and hard work was exceedingly unattractive.

There was another difficulty. Her father had recently lost most of his money and it meant a good deal of sacrifice to send her to a private school. There was not much left over for incidentals. The new clothes which at home had seemed greatly to be admired now seemed quite ordinary. They attracted no attention and boasting about them only brought ridicule. Several of the children came in cars, also a source of envy. Up to this time she had been much in the company of an adoring aunt. Her mother had taken over some of the office work in order to help over the financial crisis and the aunt, a much older woman, had "played with Sally," literally played with her all sorts of games which she always won, because "she loved to." With the children she did not always win nor was her right to such supremacy admitted.

One day she arrived with a tale of a little girl who came to see her. She wore a blue velvet coat trimmed with fur and came in an automobile. Her name was Sally also. Her father was very rich and gave Sally everything she wanted. The naïveté which she showed in choosing her own name for the playmate was amusing. Now Sally became a very important person in her life. Whenever the aunt had to be busy about her household tasks Sally was there to take her place, though there were frequent interruptions in order that Sally might be admired. If she failed in school immediately Sally acquired a new glory. Then things began to disappear, small quantities of money, trifles valued by the children, and Sally the first began to display things given her by Sally the second. This led to a dramatic revelation of the character of Sally the magnificent, and she vanished from the stage.

This might have been considered the death of Sally the second, but it was only her translation to another sphere. So far as I know her place was not taken by any other acknowledged playmate. It was only in this special crisis that I came in contact with the child and after this denouement I heard very little about her.

Some years later I was again asked to see Sally. She had followed a somewhat tortuous path but had always managed to get by, and had progressed from grade to grade. For a long time there had always seemed to be so plausible a reason for failure, so sympathetic an attitude toward the instructor who was bringing her shortcomings to the light that it was difficult to blame her. A failure always became only a near-failure before the actual day of reckoning. But now she was definitely failing both at home and in her home responsibilities. She arrived at her first interview very charmingly solicitous and desirous of being of all possible assistance in the solution of her "difficult" problem. It took only a little proving to find that Sally the second was still so much alive that she had become the dominating personality; only she was no longer objectified in an imaginary companion, she was the fantasy side of the self.

The present Sally was little disturbed by the difficulties of the immediate situation, quite undisturbed by complete failures in her English courses. She was intending to be a writer largely because one could be "such an influence for good." Already she carried on conversations with well-known people met in the dreamworld. Whenever rhetoric or geometry presented difficulties "Sally" appeared in vivid form in front of the page and conversed wittily. Sally the first went to sleep every night listening to the repartee of Sally the second or watching her dress for a party.

It was easy to obtain these fantasies because as soon as she felt that they were attracting interest she poured them forth. That she undoubtedly played them up and added to them on the spot did not make them the less revealing of the fantasy habits and their use in her life. In her identifications with Sally the second she had felt herself really quite removed from the ordinary demands of her real circumstances. Certain things quite suited to the very limited finances of the family seemed impossibly hard: teachers did not understand her real nature or noble ambitions. She had been in the habit of elaborate evasions of the point at issue. Now she had to have all this taken from her. Quite ruthlessly the situation had to be shown her, ruthlessly and briefly. The two selves had to confront one another and discussion cease. She had to confront the present crisis as a crisis and stand or fall by the actual act without being allowed even the usual explanation. Poor little Sally the first had a hard struggle and is still a feeble child, but she is growing, I am told. One interesting detail was that whereas she had apparently forgotten the childish playmate, Sally the first still dressed in blue, preferably blue velvet.

Such a fantasy life frequently takes place without an objectification in the playmate. I have known many such cases, but where we find the playmate definitely personified it furnishes us with a valuable clue to the inner life.

Take, for example, the playmate "Bill" who for many months was the inseparable companion of seven-year-old Jimmy. Jimmy was an only child but he lived in a neighborhood where small boys abounded. He would start out to play with the other boys but soon would be back enthusiastically engaged in a game with "Bill." At first Bill amused the boy's parents. Then the mother noticed that in every game with Bill, Jimmy always won. Bill was reported as being able to "lick any boy on the block," but Jimmy could always lick Bill. Bill could run faster, throw a stone farther, etc., but still Jimmy could always come out ahead. A little investigation showed that Jimmy was quite easily outdistanced in most games with boys, but as soon as he lost he came home to play with Bill. His mother heard him call out, "I'm going home to play with a feller who could beat any of you."

Bill had a rival, Jimmy's father. Jimmy would always

desert Bill on Sunday when his father was at home and their games together were the events of the week. One day, however, his father remarked that he thought he would play with Bill instead, for Bill was such a good sport. Then followed a discussion of what it meant to be a good loser. This was not received with very good grace but his father was firm. Bill was better company because he played fair. After a time Bill's standards became accepted and instead of being used as a foil he was now a model. If Bill would play fair and thereby earn the approval of the idolized father, so would Jimmy. By and by Bill vanished. His place was filled by Mr. Murphy, an inventor, and afterward by many others.

Quite recently I have come upon a nearly identical playmate, one Johnnie by name, who also was always defeated, even though it frequently took some cheating to bring about this desired result. His creator, now a grown man, says that he still remembers vividly how chagrined he was when his mother and grandmother pitied "poor Johnnie" for losing instead of admiring him for being always victor. Johnnie was a more comprehensive character, as his creator was more solitary. He acted as guide, philosopher and friend, and frequently as a projected conscience. He went away when his creator became old enough to play on the street with other boys, but he was never forgotten.

Often when the playmate changes frequently, indeed where there are a whole host of playmates, we still find that the fantasy that underlies them remains the same and is indicative of the trend of those unconscious forces which, if allowed their way, may later take control of the conscious life.

School, to Barbara, was a dreary world, a world where 4×6 must inevitably make 24, and a picture must be interpreted by silly little cabalistic signs instead of by the story that it told inside your own head. Even when there were interesting things like acting and you had wonderful ideas and knew just the part you wanted someone else got it. The real world began at home and was filled with people, princes and lovely ladies and "magics" who did as you told them. Best of all was when Father got home. The regular formula which ushered in the play hour was, "Now *you* be what *I* pretend."

Perhaps she would be a lovely princess seated in a great armchair throne while her page bowed low before her. "Open the royal door quickly!" cries the princess in a

none too gracious voice. "Don't you hear someone knock-
ing?"

"Your Majesty, a thousand pardons."

The door is opened, the page bows low, announcing:
"His Majesty, the Prince of Umphalazia, has come to sue
for the royal hand." Other suitors come till the throne
room is filled. The page repeats the words of the royal suitors, certain levity is permitted, but if he grows too face-
tious he is sharply rebuked and properly humbled. Suddenly the door is opened, not by a suitor, but by nurse announcing supper and bed. Instantly the princess vanishes,
and in her place appears a very ugly little girl fighting at
nurse. The page goes down on all fours and announces
that he is an elephant, the princess mounts upon his back
and rides to the banquet, and the elephant stands on his
hind legs and feeds her.

This, as nearly as I can remember the wording, is an
exact scene which I watched from a secluded corner.
Night after night it was repeated with varying characters
but always the child occupied the leading role and the father was obedient to her commands. When playing with
children she chose those younger and slower than herself,
and her vivid imagination intrigued them and made them
almost submit to her commands. If they were insubordinate she was quite content to fill their places with imaginary actors and go on with the drama. There was never
such a difficulty with her father who was the ideal servitor.

But this is hardly the role that a father is intended to
occupy, even in imagination. It is not surprising that this
child had "difficulties of adjustment," jealousies and tempers with her mother, night terrors and other upheavals of
the unconscious. Yet this child had a very positive wealth
in the fertility and originality of her imagination. She was
an irrational, and the formal side of studies meant nothing
whatever to her. Her father, who also hated the routine of
life and loved these play hours of escape, treated her failures at school with amusement and was really more interested in hearing of the doings of the other-world people.
In this way his love was helping her to build up a dual
personality: the princess self who could command and
bestow, and exact homage; and the "misunderstood" self
who was continually being asked to do unreasonable duties. These two selves were growing farther and farther
apart.

This is the same psychological process which is at work
in cases of hysteria and dual personality. The unconscious

begins to furnish images which take on a more and more definite personality and which derive their importance, not from the achievement of the individual, but from their connection with the images of the collective unconscious. These originate as vague fantasy products that are, in their mere perception, no personal achievement and take on value only when their perception is related to the understanding of life. The child of abundant imaginative power is far richer than the child of meager imagination, provided this gift is used constructively and not as a substitute of individual achievement. Where these images are used to build up the figure of another self, one which is not to be judged by the standards of reality nor to be subjected to the same demands which life makes upon others, we have the beginnings of dual personality. In a potential form this is the attitude of the dementia praecox patient.

This child who so ruled the puppets of her unreal world was starting a power attitude toward life which would make it difficult for her to submit to the ordinary and proper demands of human relations. Especially would this be true of the man and woman relation for she would expect the same acquiescence from other men which her father had shown. In addition to this it is impossible for anyone to fail in his normal environment without becoming conscious of the failure. This rouses either feelings of inferiority, or else bitter resentments toward those who would impose the accepted standards. In either case a retreat is made to the fantasy self and the difficulties of accepting reality are increased.

With other children we may notice a very different temperamental trend in the imaginary playmate or the fantasy life. One child is always mother and she has a host of imaginary children whom she loves and cares for or rules and disciplines, in accordance with her temperament. One gentle, loving child always had all her imaginary playmates in the form of twins so that she could lend one to any member of the family who might be going away or who might have to stay at home alone. Visually the twins were babies so that the one loaned could easily be packed in a suitcase.

The way in which the child reacts to the character created indicates his own trends.

Two boys have as imaginary playmates quite similar characters, each known as the "General," but one boy is always in the general's service, he fetches and carries and takes orders; in real life he is always allying himself to some more dominating boy and acting as "fag." The other boy plainly regards the "General" as a personification of himself. He boasts about his deeds. This general is second only to the president, indeed the president would hesitate to question his authority. This second boy when playing with others wishes to organize an army and be general himself. The former looks for a leader to whom he can ally himself.

Another boy recognized in himself possibilities of cowardice. His imaginary companions were "The Three Kings" who lived back of the radiator. He would hear them arguing and chuckling together. They were served by the white-clad hosts of steam. You had only to turn the valve of the radiator and these servants rushed forth. He thought of them as spirits of great power. By and by they seemed to him like powers that one could set free for oneself. Turning the valve became a mere symbolic gesture signifying the calling on unknown powers. If he felt afraid he would slyly stoop and turn an imaginary valve and then feel that he had obtained the courage of these mysterious servants. These were beings of his own imagination yet they remind us of the genii of old who appeared in a cloud of vapor. These genii, however, were not asked to take over the task but only to set loose the courage of the young hero.

Another child beset by fears, but having withal an underlying courage, deliberately took her figure of fear as a companion till she conquered its terrors. She saw the face first on a movie screen, then in a dream. She woke from her dream screaming and her mother took her into bed, comforted her and told her to forget about it, but she did not ask what "it" was. The child afterward said, "I think if I could have talked it out then I might have been able to bring my fears out into the light but I did try not to think of it." The result was that this figure seemed always with her and she began to be more and more afraid.

Then she did for herself what she might have done with her mother. She deliberately let this figure go with her. She walked into the dark places where she believed it was and faced it. She let it walk with her on the street, she deliberately took it as her companion until she found that not only had it lost its terrifying power but that also her unreasoned fears of dark places and of being alone were dropping from her. This shows an intuitive knowledge so rare in so young a child for we can conquer nothing till we admit its existence. Since this figure symbolized her own fear of the unknown she had to accept it in order to dispel it. It became for her the personification of her own cowardice. She emerged stronger for the experience, yet we would hesitate to subject a child to such a test for the result is often an increase of fear. It is wiser in such cases not to tell a child to go to sleep and forget, but to tell her to remember and talk it all out.

Very many of these imaginary companions are called into being by loneliness. A little girl whose father was dead and who had also to face poverty, found comfort in an imaginary father. He helped her to keep her sense of proportion. When she was unhappy about her shabby clothes he was proud of her for not minding and for so helping the family problem. He discussed with her the things that were worth while, he went out with her when she felt lonely. At times he did special little acts. When all the other children had ice cream and she had no pennies with which to buy any he bought it for her. The "ice cream" was a bit of ice dropped from the ice wagon but she could taste the flavor and find comfort in the thoughtfulness of her father.

Another child, whose mother and father were consumed by professional engagements, filled her lonely hours with fantasies which were laughed at by a prosaic governess and a highly practical family of brothers and sisters. She had a "real" sister who understood. To the rest of the world this "real" sister was the only one who had no existence but to her she was the only one who could claim true existence.

Such instances are so numerous that there is no need to multiply examples, but in every case the temperament and attitude of the child is shown in the use which is made of this unconscious material. I have known of cases where the fantasies became forms of hallucination. They vanished when they had fulfilled their purpose and apparently left no harmful result.

The imaginary playmate is really a very normal form of companion for a child whose subjective world has a living reality. Most of the children quoted in this chapter were entirely normal, but from an analysis of these fantasy selves certain phenomena appear which should be of help in the interpretation of the difficulties of the individual child who reveals the fantasy and also in the understanding of the mental processes which underlie such manifestations.

The following deductions are merely suggestive. They are not advanced as dogmatic conclusions but are offered for criticism, or for refutation if further evidence seems to point to a different interpretation. This pathway is so new that we cannot hold back till we are certain that we have conclusive proof of our way. We must be willing to follow what seems to us to be a "blaze" on the trail, and if the next explorer finds a better path be glad to see our own disregarded.

What, then, seems to be the connection between the playmate and the child's psychological processes, and how does it help in his development?

The attainment of an individuality is a long and painful process, one which is not actually achieved by many so-called adults. It is certainly not the possession of the child. He is, as we have said before, a mass of potentials. Certain ego trends may make themselves manifest with such intensity that he may be carelessly spoken of as "having a marked individuality," but these trends may be merely indications of true character traits or they may be only protests against some difficulty of adaptation. A little child is confronted by many worlds, each of which demands to be met by a different self; and the child, with a sort of psychic protective coloring, assumes these various selves for purposes of adaptation.

We all know how true it is that, "With X, Billy is a different boy." He may be a quiet and well-mannered little gentleman with grandmother and the cooky box in the offing, or with an adult assembly; he may be a good sport or perhaps a rebellious but obedient little slave with his father, depending on the relationship which they have together. Again there is the Billy with his mother, a less grown-up Billy, and there are all the Billys in school, the Billy in the classroom, the Billy at recess with the other boys or the younger boys, or still another Billy with the little girls. Billy, Billy everywhere, yet where is Billy? Then there is a whole regiment of Billys whom we glimpse but rarely. These Billys live deep inside the Billy that we know. They are called into being by inner images, half-understood thoughts, fantasies built on bits of overheard conversations, fairy, hero, or horror stories, or perhaps they owe their being to deeper springs of consciousness, they may be awakened by dream images confused with reality or daydream images arising apparently from nowhere at all. So we have "Billy," a sturdy, short-trousered familiar figure, who is really a composite photograph of a shadowy possible Billy not yet really come to birth. Out of this company of potential Billys we must help the real Billy to find himself: to integrate what is valuable in these many personalities and to eliminate what is valueless or harmful.

This process is frequently helped by the appearance of the imaginary playmate; especially if the child is original and creative, or deeply subjective. This playmate may be used in many ways. In one form it is the greatly-to-be-desired self, the hero or the lovely princess, the ideal, unselfish, much-loved being, or the very beautiful and rich personality. Perhaps it may be another child who has various qualities that are greatly admired. These may arise as naturally as the fairy story, enjoyed and forgotten yet serving a purpose in development, or they may be used as compensation.

If there is a failure to meet the demands of life, or if there is a poverty caused by loneliness or misunderstanding these unconscious products take on a deeper reality. If the conscious self does not afford sufficient outlet for certain manifestations of the developing personality, these manifestations are apt to break through in the unconscious material of fantasy. We all have, at times, thoughts tumultuous, undirected, which we would not wish to embody in word or act and then accept as the real children of our brains. Many adults have daydreams to which they return in times of discouragement or fatigue, and in these dreams a favorite character acts out parts which they would repudiate if compelled to face them as elements in their own psychology. They are really trends of the unconscious which we do not wish to claim as ours and which take on an appearance of independent personality.

In this way a child who is oversubmissive almost to the point of masochism will act out, in the assumed personality, things which his own conscious would not permit him to claim. He may choose this side in his play with other children or he may make for himself as a fantasy playmate an aggressive companion to whom he submits even in fantasies of physical submission. In identifying with this companion he can compensate for the feelings of inferiority which his own lack of self-assertion forces upon him.

On the other hand his fantasies may make him assume the role of ruler. His imaginary companion will then always be one whom he can always command, so giving his overassertive ego a chance of living in the power side.

Children's play furnishes us with many character clues if we are able to understand them. Here is a little girl who always wants the part of mother. Has she a special attitude which she always assumes in this role? Is this role a repetition of the maternal pattern, or does it show individual character traits? In one such instance a woman who was unable to make any relations with a man which did not end in disaster recalled, in the course of her analysis, her own child's play. She had habitually beaten her dolls or caused them to suffer some injury so that she "might take them to her bosom and comfort them." So, very early in her life, power and the desire to dominate had masked behind the "compassionate mother" symbol. This later manifested itself in stormy emotional acts having a hidden vein of cruelty. These outbursts were followed by a passionate desire to compensate by over-intense love and compassion, or an impulse to enter into relationships where she was the ministering mother. She was not able to accept a man on terms of adult equality. She felt herself pursued by fate in her unhappy choices, but her fate was dictated by that inner force that had showed itself in her tempestuous and emotional doll play. She was, indeed, pursued by fate, but it was a fate that rose up from the blind forces of the unconscious.

If we can understand the ways in which the unconscious of the child makes use of this imaginary companion we are greatly helped in our task of guiding him in the integration of these forces. In the case of the ideal companion we find two uses. When it is accepted as a pattern it is used positively as was Anna, the twin. Here the child works out certain problems and draws up into his own personality the desired traits. When used as an escape it furnishes a basis for neurotic withdrawal. The dream is substituted for reality and the ego assumes less and less responsibility.

There is also the playmate who represents the less desirable side of the personality. Upon this companion are projected things which are not to be accepted by the developing ego. He is a sort of psychological whipping boy who is to be held responsible for things for which the prince cannot be held to account. Where he is used to project and eliminate the undesirable he is most valuable. For example, a child who was given to bombastic lying and to finger-sucking and other regressive habits invented a figure, Mr. Montague. Mr. Montague was permitted any form of boasting, he was a worthy rival of Baron Munchausen. But as the leeway permitted Mr. Montague became greater and greater, the exactness required of Bobby became stricter and stricter. When the affair in debate was not very serious it sometimes became a nice question as to whether the tale must be claimed by Mr. Montague or could be accepted by Bobby. Through Mr. Montague a clearer sense of values was realized and Bobby sloughed off certain things that should be lived out through the projected personality. Incidentally I would mention that the regressive symptoms vanished of themselves as Bobby himself became more grown up in his attitude.

On the other hand the undesirable companion may also be used in order to escape responsibility. It may furnish a retreat to the pleasure of unadmitted fantasy, or in assuming that character the small actor may permit himself to do things not accepted by his conscious personality and yet hold himself blameless. It is this attitude which is developed in Dr. Jekyll and Mr. Hyde, a projection of the undesirable, not in order to be rid of it but so as to be able to live in it and escape responsibility. But Mr. Hyde, as he increases in power, insists upon recognition and in the final mastery the bewildered other self finds himself caught. This is the dramatization of a pathological situation, but it is this same process which we find at work in child's play and consider unimportant. The following is the simplest possible case, yet shows Dr. Jekyll and Mr. Hyde in their early infancy.

Small Johnnie had a playmate named Sam Slimmer. It was Sam Slimmer who always got into mischief. Johnnie soon discovered the advantages of Sam. Things could be done and then disclaimed. Sam Slimmer would suddenly go away and the good Johnnie would reappear. The good Johnnie was always innocent. Mother was always willing to receive the good Johnnie at once and obviously the good Johnnie was not held to be responsible. But Sam Slimmer began to appear oftener and oftener. At last Father took a hand, announcing that whenever Sam had been about the first business of the evening was with him and he would be unable to talk to Johnnie until accounts had been settled with Sam. At first Johnnie was indignant but Father was adamant. Sam must be found and his account settled before he could see Johnnie. Sam was produced and the account settled. Though the method of settlement may not be in accordance with our views, the application of the principle involved assisted greatly in the integration of Johnnie.

I have purposely closed with these childish and apparently trivial cases so as to show that the same laws hold good in these early beginnings and in the pathological cases of dual personality.

Yet can we close this chapter with trivial cases? There are companions that go with the child even unto old age. The soul, from earliest childhood, inhabits a world of brilliant darkness and numinous * mystery, and from this world a friend may come, a friend who will companion the emerging ego on its never-ending journey toward consciousness. This companion, who has risen from the depth of the inner world, is experienced rather than understood, for understanding is a faculty of the intellect and experience of the unknown and unknowable is of the soul.

"I have a friend. He is little as a Twinkle and big as Pitch Black Dark."

I do not know when this friend first appeared, for when the boy made this simple statement the friend was already his companion. The child did not explain how this friend had come to him, nor did I ever inquire, for these things are secret-sacred. They can be communicated only to someone who the child instinctively feels has also experienced the numinous reality of the soul. Then communication becomes communion and the inner experience is strengthened, becoming part of human, as well as of inner, consciousness.

But acceptance must be wordless and without question, for this experience is the child's *own* and must be left to live out its own life within the child's psyche.

In the atmosphere of stillness and of mutual acceptance the revelations continued, but the child's absorption in the experience made further revelations seem a dialogue between the child's ego and his soul, in which I was only a privileged listener.

Since no questions were asked, the boy could continue his confidences, which assumed the nature of dreamlike self-communion.

"Twinkle is littler than a star but he really *is* a star. He is like a little spark that goes up from a bonfire, but that spark goes out and Twinkle doesn't. He *stays*" . . . . "You know Pitch Black Dark can walk right into daytime. Then I have to think *hard* to see Twinkle. When I do see him sitting right in the middle of Pitch Black Dark, I am not afraid to tackle the thing I have to do and I know Pitch Black Dark is my friend too."

Is not Twinkle the light seed that may grow into the star of individuation? Heraclitus calls the soul "the essen-

---

* Numinous: Awe-inspiring, filled with fascination, fear, compelling mystery, and love.

tial spark of the star." Meister Eckhart speaks of it as "the *scintilla vitae*," the "spark of life, the soul spark" and again as "that very essence of God, the highest and the purest which is seized upon by the Holy Spirit and carried upward by the flame of love."

This world of the spark Keats calls the "Vale of Soul-making," where "as various as the Lives of Men are—so various becomes their souls, and thus does God make individual beings, Souls . . . of the Sparks of his own essence." *

But the child, with that wisdom which is beyond knowledge, realizes that Pitch Black Dark can walk right into the daytime. Fear, ignorance and evil contained in the shadow, the sense of impotence, the terror of the unknown, can overwhelm the daytime light of consciousness; the spark is threatened by the suffocating darkness of unconsciousness, and by the unknown peril that he must encounter in meeting a threatening situation. Yet the dark is also the friend, the angel with whom each must wrestle till he obtains the blessing. Then the courage to *think hard* is needed to hold to the experience; that is, to see Twinkle sitting in the center of daytime darkness and to hold fast to the light which is "a strength without limit and incorruptible." For "the spark comes higher to the truth than any human knowledge." To hold to the truth that is higher than human knowledge is the courage to hold to the essence that can behold the light of God even in hell, for it is this essence that lives in the darkness "but that faces straight up to God." It is the essence contained in the opposites, hence it is the element that is beyond good and evil.

The child sees Twinkle sitting in the center of Pitch Black Dark, that is, remaining still, waiting, withdrawn from action, as the Buddha sits within the thousand-petaled lotus, letting the light grow through meditation and contemplation. Twinkle sits in the center of darkness, where the light is at rest.

This child had his times of solitude when he loved to be alone. In such times Twinkle was formed out of his own sitting still, within the darkness where the light also is found. Twinkle was the child's vision of the light seed, the essential germ of the being, the self.

* Keats: Letter to George and Georgina Keats, from *Selected Letters*, edited by Lionel Trilling, p. 258.

When the sun has set, and the moon has set, and the fire is gone out, and the sound hushed, what is then the light of man?

The Self indeed is his light; for having the Self alone as his light, man sits, moves about, does his work, and returns.

Who is that Self?

He who is within the heart, surrounded by the senses, the person of light, consisting of knowledge.*

Forty years have passed, and Twinkle and Pitch Black Dark are still exerting their power of transformation in the soul of the child now become the man.

* The Upanishads, in *Bible of the World*, Robert O. Ballou, ed., p. 55.

9

FEAR

One day long years ago, when on my way home from school, I was attracted by the furious barking of a very large dog. Coming nearer I saw behind the open grating of an area window a very small, very starved kitten. With arched back and bristling tail, she was spitting and growling in the most ferocious and bombastic manner. So bloodthirsty was she that it seemed hard to believe that anything but the grating prevented her from tearing the dog limb from limb, even though she was almost too weak to stand. Indignantly I drove off the dog and rescued the kitten, hugging her to me in a burst of protective tenderness: and for this tenderness I received a deep scratch on my face. I can feel yet the surprise of that painful scratch and the ensuing rush of anger; but I can also feel the trembling of that terrified little bit of fur in my arms and the wild beating of that little heart. A most monstrous kitten and most inexcusable! Surely she should have purred her thanks and showed her gratitude. A kitten who could thus reward kindness undoubtedly deserved to be returned to the dog. Yet even I, a small child, could understand the terror that prompted that furious scratch. Somehow I got the tiny thing home and devoted myself to the soothing of that wild, fear-possessed, little being. It was a long task and for days I could not touch her, but in the end a soft, round, purring bit of contentment sang with joy whenever she was picked up.

A few months afterward she was amusing herself with a grasshopper when a large bull terrier got into the yard and headed straight for her. The kitten, now a self-possessed young lady cat, arched her back but did not move an inch. As the dog came nearer she lifted one paw and gave him a lightning dab on the nose. Howling he fled and the kitten settled back at peace. This time when I picked her up she began her purring song. No longer did she view life from the insecurity of the half-starved, terrified street waif, but from the security of a happy home where her own position was assured. Why bother to be either terrified or angry at a mere dog?

A few years ago I was consulted in regard to "a very naughty and unmanageable small boy." He was "a liar and a boaster and a fighter," always looking for trouble and subject to rages when he would strike out at people, or attack some other child, or perhaps break some valuable article. In school he was undependable both in work and in conduct. He seemed to be bright enough when he exerted himself, but he never kept his mind on anything, and was always doing some silly thing in the middle of his recitation or scrawling absurd pictures over half-finished work. In the playground he was always a storm center.

From the moment he entered my room his attitude was one of boastful defiance. When questioned about school he began to tell how "he could fight them all." He would "show 'em if they didn't look out." When I asked him a few ordinary questions he answered the first fairly well, the second at random, and at the third broke off and began telling me how he was going to kill tigers and people—lots of people. He did not come near me, and when I tried to come too near him he became more boastful and defiant. His movements were badly coordinated and he had various nervous habits. There seemed, beyond the very evident instability, a deep-seated sense of insecurity. Questions as to teachers, schools, and boys brought the same form of answers: "he'd show 'em." Here was another little creature with his back to the wall. Might not some great form of fear and sense of insecurity underlie his "spitting and scratching"?

When he burst forth into another tirade as to what he would do I said with much interest, "That is a good story. Do you make them up often? That makes me think of Jack the Giant Killer. That's a fine old story. Would you like to have me tell you that one some day?"

He looked at me cautiously to see if I was making fun of him, but seeing no trace of ridicule, he permitted himself to become interested, and on the basis of the tale we made our first connection. Then he told another bombastic incident, this time with the deed attached to an admittedly imaginary character. The little device served several purposes. It attracted his attention, and drew his interest away from his suspicions to something outside of himself; it changed his attitude from the defensive to one of cooperation; it momentarily disentangled him from the false personality; and it gave me a chance to make at least fleeting contact with the real child, the child behind the mask. This contact was all that I could hope to obtain in the first interview. But through this contact, where something which was presented as an aggressive defiance was received as a positive value, a new element entered into the relationship.

Space does not permit me to take up this case in detail, but the facts as they came to light bore out the first diagnosis. It was a case of defense reaction produced by fear, and that fear was based upon a sense of insecurity in relationships and upon feelings of inferiority.

At birth he had been injured. One side did not develop as strongly as the other. He walked awkwardly and one foot turned in with a shuffling movement. This physical difficulty had been given proper medical attention. Yet as the physical defects were decreasing the psychological symptoms were increasing. It had therefore been inferred that they could not have any special bearing on each other. But as psychological elements the physical influences had been growing because life was making new demands. As a baby he had found these defects to be assets because they had brought added care and attention, especially from his mother, and so had lessened the demands of life; but with the coming of school age they became liabilities. Outside the home they provoked ridicule and gave him a feeling of being inadequate to life's demands.

With some persons the fear of ridicule is even greater than the fear of physical injury, for ridicule attacks our feeling of equality in relationships and robs us of our personal dignity and competence. Well-directed ridicule leaves its victim defenseless, and the fear of it is instinctive. He could not control the physical defect that made him laughed at, so he took the natural course of trying to capitalize it, hoping in that way to escape ridicule. He pretended that he could control it if he wished, he exaggerated it; he rolled, he swaggered, he strutted. Thereby he succeeded in producing an impression, but not the one he desired. He only increased the jeering ridicule of the children, and also lost the sympathy of the elders who said he was naughty and obstinate and did not try.

Lessons brought new difficulties. He was supposed to be bright because of a certain form of glibness and a trick of memory which is often mistaken for real mental ability. He was really somewhat below the average in intelligence, but because of preconceived ideas he was expected to do work which was really too hard for him. He was afraid to say he could not. Up to now his good rote memory and ready tongue had served to cover his lack of thinking, his instability of attention, and inability to grasp subject matter. In this new world more was required. He began to "play silly" and to spoil his work before it could be discovered that he was unable to do it.

When all these attempts to turn aside ridicule failed, he took refuge in boasting and fighting lest he should show his growing fear. Like the kitten he tried to scratch first. Fear produces panic and emotional unbalance, and opens the gates to floods of anger; so blind emotional storms began and he was caught in a whirl of fear and rage.

Just at this time, when he needed more than ever his sense of fundamental security, that too was taken from him. A cousin about three years older came to live in the same city in a near-by apartment. This boy was vigorous, intelligent, and attractive, and had a great fund of intellectual curiosity. He made a quick connection with our small boy's father because of his keen intelligent interests; and the father, consciously thinking to stimulate his own boy, took the nephew on all their little excursions. Soon our little fellow found himself bodily present but otherwise quite left out. He fell back on the refuge of trying to win attention by naughtiness, but he received only punishment.

The most dangerous element of this punishment was that it had in it an unrecognized bitterness. Deep down in the father's unconscious, pride was greater than love. He had always expected to be proud of the child. When disappointed in his physical qualities he had cherished a fantasy that his son would be brilliant. Now he felt thwarted in his ambition and the boy irritated him to an irrational degree. It was very evident, when one penetrated the child's dream and fantasy life, that the boy intuited this in his father and had, in addition to a form of hero worship, a great fear of him. Many of these fears he projected upon God. He was intensely interested in the Old Testament, so his mother told me with pride. His interest proved to center in the stories of a vengeful God, who was shadowed in the figures of his terror dreams, of which he had many.

So far as actual punishment was concerned the father had been very careful and controlled. On one occasion a mild punishment had been given because of a burst of temper. The boy flew into a panic of rage and bit the father's hand. He was thereupon whipped in anger. This produced such tempestuous resentment that such punishment was not repeated. It was evident, though, that the father was continually exercising self-control to conceal irritation, not simply at what the boy did or did not do, but at what he actually was. He would not accept the fact of the boy's innate limitations because he was, in all the undercurrents of his being, determined to have a child who would be a credit to him. After the boy began talking freely to me he frequently had storms of rage against his father; and once in trying to recall a terror dream he remarked quite casually, "My father does not like me much." It seemed to be *his spontaneous association* with the night terror whose form he could not recall.

These night terrors were frequent and were increased by the fact that the little cousin, with a boy's innate cruelty and love of power, had fed his fears with gruesome tales. His dreams, his fantasies, and his bombastic stories were all a mixture of these terror imaginings.

Fear, then, was the basis of all these rages and defiant acts. He was terribly afraid of the psychological situation in which he found himself involved. To him ridicule was more to be feared than physical pain. He was constantly being ridiculed, both at school and by the little cousin who was held up to him as a model. His violent hatred was centered upon this boy to whom his father's companionship was given—a companionship which his own child so craved. He could bear a good deal of physical pain (as was shown at one time when he allowed his mother to dig a splinter out of a festering finger) but the slightest touch given as punishment or in taunting play reduced him to rage and gave him the name of being a coward. The only place where he could still keep any sense of power was with his mother. He used his rages to rule her.

Fear and the sense of insecurity had been found to be the basis of the trouble. How should such a situation be met? The child must be accepted as he really was. The father must recognize the selfish elements of his paternal pride and become reconciled to all the child's handicaps, both physical and mental. The mother must recognize that, in spite of these handicaps, he could not remain her baby and be constantly shielded. The school must recognize that here was a child needing special care and understanding. The child must recognize that the boasting, bombastic, raging self was only an effigy put between himself and the world and that the real little boy had some real tasks which he must and could face.

During the hours when he came for psychological treatment he was encouraged to turn his boastings into legitimate story material. In so doing he separated himself from the hero of his tales and was able to laugh at the adventures of the one who had once been his fantasy self.

He was kept out of school for a few days and went on several little excursions alone with his father. This not only served to strengthen the relationship but gave an opportunity to enlist the sympathy of the children of his class. Children are fairly quick to adopt a new attitude and to consider illness as a legitimate handicap when a teacher presents the situation to them fairly and simply. Such consideration helped put an end to the ridicule.

When he returned to school he was not expected to complete tasks beyond his power, but was given shorter tasks which he could accomplish without too great effort. His imagination was used in story and dramatic work. He was put in a small play class with rather young children. His mother was instructed to put him alone in a room when he had his rages. The first time he was shut up alone he threw a block through the window. He was required to pay for it out of some money which he had saved and he decided that this was not worth while.

Slowly he began to make his new adjustments, and his fears decreased as he found himself adequate to the new demands of life. The cooperation of both parents upon a quieter, firmer type of discipline did much to establish a sense of security. When one parent is overindulgent and the other oversevere, or when they alternate in the times of indulgence or severity, the child feels himself at the mercy of parental whims. This stirs in the unconscious all those instinctive fears which arise when we feel ourselves at the mercy of blind chance. To the adventurous child instability of discipline rouses the will-to-power and the desire for conflict, but to the child who is naturally fearful it but adds to life's insecurities and therefore to life's fears.

How strong this feeling is even in small children was vividly illustrated by an intensely intuitive seven-year-old girl. She had been taken from the children's court, where she had been brought because her mother, a prostitute, had subjected her to the hazards of her own uncertainties both of life and temperament. After a few months in her new home she was asked one day, "What do you like best at school?"

"Oh!" she cried, "As it was in the beginning, is now and ever shall be, world without end, Amen. I never knew that there was anything that was in the beginning and always would be. It makes you feel so nice and safe."

I shall speak later of some other cases where the sense of instability in the parental attitudes creates an underlying fear which tinges all the relations of life. Such insecurity is frequently found to exist where children are unaccountably timid. If a background of stability is lacking at the time when children have a right to its support, they are apt to go through life looking for a deadening sort of permanence on which they may rest in childish dependence.

In reviewing the case of the boy above, several things stand out quite clearly as causes for this child's fear, fear of ridicule, fear of the uncontrolled emotion of the person holding the power over the situation, a sense of inferiority, and that sense of insecurity of relationship which underlay all these other fears.

It is difficult for us to realize how deeply rooted and instinctive is the fear of ridicule. Dr. Paul Radin has stated that among many primitive people the fear is so great that a man who has been thus humiliated before the men of his own tribe may quite possibly commit suicide by wandering off alone into the night darkness of the jungle where he is almost certain to fall prey to wild beasts or human enemies. Every lawyer knows the value of discrediting his enemy by ridicule, and understands how helpless the opponent then becomes. Perhaps there are few of us who at some time have not known terrified anger roused by finding ourselves the butt of well-directed ridicule. The background of this fear, reaching all the way to primitive ancestry, links it with all the blind forces of the collective unconscious and makes us feel as though we were in the clutches of some great unknown terror.

There are many children who, like primitives, have less fear of physical pain than of ridicule because the pain does not leave them so defenseless. We are in no way surprised when we hear of nervous terrors which are the result of some brutal physical punishment, but are quite incredulous of the possibility that any permanent injury may result from ridicule. A child who receives brutal physical treatment may be taken from his parents. The child humiliated by ridicule is left to the mercy of his tormentors. Back of ridicule usually lies a desire for power, and the element of cruelty contained therein is often quite unappreciated by the one who makes use of it. The child feels the danger of this unconscious cruelty and fears also the potentials for injury that lie in these veiled instincts.

There is another form of ridicule which is often employed by adults who have kind yet blundering intentions. This is the ridicule, not of the child himself, but of his fears. In this case there is no cruelty nor desire for power peering from behind the act; yet it may have disastrous results. To laugh at another's fear does not decrease its power but it does decrease the individual's confidence in himself. It makes him feel less power over the situation and so adds to the menace of the fear. It is as though we stripped the armor off the fighter instead of drawing the fangs of the beast that is attacking him. Often in their well-meant efforts to make a child brave, older people will say, "Why, you couldn't possibly be afraid of *that!*" The child *is* afraid, however, with a fear that is perfectly unintelligible to himself, and continues to be afraid in spite of heroic efforts to the contrary. The result of this treatment, therefore, is to make him feel different, inadequate, and ashamed to tell his fears in the future. If we are afraid of something that no one else is afraid of we thereby proclaim ourselves to be less brave. We are separated from the company of others not only by the menace of our fear but also by our inferiority in the matter of courage. A child so convicted shuts his humiliated self away with his fear. It may be stated as a formula that as the sense of competence decreases the power of the fear increases.

We must recognize that the reality of another's fear is not to be estimated by our own attitude toward the object of the fear, but by the attitude of the person who fears. It is the fear, not the object, which is the reality. We must therefore accept the reality of the fear before we can deal with it properly.

A patient who was haunted at every turn by fears and feelings of inferiority described this very clearly in speaking of an experience of her childhood. She had suddenly been seized by a terrible fear of a funeral procession. If they came upon one in their walks she would run blindly. Her nurse and the adults of the family assured her that there was nothing to be afraid of, that funerals did not touch people, and never came up on the sidewalk. She need not run because nothing would follow her. It was silly to be afraid. "They used to make me feel like a fool," she said, "but they did not touch my fear. By and by I learned to walk past the processions quietly, but I would lie awake at night and tremble at the pictures that they called up." These pictures were of vague forms symbolic of death and of gigantic figures whose meanings she could not comprehend.

As a matter of fact this child was more sensitive to the mysteries of the death symbols and to other spiritual symbols than were the adults surrounding her. Death is one of those dark and mysterious forces that has always stood at the background of man's consciousness. It is the urge forever at war with the urge toward living. It is not only the fear of actual physical death but of the regressive element in ourselves. Fortunately the urge toward life, the absorption in the present business of living is so keen, especially in the young, that these fears rarely break through. Where a child is sensitive to all these inner realities we do not decrease the fear by dwelling on its folly. We only make the child feel different and queer since no one else understands. This child had no fear of being run over or physically injured by the funeral carriages but the sight of them lifted the veil that ordinarily hangs between our lighted world and the world of shadows. Since these images are so tremendous, yet so intangible, we cannot analyze the actual fear, the fear of the death element, but by our attitude of sympathetic understanding of these fears, we can give the child a sense of *security* in our companionship. In that companionship we can convey our own acceptance of life, and of death, and build up the positive values to meet those fears. In such cases the elements are too intangible to be reduced to words. The child in a measure substitutes the security of the sympathetic relationship for the unknown fear. Sometimes these death fears are found to be a fear of being put in the ground and this can be met by the actual discussion, in telling of the body as a discarded covering, but the fear usually lies too deep for that. To meet these deepest fears we must have found our own attitude toward death.

One of the more common fears of childhood is the fear of the dark. Though we, in our adult superiority, make fun of this fear we only show our ignorance, for this, like the law of death, is also deep rooted in the unconscious of mankind. It is not so many generations since the darkness was a very real menace. In the jungle one could not venture beyond the safety of the firelight. A shadow dimly sensed in the dusk might be a tiger crouching to spring; a crackling twig was in all probability the signal of the approaching enemy—human, animal, or even, to the primitive mind, demoniac—for in the darkness lurked gods and devils that must be propitiated. These impressions are stored up in the collective unconscious and produce vague but real terrors. It is, therefore, reasonable to say to a child, "I know you are afraid of the dark; lots of people have been, but that is because they lived in forests, and all sorts of beasts might be prowling round, but now we live in safe houses and it is quite different. Ever so many grown people were afraid when they were children, but they got over it when they understood and so can you." This acceptance of the fear does not separate the child from the normally brave people but links him to others who have also felt this fear and have conquered. He feels the fear is legitimate, but that he can gain power over it, and in so doing his courage grows.

Here again is a place where we must admit the thing as it really is before we can change it. We are still naïve in our treatment of the thing that disturbs us. We proceed on the assumption that if we deny the upsetting thing it thereby ceases to exist. We turn our back upon the problem and feel relieved of the necessity for its solution. This has been made the basis of certain modern creeds. We find it easier to deny the existence of evil rather than to accept the necessity for reckoning with it.

It was this same refusal to admit the disturbing thing to consciousness that led people to pooh-pooh the fears of war even when its menace was almost upon the world. Such fear admitted as a reality would upset the whole placid tenor of their lives and force upon their knowledge the existing powers of evil, poverty, anarchy, and greed. It was easier to deny that there was anything to fear.

The static attitude which desires that life shall remain as it is repudiates disturbing elements. The dynamic or evolving attitude accepts the existing thing as real, not only in its present form, but as a potential from which new forms may develop. It aims at a real understanding of the existing power that we may develop toward a greater understanding of the truth, a higher degree of consciousness. We must admit the existence of these intangible fears before we can help to conquer them. In this way we build up a sense of security which strengthens the connection with the everyday world of his own child life and gives him a feeling of mastery over his own fears. In our highly ex-traverted civilization we are apt to give reality value only to the tangible and material. The inner life with its spirit-ual symbols, its intricate psychological processes, its intan-gible realities, is depreciated. Therefore fears arising from inner images, no matter how compelling, are brushed aside as unreal. Our reality sense is attuned only to the world of outer fact.

Some children are keenly alive to all the undercurrents which lie behind the material world. They sense, in more or less dimly defined, yet monstrous outline, those forces which we all fear when we permit ourselves to become aware of them. It is these fears that are most difficult to deal with in child life. The best we can do is to keep the paths always open between ourselves and the child, so that these figures of fear will not be shut away from the light of day to grow in fantasy life.

In dealing with these irrational elements of fear a solu-tion must often be accepted that in itself seems highly irra-tional. For example, an intuitive child had been subject to frequent night terrors. One day after she had asked her mother certain sex questions which were answered with the utmost frankness and simplicity, she had the following dream: "I was riding to the gate on my bicycle with X (her dog). When I call him in my dreams he always sniffs first in the other three directions and then last of all sees me. But this time he saw me right away and came directly. We went down the road on the way home. As we passed the big tree a big green monkey came down out of the tree and chased me." After relating this she said, "Why is it I'm not afraid of the green monkey any more now that I have told you about him?"

The mother answered that all people had in their heads green monkeys, beasts, and people that stories were made about, only some people saw them more easily than oth-ers. To tell such a thing to anyone who understood about "green monkeys" and also took part in the things one did every day (such as brushing one's hair and eating three meals etc.) made the story things and the real outside world come together. At once the child said, "I think that Miss A knows about green monkeys, but I don't think that Cousin C does."

Miss A was an intuitive with a vivid fantasy life and Cousin C one to whom the fantasy life was unreal.

After telling this dream the night terrors ceased. Here there seems to be no reason for the cessation of the night

terrors, but the skillful way in which the mother handled
the whole situation produced the result. She made no attempt to deal with the symbolism of the dream, to connect
the green monkey with any sexual symbol. She did not
lead the child back into the realm of the collective unconscious. Nor is it necessary for us to discuss the symbols
here since it is the way the fear was handled which is important. In the first place, by her simple explanation of the
facts of life the mother made natural the things which are
often shrouded in mystery. By so doing she opened the approach for all further confidences. If she had turned aside
from these other questions the child would have hidden
away the dream. There would have been a sense of uneasi-
ness when the subject reappeared in veiled dream symbols.
The mother's acceptance of the dream figures made them
seem as natural as the talking animals of the old fairy
tales and put them in the land where they belonged in the
child's imaginings.

Another child had a fantasy of birth of little babies. She
would imagine blowing softly through her lips until a bubble came. This bubble was bright colored like an iridescent
soap bubble. It floated about the room like a bit of rainbow and when it burst a tiny baby came out. This baby
was sometimes a real baby and sometimes a fairy child.
She carried this fantasy till it became a truth. It became
confused with all her ideas of the real birth of children.
One day she confided it and was laughed at. She carefully
guarded her fantasies thereafter but she continued her fantasy. It rather gained in strength by becoming a carefully
guarded secret. The actual knowledge of birth became unimportant and uninteresting. She asked no further questions for fear of ridicule.

When she was about thirteen she was kissed by an older
boy and rather roughly caressed. There was some physical
excitement produced and afterward a sense of guilt. This
guilt was increased because the fantasies surrounded in the
episode roused a desire to masturbate. Then the old fantasy returned and she became alarmed lest she should have
a child. Actual knowledge and fantasy became absurdly
mixed and she suffered intensely. She developed a "queer
little trick" of blowing bubbles through her lips which an-
noyed her family greatly. She herself did not consciously
connect this with the old fantasy and her continued attempts to find out if the thing was true. After a time she
became reassured as to the unimportance of the episode

but the whole experience had a distinctly bad effect upon her and served to separate her from reality.

The trouble here was the ignorant way in which the fantasy had been received. This fantasy is closely linked with some of the earliest myths and fairy tales. There are many old stories of impregnation through the mouth. In these old stories the woman swallows a peach pit or apple pit and a child is born. In these stories the swallowing represents taking in of the seed of life. This is followed by the birth of the hero who is greater than the ordinary mortal—the one untouched by earth. So this child dreaming of the fairy thing born of the bubble had touched an old myth and reclothed it in a robe of charming fantasy. It should have been treated tenderly, reverently, and linked with other tales which have the kindred imagination. The child dreamed more wisely than the adult. Facts should be told in their own time, in their own way, not as a contradiction of myth but as the material of the tangible world, and the fantasy should be accepted also in its own place. There is then no conflict between the two attitudes. This child was left with fear because her fantasy was not sympathetically received. Had it been treated as was the "green monkey," she would have been spared much later suffering.

There is also a child born of the breath. It is the creation of the poet and the storyteller. It is the thought made manifest. We could follow this symbol on through the exquisite old symbolism of the Word made flesh, of the birth of the spirit from the breath of life.

When we so examine these fantasies we become ashamed of our easy laughter and gain a reverence for the childish intuition that is in touch with these symbolic things.

A somewhat similar, but more comprehensive fantasy was told me by a physician. His patient said that, as a child, she and her sister had invented a game called "making." In this game they blew bubbles from their mouths and then told what came out of them. In this case all sorts of desired things were born of bubbles.

Frequently when children have been afraid of things under the bed or of gigantic figures of nightmare that they feel are still there when they awake, much can be done by explaining them as self-made fairy tales and as the people whom storytellers often see. Having recourse to that old ineffective reiteration that there is nothing there and it is silly to be afraid, only exaggerates the trouble. To a person factually minded one must either deny that these images exist or else accept them as material facts. To those persons such fears are "silly."

One cannot generalize in these cases. The thing that we must continually bear in mind is that each child is unique. We must not assume that because we have found the cause of the fear of the dark in one child we can fit our findings to the next case that comes our way. In some children fear of the dark arises from images from the unconscious which must be met as this mother met the "green monkey." In another case in which fear symptoms seemed to have to do with these images a similar treatment had no effect. The case was baffling till it was found that the mother had a fear which she was unwilling to face. The child in question was very closely identified with the mother and took over this fear in his unconscious. Here the whole work had to be done in clearing up the mother's fear. Then the fears of the child mysteriously vanished.

In another case a potentially imaginative child was brought up in an atmosphere of unadulterated facts. He had never been told a fairy tale nor fed on such deceptions as Santa Claus. Nevertheless the darkness held unimaginable terrors. This child was given large doses of fairy-tale fantasy, and whimsical child poetry, until the dark became peopled with fascination and the terrors ceased. Dr. Edith Wharton told me of a similar case where in addition to the terrors the child masturbated badly. When the imagination was properly directed, instead of starved, the masturbation also disappeared with the terror. It had been used to stimulate fantasy and now was no longer needed.

Sometimes, through the workings of his own unconscious, the child continues these fears and makes use of them because they serve a very definite, though not understood purpose. A child with an overstrong mother attachment wakens in the dark, terrified perhaps by some strange noise, or by a dream image. His frightened cry brings the mother with comforting assurances of safety and love. He is perhaps jealous of the father who can remain downstairs with mother after he has been sent to bed, or who shares her sleeping room. Now by means of this terror he can control the mother. He has only to cry out and she is there. He does not reason this through, consciously intending to make use of these fears. Indeed he may feel rather ashamed of them, or he may make an effort not to be selfish and "bring poor mother upstairs," yet again he wakes in the darkness and finds some intense emotion clutches him. The conscious willing part of him decides not to be afraid, but only a small part of him is will-directed self. The rest is in that hinterland of the unconscious where vague but compelling emotional figures move.

It may seem strange to say that the child does not know what emotion is controlling him, but we do not always know ourselves. The desire for the mother rising up in the child seizes upon the fear and pushes it up into consciousness. Perhaps the child at first plays with the fear, almost enjoying it, but then the fear begins to play with him until, like a dark wave, it sweeps over him and panic begins. He calls out. Like the man who loosed the bottle imp and then found that the genie grew to monstrous proportions and could not be returned to captivity, we loose these emotional demons and find that we cannot thrust them back where they belong. In such a case the work must be done through a better adaptation. Perhaps the relationship with the father can be strengthened, and a more adult attitude be formed, perhaps the child can be taught to see his own unconscious motives and so his own conscious will be able to take control. With each child the procedure must vary.

In other cases where there is, in the mother's unconscious, a resentment toward the child because he interferes with her life and curtails her freedom, the child senses this and may use his fears to keep her near him. In one such case the mother resented the coming of the child because it interfered with her career. As he grew older any suggestion of sending him away filled him with terror and started nightmares. It is illuminating to see that the terror roused is often in proportion to the real insecurity which is sensed by the unconscious.

Sometimes when the fear is of a very real subjective danger, a fear of great forces within ourselves, we interpose some absurd little objective fear between ourselves and this force that we are afraid to face. It may be easier to make this plain through the analysis of an adult who has fallen victim to these same forces, because with the adult we can follow a more consecutive dream analysis and through free association trace the action of the unconscious.

A young woman was sent me by a physician because she was in a continuous state of terror. This made her unable to carry on her ordinarily daily work, or to sleep at

night without attacks of almost hysterical fear. She
suffered also from pain in the head and loss of muscular
control. At first she wished to talk of the importance of
the physical symptoms and of the loss of sleep because of
dreams which she "could not remember." When we had
talked a little of fear and she felt reasonably sure that my
attitude would be one of sympathy, she told me that her
real trouble was "just such a silly notion as made her believe she was going crazy."

Each day on her way to work she had to pass a little
church. One hot day she went inside to rest in the cool
and quiet. Just inside the doorway were two stone effigies.
As she stepped into the dim light her eyes rested upon
these two figures and suddenly she felt weak and cold. "I
couldn't move or go out or in," she said. "Then as I
looked it seemed as though they moved, just ever so little
but I was all a-tremble. I couldn't even have screamed.
Then I knew I was silly and by and by I got past them,
but I was all perspiration and trembly. I stayed as long as I
dared, but I had to get to work and by and by I got out
again. I could hardly get between them. When I got out
the sun seemed so bright it frightened me and I wanted to
hide somewhere, and the noise frightened me too."

These figures now haunted both her waking and her
sleeping hours. She could not bear to pass the church
where she knew they lay. In her fear she left the village
where she was employed and came home to look for
work. She besought me to assure her that she was afraid
because it was such a hot day that it made her head dizzy
and queer and the figures had seemed to move. She said
that it was so "queer" that she should be afraid of these
figures when she generally was not afraid of such things
and was not a bit superstitious. She continued to see these
figures and other ones like them.

This silly fright she said had gotten on her nerves so
that she began to be afraid of other things. One day when
walking with "her boy" she suddenly was afraid that he
would kill her and she insisted on coming back home. In
the street she was afraid of strangers. "How could you tell
what they might really be?" Several times she had thought
that some woman standing near her might be a man disguised in woman's clothing. She had been afraid to say
that the sunlight frightened her for that might make people think her "balmy." She said that strangers looked at
her and the sun made her head ache. She withdrew more
and more until now she stayed at home while the sister

went out to work. In her talks with me she returned again and again to the terror of the effigies and to her hatred of going out in the sun.

Here was a real haunting terror whose power was undermining her life and making her almost long for the retreat of insanity, an idea with which she was fascinated. We had to step behind these figures to find the fears that they were masking.

In the analysis it developed that her lover had been seriously injured in the war and at the time when this fright occurred it was quite doubtful whether or not he would recover. At any time she might receive word of his death. She assured me that this was not the cause of her fear for she *did not let herself think of this at all but made herself think only of his recovery and kept on planning their home when he should be well and able to do like other men.*

The doctors had told her positively that if he recovered from the operation he must always be an invalid. Her marriage to him would involve great sacrifice on her part as she would have to continue work and also assume the cares of the house. There was a small pension but this pension would not be enough to relieve her of the financial responsibility. She had been a rather delicate, timid child, greatly afraid of the father who had taken pleasure in exploiting her fears. On this account she had been unduly shielded by both her mother and her sister. When she had been forced to bear some part of the household expense, a very easy place had been found for her by the sister. Now she was facing a situation where she would have to be strong and carry the brunt of the burden.

Consciously she accepted this and was planning for her marriage in spite of her mother's protests. Now she needed to be very well but she found herself getting nervous. It "all began with those two figures and the queer feeling when she got back on the bright street." She repeated over and over that she wanted most of all to marry but of course she could not if she was going queer. Then she told in detail of the figures. One especially exercised a powerful fascination. It was of an old man with a face so shrunken as to be like a skeleton and with long bony hands. Whenever she thought of him she was in terror, but at once she again saw the bright street.

These two fears were *her fear of life and her fear of death.* Either way there opened before her a path she had not the courage to face. Her engagement to this man had taken place when they were hardly more than children. She could not think of life without him, yet if he lived and she married him she must put away the childish sheltered life and take her place as a strong woman, one strong enough to even give up much of a normal woman's life, children and the security of home.

Since she dared not face either possibility she had refused to think of the reality which confronted her but had taken refuge in fantasies of their life together when he should be "well and strong like other men." She had made herself "look on the bright side of things," by that method which many of us use when we mean refusing to look on the positive side of the existing situation and turning away from the real problem to hide behind a comforting fantasy. We must, even in our dealing with young children, keep clear the distinction between the fantasy which is creative and has the value that we find in poetry and works of imagination, and the fantasy which is used as a retreat from reality. Looking on the bright side by refusing to acknowledge existing conditions is another form of refusing responsibility.

In this case her love and the positive value of a real human relationship was the real "bright side." In taking refuge in the fantasy that he was going to get perfectly well and she would not have to face the problem, she pushed down her fears into the unconscious where they continued to operate and made themselves known in "pains and queer feelings." When she went into the church, these effigies appeared as symbols of the power of death and, outside, the busy street was the compelling force of life. The sudden sight of the death symbol crystallized the vague terror forms of the unconscious and made them take concrete form. They imaged the fear, and into the images she projected the fears she would not face.

She had a singularly childish and undeveloped mind but she had intelligence. She saw that she must look behind the images to the inner meaning. Seen in this way her fears were of very real and tremendous things that had been masking behind the seeming trivialities. Even her dread of insanity was a desire for it as a retreat. No one could remove the terrific burden. The question was one for her own choice. Was her love strong enough to make her willing to take up this life and to find its positive values? So interpreted, her fears were not foolish things, for she had a problem which called for the fullest measure of courage and love. The unmasking of the fears and the acceptance of the new attitude were not the simple things that this very brief sketch might seem to imply. Many inner forces that had been operative since her early childhood had to be brought to light, and much in herself had to be faced. I am here giving only the facts of the projected fear.

It is this form of projection of the feeling into the object which is the ruling factor when the primitive endows his totems with magic power. Into them he projects his fears and his awe of unknown mysteries. Then by the observance of certain forms and taboos he can propitiate the unknown force and save himself from the devastating power of the fear. So great then becomes the power of the symbol on to which the fear has become projected that the breaking of a taboo surrounding it may result in death. Men have been known to die of fright on finding that they have unknowingly broken a taboo which it was death to break, or even when they have done the act deliberately the ensuing fear and sense of guilt have resulted in death. There are many records of this in primitive tribes or in such cases as of those who touched the ark of the covenant.

In treating the fears of children we must remember that it is because the object symbolizes a situation that they fear or calls up an inner image of terror that their fear often seems out of all proportion to the object which invokes it. The fear is made concrete in the object.

Often, too, children, like primitives, will invent elaborate formulas and magic rites by which to propitiate the things that they fear. A woman told me that as a child she had a great fear of the dark. She especially hated a queer shadow cast by the top of a high bureau when the light was fading. She decided it was a "dark spirit" and invented a magic formula to keep it quiet. This, she said, became much more important than even her evening prayers. She was not supposed to be an especially imaginative child nor did she develop any neurosis, in fact she was a very normal sort of person. These secret formulas are by no means uncommon but the child rarely discloses them, and as other interests develop they are pushed down and forgotten.

I knew one especially dominating child who became a sort of medicine man to the infant tribe because of these inventions. He was able to impress his fantasies on the other children so that, though they might scoff, they had an uneasy feeling that there was too much chance of its all being true for them to dare to go against the magic dictates. Frequently the adult who is most ruthless in ridicule of these childish credulities is the one who clings most tenaciously to his own. Why should we impress upon children the Old Testament myths as true and then laugh at them for believing fairy tales? Is Tom Thumb in the cow's belly more difficult to accept literally than Jonah in the belly of the whale?

Another process which is quite nearly akin to the projection of the fear into the symbol is its projection into a substituted fear. Here again most of the process takes place in the unconscious. A young girl who was having great difficulty in her school work and in her school adjustments began to be extremely nervous, and had a fearful dream from which she awoke in a condition of terror and emotional uncontrol. She did not wish to talk of the dream in her waking hours. At first she said that she did not remember it, then that she did not want to talk of it. It had, however, a compelling power over her thoughts. She was nervous in the morning and found it increasingly difficult to prepare for the tasks of the day. The power of the dream did not decrease, and after a little the dream itself returned. We had a very friendly relationship and in the course of an afternoon spent together, she was able to tell me the dream.

"Someone living on our block has been murdered and the murderer has not been found but everyone believes that I did it. I know that I did not and am innocent, but I know that no one will believe me. Then I know that they are coming to take me and that there is no way out and that *no one will believe that I did not do it.*"

She was greatly disturbed by the telling of the dream. Then, with a good deal of emotional emphasis, she said that she understood perfectly why she had dreamed it as a man had been murdered in her neighborhood and the murderer had not been found but someone was suspected and was being watched. She said that "quite naturally" she had thought of how the poor man must feel if he were really innocent and yet knew that he was suspected and might be accused. But these "quite natural" feelings had taken on a form of identification with this unknown man. She had acute suffering in imagining his fears, and kept asking herself how she would feel in his place. Then she began to read all the murder cases in the papers and think how easy it would be for someone to come into their house and commit murder there. In this way she gave a plausible explanation of the existing situation.

Identifications involving so much of emotional effect do not take place unless the person involved represents some phase of our own personal problem. I asked her what was the thing for which she felt she might be blamed and of which she was innocent.

"There isn't anything," she said, "except that I know I can't pass my examinations and everybody will think it is my fault, and the more I try, the more I know I can't pass."

The child was in a school of very high scholastic standing, and was in the college preparatory section which was very rigid in its demands. There was a history of barely averted failure in spite of special tutoring; all this had developed a certain attitude on the part of the teachers and in her own mind. Although her mind worked slowly and it had been a constant struggle to keep up she herself had been determined to take the college course. She had a very strong relationship with her parents and was quite conscious that, whatever they might say, they would be deeply disappointed if she failed to attain this special end. This, far more than her own desires, was the influence at work. Children who are obstinately insistent upon pursuing a course too difficult for their ability at a particular time are frequently keenly cognizant of their parents' unspoken ambition and are trying to fullfill its demands.

Everyone was now trying to help this young girl by telling her that she must not be afraid of her examinations and that she would surely pass. This served only to increase her fears, for it deepened her feeling that she would be considered guilty because of her failures. It was her parents' hope that would be "murdered" and she, though really innocent, would be held responsible. Then there came to light vague doubts as to whether her own attitude was really right. There might after all be something within herself that she was murdering in continuing on her present way.

As is usual in such cases there was also a compensatory attitude. When one feels in danger of drowning one clutches at straws, and when one feels engulfed by feelings of inferiority one must have some sense of superiority in which to take refuge. In these cases the compelling forces lie in the unconscious and are often quite unreasonble in their manifestations. In this instance the girl had a very superior attitude toward her classmates. Certain matters of deportment assumed absurdly great significance. She became overpunctilious, so that a really admirable desire to do right and to hold high standards became lost in a maze of exaggerations. The other girls felt this, and, with the careless cruelty of youth, used it to torment her. A very strong loyalty to the school and a conscious desire for friendship blinded her to her underlying attitude of resentment. She had the following dream.

"We were having dinner and all of a sudden there were bugs all over everything. They were horrid; I could not eat." She had an intense dislike of bugs so that on camping trips or picnics her pleasure was spoiled by them. She talked at length of this. After a little talk on another subject I asked her to give her first association when I said a word. I then said, "Bugs." She answered "X" (the name of the school). I said, "Go on." She continued "Girls," and then broke off—"Why, how funny! That has nothing to do with bugs."

All of a sudden she became embarrassed and began to laugh in a confused way. The dream had forced its association upon her and she could not help seeing that she thought of the girls as bugs. She had been having difficulty in her athletics because in basketball, in which she took great interest, she would, at the critical time, pass the ball to the wrong side. This disturbed her greatly and she made every effort to play correctly, but always with the same result. From the analysis of this dream she was able to see that the undercurrent of resentment which she felt in the unconscious took command in the moment of excitement and made her betray her side in spite of every conscious desire to help them win.

Here we see the interplay between the sense inferiority and the compensatory feelings of superiority. Unfortunately this interplay does not result in a normal balance enabling the individual to adapt to life more successfully. Instead it produces a more unbalanced state in which first one overemphasized attitude and then the other prevails. A girl as old as this could become conscious of these forces at work, and learn to see why her exaggerated attitudes seized hold of her and made her their servant. She must first find herself and her own real values, and then be willing to give genuine effort to attain the thing which ought to be hers.

Here again we see the danger of choosing a definite goal for a child and marking failure or success by the attainment of an especial end. This results in a confusion of values, for effort, understanding, and self-development are made secondary to a particular achievement. If this achievement is not attained there may arise, as in this case, not only a feeling of failure and inferiority which seeks to compensate by suggested superiority, but also a feeling of guilt at not giving the thing demanded. In such a case the positive values are all enlisted on the wrong side. A child who has little loyalty or real love will not be so troubled by the sense of responsibility. The very strength of the bond which existed between this child and her parents increased the haunting sense of guilt in the unconscious, and this, together with the feeling of impotence, produced the terror dream of being held responsible for a murder which she had not committed. Through the identification with the suspected murderer she could project her fears as a form of sympathy without having to accept them as her own. Then the interest extended to all murder cases and the fear became transferred to a fear of being murdered herself. It is through this type of projection that the real difficulty of the situation is veiled and an obsessive fear may spring up to take its place. It was quite natural for her to be insistent that the dream was caused by having read of the murder, though she admitted that she had often read of such cases without their having made any special impression.

It is very common for people to explain dreams which have a strong emotional content as caused by something read or seen, but the unconscious seizes upon the thing which bears the special message, and which will in the most vivid way provide the symbol most freighted with meaning at the time. Therefore some apparently insignificant incident may be reproduced in a grotesque form, and yet we may feel the dream to be of great importance.

Another important element in all these fear situations is the strong influence of the parents' unspoken desire, whether this desire be in the unconscious or merely repressed from speech. In the case of the murder dream the child was more influenced by the real anxiety of the parents to have her accomplish this special course, than by their expressed but also real desire to have her do the thing that was best for her even if it meant giving up their plans. They were not selfishly ambitious but were honestly looking for the best way. In that search they made, as we all must make, some mistakes even while they were reaching out for a fuller understanding of their child.

In the first case cited in this chapter, that of the small

boy caught in the net of his fear and rages, his intuitions
were of forces in the father's unconscious which were not
apparent to the father himself. We all have a deep-rooted
feeling that our children will, by succeeding where we
have failed, justify us in our own lives. To the primitive
the child is his property, part of himself. This feeling,
when understood, is not destructive of love, but we must
be conscious of it so that we shall not have a hidden feeling that the failures of the child are a wrong done to us.
When we have such destructive undercurrents our ambition masquerades as love and whenever the child fails a
personal resentment is raised. This small boy sensed the
deeper anger which underlay his father's half-concealed irritation. His fear of punishment, when the father lost his
self-control, is also a very natural fear reaction. The
deeper emotions which seem to well up of themselves and
often to sweep us away, so that they control us instead of
our controlling them, have the roots of their being deep
down in the collective unconscious. It is not so long ago,
when we speak in terms of man's life on earth, that parents not only had the right of death over their children but
exercised it at the dictates of their own uncontrolled and
not understood emotions. Dr. Jung in *Psychological Types*
speaks of a bushman who on returning from an unsuccessful fishing trip was met by his favorite little son, and in a
fit of sudden rage wrung the child's neck. He was almost
immediately overcome with grief at the tragic result of his
own act, an act which he could in no wise understand.
There is, in the collective unconscious, an inheritance of
fear and distrust, as well as these forces of sudden rage
and hate. An instability of emotional attitudes on the part
of the adult controlling the situation is an entirely legitimate cause for an attitude of fear in the child. It rouses in
him a deep sense of insecurity. In the primitive, hate, love,
fear, anger, find their immediate relief in acts. These primal emotions lie close together in the depths of the unconscious and are sometimes hard to distinguish. So the anger
of one person may call up fear in another.

To an intuititive child the possibility is more real
and to be feared than the actuality. The mind leaps
over the existing to the becoming. Therefore such a
child especially fears the anger lying behind the act. The
mother of one such child told me that, if she was angry,
any movement that she made toward the child seemed to
rouse terror, though the child had never been whipped.
Another woman who developed a fear neurosis that had

hampered her life told me that on analysis she realized that all through her childhood she had been terror-haunted because of the sound of her mother's voice when quarreling with her father. It seemed, she said, to "sweep everything away." Since the love of the parent is the strongest emotional security of the child what wonder that a sense of instability there should fill life with fear?

Frequently a child battling with this type of fear will develop a strong will-to-power. There is a surge of desire to master the situation and to control the parent lest he escape and the child be left alone. A little girl who had a very strong love for her mother and father, and was felt by them to be a drag upon their ambitious professional and social life, developed a sudden willfulness. She was arbitrary in her demands for attention, became impertinent, defiant, insistent upon her demands upon the parents' time. These periods of autocratic behavior alternated with periods of tenderness and loving companionship. Then certain regressive symptoms made their appearance. She began thumb-sucking, at the same time stroking her own cheek and ear, symptoms unimportant to dwell on in themselves but indicative of an infantile emotional attitude.

This child had already been sent to a summer camp when she was barely six and the parents were now, when she was barely nine, expecting to send her to a boarding school for small children. The child had strong intuitions of the insecurity of her hold upon her parents' love. No one with any psychological insight could talk long with the mother without seeing personal ambition peering from behind her ardor for "a larger life" and for being of use to her husband. It was this unadmitted and unrecognized personal ambition that was the corroding influence in the relationship and destroyed the child's feeling of security in love. Therefore she tried in these pathetic little power ways to gain control of the parents. The thumb-sucking was here, as it frequently, though by no means invariably is, an unconscious attempt to allay fear. To get back into an infantile, protected state gives a feeling of security. Such feelings may be auto-erotically produced by sucking and stroking.

Again we come back to those hidden forces of relationship. I have known children who had to leave home at an equally early age because of conditions which were beyond the parental control, conditions which were courageously faced. Although there was homesickness and anxiety, the background of trust and confidence in the parents' love remained; and the integrity of the relationship furnished a sense of security which stood between the child and the nervous terrors that are so apt to fill hours of loneliness.

There are also irrational and obsessive fears which arise from association. In such cases the original fear has its origin in the trauma or shock, an experience which in itself first causes an intense emotional reaction and is apparently forgotten, but which through blind association produces recurrent fears and a sense of haunting terror.

In one case a child had times of dumb panic so that she seemed "frozen" and unable to complete simple sentences or to have any control over her thought processes. She was observed to be bewildered when there were certain types of noise, the passing of a truck, the rolling of a heavy object, the roar of traffic. It was found that when as a very small child she had been alone upstairs there had been a terrific thunderstorm. There was a sudden flash of lightning and an instantaneous peal of thunder. The mother ran upstairs and found the child clutching her crib in speechless terror. There was reason to believe that she had received a slight shock. She was handled with skill and tenderness and the ill effects apparently passed away. When, however, she went from the shelter of the home to the new atmosphere of the school all her natural timidity was awakened, for she was a very gentle, reserved, introverted child. The fears began to stir again and every passing noise exaggerated them and roused the old associations of terror. She was greatly helped by having her attention directed toward these associations and by being shown why the noises produced such fear. There remained, however, much to be done in the understanding of the child's own nature and of her attitude of withdrawal. The innate timidity had to be met and her self-confidence restored.

Freud discovered that the so-called trauma was often only a fantasy trauma, that is, an imagined happening; or was an occurrence which normally should be merely incidental but which, because of the predisposition or the arousing of some inner image, assumed unwonted proportions. Therefore, in such cases of fear it is not enough to track down this trauma. We must also see what are the inner elements that made this shock have such overwhelming consequences. This is a far more difficult task and often calls for long and patient analysis. In the case of an adult it is a direct process. In the case of a child it often involves analytical work with the parents, since it is frequently their attitude which is affecting the child. The trauma assumes terrifying proportions when it is met by an especially receptive attitude, and connected with the psychological problem of the individual. The individual must, therefore, reckon with his own inner difficulties.

Kimmins, in his book on children's dreams, comments on the fact that though in England the air raids were a very real terror, and occurred in the terror dreams of children, all trace of them seemed to have disappeared even from dream association a few months after the cessation of the raids. Contrasted with this quick disappearance of terror associations are the recurrent dreams of an eleven-year-old boy; dreams of falling from high places, being forced to jump from fast-moving trains, etc.; dreams which had a high degree of emotional effect. The association which came to light was a threat which his father had made when the boy was only about three years old, that he would throw him down an elevator shaft. The boy knew that his father would not have done this, he realized that the persistence of the terror was unreasonable; yet it persisted. A dream like this indicates that the real cause of fear still exists. In this instance it was the fear of his father's unreasonable anger and of the wrong element in the relationship. The thing he really feared, the father's misdirected authority, was still a menace: the actual trauma was used as a peg on which to hang the blind fears.

The fear of fire is a very prevalent fear with children. Often they have witnessed a fire. In our large cities, especially, there is the frequent shriek of the fire engine, the clang of the gongs, the wail of the siren—terrifying noises that split the darkness. This reasonable side of the fear can be met by reasonable means: a stress on the value of these same monsters of terror, the fire engines; a knowledge of the safety of the child's own environment; an emphasis on the positive protection.

There is another intangible fear of fire which seems to be related to the inner image. One dream which I have met with great frequency is a dream of a "little man" with fire coming out of his back, or a "little man" hidden under the bed whose back spurted fire, or sometimes a little person climbing up a hill with fire coming out of his back. In most cases, though not in all, these dreams have been dreamed by overconscientious children who are in safely conventional surroundings. Fire is the symbol of the instinctive force, the primitive power. In the early myths it is closely linked with sexual rites, also with the theft of the forbidden power; hence it is linked in the unconscious with the sense of sin. We are afraid of our instincts, hence we repudiate them. In children whose natural and instinctive reactions are suppressed these old symbols break through. This is a deduction based on such data as I have been able to gather. I should be greatly interested to have the findings of others, in contradiction or in verification.

Another interesting thing about these special fire dreams is the use of the symbol of the Cabiri, the kobold or dwarf, the "little man" who is in mythology one of the delvers in the earth, one who deals in elemental things. The fire comes out of his back. The unconscious is often symbolized as the back. Things repressed from consciousness break forth at the back. That this dream, in varying settings but with the main figure with fire coming out of the back, has appeared so frequently seems to warrant such an interpretation of the symbol.

We have an instinctive fear of the elemental forces within us. Instead of looking to them as sources of renewal as did Antaeus when he stooped to touch the mother earth we make every effort to separate ourselves from them. We do well to fear their elemental power, for, if we allow ourselves to be swept away by them, we are lost, as in an engulfing flood. When we try to cut ourselves off from them, to deny their force within ourselves, we only cut ourselves off from the original springs of life. Then in some symbolic form they may break through in projected fears. Children who repress their natural expression of energy, who are too good, too well-trained, too docile, often have these dreams.

Such fears of instinctive forces have to be reckoned with; the fear of sex, the fear of sex knowledge, the fear of sin, the fear of elemental emotions such as rage and jealousy. Often we discover such fears to be sex fears whose reverse side is a wish fulfillment. A young girl of low-grade mentality had an obsessing fear of pregnancy. She was in love with a young man who had paid her only the most casual attention. On one occasion he had kissed her. She had the fantasies so common with children, of impregnation through the mouth. She lived in fear pictures of herself and her family as being disgraced and cast off by society. She even attempted suicide. The whole sexual relation was carefully explained to her and she had expressed the most intense relief; she was better for only a short period and then returned to her fantasy. This is a fantasy deep rooted in the collective unconscious, and to be found constantly recurring in old tales, but its persistence here was due to desire. Should she be pregnant it might be that the man would have to marry her and, though her conscious denied the wish, the unconscious was continually thrusting it forward in the form of a fear.

Sometimes these symbolic forms break through in the fear of a special animal. This fear may arise because at some time when we were caught—either by ourselves or by another—in some act of which we were ashamed, some blind jealousy, some dishonesty, this animal was associated with the act. Sometimes it is because we fear in ourselves the quality which the animal has symbolized in the primitive myth. So a cat fear may exist because of certain unacknowledged possibilities of treachery in ourselves. An abnormal fear of snakes may be a fear of our own unrecognized sexuality. In the myth of Circe the magic wine turned each one who drank it into the animal whom he most resembled, and the hidden thing became apparent. There was no power in the wine to change the inner nature of the man, but only to crystallize into form what was there already. So the unconscious crystallizes these fears into projected animal form and we fear these animals. With children the animal may be identified with something feared in the parent—some cruelty or some selfishness.

I do not wish to be understood to mean that all animal fears have such a basis. Often a child is taught fear of animals by overtimid elders; but in any case where we find the obsessive fear persisting it is well to try to see further into the unconscious.

It would not be possible in this chapter to deal extensively with the various forms of fear. These cases may suggest something of the magnitude and delicacy of the task which confronts one who has to deal with fear-driven children. It may also contribute to that attitude of sympathetic understanding and of respect for the reality world of each human being which is the first essential in attempting to deal with childhood fears. Back of it all again is the security of that relationship which is founded on trust and love and sincerity, a security which is the fundamental right of childhood.

10

SEX

The first and most important question in the problem of the sex education of the child is: what kind of sex education have we had ourselves? What, as a result, is our attitude toward sex? Have we clear ideas of the place of sex in life, and in that most important department of life, human relationships? Have we become conscious of our own sexuality with all its powers for good or evil? In this realm, as in all others, mere knowledge of facts cannot replace understanding; for it is not sexuality, but the attitude toward sexuality that is the important factor.

We may have careful and accurate knowledge of sex in all its biological and physiological aspects. To this knowledge of facts we may add a consciously accepted theory that since this is the way in which children must be conceived it is beautiful and holy. This conscious assumption we may try to impart to a child. But if we have, in our unconscious, resistances that make us feel that it was rather a mistake on the part of the creator to insist upon such a method and that our cooperation with him is a concession to the lower man, we are unfit to teach sex to a child. For in this, as in all other instruction, he will not get from us what we say, but what we, in our inmost depth, believe.

We may supply all, or even more, knowledge than the child really needs; but it is inexorably true that if we dodge the deeper issues of its meaning in life, if we attempt to sublimate all sexuality, or if we seize upon it as an indulgence which we must unfortunately have because of desire, we really impart to the child our own attitude of confusion and compromise.

One who would educate a child in matters of sex must himself be educated by life to a true understanding. In addition to this he must have a real rapport with the child. Normal understanding of the natural facts of life should come naturally and incidentally. The education that comes from being with an understanding person at the right moment often proves most effective. We cannot establish rapport suddenly in order to meet a special need. If a child has been left to go his own way, especially in matters of his inner thought life, we cannot expect to break through these barriers suddenly and to be received into the intimacies of his confidence. Every time we fail to understand, every time we are too busy to talk of the thing that really matters, every time we laugh at, instead of with, him, we increase the probability that he will not come to us with questions about the next thing that is of importance to him. Throughout a long summer vacation a father used to get up early to go fishing with his boy. They were not very successful as anglers but one day he said to me, "We didn't catch many fish but those early morning hours are a wonderful time to catch thoughts."

In our lives with our children we should provide plenty of times to catch thoughts. If we have done this we can be confident that the child will ask us about the thing that he is interested in at the time that the interest first appears. It will be the most natural thing for him to do.

A child is not interested in sex matters because they are sex, but because they are a part of life, and his business is with living. He is full of curiosity; he wants to know how and why. The more intelligent he is, the more curious he is. Curiosity is a great impulse toward knowledge and, as we develop, the form and intensity of our curiosity determines the form of our development. If curiosity is satisfied quite simply at the time of its normal appearance the subject falls into its proper place and carries no overweight of mystery or repression. Anything can be made an obsessive idea by being surrounded with mystery. When children become abnormally curious it is not because of an abnormal intensity of the original interest, but because of the abnormal secrecy with which the thing is surrounded. I have seen one child drive a roomful of other children frantic with curiosity over an empty box, simply because she assumed an air of mystery over it, and refused to open the box. Pandora was a very normal young person.

We cannot give to the child our adult conceptions, nor tell him, at first, anything but the first simple facts; but during that simple telling our inner attitude shows through and illuminates or engulfs the spirit of the tale. If our attitude is wrong, a child, especially if he is intuitive, catches a sense of uncertainty or shame peering furtively from behind the curtain of the well-painted fact and immediately the center of his interest shifts. No longer is it concentrated upon the thing that is being told, but upon that queer and shameful thing that is being withheld. He may, or he may not, get the facts clear in his mind—that depends upon the strength of his interest in the intuited inner thing; but, unless he is entirely factually minded, the deeper impression is made by the thing that is withheld. The more deeply he is introverted, the greater is the value that he places upon the inner reality and the greater is the harm done, though the damage may appear greater in the child who goes out to hunt down the concealed thing in the form of more knowledge.

One difficulty which we must all encounter is that we cannot arrange to have a child's inner mechanism react in a special way at a special time. Things have a way of happening at unforeseen times. A child may ask a question about these matters when visitors are present and the adults, who are none too secure in their own attitudes, become embarrassed. There are glances of evident confusion, there is a burst of laughter, or a shocked silence. Then the child is hustled out of the room to the companionship of his own feelings of humiliation, and he resolves that he will never again consult an adult in regard to that particular question.

There are several courses, any one of which he may follow according to his own particular temperament. His curiosity may be sharpened and he may seek information from some more sympathetic source (some child more "knowing," but perhaps very much misinformed). He may try to answer his questions for himself, piecing together stray bits of knowledge and weaving about them fantasies, many of which may persist even after he has been enlightened; for these fantasies he has not only his own personal imagination as material, but also the myth-building power of the collective unconscious that comes to him in dream and in daydream. Or, he may take a third way and, finding the subject too painful because of feelings of shame invoked by the experience, he may resolve to forget it altogether. He seems then to the uncomprehending adult to be charmingly innocent and devoid of all such curiosities —a very delicate-minded child. Even if he succeeds in repressing them and driving them completely out of his consciousness, he is not the gainer but the loser thereby, for he passes an infantile period without having satisfied the curiosities proper to that period. Later they may return, in which case he will find himself confronted with infantile curiosities that should have been long outgrown. They are then apt to be linked with regressive acts. Infantile curiosities are likely to go as hard in adult life as infant diseases.

Possibly this child who asks no questions may have received information at a very early age from another child or from an ignorant servant, or from a mother who regards sex as a nasty but necessary concession to marriage. This information may have come in some very shocking way. The measure of the danger is here again to be gauged by the depth of his confidence in the parent. If there is sufficient reality in that he will tell the experience and ask the truth, or even if he does not at first tell, he will show signs of disturbance and be ready to confide, when questioned, the thing that is troubling him. If the relationship is insecure he cannot risk divulging such a secret. He hides it away, and its very horror gives it fascination.

It is well to keep in mind that it is normal for a child to want to know where babies come from and how. Much trouble will be avoided if the whole subject is treated like any other. Mothers say that if a child does not ask it seems forced and unnatural to hand out the information, but life always gives plenty of opportunities. In the child's own family, or in the home of some friend, a baby may be arriving. Then the subject can easily be talked of, and the child will be quite sure to ask what he wants to know. There are plenty of opportunities, but we are not always ready to grasp them.

It is equally important that we should not force these things. Telling too much may be as bad as telling too little. For the past few years the horrors of repression have been so dwelt upon that some of us would tumble out the whole story at once, lest we leave a lurking-ground for repression. It is this same attitude that fills some adult conversations with a form of so-called frankness that is nothing but a violation of the decent privacies of life, and a means of gratifying morbid interest. The best guide in this dilemma is the child himself. Give him a chance to question, be sure of his confidence, and then answer his questions as simply as possible, assured that if he wants to know the next step he will ask about it.

In spite of all that has been written about the necessity of early sex education and the floods of sex literature that are upon the market, anyone who deals with the problem of children is amazed to find how little impression this has made upon the mind of the average parent, and how little help has been given the average child. The little child is still considered too little long after his normal curiosity has wakened; or, if the first simple facts have been taught at the proper time, the responsibility is assumed to have been fully met, and all the difficult problems that arise during the period of adolescence and the early youth of post-adolescence are left to chance experience.

A few instances taken from a long list of similar cases may be more convincing than argument. I shall choose these cases from among the children of educated parents and from cultured homes, since it is from such homes that we expect the wisest and most advanced methods. In order that we may see clearly the outcome of this *laissez faire* method I will later in the chapter give a few cases of neurotic adults, where the neurosis has developed as a result of conditions similar to those cited in child analysis.

One of the most usual symptoms that occur when a child has a morbid, unsatisfied sex curiosity is deceit. This may take the very positive form of stealing, or the more negative form of evasion or lying. A little girl who had stolen was marked out as a thief, and "a thoroughly deceitful child." The mother protested her own lack of responsibility and told how carefully she had taught the child that she must always tell the truth and never take anything that was not hers. She had not spared moral precept. I told her that I had reason to believe that the child was full of sex curiosity, and had been trying to get information from other children. I suggested that sometimes children became deceitful because of a feeling that they were unable to get the knowledge that they desired from the proper sources, and then, being driven to get it in obscure ways, they developed a sense of guilt that made them continue the deceit in other ways. I asked about the sex knowledge of the two children in that family. She replied that they were perfectly innocent, and knew nothing about such things. No, I need not worry on that score. But I inquired:

"Have they never asked where babies come from?"

"Oh, yes, and I told them that God brought them straight from heaven."

"You know that he does not, though."

In a shocked voice she answered, "But you couldn't tell *the truth* about a thing like that," and added as a proof of her careful training, "then I told them never to ask about such a thing again, and they never have."

Since hope dies hard, I still pursued the subject, and suggested that she have a frank talk with them now.

"I couldn't," she said. "I was brought up so carefully myself that I never knew about those nasty things until I was married, and had to. I have tried to bring them up the same way."

A woman of like type dreamed. "I came into the living room. In front of the fireplace was a snake seated in a rocking chair, with a bonnet on its head. The bonnet strings were tied in a bow beneath what would have been the snake's chin—if the snake had had a chin—giving it a chaste, matronly look. I said to myself, 'I suppose as long as it sits in the rocking chair and keeps its bonnet on, it can do no harm in the house.'"

The dream was told with the utmost naïveté, and with no realization of the way in which this absurd image satirized her own limitations.

With this attitude there was no possibility of her telling the child anything that would not carry with it a false atmosphere. I could, however, get her consent to let me enlighten the child and, this having been done, we started on the constructive path with the result that the stealing stopped, and the lying and cheating steadily decreased until one day when she received a much coveted "perfect paper," she arose and faced the class and said:

"That isn't my mark. I cheated."

Then I felt no doubt about the complete clearing up of all the evil effects of the deception that had been practiced upon her.

It is difficult for us to realize how an attitude or trend once started will continue to operate in the unconscious, so that there are compelling impulses toward acts connected with it. If one thing is concealed, others will be. Here I would be distinctly understood to mean only a concealment that carries with it a sense of guilt even if the reason for this guilt be not clearly apprehended, or a willful or surreptitious deceit. Taking one thing, even information, in a surreptitious manner will start impulses toward taking other things.

A child committed petty acts of theft, both of objects for which she apparently had no use and also of knowledge about sexual matters. The head of the school sent for the mother. Told of the theft, the mother, irate and full of righteous indignation, came to consult me or, rather, to inform me of the truth about herself. I suggested that the child was really seeking perfectly normal sex knowledge, and that when she had questioned me about some of these truths, I had talked of them very simply. Indignantly the mother retorted, "She's just a little liar. I am not that kind of a mother. I have told her everything. I got the very latest book on sex instruction for the young. I took her on a picnic so I would have plenty of time to lead up to it casually (the book suggested that) and then I told her all about how babies came and I followed the book *in every particular*. She is not only a thief but she is a liar." I gently suggested that as I was seeing her that afternoon I would remind her of this picnic day.

The child came, eager and friendly. I said, "Why did you ask me all those questions? Don't you remember Mother's telling you all about it?" She was frankly perplexed and I spoke of the picnic day. "Why, I remember that picnic; but she didn't tell me what you did. What *she* told me was perfectly horrid and what you told me was beautiful." I can only add the old saying, "What you are speaks louder than what you say." Love communicates its own truth.

Space does not permit my multiplying instances of this special result of sexual misinformation, but a long list of cases has come under my observation. In clinical work and in juvenile courts this has been found true. Dr. William Healy speaks of many cases where information had been imparted in obscene language, and the remembrance of the words was enough to awaken the impulse to pilfer. Here a substitution of the decent word and a sympathetic understanding of the difficulty helped the child to free himself from the obsessive idea.

In other cases there may be no actual wrongdoing, nothing tangible. The child does no wrong, but neither does he do any right. There is no interest, he does not pay attention, he is lost in a maze, a daydreamer. At home he forgets, he is stupidly careless; at school he fails. His answers are random shots rarely hitting the mark, yet at times when he is "all there" he shows a power of reasoning or an intuitional insight that makes us sure that mental qualities are not lacking. Perhaps intelligence tests are tried, and the result confirms our diagnosis. The engine is evidently there, but the dynamic force of the electric current is lacking. We fall back on the old way of saying that it is the child's own fault, but an emphatic statement of this fact gets us nowhere, either with the child or with the situation.

The question is, what is happening? What has become of the power that should be applied to running the machine? It is very evidently diverted to some other purpose. The simple fact that a thing cannot be in two places at once is applicable here. The compellingly operative dynamic force of the interest (the libido, life-energy) cannot be in the conscious and in the unconscious at the same time. Whatever is drained off into the unconscious in fantasy is diverted from conscious use. Our task becomes one of finding out what images are exercising a fascination and holding the interest below the level of conscious thought. The unconscious has a tremendous magnetic power, pulling down interests into itself, and when this interest is drawn down into the unconscious it takes on more and more primitive forms. It regresses to primitive fantasies. The child himself does not know what is happening. He simply becomes lost in a maze. I do not wish to be understood as implying that when this condition of mind occurs, we can assume that it is a sex difficulty that is causing the confusion, for it may have a very different cause, but that particular one operates frequently enough to warrant our investigating this condition. To give a typical case, a girl with this tendency toward listless abstraction told the following dream:

"I was lost in the woods. It was dark. I was wandering round and round. I met another girl. She was lost too. We wandered round and round till we met a bear. We killed him. I can't remember how, but I think with sticks and stones. We built a fire and roasted him, and he came out a baked potato."

The dream showed her own condition. She was lost, wandering round and round in a wood. She could find no guide who was not also lost, none but another child, wandering round and round as she was. The bear who came out a roast potato probably signifies her desire to dispose of her difficulties in some such simple manner. Perhaps it was a suggestion from her unconscious that the difficulty is more simple than she has supposed.

At the time of this dream her class was studying birds. The child in question did not seem interested in the special markings or the general features under discussion, but turned the birds upside down and looked under their tails. One day a Bible story was told. A question was asked the class. She raised her hand and remarked in a dreamy voice, apropos of nothing:

"My mother says being born is horrid."

It was not difficult to infer the buried interest of this child. A talk about the birds, eggs, and baby birds, given in class, and then a very frank talk about baby animals and human babies did not seem to be enough to clear the question. She had also to receive individual instruction given in a very clear and simple way.

It often surprises us that at the first telling of the truth the matter is not cleared up, because it is difficult for us to realize the compelling power of the fantasy and its persistence. It is as though an inner voice were telling the story over and over in its own way. The fantasy becomes the truth to the child, and its frequent repetition is as convincing as an oft-told tale. We know that if we tell a thing ten times one way and once another way, the repetitions will win out unless the single telling carries with it some impressing quality of conviction and satisfaction. We may therefore have to repeat our explanation several times.

With this child more damage was done because she was a child of deeply introverted type, and fantasy exercised compelling power. Her difficulty will not cease with this single clearing of the mystery. Her own inner world is too fascinating, and it will always be easier to take refuge in this world when the outer world is too hard or too uninteresting. A sympathetic relationship with an adult who understands and who is ready to meet the difficulty and to bring this fantasy thinking into line with the truth without ridicule or blame will keep open the door to the objective world. She must also be made increasingly to face her own responsibility in using this world of easy and undirected thinking as an escape from her job of living.

Here is a striking example of what I said at the beginning of this chapter about the importance of a true attitude; for it was found that this mother had told the facts of life as an unwelcome duty. The words the mother had spoken were carefully chosen but the child's whole attention had been so focused upon the manner that underlay the words that the only thing that had deeply impressed her was, "My mother says being born is horrid." The same story told by an adult who had a different attitude, and to whom the child had a real relationship of love and confidence, dissolved the sense of horrid mystery.

It is the power of mystery that makes a child with perverted or precociously developed sex knowledge such a danger to the class or to all members of a child group. Nowhere is the sense that knowledge is power more clearly shown in child life. Sometimes this form of power is used to compensate for a feeling of inferiority.

An adopted child who had been taken by the juvenile courts from a prostitute mother was after several years sent to a new school. She was in type an extraverted sensation intuitive with keen dramatic sense and love of the beautiful, but in her earliest years she had lived by her wits and she had little balance or concentration. In the new school she found herself at a great disadvantage. All the other children possessed many things that she did not. In classroom work and in social adaptation she found herself outshone. One thing she did possess, and that was perverted sex knowledge. On this subject she could speak with authority. The thing which was her greatest separation was also her source of power, and this power she used.

She had been dismissed from her first school because of having been found in the toilet with some boys, and for other misdemeanors of this sort, but it was believed that she had been long enough under the influences of her new home to have counteracted the early difficulties. She had a keen, vivid interest in beauty, poetry, music, color; she possessed also a warm outgoing nature; but as her difficulties increased, as she saw other children surpassing her, she clutched at something to give her back her sense of importance, and this knowledge was her power. Even the story of her birth she dramatized. When she found its thrilling effect she could not resist the temptation to go on to greater elaboration. It became impossible ever to leave her alone with other children. Much as she needed the development of such contacts, the danger was too great for the others.

Such a child is a menace to an entire class unless watched every moment, and even then she exerts a fascination. She had very real and deep interest in beautiful and worth-while things, and I believe that except for her desire to compensate for her sense of inferiority by using this knowledge she need not have been a harmful influence. We see this same motive at work in a less exaggerated form with many children who peddle sex knowledge.

There are many sex dreams that should be treated with extreme simplicity. A little girl of eight who had been told about babies everything that she seemed to wish to know, brought the following dream:

"I was out with the children having a party. Then we were all on the train going to Long Beach. Mademoiselle was there. J (a little boy with whom she had played that summer) was there too. He was running around naked. I took off my clothes and ran around naked too. The children laughed but I did not care. We ran naked. Then we were in the elevator in our apartment. We were going up to the roof to have ice cream. When we got up there we saw a great big sign, 'Private Property.' We could not go any farther. Mother stood in front of us and kept saying, 'Private Property! Private Property!' over and over till it made me laugh so that I woke up."

While she was telling the dream she turned with her back to me and then began talking nonsense. I asked simply:

"What would you like to know, M?"

"Nothing."

"Oh, yes, you see you wanted to see something on the roof, and thought you must not. Now you can know about that thing as well as about any others. What is it that you want to know?"

"I want to know how little boys are made different from little girls."

I told her quite simply and then, since she was fond of lovely statues, I advised her mother to take her to the museum some day soon and let her see a boy figure. It was not long after that she lost all interest in both dream and subject.

Sometimes a child who has not been told as much as he desires and who is too conscientious to seek information from underground sources will dream or fantasy the entire story either as it actually happens or in the form of some old myth. A young boy of about eleven was becoming inattentive, and failing in his work. He had plenty of ability, and this sudden difficulty seemed unaccountable. He was unwilling to talk about it, but we took a long walk and in the course of the afternoon when we were resting by the roadside he told me that he had dreamed that he saw a girl coming toward him and had run to meet her. She had pressed close to him, and then he dreamed the sexual intercourse. He had wakened with feelings of extreme physical discomfort, and the dream had been so vivid that he had a guilty feeling as if the act had been actual. From then on at intervals the recollection of this dream experience would come to him in class and not only would he feel its compelling power but also a wave of intense shame would sweep over him, and he would say to himself:

"If they (the boys and teachers) knew about this they would not have me in the class."

He would then become confused and could not follow the questions nor think of the subject matter. The mere telling of this broke the power of the fantasy and a very direct matter-of-fact talk took away the horror and the fascination. One thing that seemed to help him was to find that a boy could talk to a woman quite as naturally and simply as to a man. Often the difficulty is not a simple sex problem, it may be complicated by the whole trend of the child's conscious and unconscious life. Mingled with it may be fear of every sort, desire for undue attention, love of exciting others, and many other confusing things.

A girl twelve years old began to have seizures almost like epilepsy. She would grow pale, rigid, insensible; she would moan and show every sign of fear and pain. After these seizures she would be much confused and have violent headaches with the most severe pain in the back of her head. She had been under a doctor's care for some time, but the seizures had only increased. She was a very lonely child. Her mother had died, and her father was a very busy man who had to leave her much of the time with an ignorant servant. After a very short time she began to talk freely.

She had two great fears. One was that her mother whom she had loved dearly might be still in the ground. She had fantasies of her being lonely and crying out through the dark earth. The other fear was that she might be going to have a baby. She knew nothing of the sexual act, but had been told by a girl that women had awful pains before babies were born and now, at the beginning of her menstruation, she was having pains which seemed to her to correspond with the description which she had been given. She had made timid inquires and the girl, who felt her importance as the bearer of forbidden knowledge, had given gruesome details of how the pains got worse and worse, but had never informed her that they did not continue for several months. Each time that her menstruation began she tortured herself with the idea that she might be going to have a baby. She had also been told that a girl who had a baby was so wicked that no one would have anything to do with her, and she might just as well drown herself. The utter absurdity of this idea from the adult point of view had no influence upon its terrifically obsessing power.

She feared being left alone in the apartment. Her father was frequently away during the evening, and the servant went home directly after dinner. There were plenty of people in the house, but none near enough at hand to reassure her. When she had had a very bad turn her father would sometimes arrange to be at home or to have someone there. Then after the first seizure at school she received a great deal of attention which was unaccustomed and very welcome.

All these threads were woven into the fabric of the obsessing fear, and whenever their power became too great the child had a seizure or at the least a very violent pain in the back of her head and neck. She had not talked of her mother, for her father "did not seem to want to." At first we talked very simply of her mother and of all that they had done together. Then we spoke of the body as a garment for the spirit, one that had been outworn, and had no longer feeling or living force. Talking of her mother seemed to bring back her real and loving presence instead of the dead thing in the ground.

After this we talked of how she had been a part of her mother, of her conception. She had known that she grew in her mother, but that the seed from the father and from the mother had to be joined before the child could begin to be formed she had not been told. Now she wished to know it all, and I told her of the joining of the two cells of the parent fish, of the cat, of the dog, and how the same law operated in the human world. She wanted to know how the seed got into the mother, and when told she said with relief, "Then you couldn't just happen to have a baby."

I told her how it was arranged so that the coming of the child could be planned for, and when she asked me why it was wicked for a girl to have a baby when she was not married I told her because it was selfish to bring a little child into the world without a home and a father and mother to care for it. She had been greatly concerned to find a good home for her kitten if she went away to camp, and I asked her if she did not think that it was even more necessary for a baby to have a real home than for a kitten. Selfishness was always wicked, and that was why people must be careful not to have little babies without trying to have everything happy for them.

We talked of her own seizures, and I told her that I thought she had them because she was afraid of things that she had not been able to understand, and that now that she understood she must not be afraid and they need not come back. I talked to her, too, of her own responsibilities, and told her that sometimes people hid behind being sick without really meaning to. I spoke of the temptations of her loneliness, and of how easy it was to use the sickness in order to make people stay with her. This helped her to see that that was childish and insincere.

It was arranged that she should not be in the apartment in the evening alone, and that her father would talk with her about her mother, and would try to stay more with her. The seizures ceased, but, from what I have learned of her subsequent history, I fear that the father did not live up to his obligations of companionship and understanding. Though the special difficulty did not return and there was for a time a great gain, the child and the father drifted apart. He evaded life in many ways, and she was reported as evasive and a bad influence in another school to which she went the following year. In such a case as this there is always danger that the hysterical tendency will come out later in some new form, unless there is established a counteracting influence which can reach over a long period.

As the child grows older the form of sexual interest changes. It is no longer merely curiosity as to the beginning of life, or the question, "Where do babies come from?"—neither is it the secondary interest in those problems of human relationship shown in the lives of the adults. The interests shown in the usually unasked question, "What do my mother and father do to make babies?" or "What is it that my father does to my mother?" changes now to a much more personal problem. Curiosity is more and more replaced by a strange and growing personal desire or a still stranger and more mysterious impersonal urge of life itself. With the coming of adolescence, with all the bewildering demands of growing up, the desire to know gives way to the urge to experience, or sometimes to the *fear* of experiencing. There arises in the adolescent a need not merely to know the physical facts of sex, or even the physical facts plus the psychic facts of parenthood and love of children and home, but even more to understand this great change that is occurring in himself. What is this great hunger growing within him, what is its meaning, and its value for good or its power for evil in his own life? Shall it obtain gratification, and if so through what means may it be legitimately satisfied?

It has been noted that at this age certain changes are apt to take place in the dream content. At about twelve or thirteen years the terror dreams of girls increase while those of boys decrease. The dream of the robber and of being chased by a man (dreams which are common with both boys and girls at about seven or eight years) tend to increase with girls. At this time, too, girls often have dreams or fantasies of death, and religious dreams and fantasies in which the element of sacrifice enters. Boys' dreams tend to become more aggressive. Kimmins says that there are fewer dreams at this period, but I have not found such to be the case. In my own experience I have noticed a great increase in dream *repression*.

It is a period of extreme self-consciousness and of apprehension in regard to these psychic changes and dream retreats. If dreams are asked for as a classroom exercise or in a general conversational way, they are harder to obtain, and the child usually says that he does not dream. I have found, however, that wherever the rapport has been established and the child tells his dreams, this element is shown to be as active in the psychic life of the child at this time as at any other time. My explanation is that there is now a period of withdrawal. The child is bewildered by the dawning of new forms of consciousness, and the awakening of greater self-consciousness, and he either represses the new images arising from the unconscious, or else holds them as immensely important but secret things.

The cause of the diverging content of the dream at this time is quite plain in the ideas of submission which sex awakens in the girl and of mastery in the boy. Boys and girls both have terror dreams in which the force itself appears as overpowering to the ego.

In the boy the sex awakening takes an earlier and more definite form. He cannot reach the age of eighteen without having had to face sexuality in its crude state and to recognize its possibility of being a purely animal urge, the war between its spiritual and animal aspects is keener, and the physical and mystical aspects more clearly separated. With him there is a natural cleavage between sexuality and feeling.

In the girl sexuality is more masked, more closely connected with her real feeling. For her bodily and spiritual values are more closely knit, or (as is too often the case) more hopelessly confused. It is normal for her to find her expression of life through relationships, and her sexuality is a secondary form of expression. Yet in the girl, too, it exists in its crude form. Sex as a biological factor and sex as a psychic factor must be acknowledged and their place accepted in the life of both boy and girl. The two aspects must be recognized, and their values and their dangers understood.

Everything connected with sex has for so long been under a ban that we must be careful now not to fly to the other extreme and preach sexual indulgence as a cure for repression. Nothing can be controlled until it is accepted. If a young girl is taught to regard the existence of sexual desire as a sin, her whole conscious effort is to deny the existence of such a compromising thing in herself. Therefore perfectly natural sex attraction is misread into terms which can in no way injure her delicate susceptibilities. If she feels a strong sexual attraction toward a man not otherwise attractive to her she tricks out her attraction in a dress of womanly love, or when a strong sexual feeling emerges in a relationship already formed, she repudiates the entire connection for fear of the existing sex element. As the very real part that sex plays in the fusing together of two natures is unaccepted, so also is the very real lure of the crudely animal craving of sexuality ignored.

If a young girl could face her own sexuality and understand its rightful place in her relationships with men, there would be fewer tragic marriages. These are inevitable while she idealizes emotional excitement or covers it with a salvation fantasy of purifying and redeeming the man through the mystic quality of her love. Her real task is not to run away from any relationship simply because it contains sexuality, nor on the other hand to form relationships on that basis through translating emotional excitement into idealistic terms.

The boy's task does not lie in an effort to deny the existence of the purely physical aspects of sex, and to try to separate them from feeling values, but rather to learn to make a real connection between the two. Since his natural adaptations of life are not in the realm of feeling, his sexuality is more apt to be distinct from feeling and he must learn to find their connecting values in a love relation.

In dealing with the subject of sexuality, repression and

suppression must not be confused. Much in the civilized relationships of our lives must be suppressed and controlled. We must suppress and control all that runs counter to the highest good of civilization as well as to our own highest good as individuals. That is quite different from the repression into the unconscious of the thing which should instead be consciously acknowledged and controlled. To repress, that is to consciously deny the existence of, sexual impulses in ourselves only serves to force them down into the unconscious where they flourish and later emerge in surprising form and power. A boy who so represses all thought of sex may associate with women believing that he has no sexual urge, but suddenly he may be swept off his feet by a consuming desire which he may yield to in its crude form of passion, or he may confuse this yielding with love. On the other hand he may turn it into a sterile idealism which prevents him from forming proper relationships since he fears the necessary contact with reality.

No one of us can deal successfully with the problems of young people without admitting the sexual need as a real need, a human hunger. We must face the fact that we all have it, and that without its satisfaction we miss one vital part of our completion as human beings. We must also recognize that this hunger in civilized man is closely knit with the finer human relationships of love and companionship, and of home and responsibility. Stripped of these it becomes a barren affair. The human being who has found normal sex life has found one of life's values. If we fear it or see no way of having it our task is not to deny its value nor to repress our human desire for it but to face this lack as a part of our individual problem, to form such a relation if opportunity offers, and if not, to learn to use this energy in another way. Otherwise our repressions may return in the guise of hatred, narrow-mindedness, intolerance, unrelenting justice and revenge toward those who have not repressed. There is no judge so vindictive as he who is beset by his own unrecognized and unsatisfied desires.

With adolescence and post-adolescence there comes a greater need of becoming conscious of the collective forces that lie within each of us. The forms of early relationship that were suitable to the period of childhood have to be abandoned. The duty of knowing one's self becomes more imperative as the individual self begins to emerge.

This brings us to another great danger in the sex instruction of a young person: our own confusion in regard to its true value as a relationship expression. We all know that the sexual act is spiritually creative and vitalizing to the entire being when it is used as an expression of a deep reality of relationship as well as when it is used as a means of procreation. (I should perhaps qualify this by saying that we all know this unless we are ourselves under the sway of fears and repressions.)

In our discussions with young people, we still persist in representing it as beautiful *only* because it is an act of procreation, and we shy away from the discussion of its other aspects. In this way we tend to build up in the unconscious a feeling of guilt when it is used as an expression of love apart from childbearing. This may later on make the woman confuse frigidity with virtue in her marriage relationship, and make the man feel that he must find satisfaction for his lower nature outside of marriage, since seeking it in marriage is a violation of his wife. It may give to the woman an unconscious feeling of self-sacrifice in participating in the sexual act, so that instead of its being a joyous act of creative love for both man and woman it is to her a concession for which she has a right to demand payment—either the kind of payment received by the prostitute; or that more conventional marriage support; or, as often happens, an overpayment of devotion from the man, for which she makes no return in kind.

There is another danger with young people of today: sensing our fears and repressions they may decide that we know nothing whatever about life, and, in their desire to be more free than we, they may rush blindly into all such experiences mistaking them for the realities of life. We must hold clearly in our minds the fact that the value of sexual experience is in proportion to the depth of feeling that accompanies it. If the higher feeling values are established between man and woman, then sexuality becomes a heightening of the beauty of the relationship and a stimulus toward a fuller expression of the whole individual.

Sexuality must follow feeling, not feeling sexuality. Sexuality is therefore an asset, contributing to the vitalizing of the life force, or a liability which must be met at the cost of the higher self, in accordance with the attitude of the individual. It is of value in proportion to the strength and understanding and reality of the relationship—an understanding which must include a realization of what are its responsibilities, its human values in our conscious life, and its compulsive forces whose roots are in the unconscious.

When we have done our best in clearing our own minds and in helping the young person who is near to us, we must again and yet again remember the great and mysterious calls of life and of the irrational elements against the misuse of which the strongest bulwark is a fearless love of truth. Even our own child may be the one to be swept away. In this case we must stand ready to help him not to forget but to live through the experience so as to gain understanding. We cannot afford to forego the value of any experience which is accepted and understood. Through such understanding must come to each of us at some time in our lives a knowledge of the terrific powers of good and evil, and of that fire of the gods which either quickens or consumes.

In reckoning with these powers of the unconscious we must bear in mind all those collective images and archetypes which are a part of our psychic inheritance, and which are also a part of our collective social life. These forces from the collective mold us from without as well as from within. We bear within us the imprint of collective evolution. Whether we are, by personal creed, Christians or not, none of us can escape the deep impression that Christianity has made upon our psychology. We are unconsciously influenced, not only by all its spiritual quickenings, but also by all its mistakes. To understand these we must first understand the degree of sensuality in the Roman civilization, from which Christianity was such a liberation.

Christianity was a violent protest for the life of the spirit which had been engulfed in the most degraded sensuality. In the revolt the emphasis was carried to the other extreme. Perhaps the greatest wrong that the early Christian church did to humanity was this separation of the body from the spirit, dragging down the one in order to enhance the holiness of the other.

Christ preached no such doctrine. For him, "they shall become as one flesh." From the time of St. Paul, whose sexual neurosis became engrafted upon the body of the church, the cleavage between the spiritual and the "carnal" became ever greater, until it culminated in monasticism with its repudiation of life itself. St. Paul's fear of his own sexuality was the basis of his attitude toward women, and toward marriage as a concession to the lower man. "Wives, submit yourselves unto your husbands for this is the will of God concerning you," and the advice to men that "it is better to marry than to burn" have remained a stumbling block in the path of understanding. His fear became glorified, and so has remained a part of our collective psychology.

Our fear of the body swung over into an overemphasis of the importance of the body. Through this false attitude it became easier to forgive a sin against the spirit than a sin against the body. Conventional relationship "sanctified" by law was accepted even though in that relationship all the laws of the spirit (of love and human sympathy) were violated; or as an alternative a sterile, life-denying love was glorified. A violation of "bodily chastity" was punished by ostracism for the woman, or accepted as one of the carnal necessities for the man, without any reference to the quality of the feeling which caused it.

Space does not permit a discussion of the differences between masculine and feminine sexuality nor of the way in which these differences have influenced our collective attitudes. Deeper understanding of this subject is important for all of us who wish to face the changing attitudes of the present age.

Now that the pendulum has swung the other way we must build up a true attitude on the basis of an understanding of relationships, and of our unconscious impulses. This cannot be suddenly done. We cannot leave the building of a road until it is time to embark upon a journey and then expect to find safe and easy going. From earliest childhood this kind of sex education must be carried on.

The child who learns that he can get the thing that he cries for, the one who sees that when she is sick she will be the center of attention, and who knows that she will not only have mother's attention during the day but also father's special care in the evening, and who learns to use this power, is learning to make use of weakness in order to exert power in the name of love. So-called adult forms of love are often only a desire to possess the beloved object in order to satisfy a sense of personal need. Fainting and hysterics used to be a woman's power weapon over her husband. The germs of false relationships are laid in childhood, and only when we begin from the first to demand sincerity from the child shall we have the attitude that makes in later years for a genuinely adult understanding of a sex relation.

Our general attitude toward life and our attitude toward sexuality cannot be separated. We cannot choose where we will build strongly and where we will disregard, for all the threads interweave to make the human pattern. Emotions are far harder things to understand than algebra and geometry, yet we spend hours in elucidating mathematics and expect such a problem as that of human relationships to solve itself. The child with a power attitude toward his childish relationships will manifest this power desire in his sexual life later on. Insincerity and inability to face the truth in questions of daily conduct will result in inability to face the truth when he comes to deal with those forces within himself that go to make up his attitude toward sexuality.

Deep in our unconscious we still cling to the belief that only the acknowledged thing has power, therefore if we do not admit the existence of a thing even to our own conscious minds, that thing is to all practical purposes nonexistent. Some people, especially women, may go through life with unawakened sexuality and think themselves the gainers, but by just so much as they have remained unconscious of one of the great forces of life, by just that much have they failed to live, and by just that much is their power for understanding and usefulness in their human contacts curtailed. Children and young people feel instinctively this lack of understanding, and do not bring sex problems to an adult who has refused recognition of these forces within himself.

Once more when we come to the study of so-called perverted forms of childish sexuality we find ourselves involved in a study of the development of relationships. Premature sex relations which make themselves manifest in early childhood are usually due to an environment not suited to normal psychological development rather than to organic predisposition. Many of these perversions are due to the holding over of childish emotional content which should have been utilized at the proper time, and so have left the interest free for more adult adaptations. So much has been written on this subject both in support of Freud and in disagreement with him that I shall take these matters up briefly.

I have said that the first relationship that a child has is with himself, with his own body; here he finds his first toy. There are certain pleasure zones, certain sensitive parts which give him keener sensations when touched than do others. The genitals are especially responsive in this respect. At first they are not so apt to attract his attention as his toes. Fortunately for the baby no one has yet tried to find a sexual significance in a child playing with his toes, although the foot has been accepted as a phallic symbol.

He is interested in his fingers, in his toes, in all of his body. Frequently he discovers the genital region and contact there gives a different and more pleasurable sensation. Therefore, if he has once experienced the pleasure that comes from touching this region he is likely to continue it.

Sometimes very young infants have a habit of masturbation. Usually this habit disappears of itself. It can often be corrected by arranging the bedclothing so that it is difficult for the hands to come in contact with this part of the body. Later on, masturbation in some form (whether of rubbing with the hands or pressing these sensitive parts together or of various other movements of the legs) is apt to make its appearance.

We are wrong to consider masturbation as a single type of act, always carrying the same consequences. Its importance, like that of most other acts, depends upon its roots in motive both in the conscious and in the unconscious. It should not be unduly emphasized. The sense of guilt that comes from a reproof or punishment is far more injurious than the habit itself. The greatest danger from masturbation is that it tends to isolate the doer, either through providing him with a means of short-circuiting his emotions through self-satisfaction, or because the act calls up fantasies which tend to separate him from a world of reality. In the latter case he can find satisfaction without having to make genuine effort.

If a sense of guilt is attached to this act and the child is made to feel that in some strange way he has committed an unpardonable sin, he becomes immediately isolated by that sense of guilt. The consequent sense of inferiority separates him from his fellows; he is driven back into his fantasy world, and masturbates to call up the fantasy. With each return to the masturbation the sense of guilt is deepened, and so a vicious circle is formed, isolation and guilt constantly increasing. Yet the fascination also grows, for the fantasy exercises more and more compensatory power. The best way with a child of this type is to speak of the habit as unwise because of the sensitiveness of the organs, and then to try to find out the fantasy which is occupying the child's mind and to lead him back to reality contacts. Dwelling upon the masturbation, giving it undue importance, or attaching to it a sense of guilt, gives it increased power.

A young boy was brought to Jung. He was pale and fearful, his attention wandered, he had not been able to maintain the standards of any school. His parents had devoted themselves to a psychiatric pilgrimage in quest of help. Dr. Jung was the last resort. In the first fifteen minutes Jung had established a friendly human atmosphere in which the dark secret could be revealed, a secret in which the boy felt he was alone. He it was who had discovered the guilty secret of masturbation. This set him apart from all others of the human race. Dr. Jung smiled. "Well," he said, "what is so strange about that?" "But, Dr. Jung, you don't understand. I have to do it every night and then I feel so guilty, so alone." Dr. Jung put his hand on the boy's shoulder and smiled down at him. "Well," he asked, "if it makes you feel guilty to do it at night why don't you do it in the daytime?" The temple of darkness and of secret rites fell with a crash and let in the sunlight; and there, smiling at him, was a friendly world in which he was not alone. With that one question Jung had lifted the burden of solitary guilt from his shoulders, and with the lifting of the burden the obsessive desire for masturbation vanished and the psychiatric quest was over.*

With another type of child the sense of guilt leads to a repression of the act itself, but the feeling of horror which has been imparted makes the abstinence an almost obsessive idea. A little boy was brought to me for various mental tests. He gave me the impression of a person who talked continuously for fear he might betray his thoughts. In the word association tests he answered with great rapidity, paying little attention to the word given but saying the name of anything on which his eye lighted. Whenever such a word as *touching* or *rubbing* or *handling* was given the emotional confusion was so great that he could find no word—his mind went blank in a panic.

This child had been trained by an overconscientious mother never to touch the genitals. He did not know their function but had a deep fear of the guilt of such an act. Sometimes if his hand came in contact with the genitals he would ask anxiously, "Did I do anything wrong?"

In this case the real obsessive idea was the mother's fear of sexuality, which quite unconsciously found its expression in the careful overtraining of the boy. His unconscious caught all the fears which she did not intend to express, but with which her unconscious was filled, and the boy concentrated them all in his attitude toward masturbation.

Of primary importance was the mother's attitude. She

* Told the author by Dr. Jung and used by his permission.

had many repressions dating from early childhood. Her own mother had no real relation with her father, and during most of her girlhood the mother and father had been living virtually separated lives. The mother had lived fantasies of martyrdom and saintliness which had not prevented her from being in many ways a good mother and a useful person, and in other more important ways as maddening as a gadfly; but in the way most needed, in the way of preparing her daughter for her own adult relationships, she had failed because she had never solved her own problem.

The girl had suspected her father of relations with other women, and the mother, while never openly accusing him, had hinted at this as the cause of her unhappiness and had warned her daughter against "the animal nature in man." Her own sexual relations she had regarded as a concession to this necessary evil, and though in her conscious attitude she appreciated her husband's love she could not repress fears that her mother's unhappy history might be repeated in her own marriage.

When her boy was born she projected all these fears upon him and was determined to save him from growing up like her own father. She had to face the fact of her identification with her mother for whom she had a passionate attachment, understand that a full share of the responsibility lay with the mother who had, according to her own account, contracted a loveless marriage, and had never had the courage to face the consequences in the open.

Here the false attitude had reached out to clutch even the second generation, and this little boy was being made to suffer for the sins of his grandparents. In this case practically no time was spent on direct work with the child. When the mother's attitude changed the child obtained relief from the obsessive fears which were the chief factors in his neurosis.

In masturbation are bound up many fantasies of creation from the self. On the physical plane it is not only a short-circuiting of the emotional content, but sometimes a means of creating a feeling of self-sufficiency. Often it is used when a young person feels inadequate to perform some task which calls for all his forces, and at times the act has apparent value as a release of energy. It is, however, only a substitution for reality and for the truly adult attitude. The adult attitude could utilize this energy in a direct attack upon the difficulty that now demands the whole force of the libido.

When the habit persists into later life, or when an adult returns to it, there is indicated a regressive tendency of the libido which seeks a retreat in childish adaptation. Life is too lonely, or too hard, the task of forming adult relationships too difficult, or the demands of adult thinking are too taxing to the mind that loves to live in fantasy, so there is a return to the easy way of self-induced physical satisfaction or of fantasies which, called up by this method, provide a retreat from reality.

Another problem which many mothers and all teachers must at some time face is the problem of homosexuality. This word has come down to us so overweighted with sinister import that many of us are afraid of the mere sound of it. Its simple meaning, as we all know, is love of a member of the same sex. Its germs may blossom into friendship.

Often homosexuality is an overemphasis of a normal desire which has been thwarted in its attempt to find its true and natural expression. This causes a damming up of the emotional stream, the proper causeways are stopped up and the stream overflows in the wrong direction.

A young girl of fourteen was reported as moody, unsocial, slovenly in her schoolwork. She showed signs of nervous disturbance, jumping and starting when spoken to. She was often found in one of the empty classrooms and would show symptoms of guilt when found there which were out of proportion to the trivial nature of the offense. She was described as furtive and shifty, though there were no actual charges against her. She was fond of hovering around certain teachers, one especially, and this was described as "a sort of clumsy calf love." She had also been found caressing one of the children, and had appeared so confused that a suspicion was roused that something wrong was happening. At times, when she was asked a question she would blush, stammer, and become too confused to answer. The girl's manner when I met her was a mixture of fear and defiance. Quite early in the course of our conversation she found herself caught in an evasion which she knew that I had recognized. Her eyes were full of defiance. I put my hand gently over hers and said:

"I am sorry that you are afraid. Was it something that I said?"

She shook her head.

"Then was it something that came inside yourself? I

would be glad if you could tell me. I think I could help you, and you see I don't want you to be frightened, not by me nor by yourself."

Her answer was to throw her arms around me in a violent caress. There was something repellent in it, almost like the demonstration of a little animal, but there was also a revelation of a hunger that had to be appeased. One cannot criticize the table manners of a starving man who suddenly sees food. Here was some terrible flooding of the emotions that had been restrained by some evil means. It must be carefully met, but not turned back upon itself.

As we went on together she revealed to me a fantasy life that was to her both revolting and compelling. The thing that had come up when she had evaded my question was a sudden shifting of her interest to a distinctly homosexual fantasy about me. Such fantasies were a part of her daily thought life. The sudden realization that I had recognized this terrible inner being who filled her with fear, and that I could still be sympathetic broke the immediate power of that special fantasy and relief was sought in an emotional outburst. Usually the feeling content had found no outlet except in furtive ways or in a deepening of the fantasy. At first she had called up these fantasies in a mild form for the pleasure they gave her when she felt lonely or neglected, but now the fantasies called her up and took possession of her.

This is the terror of the unconscious—that we cannot measure the strength of the forces that we are calling up. If we give ourselves over to the images invoked the time may come when we shall be swept away by their mighty force. When the images from the unconscious can command us, then we have stepped across the threshold into insanity. This child had a growing terror of these fantasies and an ever-increasing sense of guilt because of their appearance, though she was of course unconscious of what it was that she really feared.

The first step was to separate her from the identification with the fantasy and to break the sense of guilt. To do this it was necessary to find out what had caused the life stream to turn in the wrong direction. Here again we came upon the parent-child problem, and the unsolved problem of the parent. It was the failure of the parents to face their own difficulties and to solve their own relationship which had acted so disastrously in the child.

The mother was an intensely ambitious woman who had through marriage annexed a gentle, lovable, rather ineffective man. She herself was unaware that it was her unconscious desire for power that had led her to "fall in love" with this easily dominated personality. Since she had identified with her own masculine adaptation to life the pull of her unconscious was all toward the apparently feminine qualities which he displayed. She had at first given all her energies to the task of trying to advance him in his profession, but since he had very little desire to advance and cared far more for the life of withdrawal, her attempts were not attended with success. Then contempt entered in.

It is not possible to give any of her inner processes, for she was unwilling to face them, but in her anger toward his "laziness" and toward the child for failure one could read much. Then, too, if one is trained to see these things one frequently catches figures from the unconscious peering through the mask of conscious personality. In this way, and from the revelations of the child's dreams where it was plainly shown that the problem had been intuited by her unconscious, it was possible to obtain material to warrant the drawing of conclusions. Since the child resembled the father far more than the mother and continually reminded her of him she projected much of her buried animosity upon the child.

The mother was a handsome, brilliant woman, in a hard sort of way, and the child adored her. She exerted a fascination over her and could reduce her to tears by her sarcasm, or fill her with emotional excitement by some careless caress. When the caress was returned she repulsed the child, making her feel as if she had committed some crime. She made fun also of the child's show of affection for the father, so that the child had a sense of guilt even at feeling affection for him. All the mother's libido had gone into power. Through this power she was compensating for what, to her, was the wrong done to her pride by the father's failure to obtain worldly success.

I do not mean that all this was done as crudely and openly as this brief statement would imply. Her acts were often masked under the guise of "trying to make the child amount to something." All bodily needs were scrupulously cared for. Food, exercise, care of teeth, dancing, were all provided. Material provisions were of the very best; but the one thing most needed, a loving understanding of the child's human needs, was lacking. The child was starving for love. Since she had never had the experience which should have come to her as a little child, she still craved the infantile forms that should have been lived through.

In making her relation to the analyst she had therefore to go through a most infantile stage of affection. Since she had repressed these desires from her conscious, linking them with a sense of guilt, the repressed emotions went down into the unconscious, and lived their life in regressive fantasy form. It is of interest to note that many of these fantasies took forms quite unimagined by her conscious. They rose unbidden as do dreams, and went their way undirected by her ego. She felt that she was responsible for them and yet that they were not hers. They were products of the collective unconscious, for the fantasy had retreated to deeper and deeper levels.

The saving factor in this case was the father. It was not possible to tell the mother anything of her daughter's fantasy life. She would have considered it a sign of sexual perversion and would have increased the child's sense of shame. The father, however, could, and did, face it with the child. It was not an ideal solution, for he was still compromising with life. He had not the strength to bring his own problem into the open with the mother, and even if he had done so he could not have accomplished much while she was unwilling to face herself. Through establishing a real relation with his daughter he gave her a reality in her feeling world besides the sense of reality which she received from the analyst.

She was old enough to have an intelligent attitude toward her own psychological task. To bring up the buried hatreds and to let in the light of the conscious upon the unconscious resentments took much courage. A strong transference reinforced her own strength and she made a very good adjustment. The fantasies ceased and she could use this released energy in the service of her conscious demands.

This was one of the cases where analysis cannot work the miracle of change in circumstance. The relationship with the mother, to which every child has a right, could not be established because of the mother's self-love. The girl's path to womanhood has not been an easy one. The dragons from the unconscious have at times returned in varying forms, but her progress has on the whole been steady. In this case homosexuality was clearly only a result of an unsolved normal relationship, a condition for which the child was not herself responsible.

I have given the case in detail because it shows how deeply buried are some motives and how far beyond the child's conscious control. In this child the escape from reality took the form of fantasy but, in a more aggressive type, the wounded and outraged feelings might have found their release in acts. Then the child would probably have been turned out of school and branded as a pervert. The influence of such a child is, we must admit, like a subtle poison in a collective group, but the guilt is that of the parents who refuse to face their own lives.

In every school, especially in boarding schools, this factor has to be reckoned with. There are several elements which enter here. The segregation of the sexes plays an important part, the relationship of the pupils to the teachers, and another very important but often ignored factor, the number of pupils who are in the school because they have no real relation with their parents. This is especially true of the younger pupils. There we always find a percentage who have been sent away from home because their parents found them in the way in their own lives, or were unable to make the proper relationship with them.

I remember meeting one of these mothers. She was looking tired and distraught, and she bleated, "Children are such a responsibility, don't you think so? The boys have just been home for the holidays and I find it such a strain to be a mother. Of course they are at boarding school in the winter, and at a fine boys' camp in the summer. You see I believe in companionship for young people, but I do try to give myself to them in the times in between, and with all the other things one has to keep up (one *mustn't* let one's own life go, you know), it really is a tremendous responsibility. It all comes to me. Their father is no use at all but then one must expect that being a mother." I have tried to put down her words exactly as I recall them.

Further conversation showed that the "responsibility of being a mother" involved giving a certain number of theater parties sandwiched in between her own, and letting them have friends for lunch, at which times she was frequently absent, and in propitiating the cook. Of times of real companionship there was no suggestion. With such a foundation for relationships would it be very surprising if the emotional element went astray when some violent attachment was felt for a chum or a master?

The boy and the girl who can find sufficient release in athletics and constant activity are in less danger from morbid fantasy, but they are open to all sorts of suggestion. My plea is that should we find children who have gone astray in these matters we should not render judgment upon the act, nor treat the symptom, but should investigate the underlying causes and place the responsibility where it belongs. This is frequently not with the child himself.

Before we condemn let us remember that neurosis is a result of maladaptation and does not mean inferiority any more than it implies superiority. It is a struggle between opposing forces of the personality. It is resolved when these warring forces make peace. This may be done by yielding to either of the opposing sides. A boy, therefore, who habitually masturbates and has no sense of guilt is not rendered neurotic, but he rarely seeks help. It is a harder task to change the adaptation of such a child because the existing one is found satisfactory.

In cases where the physical pull is unduly strong and the boy or girl is oversexed, we must help the young person to accept this fact as something for which he is not responsible, any more than he is responsible for the color of his hair or for being born with blue or brown eyes. The problem is to recognize the physical condition and consciously to reckon upon its influence.

A girl who is oversexed and who is consequently disturbed by physical sensation is especially apt to feel a sense of humiliation or inferiority. This tends to separate her from life. She should be helped to see it as a handicap for which she is in no wise responsible, but also as a danger since she has the ever-present temptation to misread physical excitement into terms of love. Such girls frequently masturbate, and if the practice is only occasional it should be treated casually.

The question of homosexuality in schools leads us to the consideration of the emotional life of the teacher. The greatest safeguard which a teacher can have is a well-balanced emotional life of his own. Again I would repeat we cannot give from poverty, but only from wealth. A teacher who is emotionally starved is reaching out to be fed, and this reaching out often takes the form of a great unconscious urge. As a jellyfish sends out its tentacles so the unconscious sends out little invisible tendrils to catch and hold the thing for which it craves. The child should not feed the teacher, but the teacher the child. Yet often teachers who have no life of their own outside the school make their love of the children a possessive thing. The crushes of adolescents are often called into being by the teacher's unconscious desire for love and admiration. For a teacher to have the love of the children is a tremendous asset, but it is not enough that we should be able to inspire love, we must know what to do with it when we get it.

Analysts know that it is a great problem to understand how to receive the transference: that is, how to accept and direct the emotional stream which is pulled up from the unconscious in this intimate personal relationship which must have for its foundation the love and trust of the patient—a love and trust which will carry him through the maelstrom of the unconscious and give him courage to face the thing that he most fears in himself. A strong love is needed. Much of this love does not belong to the analyst personally, for the very circumstances of the analysis often do not permit the forming of such a personal relationship. Nevertheless the reality of the feeling must be respected; it must be received and made a valuable asset in the working out of the problem of the patient. To repudiate love only turns it back upon the giver, and the emotion is apt to retreat to the unconscious.

So a teacher cannot repudiate the love of a child. She must receive and direct it. That is one of the responsibilities that her position forces upon her whether she likes it or not. There are teachers who with an unconscious love of power find satisfaction in stimulating the love of a child, and then feel at liberty to repudiate the affection. Of one such teacher I heard it said, "Many of the girls adore her but she won't have any crushes; there is no danger of anything of that kind with her." As a matter of fact the danger with her was twofold, both in the type of love inspired and in the fact that it was frequently turned back upon the giver, so calling up feelings of humiliation and hatred and rendering harmful that which should have been turned to good account.

The woman herself had never outgrown certain adolescent attitudes. She had never accepted the fact of middle age nor arrived at its maturity of outlook. The adoration of certain girls administered to her vanity, to her sense of being young, but she permitted it only when its expression did not bore her. Her love was not called out by the child's need. In such cases waves of unused emotion are apt to sweep through a group and lead to undue sexual interest or homosexual manifestations.

There are emotionally starved people who try to blind themselves to their own lack of personal life by an overbalanced attitude of conscious service. Sometimes a life which denies the emotions is chosen, quite deliberately, but then the unconscious has its revenge through growing bitterness and narrow-minded intolerance. It is this which makes the unsatisfied older person such a dangerous guide and companion for the young. If one awakens too late to a sense of life's values, and there is a feeling of futility and hopeless loss, the conscious attitude will often seek compensation through unconscious envy, and a desire to destroy the thing that is no longer attainable.

Since so much of the real education of young people comes from relationships it would be well if we could have teachers with more experience of life even if it meant less intellectual attainment. A plea might be put in here for summer living instead of summer school, and for such material recompense as will attract a live teacher with a fair method rather than a dead teacher with a method irreproachably modern.

Let us try to look behind existing sex manifestations to the underlying conditions of relationship, and to the inner attitude toward life, and not attempt to consider sexual difficulties as things in themselves, apart from the whole psychological attitude.

11

DREAMS

The dream world is very real to the child. In fact, the events of the dream are often even clearer than those of the hours of daylight. And yet we cannot submit the child's dream to the same type of analytic treatment that we use in the analysis of the dream of the adult. With the child, there is always danger that premature interpretation will either put upon him burdens that are not his own, or else that even greater danger, that we will, in our clumsy efforts to understand the child, injure the mysterious process by which the dream is living itself out in his psyche and silently effecting its own power of transformation. Let us therefore be willing to do too little, rather than too much, and to treat the dream reverently as a gift that the child has given us, rather than as an object to be dissected, or even vivisected, in the interests of our own attempts at scientific classification, so adding to our own understanding at the expense of the child.

We must also remember that the dream *belongs to the dreamer*. It is not, from earliest childhood, to be submitted to our "scientific interest" or desire for classification. What is the attitude of this particular child in relation to this special dream, and what is the reason for confiding it to us? Does it deal with problems not his own? Is it part of his own immediate problem of growing up?

We already have discussed dreams that arise from intuitions of the unsolved, and consciously unknown, problems of the parents or their surrogates. To analyze these childhood dreams as we would those of adults would only fasten the burdens of the parents upon the psyche of the child. Such dreams (see Chapters 2 and 3) really belong to the parents. But there is another type of childhood dream that must not be submitted to the analytic process but left to work out its life of transformation within the child's psyche. These are the Great Dreams that spring from the depth of the psyche, where archetypal images move, and through such dreams, if they are left in reverent admission of their numinous quality, the child becomes aware of unknown and unknowable truths of the soul.

Such a dream came to a three-year-old child and lived on in the psyche of an old, old woman until it blossomed into a faith by which, in her old age, she lived; a faith in life itself, to which she sought to give testimony. She did not tell the dream; she knew that her life must be a revelation of its truth if she would give testimony to its reality, if it were to live.

Sometimes the first remembered dream retains this numinous quality throughout long years. To an old, old woman the dream which came to her at the age of three retained the numinosity of mystery and of unknown and unknowable truth.

The dream journey was long. All the details are forgotten. Only the final picture remains clear. "I am in a high meadow, unknown yet strangely familiar. In its center is Behemoth: huge, terrifying, evil. By his side, unafraid and rooted in its own serenity, is a single bluet, that smallest flower of meadow or woodland, tiny, fragile, perfect in its four-petaled innocence."

I am sure that I made no interpretation of the dream, certainly no identification with the fragile flower. I already knew bluets, Quaker ladies, we called them. I had seen them carpeting a meadow or a woodland clearing, but I had never seen one growing in solitary and self-assured rootedness. Yet again and again the image returned to me when I woke in night's darkness and the four-petaled flower became associated with the pinpoint of light (the night light) that was always there. Was it my first unrecognized experience of "the smaller than the small, that is greater than the great?" The image has companioned me throughout the years and the smallest of small flowers is rooted in the garden of my heart.

Nor do I recall whence the image of Behemoth arose. Was a copy of Blake's visions already in the house? I was certainly familiar with the picture of Behemoth and also of Leviathan. In the dream the image was definitely Behe-

moth. Perhaps that was because the word Leviathan had a
musical sound, whereas the word Behemoth was bumpy
and intrusive and evil in its very clumsiness. Behemoth
and the Quaker lady lie together in that high meadow of
truth where the soul is pastured. And so they will exist
side by side until "the day breaks and the shadows flee
away."

An attempt at interpretation of such a dream by one to
whom the dream is entrusted may destroy the inviolate
mystery of the experience. To share a mystery with one
who knows the reality of the inner world is to reaffirm its
power and also to impart to the sharer an increased sense
of love and trust. Remember the dream fabric is not only
strong but fragile as fine-blown crystal. Do not let a
clumsy breath destroy it, for with its destruction all lines
of communication between you and the child will be forever destroyed.*

Such a dream as Behemoth and the smallest bluet
rooted in its own serenity lives on in the soul of the child
and its message, like the message of all great dreams,
deepens with the passing years, though its numinous mystery remains insoluble. The problem of good and evil
which has occupied minds of theologians and philosophers cannot be solved by a three-year-old child but its
eternal quality can be experienced. Its truth can be lived
and, slowly, its meaning is confirmed by life itself. This is
the fragile yet indestructible flower that blossoms in the
soul of man and was not destroyed by the Behemoth of
the concentration camp but only transplanted by the exter-
mination of the gas chamber.

And to the child become an old, old woman who still
held the dream in remembrance, it became a symbol of
the faith by which she lived. It was a truth so far beyond
the personal that she did not question whether she could,
herself, endure the torments of the concentration camp—
that, thank God, was not her destiny; but she could in her
own life nurture the faith in the indestructible power of

_____

* To children still poised between the worlds of inner and outer
realities, dreams are more than events of the daylight world. Two
sisters, five and three-and-a-half years old, used to wake early and
tell their dreams. One morning the three-and-a-half-year-old said: "I
don't need to tell you my dream, for you were in it, so you already
know." "But it was *your* dream, I was in my own. I don't know
anything about yours till you tell me." "But you were *there*. I saw
you with my own eyes." As the argument continued, the small child
burst into tears. "Stop teasing me. You were *there*. I saw you plain
as I see you this minute. You are making fun of me."

the good within the soul that, in spite of chaos and disorder, is still rooted in the high meadowland of truth. She could also search out this flower in every human heart and nurture it in all the unlikely places where frail humanity might transport it.

These childhood dreams are not so rare as our rational mindedness would have us believe. In *The Inner World of Choice,* especially in the chapter on "Childhood and the Friend of Choice," a number of these dreams are given. The dream of the golden baby with a silver star in the middle of his forehead came to a very young child and companioned her over many years as she again and again faced the recurrent problem of rescuing her own essential value from the dragon of regression.

The blue starfish appeared "with the eye in the middle of him who saw the 'me-myself' "—that is, herself as she really was with all her good and her evil, her potentials that were still only possibilities. These she must, in spite of her resistances, face and do the best she could about them, and acting upon the dream, she took the starfish home.

The childhood dedication of the boy on the lonely road who perceived the north star as *his* star that he must follow; the blue flower that must be sought in the high place; all these lived on in the souls of the children to whom they were vouchsafed. Many of these dreams were known to me at the time I first wrote this book, but their power of survival was not known to me then; now after forty years I can bear witness to their abiding power of transformation within the human spirit.

And there are other frequently recurrent terror dreams that show the ominous forces confronting even a very young child—forces that he must face and understand before he can live freely in his adult life.

A man wakes in the clutches of nameless fear. In his sleep he has been running, running across an endless desolate plain. In sharp memory he is back in the room where he slept until he was five years old. He is also back in a recurrent childhood dream that first made darkness a region of terror and dread.*

My mother is the moon; she is a huge funnel. She is chasing me across a great empty space to suck me in; I run and run, faster, faster, but always she is just

* The moon-funnel mother dream is from the author's *The Inner World of Choice,* pp. 111–12.

behind me. I come to the edge of the world and jump off. I am falling down, down into darkness. While I am falling, I wake in terror.

The mother *is* the moon, ruler of night with its luminous magic and its dark withdrawals. The moon in its negative aspect is the land of dead souls. This moon mother *is* the funnel whose insucking breath tries to draw the child back into death in the darkness of her womb of night.

Running was the necessity for this man, whose recurrent dream began when he was three; he was twenty now. I had taken a house for the summer. It was about an hour's drive from New York, and I had asked him to spend as much time there as he cared to. He had come into my life in a strange way—a legacy, almost, from a loved friend who had died on the very night I had promised to accept this young man in my life. I knew his instability, his fears, I even knew the dream that had haunted him.

He drove me up, the first day that I spent in the house in the country. He was restless, edgy, ill-at-ease. In the afternoon he said, "I am going to the village to get a paper. Is there anything I can get for you?" I mentioned some small item and said, "My purse is upstairs, get what you want from it." (I had brought $125 for preliminary expenses.)

When he came back he threw the open purse between us. It was empty. "I got some things that I wanted," he said. "They are on the kitchen table—caviar, pâté with truffles, and other things. You will find them there. I also got a bottle of whiskey. I want a drink tonight."

"Be still; very, very still; something you do not understand is happening," my inner voice told me. At that moment I felt we were not alone. A presence had entered and stood, sinister and silent; waiting—waiting.

Aloud I said, "What would you like with your drink, caviar or pâté? Shall we have dinner in here?" (I had brought food from New York.) I made no comment as we put away the things that he had bought. I do not remember the evening—does it matter? The next morning he left early for New York. He had waked, he said, remembering the house where he had first dreamed his recurrent dream—that now far-away house from which they had moved when he was only three.

He came back that Friday. A roll of bills was in his hand.

"You understood," he said. "I had to do what I did. The night before we came, I dreamed the dream and woke feeling that you were now the moon-funnel mother. The dream, coming back that night, seemed a proof. I had to defy you. Money was one of the things she used against me. If she sent me to the store with a dime, she accused me of short-changing her and stealing a penny, and beat me up. I had to defy her. I had to spend all the money in defiance of the image that I thought the dream had put upon you. I was so tired, so tired of running. I had to stand still and defy her. And then you refused the image; you broke the spell and I was free."

The moon-funnel mother had gone and taken the dream with her. He never dreamed that dream again.

I do not mean that this single incident miraculously solved his problems. Childhood wounds are too deep for such a miracle. But the incident set him free to face them. It was a long and difficult way that lay before him. But it was, at least, his own.

With the adult we can analyze the dream and through the dreamer's associations arrive at the understanding of the dream symbols. This method can be used with a child only in certain instances and then with greatest care. As is shown in an early chapter, many of the child's problems are the intuited problems of the adults by whom he is surrounded. The dream shows these problems which should be considered in helping him but which should not be raised for his own conscious consideration since the responsibility for their solution is not his.

D. H. Lawrence describes this in *The Rainbow*, concerning the child Anna:

> Anna's soul was put at peace between them: She looked from one to the other, and she saw them established to her safety, and she was free. She played between the pillar of fire and the pillar of cloud in confidence, having the assurance on her right hand and the assurance on her left. She was no longer called upon to uphold with her childish might the broken end of the arch. Her father and mother now met to the span of the heavens, and she, the child, was free to play in the space beneath, between.*

* As used by Dr. Edith Wallace in *Childhood Dreams: A Door to the Past and a Message to the Future*, reprinted from International Monographs on Child Psychiatry by the Pergamon Press, New York, 1964.

If trust in the parents is established, the child is free to play under the rainbow arch.

The security of childhood lies in *trust*. Where the parents are living their own lives, the child can live hers.

The picture which is so vividly presented in a dream is frequently not one which we can discuss directly with the child. The person who holds the father or mother image has a tremendous influence on the unconscious of the child and the form of this influence is often shown by the character of the dream. Where we cannot analyze the dream with the child we must take up the problem with the adult who holds the power over the situation.

If the child himself is conscious of some great difficulty of adjustment, a dream may be interpreted as a self-made fairy tale illustrating his conflict between regressive desire and the more adult acceptance of his task, but we should be careful always to do too little instead of too much in this dealing with unconscious material. We must never vivisect the mental life of the child for the sake of verifying our own deductions. If we cannot get a simple statement of the problem from the child or verify our deductions through the analysis of the adult involved, then we must be content to go without the desired knowledge.

We must, therefore, be content to go slowly, to amass material in indirect or other natural ways, and gradually to sift our evidence as connections come to light of themselves, drawn up by the bulk of the evidence.

The choice of the way lies with the conscious. The unconscious merely presents the problem, pulls it up into the light so that it may be examined. The acceptance of the task and the choice of the new way to be followed lie in the conscious. Analysis, therefore, does not solve our problems but merely presents them for our inspection. If we prefer to remain childish, swayed by insincere and unworthy motives, we have the choice and may do so, but most of us desire the more adult way when once we see it, though we may trick ourselves over and over. The dream shows the problem, sometimes in a very veiled and fantastic way, sometimes with a vividness or humor of almost unbelievable clarity.

The dreams of children seem to be singularly vivid and simple. As a whole, they have fewer confusing details. They have often a naïveté in the way in which they hand out a secret. The dreams of rather infantile adults have the same pictorial quality. Some patients present dreams which tell the story humorously in a few clear strokes

without being at all aware of how graphically their unconscious is presenting their hidden reactions, resistances, or
infantile emotions. Such dreams have the truth-telling
quality of a fable. With very neurotic children there is
often a greater intricacy of detail, as is also true with
post-adolescents. There is such a wealth of imagery and
such frequent beauty of detail in the child's dream that we
cannot doubt that in the unconscious lies stored up for
him a vast accumulation of that precious material from
which poetry and painting have been born. Very interesting
work remains to be done in helping the child to make use
of this myth-making material which lies within himself.

The real value of the dream lies in its relation to the
conscious of the dreamer and its bearing on the problem
which he is facing at a particular time. No matter how
well-substantiated a theory we may have formed in regard
to types of dreams we must be prepared to abandon it at
the first hint of its unsuitability in any individual case. We
cannot force our own interpretation upon the dreamer.
The unconscious is a cunning and skillful craftsman selecting just the symbol needed for the individual at the special
time, but the value of the symbol is not a fixed and definite thing in itself. It lies in the relation of the symbol to
the dreamer.

Since, as we have said elsewhere, the psychic life of the
child is so closely linked with that of the parent, it is often
difficult to distinguish whether a dream is really a portrayal of his own psychological condition or a picture of
an intuited parental problem. Often the dream shows the
failure of the parent and not that of the child. So keen are
these intuitions of the unconscious that the dream may be a
mirror of the parental unconscious. Jung told of a case
where he analyzed a man who had great difficulty in making conscious his psychological problems. He did not see
below the surface of things nor did he dream. His little son
had a very strong relationship with him. So complete was
this psychic identification that the child dreamed the father's problems, and the parent's analysis was conducted at
one time through the child's dreams.

The following are a few instances of such dreams:

"I was sitting on the floor playing with my mother. We
were both playing with toys. My mother had on a little
girl's dress. Then the door opened and a great beast came
in."

This portrayal was uncanny in its vividness. The mother
was, metaphorically, playing with toys. She had never

made an adult adaptation to life. The relationship with her husband was breaking and the security of the home threatened because she really wished to be treated, not as a wife and comrade sharing the responsibilities, but as the favorite child. Her own little girl was a sort of doll to be petted and played with when it suited her but thrust aside when she became interested in other things. This childish attitude on the part of the mother opened the door to the beast who might devour the security of the home.

An older patient told of a dream which, in varying forms, had haunted her childhood. She had a recurring terror dream of meeting a woman who had big feet like a man. The first time that she remembered the dream was when she was about seven years old and the details were not clear, but as nearly as she could recall it she was going berrying and saw, in the field, a woman who was also getting berries. She was going to speak to her when she noticed that she wore a very long dress and from beneath the skirt protruded the very large feet of a man. She was terrified and woke shrieking. After that, at more or less regular intervals, she would dream of a woman who had the feet of a man. She did not remember anything else that terrified her in the dreams but even as an adult she felt a curious sense of panic when she saw a woman with unusually big feet.

In her associations she recalled the phrase "putting one's foot down" though she did not remember having heard her own mother use it. The mother was an extremely masculine type with a strong will-to-power. The whole household stood in awe of her. She spoke of her father, of whom she was indulgently fond, as unobtrusive. "I remember," she said, "that whenever there was an argument he would just seem to melt away." All the children were more or less neurotic and unable to break away into independent life. It is not necessary to elaborate the dream symbolism as it was revealed in all the associations, but clearly the terror was of the overmasculine mother who could not control her own power devils.

A terror dream told by a ten-year-old girl clearly shows the family problem.

"My mother and I were in the apartment and we heard a great noise in the hall. We ran out and found the hall full of rough men. They were throwing all the women and children out of the window. One dreadful-looking man came for me. Mother begged them not to throw me out. Then one said to let me go. I ran downstairs and the street was full of women and children lying all in heaps where they had been thrown out of the window."

The father and mother were separated. The father had injured the family by dishonorable acts. He appeared at the home occasionally and both the child and the mother dreaded him. The child looked to the mother for care and protection as is shown in the dream. Also her fear of men was here clearly portrayed. But she had projected the acts of the father upon all men. It was necessary that the mother should separate her personal problem, her mistake in choice of a husband, from the general problem of man's relation to his family. The child must, with the mother, courageously face the fact that it was as an individual that the father had failed. If the psychological causes for this failure could be found and made clear, so much the better, but in any case the father's act must not remain in her mind as representative of the masculine character, otherwise she would be unable later on to form any true relationship with a man and her life would be overshadowed by fear and distrust.

Here is one of the situations that must be faced in the open. The unpleasant truth must be acknowledged and the sin of the father discussed as his individual failure and not as something to be hidden. If it is not faced it may remain in the unconscious of the child, there to become a father imago which will be a standard for the child in her judgment of all other men. The problem must always remain a problem, but in the light of its conscious acceptance it has not half the menace that it was when left in the dark of the unconscious. If the child can make a father transference to some other relative, or to a friend, or teacher, this may furnish the solution.

Often with the death of the father or in case of separation, either actual physical separation or a spiritual separation of the parents, the mother makes too great demands upon the emotional nature of the child and threatens its individual development. In such a case the child is in danger of being devoured, swallowed up by love. In one such case a mother lavished devotion and demonstrative affection upon the youngest child. She could not leave her for even an hour or two without coming back three or four times to kiss her and assure her of her love. The child dreamed: "I was out in the street in a big city and there were lots of bears and they were all chasing ladies, and a little bear came up to me and when he said that his name was 'Mama,' I was so frightened that I woke right up."

The humor of the unconscious is illustrated in this dream, for the mother looks like a gentle and humorous little bear. The child is continually dreaming of little bears.

These intuitions of situations are not always confined to the important family problems but sometimes are amusing illustrations of how the undercurrent is sensed by the child's unconscious. When these are intuitions of passing events which are not of great moment to the child they do not rouse any emotional reactions of fear or apprehension. In such instances I have found that the child had a good feeling rapport with the person involved in the situation.

At one time the principal of a school came several times to visit a special grade. She was quite frankly there for the purpose of seeing how certain scholastic results could be more efficiently obtained. Though there was no conscious change in the teacher's manner with the class nor any attempt to limit their usual freedom nor to change any part of the usual program, the teacher felt the undercurrent of strain. A child who was very fond of her announced one day:

"I had such a funny dream. I dreamed that we were in school and a funny little man was there all the time. You made us sit with our legs straight out in the air till we were so tired. You made us, Miss X."

Since the atmosphere of that room was very free and happy and the children ordinarily felt no restraint the child was struck by the absurdity of the situation. She had of course felt all the strain of that special situation which Miss X was trying not to let appear in her conscious attitude. Was the "funny little man" the animus of the principal who came to criticize?

In another instance a teacher who was especially loved by the children encountered the wrath of a parent who insisted that her child, a little ten-year-old of very slow mentality who had been injured in her proper adaptations by constant pushing at home, should be rated as a "bright child" and recommended for advancement in a type of work for which she was not fitted. There had been several stormy encounters with efforts to carry the matter to higher authorities. When the term reports were ready for mailing this teacher said to a colleague with a good deal of anxiety, "When Mildred's report reaches home I see my end." The children were not present when the remark was made but the next day one of them said, "What do you suppose I dreamed last night? That Miss A was killed in Mildred's house."

These are only amusing little incidents but they do show how the unconscious of the child registers the unspoken difficulties of those with whom he has a relationship.

A dream carrying a much greater affect was the following: "I was out in a boat, way out in the middle of the ocean. Then the boat turned over and I went down and down." In this case the child had everything that love of the two parents could give him but the mother had not found her own adjustment to life. She was haunted by vague fears, and had a sense of insecurity. She was often full of apprehension which she could not formulate but which undermined her coveted contentment. These unfaced fears, which rose from the sea of her own unconscious, were registered also by the unconscious of the favorite child.

Where the affect is very great we may consider that the dream has special significance. This significance is usually a purely psychological one, not a prophetic one. Sometimes a dream, apparently most trivial and commonplace, will intrude insistently upon the waking consciousness. We can then be quite sure that it deals with something of true importance for the dreamer.

Often problems interlock and the dream which quite clearly states the child's problem also gives that of the parent; sometimes in a process of identification the child repeats in his own life the problem of the parent.

There are frequently dreams that simply, and often humorously, illustrate the child's immediate problem. Such a dream may be discussed with the child as a self-made fairy tale with its own little special moral made for his own little special self. To illustrate; a little girl of eight told the following dream:

"I was walking with my mother and I saw a little ball and I started to pick it up, and my mother didn't seem to think I could but I did and I started to pick it right up but it grew and grew and it popped out all over my hands and I got mad and dropped it and then it got small and I went to pick it up and it got big and then I was mad and went away."

This is an amusingly clear statement of her own problem in connection with any task. She flies at it without much thought or any regard to advice; she is quite sure she needs no explanation of any difficulty before beginning; she has tremendous self-confidence in her approach but at the first difficulty is impatient. Then the task begins to look impossibly hard; she drops the ball, perhaps a little

encouragement makes it seem small again; but another difficulty appears and she "gets mad and walks away." Her
attitude is always that it is the fault of the task, not her
own fault. That is to say, the ball has grown big, it has
played an unfair trick. She does not look at her own responsibility in the matter. This child is a delightfully humorous and friendly little extraverted intuitive. She was
quite capable, not only of understanding and enjoying the
dream, but also of applying it. She had a sufficiently
friendly relationship to make the little joke between us a
cordial bond, not an impertinence on my part; so, when
the dream had been explained and she had discussed it
with a good deal of intelligent interest, it was possible
thereafter when the quick, impatient discouragement appeared to say, "My, how that horrid ball is growing!" or if
there were others about, to merely give a friendly smile
and make a ball of my hands, whereupon there would be
a little grin in response, and a new attack. I do not mean
that this dream magically obviated the difficulties, but it
did help in raising and facing the problem.

Sometimes in these dreams which deal with the immediate problem a part can be discussed with the child and the
rest must be taken up with the parent. The following is an
illustration of such a dream:

"I had a little pony all my own and I rode on it all
alone where I wanted to, and I went to my grandmother's
house in B and it seemed very nice, but when I got there
the garden was all full of buffaloes and I thought I would
climb a tree away from them. But great big elephants
flew right out of the trees and I woke up all frightened."

This child had an insecure relationship with her mother
for which she compensated by an attitude of cocksureness
and obstinacy. She was very anxious to go her own way
and was resentful of criticism. She also had fears that
seemed to come upon her suddenly, and night terrors. She
had a very strong relationship with her grandmother
whose "baby" she was. Here the horse is her libido, it is
her own way. She rides it all alone and where she wishes
to. There, quite clearly, is her own attitude in her conscious life. She wants to go her own way alone. So far as
adult control is concerned, she wants no help nor interference. She is, however, very infantile in her independence,
she is not ready yet for the way that she demands. Her
horse, therefore, takes her back to the grandmother where
she can exercise the authority in the most infantile form.
This, in the dream, "seemed very nice at first," as it does

to her in real life. But it is a regressive way back to her babyhood, hence come the beasts that beset her path. She makes efforts to get away from them; that is, instead of trying to conquer her difficulties she tries to get into some other place where she will not have to meet them, she climbs a tree off the solid ground. But this, too, is unsuccessful, in fact it is even more disastrous for "great big elephants fly right out of the trees" and she awakes "all frightened."

In this dream the child's own part of the problem is clearly stated. She must not only try to conquer her own difficulties but she must be willing to accept the guidance of those who know the way better than she does. Her little pony cannot yet go his own way all alone. If he does there will be strange and unnatural beasts to be encountered. It is nice to go back and be a baby at grandmother's, and at the same time to have her own way, but she is too big a girl to take that baby way of seeming grown up. She cannot get away by pretending. That only makes the beasts grow bigger.

The other part of this dream belongs to the mother. Clearly the child needs a surer relationship with her. The retreat to the grandmother is not only an actual fact, but it indicates also a regression into the too infantile attitude. In many dreams the grandmother symbolizes this retreat. Where the child makes this type of relationship with the grandparent it carries still greater weight in the unconscious and results in an identification that is even harder to break than the parent-child identification. In this case the grandmother had been overindulgent but the mother had demanded too much. In her efforts to keep the child from being spoiled she had been overstern. There had not been a deep enough bond of comradeship and understanding. The child questioned every step of the way, not only in this matter of authority but also in matters of information. She was impatient of explanations even when her own questions indicated a real desire to know and understand. Often these questions were irritating and made demands on time and patience, yet they could not be brushed aside. They had to be dealt with, and a discrimination made as to their values. The confidence and trust needed to be strengthened in the mother-child relationship. The dream therefore belongs to both the parent and the child. For each is a new way indicated.

A child who was overcome by fears, who was failing in

her schoolwork, especially in all group work, brought the following dream:

"I climbed a tree and went out on a limb. It seemed all right but I kept feeling funny as though it were rotten, you know. Then I got way out on the point and it broke and I dropped down, but I dropped right into water, and my head was way down; and I came up and there was a great fish who said, 'This is my ocean,' and I was frightened and tried to get to land and I woke up."

She was an only child whose mother married late and had feared that she would never have children. Her whole life was bound up in this child. From the time of her birth she watched over every moment and even worried all the time she was in school. The child had no confidence in herself and the slightest criticism was enough to make her so nervous that she was almost unable to work. She was the embodiment of her mother's fears. This dream shows the insecurity of her own attitudes and the fear of being swallowed by the mother.

Analyzing the dream with the mother made her see how the child's life was being undermined by the overcautious atmosphere by which she was surrounded. A change in the mother produced an entirely new attitude in the child. The fears decreased rapidly until a spirit of almost tomboy venturesomeness set in as a reaction from the old timidity. The schoolwork also improved steadily.

There come to children and to adults as well dreams that are undeniably important messages from the collective unconscious. So little material of this sort is available that it is difficult to draw conclusions, but many dreams present striking mythological symbols, or repeat experiences that are tribal primitive rites which have great significance for the individual yet which are completely unknown to his conscious. Also at a time of very great significance when a decision must be made or a crisis is approaching, such dreams rise out of the collective. Jung has said, "When the way of life forks before us and we are confronted with the necessity of choosing irrevocably, and also in moments of great danger these superhuman figures of our own Fate come to gently tap us on the shoulder. Such a dream from the collective unconscious is a *memento mori*." It is to be expected that with children these dreams should be comparatively rare and closely guarded, for a child normally is not confronted by these moments of fate, yet should the occasion arise the dream may come even to a comparatively young child.

A boy of twelve was brought face to face with a decision which he felt to be of great importance. He had been an invalid and necessarily guarded in many ways. He was sensitive, and failures had made him fearful of new situations. An opportunity came for him to enter a school which would give him the training which he greatly desired but the head master, while saying that he would give him a chance, also said frankly that he felt that the school was too difficult and that with his poor health the boy probably could not keep up with the requirements and advised his not entering. While the subject was under consideration he dreamed the following dream:

"I was in a great hall. There was no furniture except a bare table behind which sat a very old man. He looked ages old and had a long gray beard. In front of him on the table was a dice box. Just back of him was a clock which pointed to two minutes of twelve. Not a word was spoken but as he looked at me I knew that before the hands of the clock reached twelve I must throw those dice and that all my future life depended on the throw. I looked for someone to help me and then, as I looked at the old man, I knew that I must throw the dice myself."

So deep was the impression made by the dream that he refused to discuss the situation but went off by himself until the decision was made. He decided to take his chance of making good against the odds, and the result justified the decision. Quite clearly this was the figure of fate risen from his unconscious to emphasize the importance of the event and to warn him that he himself must decide his own life and abide by the results of his own decision. As an illustration of the significance of the details of the dream, the hands of the clock pointed to exactly two minutes of twelve and the head master had written that he might have two weeks to decide.

Another boy was having difficulty in making his adult adaptations. He dreamed that he was on the athletic field and knocked out two front teeth. He saw them lying on the ground in front of him and stooped down to pick them up and put them in again. His instructor said, "Don't do that, if you do you will never grow up." The dream impressed itself so by its vividness that he repeated it, though it seemed mere nonsense. In reality it was a portrayal of his own situation. In many primitive tribes one of the ceremonies of initiation when the youth ceases to become a child and takes his place among the men of the tribe is to knock out the two front teeth. In his dream he tried to pick up the teeth and put them back. In reality he was trying not to accept the initiation into adult life but to remain a child. His instructor, who in the dream took the part which would have been taken by the medicine man, says to him when he would put back the teeth, the childish attitude, "Do not do that or you will never grow up."

The following dream was brought me by a little eight-year-old girl. This child was curiously remote. She rarely played with the other children in a whole-souled way. The children, for the most part, shunned her. If possible they never took her hand or chose her as partner. If they were walking in pairs she always seemed to be shifted to the end of the line so that she would be alone. She was a deceitful child, often cheating for the sake of appearing to have done good work, and her teachers accused her of petty theft. The mother was a frivolous little woman who left her mostly to the care of an ignorant nurse. Her sole duty as a parent seemed to be summed up in the hope that she would be "nice and not know anything that she ought not to." She considered all sex knowledge nasty and had punished the child for asking questions that were about "things that a nice little girl does not talk about." The child dreamed:

"I was with my nurse and she had short red hair, and it grew and grew and it grew and it got grayer and grayer and it was Miss X and she was ironing and there was a pool of water down by her feet (here she drew a round circle with her hands) and I had to put my head in and it was boiling and she said, 'Ha! that hurt you!'"

In certain tribes of the Congo where cannibalism was practiced the primitives selected a victim for the sacrifice. If an adult, the victim was killed with a spear. If a child, he was held head downward in boiling water till dead. This child was set apart, the sacrifice. The part of her that belonged to the tribe, that is the community life in the little class life which she lived, was being devoured by the misunderstanding of the mother. Her first sense of separateness came when she went to school where her teacher was Miss X who had abundant gray hair, hence Miss X in the dream stands by the pool of boiling water into which her head is thrust.

Here is a case where the child is deceiving and cheating because she cannot get in the proper and normal way the instruction and love and approval which she craves. Her knowledge must be obtained through underground channels, thus building up an attitude of secretiveness. Since so much of her conscious is drawn down into the consideration of these mysteries she has not enough power of attention to solve the small matters of daily classroom demands, the attention is focused on these other problems. Yet she feels the injustice of disapproval and cheats in her work in order to gain some standing in the eyes of the class. Since in one important department she must satisfy her needs by devious and tortuous ways, she applies these methods to other needs.

The great difficulty in such cases is that the real need, the establishing of the proper relation of love and trust between the mother and child, cannot be accomplished because the mind of the mother is closed. A substitute must be found and some adult must stand ready to answer questions. After establishing a friendly relation with the teacher and asking various questions, and discovering that things could be brought up into the light and discussed freely, she began to attack her own problem of honest work, and her attitude became more friendly. As she advanced in comradeship and trust she lost her deceitful, secretive manner. The dream problem had been worked through, she was no longer set apart to be devoured by the primitive prejudices and attitudes of the mother.

Strange figures of fate sometimes appear and we, in our ignorance of their import, may treat them as foolish fantasy and of no consequence. One deeply introverted child of the creative type would become lost in a world of her own. So deeply withdrawn was she that even when her name was spoken it did not always rouse her. She was reported as inexcusably inattentive and terribly stupid. The first task was to find out what was going on. I could obtain conscious fantasies after the early establishing of friendly relations but there was something more important. It was very evident from the child's manner that here was a carefully guarded secret, a something more real than our reality, a subjective reality more vital than anything which the objective world could offer. That it had its origin in a dream or was founded upon dream content I soon became convinced, from the very evident agitation and consequent withdrawal which occurred whenever the dream was mentioned.

First the child was made to realize that in the eyes of the psychologist as well as in her own, the school work was of minor importance, it was the reality of the compelling factor in her own mind which must be considered as vital. After the rapport was established there was an open-

ing of the doors into her fantasy world, but still the way
was guarded. First came the less important material which
was always told with an air of watching to see the effect,
and with a wary expression as though ready for retreat at
any moment.

The father was away from home most of the time. The
child saw very little of him and he took little interest in
her since she was obviously not bright. The mother was
oversolicitous as to the child's progress and clothes and exercise but angry that fate had given her a child different
from the other two. Failing to find the understanding at
home she had lived in a fantasy of being an adopted child
and of having real parents who would find her some day
and show everyone what a lovely little daughter she really
was. The mother figure was hazy but the father became so
real as to be the ruling image of her life. She masturbated
when dreaming of this figure. Every test showed a subnor-
mal intelligence unable to do the work required and the
fantasy had become her retreat.

But this fantasy, no matter how alluring, could not account satisfactorily for the combination of terror and fascination which was apparent in her periods of complete
absorption or when the subject of dreams was mentioned.
It became more and more evident that she wished to confide in someone if only she could be quite sure of complete understanding. At last one day it came, a recurrent
dream. "There is a woman. She is very tall—very, very
tall, and she stands straight in front of me. Whichever way
I go she stands in front of me, and she nods her head—
she always nods her head, just as if she knew something
awful about me."

This figure had come night after night in her dreams
and now was forming part of her waking fantasy life.
Masturbation called up this figure and the consequent terror, yet she masturbated habitually. She had been punished for a very obvious form of masturbation but now
produced the desired result by sitting half over the edge of
her chair and with slight apparent movement pressing the
edge into the genitals. In spite of her terror of the figure
its fascination was apparent in that she continually resorted to masturbation to invoke it, for the terror was also
mixed with desire, the desire to retreat to that world of the
collective unconscious. The dream apparently came nearly
every night and she waked in terror.

One day she came in a condition of fear and excitement. She was reported as having done nothing in school

all day, "even the things that she knew perfectly well." For a long time she would not talk. Then she burst out: "I met Mrs. S on the street and she nodded her head up and down, up and down, and the woman who comes at night has a face like Mrs. S and my mother says that she was in a crazy house."

Now the figure of the dream was openly identified as the personification of the collective unconscious, the loss of the objective reality and the retreat into psychosis. The figure of the dream nodded to her, knew and shared her secret, and had grown so real as to produce an actual hallucination.

There was release from the fear after this confidence and a sympathetic talk which helped her to laugh at this special hallucination. Some progress was made in objectifying the figure through connection with fairy tale and myth and she was helped by having more handwork and a change of curriculum. Her doctor did not consider the dream of importance but the subsequent history bore out the diagnosis. The family moved to another town but later information showed a progress of the symptoms. She had become known as queer and defective. She withdrew more and more and it was evident that this dream figure was like a foreshadowing of the coming of her fate.

Though we must be careful of putting our own interpretation on the dream symbol yet it is legitimate to recognize that there are symbols which have been used by the race for many ages to express certain spiritual ideas. When we find these symbols in dreams of arresting interest it is fair to assume that they are of special importance in indicating a psychic stage of development where a new need has arisen, and that this message from the collective indicates the new way.

The dragon figure in mythology is the old and regressive attitude which must be slain before the hero can be reborn and can enter into his inheritance of adult power. So, also, the descent under the sea, the entrance into the dark caverns of the deep, the being swallowed by the great fish, all portray the reentrance to the mother's womb that there may be a rebirth into a new and finer attitude. A young girl of thirteen, who was having great difficulty in giving up an adaptation of extreme childishness and dependence, dreamed that she was bathing with some very little children. They were all naked in the sunshine on the bank of a large lake and were diving in. Suddenly as she dove she saw before her a great black shadow in the water and knew, rather than saw, that it was a huge fish with mouth open like a cavern and that she was diving straight into the black void. Here was her problem. She was on the bank in the sunshine. Her companions were very little children; even in the dream she was conscious of how much younger they were than herself. She feared the separation from these too childish companions and the sunny bank of childhood yet if she was to grow up she must dive off this safe sunny bank and the childish attitude must be swallowed by the monster in order that the new adult attitude might be born.

The snake is clinically used as the symbol of sexuality yet in certain dreams it may appear as fear. One child who had a very low threshold was afraid of the dark which, to her, was peopled with strange forms of terror. She was afraid of strange people, of new situations, of everything that demanded a new adaptation to the outer world. She had difficulty in talking of her inner thought life. At this stage she had the good fortune to be in the care of an unusually sympathetic teacher who always talked quite simply of any questions that might arise, whether of sex or of fear or of childish misconduct, that might be misunderstood and so carry an overweight of shame. The atmosphere of the classroom was one of happiness, understanding, and success. One day the child produced the following dream:

"I was at my desk. The floor opened and there was a big hole. The desk went down and I went too. Then the desk stopped and I went on. There was a passage that was underground. There was a snake, black with yellow spots. I walked right down his mouth. I walked all around inside him, and then I walked out again and I came right out into bright sunlight."

Here, quite evidently, was an indication that the unknown terrors had been investigated, the monster had been explored and she had come out into the sunlight. It was significant that in the dream she had been seated at her desk for it was in the atmosphere of the schoolroom that the monster had been rendered harmless. Not only were any questions of sex and of fear dealt with very simply, but also in this class much attention was paid to the myth and folk tale with as much interpretation of the underlying symbol as the children were capable of comprehending. In this way the monsters of the unconscious were robbed of some of their mysterious terror and the collective images which so often haunt children were treated impersonally.

This had had its effect on this child without there having been any special reference to her own terror images that rose from the collective in dream and fantasy. A little while after this dream I had a talk with the mother. She spoke of the child's improvement at school and said, "She seems to be doing very well now in her work, but I have noticed, too, that she does not seem to be so afraid of things and she sleeps so much better."

Another child who was still beset by terrors of the unknown told with some reluctance yet evident relief this dream: "It was way in the woods and it was night, and it was all dark and I heard big drums go boom, boom, and I was afraid and ran and some things caught at my feet and I couldn't see anything but I could hear drums all around and I was so frightened that I woke up." Here one can hardly fail to catch the beating of the tom-toms, the darkness of the jungle and the strange unreal terrors with which these forests were peopled to the superstitious mind of the primitive, the "things" clutching at her feet in the tangle of the jungle.

Where the dream touches deeply buried content or deals with some frequently recurring mythologic symbol intuitively felt to be of great import, or is a form of personification of a haunting terror, it is especially hard to get the child to tell the dream; and if any undue pressure is exerted a fabrication will often be given. It is quite right that this should be so for such dreams are of utmost importance and should not be given out where they may be misinterpreted and their true value destroyed or, worse yet that they should be turned back to act as elements of destruction instead of construction. It is, therefore, a true instinct which bids the child guard these secrets.

The primitive has the same instinct in guarding the treasures of his collective unconscious which, in his case, have been formulated into tribal taboos and ceremonials. Elaborate stories of imaginary rites and ceremonies have been told to gullible explorers, and to missionaries whose unsophistication in these instances seems greater than that of the childlike savage whom they are observing. One anthropologist tells of how a native whose confidence he had gained referred to various elaborately related tales of customs as "words to fool the old sheep," the old sheep being the long-bearded missionary. In the same way children will often safeguard their defenses by a silence that can be broken down only at the expense of the rapport, and at the price of future ill-feeling; or by a fabrication which also breaks the rapport but which, in addition, gives the child an undesirable sense of superiority in having outwitted the analyst.

A child upon whom constant demands of extraversion were made had a very beautiful dream on which she wove a fantasy which she called "The Dream of Beautiful Things." Into this she incorporated much that acted to her as spiritual compensation for the too-crowded life.

To dream this dream she had to be transported in imagination to "the-island-where-it-is-always-spring." There things were always beginning all over again and she herself could begin all over again without any of the mistakes that she was always stumbling over.—Oh dear! There were so many things to do in that outside world that grown-ups called "Reality."—But on the dream island she didn't have to do; she just had to *be*. One day when she was on the island the dream of beautiful things wove itself into a song.

She thought she was alone, and sang the song that had come out of the dream. She knew that she must keep her eyes shut while she sang or the island might vanish and the grown-up world might crowd into its place. But on that special day a voice broke in on her aloneness.

"What are you singing?" It was the voice of a child whom she avoided whenever it was possible.

"Just something of my own—my very own." She kept her eyes tightly closed; the dream island must not vanish now or she would be face to face with "Reality" in its most repulsive form.

"Open your eyes at once. You are being a very rude little girl."

The grown-up command must be obeyed. She opened her eyes.

"What were you singing? Tell your little friend." Again the grown-up voice.

Frantically she groped for something—anything—to protect her inner reality. She tried tonelessly to chant a nursery rhyme to the rhythm of the song.

"It didn't sound like that."

"Well it was that—just that."

A lie might be "an abomination to the Lord" but surely it was "a very present help in time of trouble." She felt very grateful to the lie that had kept her from violating her inmost truth.

It was not till long years afterward that she evolved her definition of a real lie. A lie is something false that you tell to a person who has a right to know the truth and who will use the truth with loving understanding. But the truth should *not* be spoken at all times. To lie to a person who would misuse the truth is a righteous act, for it defends the inner truth of another human being.

We must be content to take only what is given to us willingly and never to force confidence. Insight into these dreams depends, as does everything else in analysis, upon the transference. Trust and friendship must come first and we must await the drawing near of these confidences as the bird lover waits for the shy things of the woods to come to his hand, knowing that a single move on his part may make the wild thing take flight forever.

Sometimes, when the transference has been established, a device helps with a small child. With one child I built a "house of dreams" out of blocks and out of each window looked a dream. First I chose a window for my dream to look out and then he chose one. First we had pretend dreams, then, very warily, real ones began to creep to the windows. Still the one we wanted, a recurrent terror dream, would not come though I could feel it creeping nearer and nearer. At last, after several days of play, he put his finger on the window that he had called "that window." "There is a man there," he said, "he is the man who comes at night. He has something in his hand all made of ropes, something to catch me. He comes nearer and nearer and sometimes I run away and he runs after me, and then I can't run any more and then I wake up."

This child (a boy of seven) suffered from physical handicaps both in his walking and his speech. He felt bound and limited by these circumstances that were not of his own imposing. Often when he was trying to do things like other boys he would have a feeling of powerlessness and then would take refuge in rage or in domineering actions. They were the only things that could give him back his sense of adequacy which had been crushed by defeat. The man of this dream was not like the figure of fate which came to the little girl mentioned in this chapter. This figure was the personification of his own feeling about his impotence. It lost power by being talked of, but much more when outer conditions were changed so that he was not continually confronted by a sense of failure.

To this child I could explain the figure in so far as the explanation would help him in the adjustment which he himself had to make in self-control and directed effort. We discussed the man as part of himself that wanted to tie him up so that he could not do the things that he should. We discussed his tempers, etc., as the wrong way of trying to get out of the ropes. In this way he learned to vanquish the man by understanding. In this case there were no symptoms that showed the predisposition of psychosis. The figure was not the monstrous one of that strange world of symbols. The figures from the collective are apt to be great of stature like the giants of olden myth. There was a different feeling in describing this figure, it had a different spell. It could be exorcised through understanding.

Jung has stated that the cosmic dream, or the dream of the moon or stars, or the embodiment of the great forces of the universe, is very common in childhood. Personally, I have not found many examples of this, though these dreams do occur. Usually they have been told me by children who had not a very good conscious adaptation to their surroundings.

The following dream contains an element of the well-known fantasy of destruction of the earth by the falling of all matter into a great void. In this there is, beside the collective content, a distinct link with the conscious personal problem, for the child had received the old-fashioned idea of hell and had read with fascination the Biblical descriptions. This dream came after an act of disobedience which she had not regarded with great seriousness during the day but which assumed terrific proportions when she was in bed in the dark:

"I was in the kitchen and my mother asked me to do something and I said, 'I won't,' and then one night I dreamed that I was in the kitchen and there was a big black hole that grew bigger and bigger and then there wasn't any kitchen any more but it was all a big black hole and everything was falling into it, all the houses and all the trees and everything was falling into it, all the houses and all the trees and everything in the whole world. And I tried to run and something butted me from behind and it was the next-door billy-goat only he was big as an elephant. And he butted me and he butted me and every time he butted me he said, 'Won't you? Won't you?' And he butted me to the edge of the hole. I could not see the bottom but everything was falling in. And then the billy-goat was at the bottom, only he had great green eyes and big horns and he didn't look like a billy-goat at all. And then something began to pull me and I fell in and then I woke up."

This became a recurrent terror dream except that the detail was not always repeated, but there was always the great black pit and the beast that pushed from behind, and a force that drew from below and was one with the beast that exerted a magnetic power in the darkness of the pit. It became to her a symbol of universal destruction and as such remained with her.

The dreams of defective children are frequently filled with details of cruelty and gruesomeness. This seems especially true when the conscious life is full of gentleness, acquiescence, and negation. This type of dream is also present in more exaggerated form the more the child is confronted with a sense of failure and of indifference. Even as a dog tied continually will tend to become fierce, so a child who is physically tied by an inferiority sense or a sense of impotence will develop desires for the assertion of power even through channels of cruelty. Often when the conscious has been educated into a sense of "goodness" and gentle expression, the power instincts run riot in the unconscious and find their expression in the dream and night terror.

A little girl of nine who was mentally about six had been trained in habits of obedience and outward consideration. She had also an overpowering feeling of personal responsibility for her own defects. She had been contrasted with a sister a little over a year younger who was a rather precocious child. Though the mother tried consciously to be just yet her strongest feeling was of hurt pride. She was constantly warring between the desire to keep the child out of sight because she was a source of humiliation, and the effort to do her duty and make the child one of the family. This often resulted in her actually thrusting the child into positions of unwarranted prominence in order to satisfy her conscious desires for martyrdom and self-approval, instead of accepting the real situation and trying to find ways in which the child could function without undue strain. The child was apparently submissive and acquiescent, but awkward, stupid, and unresponsive. In reality she suffered tortures from her continuous sense of impotence. Her sleep was restless and though she rarely cried out she often waked trembling, or got up in the morning heavy-eyed and apprehensive. She produced many dreams of the following type: "I was walking along the street. There was a big crowd. I was frightened but I went up, and there was a woman who had been killed and been cut up and the blood was all spurting out and it was running all over everything and there was a knife and I picked it up and I jabbed it into her and some more blood came out." "I saw a dog and he was running down the street and he was all cut open and his paws were cut off and he was all bloody." "I was walking down the street with M (a little neighbor) and there was a girl run over by a car and she was all squashed and the blood was running down in the gutter and I stepped right into it." In most of these dreams there was shown a desire to participate in some way, to step into the blood, to draw the knife and stick it into the dead woman. Though the dreams gave her fear and horror, it is also quite evident that they gave her a form of satisfaction. That the woman in the dream personified her mother and the maimed dog her own maimed functions is quite probable, but in such a case it is most unwise to try to establish the truth of such assumptions by getting the child's own associations since our task is to place the responsibility upon the adults who are in charge of the situation, to make them conscious of the problem not only in so far as it concerns the child himself, but also cognizant of their own inner adjustment to the hostilities aroused in their own unconscious. The actual situation must be accepted and they must see wherein they are trying to make the conditions administer to the good of the child or where they are influenced by undercurrents of personal ambition or wounded pride.

Sometimes the dream is so clear that the child herself makes the associations and finds relief in doing so. A child of very retarded mentality who also was handicapped by the constant comparison with a brilliant younger sister brought the following dream: "I dreamed about Martha and Ann [two little friends]. Well you know Ann was going to be killed because she had killed her mother that morning, and we were all going to the cemetery together in a carriage, Mother and Martha and Ann, and Ann had to be killed before we got to the cemetery, and Martha said that she was glad that Ann had to be killed because Ann told lies. I said that Ann ought to kill her mother because her mother does like Martha best and when Martha tells things about Ann her mother spanks Ann and she ought to kill her. So Ann had to be killed. She had two bright knives, and she said, 'Shall I commit suicide?' I said, 'Yes do. Just stick the knife in here [pointing to the heart], just stick the knife right in, jab it in, *jab it!*' And Mother said, 'Turn your eyes away, Alice, I don't want you to see such things' (just like Mother she always talks).

So she did jab it in and when we got to the cemetery she was all bloody, all dead and bloody and they took her out and they took her down cellar and it was a Catholic Church and the priest said, 'Martha, would you like to read the Bible?' and Martha said, 'Oh that would be great fun,' and then we had a great time."

"What did you think about your dream when you woke up?"

"Nothing."

"What do you think about it now?"

"I think that Ann ought to kill her mother." (A long pause.) "I'm not going to talk any more."

"Are you thinking about your mother?"

She turned away so that I could not see her face, then suddenly burst out in great excitement turning back and looking at me with blazing eyes, "My mother isn't fair either. She believes Julie and Julie lies."

"What would you like to do?"

"I would like to run away."

"Would you like to do anything else?"

"I can't tell you. It's something that I can't tell."

"I think you can."

"Well I would like to kill her, I would like to kill her very often. I ought to kill her, she is not fair. Then I would like Julie killed too. I often want her killed. I would not kill Father, only if he punished me I would run away, I would run away and then come back." (A pause.) "Then I would have a baby brother."

The content of this dream is of course too clear to need comment. It was followed by a burst of rage against the mother. Up to this time she had always spoken of her mother with overaffection, but she had kept away from her a good deal and had not confided in her. This outburst seemed to help clear the air. The part of the father with the birth of the baby brother was also entirely obvious with its jealousy of the mother and the desire to have a baby by the father. The father was very proud of the younger child and tried to compensate to this older one for lack of comradeship by physical demonstration, which was of course the worst thing that he could do for her. He was proud of the cleverness and quickness of the younger child and delighted to take her about with him and to talk to her and enjoy her developing mind. Since he could find none of these satisfactions with the older child he tried to pretend to himself, to her, and to everyone else, that he was equally fond of both by petting and caressing her. She

was physically rather overdeveloped and, in a purely animal way, very pretty, and all her latent sexuality was fed
by this treatment. She was, however, conscious in a confused way that this was not as real an affection as that
which he gave the younger sister. She would try to attract
his attention by showing off for which he always rebuked
her, or she would bring to him attempts at lessons with
which he always found fault. She, therefore, had no means
of obtaining his attention except when he petted her.

For a long time her dreams were full of killing, of cutting up people, and of dismembering animals. These
dreams grew less frequent when she was placed in another
school where she was not contrasted with her sister and
where in special classes she was taught the simple things
that she could do. Gardening, care of animals, and simple
handwork gave her more normal interests. A change of attitude on the part of the parents and consequent change of
environment in the home seemed to produce a change in
the type of dream.

Quite frequently I have noticed that the night terror and
dreams of cruelty seem to increase in strength in proportion to the amount of conscious repression exerted in the
daytime; this is true even when the repression is of a nature that involves a fair degree of conscious control, but a
control that is at war with the unconscious undercurrents
of rebellion and with a sense of injustice. These undercurrents must then be dealt with.

One small boy who was given to fits of violent rage in
which he tore like a whirlwind through the house, often
throwing things at his small brother and sister or suddenly
destroying some bit of treasured property, had occasional
night terrors. When under treatment he began his struggle
toward conscious control the night terrors increased in frequency and violence. They became a substitute, draining
off the tremendous excitement which had been in the habit
of finding its outlet in the volcanic eruptions of the rages.
This same interrelationship of dream and conscious control I have noticed in enough instances to make me feel
warranted to speak of it as a real connection to be taken
into account in the consideration of such cases.

It would be of great value both for the study of the
adult and of the child if we could have a collection of earliest remembered dreams in order that we might see if
those which were especially compelling, whether isolated
or recurrent dreams, were indicative of the psychological
type and therefore of use in determining the predisposition

of the individual and so indicating the best way of helping him to fulfill himself. In such a way dreams might be spoken of as prophetic of the coming individuality.

A deeply introverted patient had dreams as a child that she was in a sphere of glass suspended in space. As she sat there, isolated and yet able to see out, the glass gradually changed so that although it was still, to all appearances, the same clear substance it had lost its actual transparency. It became increasingly difficult to see through, and at last completely shut her off from the outer world. This was somewhat the process which she had followed in her life history, withdrawing more and more deeply until her contacts with the outer world were lost. This type of dream is prophetic in the psychological, not the superstitious sense. It shows the potential as already existing within the child; it indicates the tendencies and points out the dangers; but it is not an assertion of a blind fate that must have its way. This dream was a recurrent one. It came over and over, always with intensity and deep significance.

Had some understanding person been able to use that dream as an index to the inner nature of the child, many of the difficulties of later life might have been avoided. The history of this child's early life was one of conflict in adjustment to two worlds that seemed to her immeasurably far apart. Her fears, her imaginations, her questionings were laughed at so that she early learned to hide the things that really mattered. Much of her adjustment to the outer world became a disagreeable duty, not a delightful adventure to be met with happy curiosity. Of course she retreated farther into her own fantasy life whenever she could. She was known as an antisocial child, inattentive, difficult, a daydreamer. As she grew older she withdrew more and more and when, in adult life, she came to analysis she seemed to have completely lost her way in the world of objective reality.

"I am at a circus but I am not in the audience. Instead my sister and I are walking on a tight rope very far above the other performers. My uncle and my two cousins are performing on high trapezes and every time they swing, their feet go through great windows and smash them."

The dreamer was the child of a fundamentalist minister who was well-versed in the letter of the law and of the literal interpretation of the once-for-all revelation of the Bible. The child was a prig and was shunned by her classmates. She was intent upon showing her classmates where they had strayed from the tight rope of professed piety. Her uncle and her two cousins were also fundamentalist ministers who felt it their bounden duty to crash into the windows of any person they felt was living in a "glass house." When it was found that I was teaching such incontrovertible and literal truths as Jonah and the whale as myths containing symbols by which men had groped their way toward truth, the child was immediately withdrawn from a school that contained such misuse of never-to-be-altered factual truth, and she was put in a small school conducted by a Sunday school teacher who had been under her father's guidance. So far as I know she is still precariously balanced on the tight rope and has never let her eyes stray to the contemplation of worldly pleasures.

Another introverted child dreamed that she was in a dark passage. Suddenly she was attacked by "tens, hundreds, thousands, etc." These creatures had no tangible form nor substance; for that very reason they were immeasurably more terrifying, and intuitively she knew them to be "tens," etc., pressing all about. Then as they came nearer and nearer, she awoke in terror. This was a recurring terror dream. It came over and over till it came to be part of her experience. This dream continued over a period of many years. When she made her free associations, the tens, etc., immediately brought to mind the round Goops of the Gelett Burgess book. These had personified in her childhood all the stupid and inexcusable blunders which one might at any time make. "Don't be a Goop," was sufficient to throw her into a state of inner panic.

She had a great fear of the outer world and especially of drawing any attention to herself. She was divided between a desire to conform to the conventions thrust upon her by rigid family tradition and the compulsion to follow her own thoughts and inner way. There was the ever-present conflict between the inner thought life and fear of breaking "the law."

There were also associations with the time when she was being taught decimals by a governess who "broke" her of her fear of the dark by putting her to bed in an upstairs room, putting out the light and leaving her in a dark room, forbidding her to open the door. She had never opened the door. Since she had been told that this self-control was "good for her" she had acquiesced in the thought; but that same type of acquiescence had been carried into all her adaptations. She had done the things that were "good for her" and, especially when they were disagreeable, had believed them to be good. The inner life persisted in spite of the other adaptations and increased in fear and compelling power. Her thoughts were not the thoughts of her family; therefore, though they persisted, they must be evil. Fear of hell (real literal hell as the proper home of the nonconformist) became one of the formless terrors of the dark passage. Conscious love of family was at war with rebellion deep buried in the unconscious, never faced but every now and then raising its head to appear in some strange thought that filled her with self-reproach; another form of the dark passage. In her analysis, where she explored the dark passage of the unconscious, each of these "tens, hundreds, thousands," with its compelling terror had to be met, identified, and overcome by understanding. Then she had to find how her own way could be brought into happy conformity with the outer world, a world she learned to choose for herself. Not without any struggles is she gradually putting aside her own childish adaptations and growing up in her own right way.

Another introverted child used to dream, over and over again, that she was going up in the garret to find something that she could never find. After a long search came a baffled feeling, and as this feeling grew she became confused; till at last she not could even remember what it was for which she was searching.

In telling this dream she recalled that at one time when quite a small child she had been extremely naughty and had complained that there was nothing to do and that no one provided anything for her. Her mother suggested that she should go up in the garret and see if she could find anything. At last she went up, though reluctant and with feelings of rebellion. In the garret she found carefully arranged some little piles of bright silks for doll clothes. She felt greatly ashamed of herself to think that when she had been complaining of unkind treatment her mother had already prepared this little surprise for her. Suddenly she heard a voice say, as plainly as though an outside person were speaking, "Now you will be good and say that you are sorry, won't you?" Then something dark rose up inside her and she answered out loud, "No, I won't!" and she stayed up in the garret.

After this she was engulfed by a sense of remorse and guilt. She felt that a choice had been offered her and that she had taken the wrong way. She had committed the unpardonable sin in deliberately choosing the wrong, she had

offended against the Holy Ghost for she had denied the
voice that came to her. One can see here the deep and
true quality of her introversion in that the denial of her
voice (the God within) was the supreme sin. She told no
one, for such children do not tell these vital inner experiences unless they have some deep bond with someone who
they feel sure will understand, but the sense of guilt remained. Thereafter in her dreams she went back to the
garret always searching, searching for the lost way, the
thing that she had lost when she turned from the voice
within.

As she grew older she developed a tendency toward
self-destruction, to destroy the thing that she created and
loved. Often when she had nearly completed some lovely
thing she would work on after her hand had lost its skill
and by some careless movement ruin the object. All the
time she was working she was conscious that if she went
on she would spoil it, yet something drove her on. It was a
repetition of the experience in the garret when she had let
herself be driven by the blind force instead of the guiding
voice. She had to become conscious of this compelling
force of destruction, and to make her peace with the God
within.

How much would have been saved if someone who understood the tremendous power of these images from the
unconscious and who had a true relationship of love and
trust could have heard that dream when it first came to
her, and could have helped her to go back and find her
true way.

An overextraverted child who had yielded to the demand made upon her by her family and by the environment dreamed over and over of a house. It was like no
house that she had ever seen or of which she had ever
read. There were sunny rooms on each side of a wide hall.
This hall went all the way to the top of the house and on
each side was a stairway. She would go through this hall,
never stopping in the sunny rooms so intent was she on
her quest. At the top of the stairs was a door which she
would try to open but always it was locked. Then, disappointed, she would go down the stairway on the other side
and halfway down would meet a person who would say,
"Have you seen them yet?" Always she would answer,
"No, the door is still locked," and then would wake with a
feeling of frustration.

As a very small child she had compensated for her extraversion by a world of fantasy. Indeed this inner world

was almost more real than the outer, but as she grew older many demands were made upon her. She was the only child in a large family of old people and her attitude became that of a general mother. She, too, was troubled and careful about many things. Gradually she began to attach a sense of guilt to her thought life. When she fled to inner things, as she still did when opportunity offered, she felt that she was taking time that belonged to someone else. So the inner door became locked, for, endeavoring to "do her duty," she had locked the door of the inner world upon herself. During her analysis she dreamed that she saw a little door near the larger one and, creeping through a passage, came into rooms, simply furnished with such furniture as her colonial and English ancestors had used. She exclaimed, "Why all that I was looking for was under my own roof all the time!" In the analysis she found the world that she was looking for behind the locked door, the inner world of spiritual symbols, her own meaning of life—not the end of problems but a guide in solving them.

Another extraverted child who was engulfed in multitudinous demands, dreamed frequently that trains were "off the track" and rushing about the country. This filled her with terror. She also dreamed of a tidal wave that rose and engulfed the whole land. The dream of the tidal wave is by no means unusual. Frequently it has the import of being overwhelmed by the unconscious. In dreams the unconscious is often depicted as the sea, for it is in truth the sea from which arise the islands of consciousness. An adolescent girl used to dream frequently of seeing a great tidal wave rising to engulf them all. She would run before it in terror and succeed in finding safety on a hilltop but all below were submerged. The dream had a fearful power, and in her waking hours she could see the great wave and feel the terror. This dream began when she was about eleven and continued over a long period.

In this case the mother of the family was the typical "terrible mother" whose enslaving love threatened to swallow them all. It was the destroying force of the mother's unconscious which was depicted in the wave of the dream. The other children were all caught by it. She sensed, though she did not understand, the danger, and knew that she could never be herself unless she could get away from home. This she managed to do. She was the only one of the children who succeeded in establishing a life of her own. The brothers especially remained enslaved by their infantile attitude and were never able to break from the mother or to form a relationship with another woman.

Since I had tried in this chapter to deal with dreams which, in their analysis with either the child or the parent, show clearly the relation between the unconscious material and the problem which at that particular time is threatening the child's normal development, I have not taken space to consider or even to enumerate certain very common types of dreams; for instance, the terror dream of the old man or the burglar so common with the young child and reappearing, especially with the girls, at adolescence; or the kinesthetic dreams of flying, floating, falling, walking on air or water, which show the desire for the escape from reality so common with both children and adults.

Many of the dreams which we have considered are those of very young children, yet they deal clearly with fundamental problems. Such a depth of insight is far beyond the conscious ability of the dreamer. It can hardly be explained in any way except by accepting Jung's theory, which grew out of his new discoveries in analysis, the theory of the collective unconscious, that substratum which we all possess and which through archetypal images hands down to us our inherited wealth of inner life.

It makes us feel also the tremendous importance of keeping wide open the doors of sympathy and understanding in all our relationships with children, so that these vitally important things shall not be shut away from us.

A CORRELATION OF DREAM AND FANTASY

The words "let's pretend" are a key that opens the door to a world where fantasies throng. Children whisk in and out of the personalities that inhabit this well-known yet surprisingly unfamiliar country where anything may happen. Here, on the threshold of this magic land, the child may choose the fantasy that will companion him on his journey and the choice of this companion may give us a clue to the child's own innate nature, to the problem, inner or outer, that he is facing and to the deep-buried but centrally impelling attitude toward these problems, even to the problem of life itself. For very small children have an attitude toward life that impels them toward creativity or destruction. Surprising and revealing things happen in this magic land of "let's pretend."

To penetrate the fantasy side of child life without doing violence to the child is a most difficult task. Always the child's welfare must take precedence over the desire for scientific knowledge. A knowledge of our own problems, and a relationship of love and trust with the child, and a continuous effort toward greater consciousness first for ourselves then in his own developing life, are the things that we must seek after if we are to have a helpful part in shaping the lives of children.

A class of seven-year-olds delighted in exploring this country, and often we entered it and wrote stories of their adventures.*

* Here I would interject a word as to the freedom needed for the writing of these spontaneous tales. No thought was given to spelling

The correlation of these fantasies with "the dream that dreams itself" is often startling in its revelations.

One winter's morning a child told of how, on her way home the day before, she had found a lost dog, hungry, cold, shivering and forlorn. Cheered by a sympathetic word, he had followed her home. Her mother had fed him and then had sent for "the man who takes care of lost dogs."

Another child, always near to the magic land of fantasy, said, "I am going to pretend I am a little dog who went with his master for a walk in the forest and got lost in a snowstorm." The world of the lost dog became an alluring one. The children went scampering into it; but how different were the tales they told.

One child's story ended, "It was dark; very, very, dark. It was cold; very, very cold. I was lost; very, very lost. There was nothing I could do about it, so I just lay down in the snow and died."

Very different was the denouement of another tale. "I felt cold white feathers falling on my nose and it was fun and I chased them farther and farther into the forest and it got dark and I couldn't find my master and I was lost. So I crawled into a hollow log to wait for morning. *But it was all worthwhile,* for that night another little dog crawled into the other end of the log and next morning we had eight puppies."

Then I remembered a dream that the child who "just lay down in the snow and died" had told me in a quiet hour of mutual confidence.

"I came home from school but the door was locked, and all the blinds were down *tight,* and I knocked but no one came and I knew Mother had gone away forever and forever, and there was no place to go, and *there was nothing I could do about it.* Then I woke up in the dark and there was the dream staring at me."

Dream and fantasy met in the despairing sense of doom. But what in the child herself contributed to this feeling of inevitability? What could be done to help her? Little could be accomplished in her life of circumstance, for her mother had indeed "gone away" and a divorce was imminent. This the child did not consciously know, but her intuition was subtly aware that the house of love was

---

or punctuation. These matters would come later in formal class-room work. In transcribing these stories, I have myself supplied a sufficiency of these boring details in order that the reader might not get lost in the confusing onrush of the tale.

already empty and dark, and the deepest undercurrents of her nature flowed into this dark sea of no return. She "just lay down and died."

I saw how this attitude permeated every experience. Even the smallest schoolroom task could defeat her. At the first challenge in relationship, in lessons, even in her games with the other children, she "just lay down and died"; that is, she completely repudiated the idea that she, her own small self, could do anything about it.

She was constantly defeated by her own sense of inadequacy and her terror of life itself. This sense of doom was the deepest undercurrent of her nature. The first prerequisite was that someone should believe in her potentialities and love her *as she was,* without waiting for the transforming touch that should make her possibilities into actualities. This love and understanding I could give to her but it was so little, so little as measured by the enormity of her need. But we could try. And we began, not with the dream, but with the fantasy and its power to evoke understanding love. This was not said in words, but through the acceptance of the dramatic quality of the "let's pretend" and of its power to evoke sympathy. It had already brought the other small children nearer to her in small overtures of friendliness. Here was a potential that perhaps she could do something about. Could the stark, bleak reality that it stated be turned into acceptance of love, and so into upspringing life that one could do something about? We went slowly, very slowly, step by step, cautious as tightrope walkers. The child who had "found it all worthwhile" had made a tentative gesture toward this little one who had lain down and died; tentative because these gestures had so often been repulsed; but now her own fantasy had awakened response in the other, so different, child. Would she like to ask this child to stay after school and feed the tadpoles with her? No, she couldn't possibly do that. None of the children really liked her, and she could do nothing about it. "I'll ask her then, and now I ask you, and after the tadpoles are fed, I'll tell you a story, not perhaps as good as yours but a true story about a little girl I once knew." That afternoon we made our first step, and slowly, very, very slowly, we together took other steps on the road that might lead to a new attitude. Then the divorce became a reality. The child was put in a boarding school; the father moved away; and our relationship seemingly ceased.

Yet such is the mystery of life that nearly forty years

after, I met "casually" (are such events ever casual?) on a street corner the child who had dreamed of puppies, and recognition leaped between us, and we began where we had so long ago left off.

Thus forty years after these lost-dog stories were written a miracle occurred! These two children had come back into my life. The eight puppies had not been born in the light of the new morning. Yet the sorrow and the lostness had "all been worthwhile," for an inner wisdom had been born to the child now a woman, and the truth was verified, for "after all comes wisdom by the aweful grace of God." Though life had denied her the early desires of her heart, children came to her with their joys, their sorrows and their perplexities and "it was all worthwhile," for she became the spiritual mother of more than eight times eight carried to uncounted numbers.

The other child had drifted away many years before, and then through a chance meeting something between us was renewed, and on my cordial invitation she came to see me. The death wish was still the compelling motive, yet through a relationship now lost, she had gained an insight into what life might be, and even into what she might do about it. This relation was now over in factual reality, but she found herself on the threshold of life, even though deep within she was still lured by death. Several times she had stepped in front of a taxi, and only the brakes suddenly applied had saved her from "accidental" death, which really would have been suicide. Now the very sorrow of her loss worked its miracle, for what we have truly experienced is ours forever, and this she was discovering within herself. The question again confronted her: What can you do about it? Could she really do nothing? Dream and fantasy met once more as we together entered the waters of the unconscious, and a pinpoint of light, on an analysis that went back to the days of "let's pretend" like a star, not descending from the heavens but rising from the darkness of the unconscious, shed its ray of hope. She had, and could "do something about it": that is, she could decide for life as against death. She struggled for days to make the decision; but the numinous experience that had been hers wrought its miracle of transformation. She had said Yes to life, and since death is part of life she could say Yes to him and meet him as a friend, for he would open a door into the unknown and unknowable house of life. She has now met death, not as self-chosen obliteration, but as a friend. She had done "something about" the inner attitude, and I feel her death was only a step across the threshold of a new morning that she herself had made possible by her own deep change of attitude toward the force that works in every human heart and makes for the transformation of the spirit.

INDEX

Contents

MILTON FRIEDMAN

Bright Promises Dismal Performance:

AN ECONOMIST'S PROTEST

Edited, with Introduction and Notes by
WILLIAM R. ALLEN

A Harvest/HBJ Book
Harcourt Brace Jovanovich, Publishers
San Diego   New York   London

Copyright © 1983, 1975, 1972 by Thomas Horton and Daughters

College Edition published by Thomas Horton and Daughters 26662 South New Town Drive, Sun Lakes, Arizona 85224

Trade Edition published by Harcourt Brace Jovanovich

Grateful acknowledgment is hereby given to *Playboy* magazine for the material on pp. 9–59; to *The Alternative: An American Spectator* for the material on pp. 60–75; to The Standard Oil Company for excerpts from *The Economics of Freedom* on pp. 141–152, and 161–168; to *U.S. News and World Report* for material on pp. 193–197; to *Wall Street Journal* for material on pp. 241–249; and to Newsweek, Inc. for all other articles appearing in this book. All material reprinted with permission.

Book designed by Mark Likgalter

Library of Congress Cataloging in Publication Data

Friedman, Milton, 1912–
  Bright promises, dismal performance.

  (A Harvest/HBJ book)
  1. Economics—Addresses, essays, lectures. I. Allen, William Richard, 1924–   II. Title.
HB171.F77 1983   330   82-21390
ISBN 0-15-114152-5
ISBN 0-15-614161-2 (pbk.)

Printed in the United States of America

C D E F G H I J

CONTENTS

Contents

Contents

PREFACE

When my friend and publisher Thomas Horton pressed me for permission to bring out an updated collection of my columns from *Newsweek*, I was amazed to find that I have written more than 275 columns since starting my tri-weekly column in 1966—half of them since an earlier collection, *There's No Such Thing as a Free Lunch* (1975) (itself an updating of *An Economist's Protest* [1972]) was completed. I recalled with amusement my initial concern that I would soon run out of subjects to write about. No such thing. The problem has rather been an embarrassment of riches generated by the course of events—subjects displaying a fascinating mixture of sameness and novelty. The same principles and fallacies recur, always in a new and frequently deceptive guise.

Nonetheless, my wife and I, who had shared the work of selecting and organizing the two preceding collections, were reluctant to undertake the preparation of a new one. As the years pass and the time left shrinks, what economists call the marginal utility of time has risen sharply. In addition, we felt that an independent editor would do a better job than we could in selecting the items that deserved inclusion.

Tom came to our rescue by persuading William R. Allen to edit the book. Whatever credit or blame attaches to the selection of items is his, not ours—though, of course, any errors of content are mine alone. We saw the proposed table of contents only after it was complete and suggested no changes in it. Our only contribution has been this preface plus some input into the choice of title.

Bill Allen's agreement to edit the book was a godsend to us. Like us, he combines a conviction that economics is a positive science capable of predicting many of the consequences of public policies with a fervent belief in individual freedom as the criterion by which to judge the desirability of those consequences. He has made important contributions to positive economics. He has also been extremely effective in communicating his analysis and his values to the general public—through books and articles and especially his "Midnight Economist" series of radio and TV commentaries.

My debt to Tom Horton and Bill Allen is matched by my continuing debt to *Newsweek* for offering me so effective a forum for communicating with the public—a two-way forum with a steady flow of stimulating feedback—and for giving me complete and absolute freedom to determine what goes in my column. I owe a debt also to William and Peter Jovanovich who have become warm personal friends, and valued counsellors, in the course of the publication, first, of our earlier book, *Free to Choose*, and now of the trade edition of this book. No authors could ask for better treatment from publishers than we have received from both Tom Horton and Daughters and Harcourt Brace Jovanovich. Our other debts are too numerous to list—to colleagues and friends who have read and criticized early drafts and have suggested subjects; to readers of the columns and other articles who have volunteered encouragement and sometimes abuse, and have added a sense of personal involvement and interest; and especially to those of you who have read this far.

Milton Friedman
San Francisco, California
November 20, 1982

INTRODUCTION

Milton Friedman is a superb economist. There are not, and never have been, many.

There is little point, if any point at all, in grading and ranking the best of economists, and there are good reasons not to try. It is surely unseemly to argue in public about whether one scholarly giant is "better" or "more valuable" than another. Not only will estimations and impressions differ in the gallery in making comparisons on the basis of a given criterion, but opinions will differ also on the weighting of various criteria.

What is it that superb economists do so well?

"Pure theory" generally has been the most glamorous realm of the economist, and the elegant "logic machine" has been the most conspicuous hero. This has resulted partly from the awesomeness of mental gymnastics which few can do. But it stems also from the substantive fact that economic analysis is "a way of thinking." Economics without economic theory is likely to be mere ideological fluff and certainly not more than unsubstantial blank verse.

But theory is only intellectual scaffolding—clearly essential but obviously not the end of the project. The community, which subsidizes economists, understandably has little interest in theory for the sake of theory. But appropriate, well-directed theory indicates the questions to ask and the information to seek. Then, to apply the theory, to use it effectively in explaining aspects and phenomena of the world, calls for effort and ingenuity matching that in the construction of the theory.

In addition to creating theory and empirically using it in real problem solving, there is a teaching and advising function to be performed. Analytic methods and research results are to be explained systematically to colleagues, the tribal elders are to instruct the young braves on college campuses, and somehow the community at large and its governmental representatives are to be soberly (but not too soberly) reached with fruitful applications of elemental analytics.

The teaching function—especially "economic education" for the community and its government—is not often deemed glamorous. It requires patience, good judgment, and catholicity of interests more than quiz-kid brilliance and arcane genius. It is rarely attempted by leading scholars, who generally confine themselves to the dreary professional journals and the intimidating classrooms, and it is even more rarely done well: the typical disinclination of giants of the economics fraternity to communicate with intelligent laymen is paired with innocence in how to do so.

Milton Friedman has long been acknowledged as a master of theory—in particular, ingenious theory for tough empirical purposes. Such pathbreaking, seminal work as is found in A Theory of the Consumption Function *(1957),* A Monetary History of the United States, 1867–1960 *(1963, with Anna J. Schwartz), and* The Optimum Quantity of Money *(1969) was recognized with the 1976 Nobel Prize in economics. Although now retired from the University of Chicago, Friedman's scientific work has continued, evidenced in* Monetary Trends in the United States and the United Kingdom *(1982, with Anna J. Schwartz).*

Dr. Friedman has become as influential a teacher and public adviser as he has been a scholar. Not only extraordinarily effective in the graduate classroom, he has caught the attention of the general community. Among his presentations for nonspecialists are Capitalism and Freedom *(1962) and* Free to Choose *(1979, with Rose Friedman), the latter effort a popular television series as well as a book. In 1966, he began contributing a column every three weeks to* Newsweek. *Some of those splendid* Newsweek *commentaries, none more than a page in length, provide the bulk of this small volume.*

Essays which are very brief, self-contained, and intended for a diverse audience, but which responsibly provide genuine economic analysis, are an extraordinarily difficult art form. One cannot look to such essays for definitive scientific treatments. Still, the reader of the Friedman commentaries will be impressed that he is observing an economist—not an ideologue or a poet—employing his craft.

This selection of articles, along with a famous interview, hardly constitutes a full-blown textbook. But the range of subjects is very wide—the philosophy of freedom and efficiency, the market and governmental workings of our mixed (and sometimes mixed-up) economy, the monetary and fiscal contexts within which we earn and distribute our daily bread, the international setting of our economic activity.

This is a splendid sample of interpretation and guidance from a superb economist.

William R. Allen
UCLA Department of Economics

I. Economics, the Economy, and Political Economy: Surveying the Territory

INTRODUCTION

If "economics" is described simply as concern with and practice of economizing, then everyone needs be an economist. Ever since the serpentine fiasco in the Garden of Eden, when we blew our opportunity to live in a world of abundance and were relegated to perpetual scarcity, all of us have had to economize. Resources are not available to satisfy all wants of all people all the time.

Unavoidable and pervasive scarcity has fundamental consequences. One is conflict and competition as we struggle, not only with niggardly nature but with each other for bigger slices of a finite pie. Since we cannot avoid scarcity, we cannot eliminate competition. Nor can we escape the necessity of making choices in using our inadequate resources—and thereby the inevitability of confronting costs. But there are ways and ways to cope with scarcity, different ground rules by which we conduct our competition, different means of registering preferences and of assigning gains and bearing costs. Some institutions and procedures conduce efficiency and freedom; others generate waste and tyranny.

While everyone is a practicing economist, we are blessed with professional specialists who more or less systematically and with greater or lesser rigor brood over the sorry societal implications of scarcity. But—as with lawyers, doctors, and horse trainers—there are economists and economists, and good economists are scarce as well as useful.

Economists analyze some types of cause-and-effect and de-

7

duce conditional predictions of if-this-then-that. They offer seminal, even if partial, explanations of a wide variety of phenomena. But to account for something is not the same as to justify it. To assess a policy or alternative policy proposals by well-delineated but nonexhaustive criteria is not to decree what surely should be done. Still the free society can gain guidance from the economists it subsidizes. With that guidance, citizens may avoid doing some really dumb things they would otherwise have committed. If so, economists earn their keep.

It is unlikely that any other economist more certainly earns his keep than does Milton Friedman. The scope of his interests and the insightfulness of his view of the world and its processes and history are suggested by the two items in this opening survey. Without aid of centerfold, the Playboy interview touches incisively on a wide range of topics—inflation, monetary and fiscal policy, and price controls; minimum-wage laws and the condition and prospects of the poor; consumer protection and government regulatory agencies; private and public monopolies; environmentalism and the "social responsibility" of corporations; Social Security; taxes and tax reform; welfare programs and a possible negative income tax; greed, prejudice, coordination, and social organization—and then a number of distracting and diverting myths, embraced in many political and educational circles, are shown to be without clothes.

Playboy Interview

February 1973

Playboy: In every public debate on an issue involving economics, there seem to be nearly as many conflicting opinions as there are economists. Why can't you people get together?

Friedman: We do. But that seldom makes news. It's our disagreements that receive attention. For example, how much attention is paid to agreement between Galbraith and myself in opposing a draft and favoring an all-volunteer armed force, or in opposing tariffs and favoring free trade, or on a host of other issues? What is newsworthy is that Galbraith endorses wage and price controls, while I oppose them.

Playboy: Yet in the past election, you supported Nixon despite his imposition of controls. Have you changed your mind?

Friedman: I haven't—and neither has Nixon. I'm still opposed to wage and price controls, and so is he. Incidentally, going back to Galbraith, in a note that I wrote to him shortly after Nixon imposed the controls, I said, "You must be as chagrined as I am to have Nixon for your disciple." So far, he hasn't replied.

I regret that he imposed them; yet in doing so, I think he behaved the only way a responsible leader of a democracy

9

could. He resisted controls for nearly three years when there was strong pressure for their introduction. He tried to make the case against controls, to educate the people about the causes of inflation, and the best methods of fighting it—namely, reduced monetary growth and lower federal spending. But he failed, and finally gave in to the popular demand for some kind of immediate and extreme measure to halt rising prices, and controls were the measure most people seemed to agree on. As a leader, that was a proper thing for him to do, even though he felt it was the wrong solution. He behaved the same way with regard to the war.

Playboy: Aren't you saying that there's been a large element of political opportunism in Nixon's reversals?

Friedman: One man's opportunism is another's statesmanship. There is a very delicate balance between the two in our society. Good politics is what we should demand from our politicians—to a degree. We don't want our leaders to charge off in every direction trying to satisfy the latest public whim, but neither do we want them to completely ignore the will of the people. I think Nixon acted properly. The real problem is educating the public, and there he was unsuccessful.

Playboy: Isn't it possible that Nixon was wrong? Wasn't inflation at a level that demanded drastic action such as controls?

Friedman: No. Inflation was already tapering off as a result of earlier monetary and fiscal measures when the President imposed controls. In any event, controls are the wrong way to ease inflation.

Playboy: Why?

Friedman: Because they never work. We've seen that throughout history, ever since the time of the emperor Diocletian. If controls are administered with any real zeal, people find ways to get around them. The current controls cover only about one-third of all prices. Suppose those prices were kept down by controls. That would simply mean people would have more money to spend on the products represented by the other two-thirds and would drive up the prices of those goods and services.

In the case of wages, there are any number of ways of getting around the controls. If an employer wants, for some reason, to pay a higher wage, he can promote the wage earner, offer him fringe benefits, give him a car—all sorts of things. This takes place especially at the higher income levels, with corporate executives, and so forth. So the people who are hurt most by wage controls are those the program is said to protect: the hourly wage earner, the employee on a low salary—production-line workers and secretaries.

If the controls are tightened or expanded, people will find new and more ingenious ways of getting around them. And as the power of enforcement increases, you move farther and farther from a free society; this is the most damaging effect of controls. The apparatus required to make them effective in even a limited way will be unpopular in a free society. We saw that in World War Two; even then, when there was fairly broad agreement on the need for controls, there was resentment and there were black markets.

Playboy: Why does inflation seem to be such a perennially insoluble problem?

Friedman: Technically, inflation isn't terribly difficult to stop. The real problem is that the favorable effects of inflation come early, the bad effects late. In a way, it's like drink. The first few months or years of inflation, like the first few drinks, seem just fine. Everyone has more money to spend and prices aren't rising quite as fast as the money that's available. The hangover comes when prices start to catch up. And, of course, some people are hurt worse than others by inflation. Usually people without much political voice—the poor and retired people on fixed incomes. Some people aren't hurt at all. And others profit enormously.

When you start to take some action *against* inflation, on the other hand, the bad effects are felt right away. People are out of work. Interest rates go up. Money gets tight. It's unpleasant. Only later do the good effects of an end to rising prices show up. The problem is getting through the painful cure without wanting another drink. The greatest difficulty in curtailing inflation is that, after a while, people begin to think they'd rather have the sickness than the cure. What they don't realize is that once the cure has taken effect, it's possible to have both economic growth and price stability. But as we saw with Nixon, there is terrible public pressure to junk the cure and go back to being sick—or drunk, to continue the metaphor.

Playboy: Why is it so difficult to make the public understand this?

Friedman: That has to do with the rather complex causes of inflation. When a shopper goes to the grocery store and sees that the price of meat has gone up 10 percent or so, she screams bloody murder and demands that something be done about it. She writes her congressman. Well, perhaps she's been admonishing that same congressman to vote for Medicare and increased Social Security and federal housing assistance—and, naturally, for no increase in the income tax. The congressman has voted for all these things and the Federal Reserve Board has made it possible for her congressman to pay for these measures, without increasing taxes, by expanding the money supply. Those are the basic sources of inflation and they are hidden. The shopper thinks the butcher is stealing and she wants it stopped. The butcher thinks his landlord is stealing when he increases the rent by 15 percent. The landlord, in turn, is upset about the increased costs of maintaining his building, and so on.

Playboy: But why have costs and prices risen?

Friedman: Not because of greedy wage earners or avaricious

12

businessmen. Prices have risen by 25 percent in the past five years because of what nineteen identifiable men, sitting around a table in Washington, did with respect to such arcane subjects as reserve requirements, discount rates, and purchases on the open market.

Playboy: You're talking about the Federal Reserve Board?

Friedman: Of course. Now, I'm not talking about any kind of conspiracy, or even dereliction of duty. These men did what they thought best for the country. They would have acted differently had government expenditures gone up less rapidly, had the deficits been lower.

Playboy: But how does the Federal Reserve System cause inflation? Isn't it simply the government's bank?

Friedman: That "simply" covers a lot of ground. The Fed, because it's the government's bank, has the power to create—to print—money, and it's too much money that causes inflation. For a rudimentary understanding of how the Federal Reserve System causes inflation, it's necessary to know what it has the power to do. It can print paper money; almost all the bills you have in your pocket are federal reserve notes. It can create deposits that can be held by commercial banks, which is equivalent to printing notes. It can extend credit to banks. It can set the reserve requirements of its member banks—that is, how much a bank must hold in cash or on deposit with the Federal Reserve Bank for every dollar of deposits. The higher the reserve requirement, the less the bank can lend, and conversely.

These powers enable the Fed to determine how much money—currency plus deposits—there is in the country and to increase or decrease that amount. The men with this power are appointed by the president and approved by the Senate and are leading financial experts. But this is tremendous authority for any small group of men to have. These men have attempted for the past sixty years to predict where the economy is headed and to keep it on an even path of growth. I have studied the monetary history of the United States and written a book on the subject, and it's my opinion that there have been more severe crises in the years since we've had a Federal Reserve System than in the years from the Civil War until 1914. Even if you leave out the years covered by the two world wars, the Fed seems to have failed in its mission of keeping the economy on a steady plane.

Playboy: Why?

Friedman: Basically, I think because it's a system of men and not of rules, and men are fallible. The decisions of the people who run the Fed, as I said, are made in good faith. They want to do the right thing. But the state of our knowledge is incomplete. Often they don't have all the facts or they see one particular phenomenon out of proportion. In the Great Depression, they managed to shrink the total money stock by a third. They did this for the most honorable of reasons, but it was exactly the wrong thing to do. Just as banks all around the country were closing, the Fed raised the discount rate; that's the rate they charge for loans to banks. Bank failures consequently increased spectacularly. We might have had an economic downturn in the thirties anyway, but in the absence of the Federal Reserve System—with its enormous power to make a bad situation worse—it wouldn't have been anything like the scale we experienced.

Playboy: Has the Fed's recent record been this bad, or have we learned from past mistakes?

Friedman: We've learned a great deal from past mistakes. Two decades ago, I argued that the U.S. was depression-proof because the monetary authorities would never again permit a collapse of the monetary system like the one that occurred from 1929 to 1933. But I went on to say that the danger now was a swing in the other direction, that in attempting to avoid recession and unemployment, the system would overreact and produce inflation. Unfortunately, that is exactly what's occurred. Even so, the record for the post-World War Two period as a whole is enormously better than for the prewar period. We've had a quarter of a century without a really serious recession or depression, and our inflation, while we regard it as serious, has so far been mild by world standards. We've done better, but not as well as we easily could have done.

Playboy: What's the answer? Should we junk the Federal Reserve System and go back to private banking?

Friedman: No. But we can take some of the discretionary power away from the Fed and make it into a system that operates according to rules. If we're going to have economic growth without inflation, the stock of money should increase at a steady rate of about 4 percent per year—roughly matching the growth in goods and services. The Fed should be required to take the kind of limited action that would ensure this sort of monetary expansion.

Playboy: Wouldn't the Fed lose its emergency powers—powers that would be useful in a crisis?

Friedman: Most so-called crises will correct themselves if left alone. History suggests that the real problem is to keep the Fed, operating on the wrong premises, from doing precisely the *wrong* thing, from pouring gas on a fire. One reason we've so many government programs is that people are afraid to leave things alone when that is the best course of action. There is a notion—what I've called the Devil Theory—that's often behind a lot of this. The Fed was supposed to take power out of the hands of the conniving bankers, who were supposed to profit when the economy fluctuated wildly. The idea is to pass a law and do something about it. Put good men in charge; that's one line. The competing line is that there are problems in the world not only because of bad men but also because it's an imperfect world. People are imperfect. There are scarcities. Shortages. You can let things work themselves out or try to do something about them by passing a law. Of course, you know which idea is easier to sell.

Playboy: But you prefer the laissez-faire—free enterprise—approach.

Friedman: Generally. Because I think the government solution to a problem is usually as bad as the problem and very often makes the problem worse. Take, for example, the minimum wage, which has the effect of making the poor people at the bottom of the wage scale—those it was designed to help—worse off than before.

Playboy: How so?

Friedman: If you really want to get a feeling about the minimum wage, there's nothing more instructive than going to the congressional documents to read the proposals to raise the minimum wage and see who testifies. You very seldom find poor people testifying in favor of the minimum wage. The people who do are those who receive or pay wages much higher than the minimum. Frequently Northern textile manufacturers. John F. Kennedy, when he was in Congress, said explicitly that he was testifying in favor of a rise in the minimum wage because he wanted protection for the New England textile industry against competition from the so-called cheap labor of the South. But now look at it from the point of that cheap labor. If a high minimum wage makes unfeasible an otherwise feasible venture in the South, are people in the South benefited or harmed? Clearly harmed, because jobs otherwise available for them are no longer available. A minimum-wage law is, in reality, a law that makes it illegal for an employer to hire a person with limited skills.

Playboy: Isn't it, rather, a law that requires employers to pay a fair and livable wage?

Friedman: How is a person better off unemployed at a dollar sixty an hour than employed at a dollar fifty? No hours a

16

week at a dollar sixty comes to nothing. Let's suppose there's a teenager whom you as an employer would be perfectly willing to hire for a dollar fifty an hour. But the law says, no, it's illegal for you to hire him at a dollar fifty an hour. You must hire him at a dollar sixty. Now, if you hire him at a dollar sixty, you're really engaging in an act of charity. You're paying a dollar fifty for his services and you're giving him a gift of ten cents. That's something few employers, quite naturally, are willing to do or can *afford* to do without being put out of business by less generous competitors. As a result, the effect of a minimum-wage law is to produce unemployment among people with low skills. And who are the people with low skills? In the main, they tend to be teenagers and blacks, and women who have no special skills or have been out of the labor force and are coming back. This is why there are abnormally high unemployment rates among these groups.

Playboy: How can you be sure that the minimum-wage law is the cause?

Friedman: In 1956, I think, the minimum was raised from seventy-five cents to a dollar—a very substantial rise. In the early fifties, the unemployment rate among male teenagers was about the same for blacks as for whites. Both were about 8 percent when the overall unemployment rate was about 4 percent. In the late fifties, after the minimum-wage rate was raised from seventy-five cents to a dollar, the unemployment rate of black teenagers shot up from 8 percent to something like 20 to 25 percent. For white teenagers, it shot up to something like 13 percent. From that day to this, the rates for both black and white teenagers have been higher than before 1956. When they start to decline, a new rise in the minimum-wage rate comes along and pushes them up again. The black teenage rate has been very much higher than the white teenage rate, for reasons that are highly regrettable and that we ought to be doing something about: blacks get less

17

schooling and are less skilled than whites. Therefore, the minimum-wage rate hits them particularly hard. I've often said the minimum-wage rate is the most anti-Negro law on the books.

Playboy: Couldn't those who are hurt by minimum-wage legislation be trained for more skilled jobs at better wages?

Friedman: The minimum wage destroys the best kind of training programs we've ever had: on-the-job training. The main way people rise in the labor force is by getting unskilled jobs and learning things. Not merely technical skills: they learn such things as being at a job on time, spending eight hours a day at a job rather than standing around on street corners, having a certain element of responsibility, letting their employer know when they're not going to come in. All of those traits are very important. In an attempt to repair the damage that the minimum wage has done to traditional on-the-job training, you now have a whole collection of programs designed to take up the slack. The great proliferation of governmental programs in which employers are subsidized to provide on-the-job training gives employers an incentive to hire people and then *fire* them in order to get other people for whom they can get more subsidies.

Playboy: Even if minimum-wage laws have been as counterproductive as you say, isn't there a need for some government intervention on behalf of the poor? Laissez-faire, after all, has long been synonymous with sweatshops and child labor—conditions that were eliminated only by social legislation.

Friedman: Sweatshops and child labor were conditions that resulted more from poverty than from laissez-faire economics. Wretched working conditions still exist in nations with all sorts of enlightened social legislation but where poverty is still extreme. We in the United States no longer suffer that kind of poverty because the free-enterprise system has allowed us to become wealthy.

Everybody does take the line that laissez-faire is heartless. But when do you suppose we had the highest level of private charitable activity in this country? In the nineteenth century. That's when we had the great movement toward private non-profit hospitals. The missions abroad. The library movement. Even the Society for Prevention of Cruelty to Animals. That was also the era in which the ordinary man, the low-income man, achieved the greatest improvement in his standard of living and his status. During that period, millions of penniless immigrants came in from abroad, with nothing but their hands, and enjoyed an enormous rise in their standard of living.

My mother came to this country when she was fourteen years old. She worked in a sweatshop as a seamstress, and it was only because there *was* such a sweatshop in which she could get a job that she was able to come to the U.S. But she didn't stay in the sweatshop and neither did most of the others. It was a way station for them, and a far better one than anything available to them in the old country. And she never thought it was anything else. I must say that I find it slightly revolting that people sneer at a system that's made it possible for them to sneer at it. If we'd had minimum-wage laws and all the other trappings of the welfare state in the nineteenth century, half the readers of *Playboy* would either not exist at all or be citizens of Poland, Hungary or some other country. And there would be no *Playboy* for them to read.

Playboy: Aren't there any government programs that can successfully improve the lot of the poor?

Friedman: The actual outcome of almost all programs that are sold in the name of helping the poor—and not only the minimum-wage rate—is to make the poor worse off. You can take one program after another and demonstrate that this is the fact. Indeed, by now, I'm getting a lot more company than I used to have on this point. In a recent Brookings Institution report, the authors of Great Society programs such as the War on Poverty now admit that those programs spent a lot of money but accomplished very little except to create employment for a lot of high-priced poverty fighters. Sometimes these programs have been well-meaning—those who are naïve about the laws of economics think the best way to help the poor is to vote them higher wages—but often they are outright subsidies to the middle class and the rich at the expense of the poor.

Playboy: Please explain.

Friedman: Take aid to higher education. In my opinion, that's one of the country's greatest scandals. There is an enormous amount of empirical evidence that subsidies to higher education impose taxes on low-income people and benefit high-income people. In the state of California, over 50 percent of the students in government-financed institutions of higher learning—the University of California, the state universities, junior colleges and all the rest—come from the upper 25 percent of families by income. Fewer than 5 percent come from the lower 25 percent. But even that understates the situation, because what really matters is what the incomes of the people who go through college will be after they get out of college. If you have two young men, one middle class, who goes to the university, and the other poor, who doesn't—who goes to work as, say, a garage mechanic—the one who goes to college will obviously make more money over his lifetime. But the man in the garage will be paying taxes to support that other man's education—and perhaps his draft deferment. When I'm being demogogic about this, I say that the system in California is one in which you tax the people of Watts to send children from Beverly Hills to college.

Playboy: There are probably liberals who would agree that some well-intentioned government programs aimed at helping the poor don't work and are demeaning or unfair to the people they're supposed to help. Would you agree with *them* that the government has a responsibility to protect the public—via consumer protection, for example—from the excesses of capitalism?

Friedman: The basic premise of the consumer "crusade" is that unless the government moves in with inspectors and agencies, consumers will be defrauded by unethical producers and sellers. I can't accept that kind of solution. If a consumer finds he's being sold rotten meat at the grocery store, he has the very best protection agency available: the market. He simply stops trading at that store and moves to another. Eventually, the first seller gets the message and offers good meat or he goes out of business.

Playboy: Isn't the issue more complex than that? One of the most serious consumer problems is mislabeling and misrepresentation of products that only the most sophisticated shopper can spot.

Friedman: Yes, it's more complex, but the model is valid. If there is devious misrepresentation—which isn't likely, because the return isn't that great—a few shoppers will spot it. Producers work on a margin, like everybody else. If the 5 percent of shoppers who are careful spot a clever misrepresentation, they'll leave the store. That's enough pressure on the store owner. The infrequent shopper assumes this when he goes to a store that's popular. There has to be a reason for its popularity, he decides. The reason is that it appeals to those who are very careful about measures and labels and that sort of thing.

Playboy: Without some kind of consumer safeguards, how is the public to be protected from such things as injuries caused by faulty products?

Friedman: You sue. That's why we have courts. But in the case of a consumer-protection agency, that might not be so simple. Do you sue the manufacturer or the agency that didn't find the error and approved the product? I think most people would rather be able to sue General Motors than an agency of the government.

Playboy: But there *are* consumer frauds and there are dangerous goods put thoughtlessly on the market. Isn't there a way to prevent that rather than inflict punishment after the fact?

Friedman: The most effective deterrent a producer can feel is loss of profits. He's going to be careful about what he puts on the market becaue he doesn't want to lose business. He doesn't want to be sued, either. People like Ralph Nader are always talking about misleading advertising and mislabeling, but I believe it would be very hard to find any examples of mislabeling that can approach what is practiced by those of us who write for the public at large. We're the worst advertisers of the lot. We screech about how important our own products are, how good they are, how they'll cure every ill, and yet some of us complain when businessmen do the same thing. We don't want an agency to assure the public that we do or don't measure up to our claims. Critics and consumers do that.

One of the most dramatic failures of government has been the case of the regulatory agencies. Even the strongest critics of the market and the warmest supporters of government will agree that these organizations have become the servants of those they were supposed to protect the public *from.* Yet there is now a demand for a federal consumer-protection agency. We never learn.

Playboy: Do you discount the possibility that John Gardner or Ralph Nader might put together an honest-to-God consumer coalition—outside the government—that would get effective legislation passed?

Friedman: Do I discount the possibility that water can run uphill? They're working against the fundamental nature of things. The interests of consumers are diverse and diffuse. You buy a thousand things, but you make your living producing a single product—let's say a magazine—and you spend the income from that on the thousand different things. When the chips are down, your willingness to promote your interest as a consumer of the thousand things will be far less than your willingness to engage in something that will promote your interest as a producer. You're going to lobby for postal subsidies for magazines, and you're going to make a much harder case than the people who only *read* magazines. That's in the nature of things.

Playboy: You're talking about the assertion of individual self-interest. But you also seem to feel that it's in the nature of things for a governmental agency—even one specifically created to protect the public from corporate self-interest—to put the welfare of industry before that of the consumer. Why?

Friedman: Because it's in the clear and immediate interest of the regulated industry or industries to either neutralize the effect of that agency or use it to their advantage. Since the interest of an industry is direct and focused, it will spend a lot more time, money and energy to accomplish its goal than the public will to protect its interests. The public's interest is diffuse, as I said. A consumer-protection agency might work for a brief period of time, but after the initial, faddish interest in the project dies down, the producers will move in with pressure for exemptions and other special rulings.

Take the historical example of the Interstate Commerce Commission, which was established to protect the consumer from exploitation by monopolistic railroads. In actual effect, this created a tight cartel that was able to keep rates up. The railroad people themselves had been trying to set rates, to establish a cartel, but every time they got an agreement, some chiseler would break it and they'd be back in competition again. So the ICC was created, and its initial effect was to enable the railroads to keep rates up and competition out.

Then trucking came along, which would have competed with the railroads. There was no monopoly argument whatsoever for including trucking under government regulations. Nobody ever argued that, because there was an enormous amount of competition in the trucking business. Yet trucking was brought under the ICC on the claim that consumers had to be protected from unscrupulous truckers. Of course, the real reason for bringing trucking under the ICC was to protect the railroads from competition.

Or consider the control of air fares by the Civil Aeronautics Board. Now, it's perfectly clear that if you didn't have governmental price fixing, air fares would be roughtly 60 percent of what they are now. We know that because California is big enough to support rather a sizable airline, within the limits of the state. It is, therefore, not controlled by the CAB. If you compare the fares from Los Angeles to San Francisco on Pacific Southwest Airlines with the CAB-controlled fares from Los Angeles to Reno or Phoenix, which are roughly the same distance—or even with the earlier CAB-mandated fares between Los Angeles and San Francisco—you will find that the Pacific Southwest Airlines fares are roughly 60 percent of CAB fares.

Playboy: Do PSA and the other federally unregulated airlines make a profit?

Friedman: PSAs rate of return on capital is as high as, and I believe higher than, that of the other airlines. It's clear that a large part of the effect of higher fares is simply to cause the commercial airlines to waste money. Since they can't compete on fares, they compete with free drinks, fancy meals, attractive hostesses and, most important, with service—all of which keeps the fares up, which means half-empty planes. If you look at the occupancy rate on PSA, it consistently averages much higher than that of the main-airline planes on similar heavily traveled routes.

Playboy: So the CAB-regulated airlines aren't really benefiting from higher fares?

Friedman: Most of this "benefit" is eaten up in higher operating costs. But let's suppose some of it does trickle through. Where does it trickle through to? It trickles through to airline profits. Who owns the airline stock? The same income class of people that does most of the flying. Perhaps they don't realize it, but all they're doing is taking ten dollars out of their left-hand pocket in order to put one dollar into their right-hand pocket.

Playboy: What about areas in which there is nearly a universal public interest? The regulation of television, for instance? Shouldn't the government have some authority over the airwaves?

Friedman: TV is a more complicated case. The Federal Communications Commission has tremendous power over the networks, which are few in number, and the broadcasters have an ultimate interest in the decisions of the FCC. Consequently, they can and do exert influence on that agency. And the FCC has done a great deal to keep the big networks in business and to protect them from competition. Many liberals want stronger FCC regulation to improve programming and reduce advertising. Yet cable television would allow people to watch Shakespeare uninterrupedly if they were willing to pay enough so that a producer could make a profit by supplying it to them. But the FCC has held up cable TV with regulations and delaying tactics that are completely acceptable to the big networks, which make their money through advertising. If you want to watch television, you watch what the networks provide—complete with the advertisements. So, in a way, the advertisers are being federally subsidized. Of course, there are still substitutes. You can read or go to the movies. And even in television, which has been shackled by government regulation, the free market is close to surmounting the problem. Technology spurred by competition will soon make video cassettes available. Since they don't require use of the public airwaves, they won't be subject to federal regulation.

Playboy: Do you think there's a constructive purpose to *any* governmental regulation of commerce?

Friedman: No, I don't. All of these interferences with the market are justified as protection of the public interest, but, in fact, they endanger the public interest. In the absence of regulation and protection, we are told, we would be exploited and overcharged for shoddy service and unsafe products, degrading the quality of our lives and jeopardizing our safety. I've always found it amusing and paradoxical to behold the enormous success Nader has had in selling the idea that capitalism degrades quality.

Picture one of these dupes whom Nader feels for walking into this home and turning on his magnificent hi-fi set. Stop and think about the improvements that have taken place in electronics and hi-fi and ask yourself whether that was through governmental action, whether it was due to regulation, whether it was due to standards set up by the government. The answer is no. It was due to straight private competition. He turns on his fancy stereo FM—which is living proof of a proposition contrary to Nader's—and listens to Nader telling a Senate subcommittee how production under capitalism, by business enterprises, is synonymous with reduction in quality, with shoddy goods. If Nader tried to carry that same message through letters handled by that efficient government monopoly, the U.S. Postal Service, he would never be heard.

Playboy: Why *do* we have such poor postal service?

Friedman: Precisely because it *is* a government monopoly—

and performs exactly like one. But we can't eliminate it, because a very strong interest group lobbies against its elimination. And that group, like all interest groups, has a focused interest as opposed to the diffuse, general interest. We've seen in the case of parcel delivery, which can be undertaken by private firms, that there is an opportunity for profitable and efficient delivery. United Parcel Service makes a profit and provides good service. But the postal union and the government employees in the Postal Service aren't going to give up their monopoly on first-class mail.

Playboy: How do you feel about *private* monopolies? Should they be either broken up or closely regulated by the government?

Friedman: The problem in this kind of discussion is making a distinction between the real world and the ideal world. For an ideal free market, you want a large number of producers. For an ideal government, you want a saint. In the absence of both, you have three choices: unregulated private monopoly, private monopoly regulated by government and government monopoly. All three are bad, but, in my opinion, the best of the bad lot is unregulated private monopoly. The ICC and the railroads provide a good example of regulated private monopoly; the Postal Service is a good example of public monopoly. Those aren't really appealing cases.

Playboy: Is there an unregulated private monopoly in existence?

Friedman: A recent historical example would be the stock exchange before 1934. You have so much regulation now that you'd have to take a total industry to find a good example. Iron and steel, perhaps. But there really is no such thing as pure monopoly, since everything has substitutes. Even iron and steel. The telephone is a monopoly, but it has substitutes in the other forms of communication.

There's never been anything like the monopoly domination of the economy that some people claim exists. It's a matter of relative size. While some people point to the automobile industry as a giant monopoly that disproportionately influences the economy, they don't recognize that the wholesale-trade industry is twice the size of the automobile industry. Studies of labor unions indicate, similarly, that their influence is relatively small and unimportant—though obviously some of them have great power in limited areas.

Perfect competition is a theoretical concept like the Euclidean line, which has no width and no depth. Just as we've never seen that line, there has never been truly free enterprise. But the examples of monopoly that can be found in this country are nothing like the threat to our imperfect free-enterprise system posed by the government's attempts to control monopoly "in the public interest." The examples we've been talking about are a case in point. Another very good example is the whole system of agricultural programs. Agriculture would be entirely competitive if it weren't for government control of prices, which has hurt the consumer without benefiting the farmer.

One final thing on this subject: free enterprise isn't necessarily strongly supported by one group in our economy and denounced by another. Both business and labor would like exemptions that would work to their advantage and against the public good. Both would like to behave as monopolies and receive special government considerations. The oil industry fights hard for import quotas to keep foreign supplies out and its own prices high. All the while preaching the virtues of free enterprise. Tariffs are supported by certain elements of labor for the same reason. The essence of the problem is that once we begin to allow exceptions for special interests, we move from a system of private arrangements to a political system where everyone's freedom is limited and government becomes a matter of trying to balance those interests. Nobody really wins under these terms.

Playboy: If consumer protection—even from monopoly—isn't an area that is legitimately the province of government, what about pollution?

Friedman: Even the most ardent environmentalist doesn't really want to stop pollution. If he thinks about it and doesn't just talk about it, he wants to have the *right amount* of pollution. We can't really *afford* to eliminate it—not without abandoning all the benefits of technology that we not only enjoy but on which we depend. So the answer is to allow only pollution that's worth what it costs, and not any pollution that isn't worth what it costs. The problem is to make sure that people bear the costs for which they are responsible. A market system rests fundamentally on such an arrangement. If you hit me with your car and you damage me, you are obligated to pay me—at least until we have no-fault insurance. The problem of pollution is that if you emit noxious smoke that damages me, it's difficult for me to know who's done the damage and to require you to be responsible for it. The reason the market doesn't do it is that it's hard to do. The resolution does have to be through governmental arrangements, but in the form of effluent taxes rather than emission standards. I prefer such taxes to emission standards because taxes are more flexible. If it's more expensive for a company to pay the tax than emit the pollutant, it will very quickly raise its own emission standards.

Playboy: At its own expense or the the consumer's?

Friedman: The consumer's, of course. There is a romantic notion that by cracking down on the producers, we will somehow end pollution without any increase in prices. Nonsense. We've already seen some firms go out of business because of antipollution legislation. They couldn't afford to stay in production. Why shouldn't consumers bear the increased costs of a company's effluent tax or of antipollution devices? They themselves are the only real producers of pollution. There is pollution from steel mills because people—consumers—desire steel. Otherwise, it wouldn't be produced. So those who desire steel are responsible for the pollution that's caused by its production, and they should bear the cost of reducing that pollution.

Playboy: Suppose the effluent tax on, say, a paper mill isn't as high as the cost of reducing water pollution. Won't the customer pay higher prices for the paper—and won't the water still be dirty?

Friedman: Not necessarily. That depends on how the government uses the revenue from the tax. The money could be spent on treatment plants—cleaning the water. Insofar as it's feasible, the effluent taxes collected could also be paid back as a tax reduction to the people who are harmed, if it can be proved who did what to whom. Which is preferable depends on whether people would rather have the money or the clean water.

Playboy: Then the tax isn't really a solution?

Friedman: There *is* no perfect solution. It's a fact of life that there are hard, nasty problems that can be mitigated but not eliminated. This is one of them. The tax is the best—or, if you prefer, least bad—of the ways to mitigate pollution. Let me add that there are some ways in which the market works to resolve the problem of pollution, or at least to lessen its effects. Take a town like Gary, Indiana. To the extent that the pollution caused by the U.S. Steel plant there is confined to that city and people generally are truly concerned about the problem, it's to the company's advantage to do something about it. Why? Because if it doesn't, workers will prefer to live where there is less pollution, and U.S. Steel will have to pay them more to live in Gary.

Playboy: Quite apart from emission standards and effluent taxes, shouldn't corporate officials take action to stop pollution out of a sense of social responsibility?

Friedman: I wouldn't buy stock in a company that hired that kind of leadership. A corporate executive's responsibility is to make as much money for the stockholders as possible, as long as he operates within the rules of the game. When an executive decides to take action for reasons of social responsibility, he is taking money from someone else—from the stockholders, in the form of lower dividends; from the employees, in the form of lower wages; or from the consumer, in the form of higher prices. The responsibility of a corporate executive is to fulfill the terms of his contract. If he can't do that in good conscience, then he should quit his job and find another way to do good. He has the right to promote what he regards as desirable moral objectives only with his own money. If, on the other hand, the executives of U.S. Steel undertake to reduce pollution in Gary for the purpose of making the town attractive to employees and thus lowering labor costs, then they are doing the stockholders' bidding. And everybody benefits: the stockholders get higher dividends; the customer gets cheaper steel; the workers get more in return for their labor. That's the beauty of free enterprise.

Playboy: We've been discussing government programs aimed at protecting the public. Do you reject the kind of programs by which the government attempts to aid individuals directly? Social Security, for instance?

Friedman: If you talk about misleading labeling, Social Security is about as misleading as you can get. It has nothing to do with social and it has nothing to do with the security of society. What's called Social Security is a program that links together a particular set of taxes and a particular set of benefits. It involves an 11.7 percent tax on wages up to a maximum that is now $10,800. The employer and the employee each supposedly pays 5.85 percent, but since the employer's half is part of his total wage cost, it's the employee who's really paying the whole bill. So here you have a regressive payroll tax.

On the other side of that, you have a benefit structure under which people above a certain age receive certain amounts. There are many things that can be said about it, but let me try to say the most important first: is it a good buy? The answer is, if you take the law as it now stands, it's a very good buy for people in the older age groups, and it's a very lousy buy for people in lower age groups. If a person below about forty-five invested the same amount of money in a private annuity or just put it in the bank and let it accumulate interest, he would end up with a much larger annuity than he is now being promised by Social Security. On the other hand, older people are getting a larger annuity than their taxes would have paid for. They're getting it partly because many of them didn't pay during the whole of their working lives, since Social Security is a relatively new thing. The number of people who have been paying taxes has been growing more rapidly than the number of people receiving benefits. Also, when they started paying, the tax rates were much lower than they are now.

In addition to the old/young discrepancy, which is the most serious, there is also a poor/rich discrepancy that works to the benefit of the rich. People who have high incomes from property don't lose their Social Security benefits when they reach the age of sixty-five, while those who have to keep working lose all or a part until they reach seventy-two. But there's a much more important bias. The lower-income person will be likely to go to work and start paying taxes at something like seventeen or eighteen years of age, while the upper-income person might go from college to graduate school and not start working and paying taxes until he's twenty-three

32

or twenty-four. That means the low-income person will pay taxes for more years and, when you take account of the effect of compound interest, he will pay the economic equivalent of roughly a third more than the well-to-do person.

It's also an established fact of demography that upper-class people live longer than lower-class people, so the lower-class person not only starts paying earlier but he's less likely to receive benefits and, if he does, it will be for fewer years. So he pays more taxes and gets less in benefits. This biases the whole program in favor of the well-to-do, who don't need the money, as opposed to the poor, who do. This is offset only somewhat by the fact that the benefit schedule is biased in favor of low-income people.

Finally, it really is misleading to think of Social Security as an individual purchase of insurance, as if your payments were buying your benefits. There is almost no relationship between what you pay and what you get. What we have in Social Security is a tax system and a separate benefits system. I don't know anyone—whatever his political persuasion—who thinks that a flat-rate wage tax with a maximum on the amount of wages taxed is a good tax. It's equally hard to find anybody who would accept it as a satisfactory benefit system. If somebody happens not to have worked in a covered industry, for example, he gets nothing, no matter how severe his need. A man over sixty-five who is qualified can have an income of $1 million from investments and still get his full benefits. A man of the same age, with no income from property, who works and earns over a certain amount, gets nothing. To add insult to injury, he has to keep paying the taxes. It's always been a funny thing to me that people who don't have a good thing to say about Social Security as a tax system or a benefit system regard it as a sacred cow when you tie the two together.

Playboy: Would you be in favor of a Social Security system that eliminated the inequities by linking payments more closely to benefits?

Friedman: Let me accept, for the sake of argument, the false claim made for this system: that it really is an insurance program. There are still two strong reasons for objecting to it. One is that it involves *compulsory* purchase of retirement. Second, it involves compulsory purchase of that retirement *from the government.* Suppose you're a young man of thirty, but it so happens you come from a family that has a very short life span. Everybody in your family has inherited cancer, heart disease, and whatnot and you look forward and say, "Hell, I'm not going to live beyond fifty." Is it irrational for you to decide that you want to spend your money on living now and not put it aside for retirement at the age of sixty-five? What justification is there for the government to say it won't let you do that? On the other hand, say you're going to live a long time—at least you think you are—but you just enjoy the present and you'd rather live it up now, knowing full well that this may put you into difficulty later on. The argument is that when you get into difficulty later on, you'll be a charge of the state. But you'll only be a charge of the state if the state wants to take you as a charge. If you decide to live it up now and take the consequences later, it seems to me that should be your right.

Playboy: Realistically, the state would probably take care of someone under those circumstances.

Friedman: All right, let's suppose we're going to compel him to provide for his old age. Here I've got two people. Mr. X, a saving type, is going to be accumulating wealth and is buying a retirement annuity on his own. Mr. Y is not. Why, in addition to what X is doing on his own, should he have to buy it through the government? If you're going to have compulsory retirement, shouldn't the government specify that every individual in the community must demonstrate to the satisfaction of the authorities that he's providing for a retirement benefit of a certain kind, then let him do it however he wants? If you want government to be in the business, let's require it to compete with private enterprise. Let it offer the terms on which it's willing to give a retirement benefit and let it be a self-supporting concern.

Playboy: Even if your objections to Social Security were shared by a majority of the voters, don't we have too much at stake to abandon it for the program you suggest?

Friedman: We have too much at stake *not* to abandon Social Security. Replacing it would take some time, of course; we couldn't in good conscience renege on the obligations we've already undertaken. I have outlined elsewhere a program that would get the government out of the business of providing for people's retirement while, at the same time, honoring present commitments. It's an involved program, however, too complex to get into here, but entirely feasible.

One final thing: like any number of government programs, Social Security was conceived as a method of dealing with special problems involving the poor. Like the other programs, it has expanded—as we've become wealthier as a nation—more rapidly than the nation's wealth. There is a reason for this. There is a particular group with a strong interest in maintaining and strengthening Social Security: the people who administer that program. As poverty declines, the pressure for more and more poverty programs increases. That pressure comes from the people who administer the programs more than from the poor themselves. This is just one more reason I propose a simple solution—a negative income tax—for the problem of poverty. It would eliminate this whole business of special categories and special programs.

Playboy: Before we deal with the negative income tax, let's talk about your more fundamental suggestions for reform on the income tax itself.

Friedman: Well, I'd like to move toward an enormously simplified income tax, by eliminating all present deductions except for a personal exemption and substituting a flat-rate tax for the current graduated schedule. Let's consider the deductions first. I would eliminate *all* personal deductions, except for strictly occupational expenses. There would be no more tax deductions for charitable contributions, for interest payments, for real-estate taxes; no more special treatment for capital-gains income, for oil depletion or for all the rest. The income tax would then be based on what it was supposed to be based on all along: individual income.

From this figure, representing his total receipts in excess of business costs, each taxpayer would be entitled to deduct a sum—a personal exemption—that reasonably reflects the cost of a survival existence in the 1970s. When the income tax was enacted, the personal exemption was supposed to assure that there would be no tax whatever on people with very low incomes. The assumption was that everybody deserved a subsistence income before he was taxed. But today, this concept has become a joke. We still have a personal exemption, but—considering the effects of inflation—it's lower now than it's ever been. I would double the present personal exemption, to $1,500, or $1,600 per person.

Playboy: At what percentage of income would you place the flat-rate tax?

Friedman: If you eliminate the present deductions and retain the present personal exemption, you could scrap the current graduated rates—which run from 14 percent up to 70 percent—and raise the same amount of revenue with a flat-rate tax of around 16 percent. This sounds unbelievable, but it's true. Our current graduated rates, while they supposedly go from 14 up to 70 percent, are fraudulent. Very few people pay taxes in the higher brackets, largely because of the loopholes we've heard so much about.

36

Playboy: According to the conventional wisdom, the graduated tax is a good way to democratically redistribute wealth by allocating the revenues to social programs. Doesn't it do that?

Friedman: The graduated tax, to the extent that it works, doesn't redistribute wealth. Not only does most of the tax revenue from the higher income brackets not go to the poor in the form of social programs, the graduated tax also *protects* rather than redistributes wealth. It is, in effect, a tax on *becoming* wealthy. It doesn't affect people who are already wealthy. All it does is protect them from the competition of those who would share the wealth with them.

Playboy: Do you think a confiscatory inheritance tax would better solve the problem?

Friedman: There's no such thing as an effective inheritance tax. People will always find a way around it. If you can't pass $100,000 on to your children, you can set them up in a profitable business; if you can't do that, you can spend the money educating them to be physicians or lawyers or whatever. A society that tries to eliminate inheritance only forces inheritance to take different forms. The human desire to improve the lot of one's children isn't going to be eliminated by any government in this world. And it would be a terrible thing if it were, because the desire of parents to do things for their children is one of the major sources of the energy and the striving that make all of us better off. Even an effective inheritance tax, if one could be concocted, wouldn't prevent the transmission of wealth, but it would put an enormous damper on progress. I've never been able to understand the merit of the sort of equality that would chop the tall trees down to the level of the low ones. The equality I would like to see brings the low ones up.

Playboy: Would your flat-rate tax bring the low ones up or would it—at the expense of those in the lower brackets—

37

benefit primarily those who would pay less under your system than they do now?

Friedman: I think it would be fairer to almost everyone than the present system, assuming you eliminated the loopholes. After all, loopholes are nothing more than devices that allow people with relatively large incomes to avoid high taxation. The Brookings Institution, which has been looking into this, estimates that if you eliminated all the loopholes, you would increase total taxable income by something like 35 percent. Given a 21 or 22 percent average tax rate on the current base to collect current revenues, you can see that on a base a third again as large, a flat-rate tax of around 16 percent would raise the same amount of money. Personally, I can't imagine many people saying that such a tax would be unfair. As you suggest, people who are very poor might make such a claim, with some justification. That's why I'd also like to double the size of the present personal exemption. Then it would take a flat-rate tax of around 20 percent to yield the same amount of revenue that the current system raises.

Playboy: You make it sound almost simple. Yet few knowledgeable people besides yourself have ever seriously considered such a proposal.

Friedman: That's not necessarily an indictment of the soundness of the idea. But you have a point. The current system, with all its loopholes, makes many taxpayers—especially the influential ones, who have a large voice in government policy—think they have a vested interest in the status quo. Probably most present taxpayers would prefer the current system of taxation to the one I've proposed. Yet the one I propose would probably save everybody money.

Playboy: But tax reform can't save *everyone* money; the revenue has to come from somewhere. Surely the rich people who pay little or no taxes under the present system wouldn't benefit by the elimination of tax loopholes.

Friedman: You're wrong. You're not taking into account what it costs people to avoid taxes. This is one of the most important—and most overlooked—points in the whole field of taxation. Let me give you the simplest case: municipal bonds. As you know, the income from municipal bonds is tax-free. You're not even required to report it. For this reason, municipal bonds pay a much lower return; if corporate bonds are paying 8 percent, municipals might be paying 5. Suppose you buy some municipal bonds. You get the income from them, yet on the government books, no taxes on this income are recorded. But still, you *do* pay a tax. You pay three dollars in eight—the difference between what you could have got if you had bought corporate bonds at 8 percent and what you did get buying municipals at 5. That's a 37.5 percent tax. It's not recorded, but you're still paying it. What happens, in effect, is that as a buyer of municipal bonds, you pay a 37.5 percent tax to the federal government, which turns your money immediately over to the municipality.

A better example is the oil-depletion allowance. A man drills for oil. It costs him $100,000 to drill the hole, but he expects to find only $50,000 worth of oil. Still, he drills the hole because of the tax advantage of being able to deduct the drilling cost from other income. That makes it worthwhile to drill. But understand, he's not really drilling for oil, he's drilling for tax advantage. If it weren't for the tax laws, nobody would spend $100,000 to find $50,000 worth of oil. So there's $50,000 of pure waste in such an undertaking. Businessmen call it buying a tax shelter.

Playboy: Who actually bears this cost—the entrepreneur or taxpayers at large?

Friedman: A good question, and one not easily answered. Individuals enter such transactions, obviously, because they think others will bear most of the burden. If they thought they'd have to pay the cost themselves, they would probably never get involved. But when you have a whole nation of entrepreneurs, each seeking tax advantage, it's impossible to say just who pays the bill. In essence, we all do. All you can say is that when a man pays $100,000 to drill a hole that will produce $50,000 in oil, $50,000 has been wasted. Given a better tax system, this waste would not have occurred. And that alone justifies changing the tax system.

Playboy: The oil companies defend the depletion allowance on the ground that it encourages exploration for new oil reserves in the U.S.—reserves that might be crucial in a national emergency.

Friedman: They do, but have you ever seen them give an estimate of how much it costs to provide emergency reserves by this device rather than by others? Two different questions are involved here. First, do considerations of national defense require a large oil reserve for emergencies? Second, what is the best and cheapest way to provide such a reserve? The answer to the first question is far from clear, given the likelihood that any major war involving nuclear weapons would be extremely short. But even if the answer is yes, there are ways of providing a reserve that would be far cheaper than requiring consumers year after year to pay unnecessarily high prices for oil in order to finance exploration for additional wells, and then using the oil from these wells for current consumption, so you have to explore for still more wells.

But I'm getting away from the question you raised: whether the rich could benefit from getting rid of the loopholes. My main point is that all these wasted expenditures, tax shelters—whatever you might label these evasive maneuvers by the well-to-do few—are largely at their own expense. True, they reduce the taxes they pay, but only at a high cost. Philip Stern wrote an article in the *New York Times Magazine* a few months ago entitled "Uncle Sam's Welfare Program—

For the Rich." His argument went like this: people like H. L. Hunt, let's say, pay $2 million a year in taxes. But if the loopholes were closed, he'd pay $20 million. Therefore, Stern said, the current system is the equivalent of Congress' enacting an $18-million welfare grant for Mr. Hunt, paid for by the public. This is sheer demagogic nonsense, because it completely neglects what it costs Mr. Hunt to avoid the taxes. Maybe Mr. Hunt, to avoid paying $20 million in taxes, paid $16 million—by buying municipal bonds, digging uneconomical holes, paying high-priced tax lawyers to find new loopholes. There probably *is* an element of welfare for the rich, but it's much less than many people imagine.

Joseph Pechman of the Brookings Institution has estimated that the loopholes reduce tax collections by $77 billion a year. My guess—and it's just a guess—is that this $77-billion loss in taxes through the loopholes produces no more than $25 billion for the people who use them. In fact, I'd be surprised if it produced that much. The rest, as I've tried to explain, is simply wasted.

Playboy: Under the graduated-tax system, the wealthy pay far more—in theory, at least—than those in any other income bracket. Under your proposed flat-rate system, they and everyone else would have to pay only 20 percent. But with all the loopholes at their disposal—even though you say they save less than they think by using them—don't the rich stand to lose more than anyone else under your system, with its no-loopholes stipulation?

Friedman: Not necessarily. If I were Howard Hughes, I'd rather pay 25 percent in taxes than buy a tax shelter that costs me fifty cents on the dollar. Wouldn't you? The only people this change would actually hurt are those who make their living by providing tax shelters for others. Statistically, these are a tiny minority. Moreover, money would be more economically invested than it is now, and these better investments would create more wealth, and thus generate more taxes, all up and down the line.

Playboy: Most people would have less quarrel with the flat-rate tax than with the elimination of all personal deductions other than provable business expenses. Doesn't a man who's hit, say, with tremendous medical expenses one year deserve a tax break?

Friedman: I have a good deal of sympathy for the deductibility of catastrophic medical expenses—more than I do for almost any other deduction. Medical expenses are a sort of occupational expense—the cost of earning an income. But for the sake of this proposal, I'd eliminate *all* deductions. For any income tax to really work, it's got to be simple and straightforward—something you can fill out on one side of one page without too much trouble. Admit one loophole and you admit them all.

As for how to cope with medical expenses if they're non-deductible, the solution is a simple one: buy insurance. When a man buys medical insurance, he's betting the price of the premium that he's going to get sick and the insurance company is betting the cost of his medical bills that he won't. If he wins, he gets his bills paid for; if he loses, he's out the premium. But it was his own decision—and responsibility—to buy the insurance. If he *doesn't* buy insurance, on the other hand, he's betting that he's not going to get sick. If he loses, my question is: why should the rest of us have to pick up his expenses by paying in taxes for the medical bills he deducts from his return? Let *him* pay the bills; that's what he risked when he bet.

Playboy: But you assume that this man is a gambler, that he makes a calculated decision not to to buy insurance. Don't most people fail to buy insurance because of either ignorance or poverty?

Friedman: We're not talking about poverty-stricken people here, we're talking about taxpayers. As for ignorance, that's not a valid argument. My fundamental belief is that you've got to hold people individually responsible for their actions.

Playboy: Even as nontaxpayers, the poor can afford neither insurance nor medical expenses. Would you hold them individually responsible for such costs?

Friedman: Obviously, it bothers me, as it bothers anyone else, to see people destitute, whether through their own fault or not. That's why I'm strongly in favor of charitable activities, whether individual or joint. One of the worst features of the current system of Social Security and welfare arrangements is that it has drastically reduced the feeling of obligation that members of society traditionally felt toward others. Children today feel far less obligation toward their parents than they did fifty years ago. If the state is going to take care of the parents, why should the children worry? Similarly with the poor. Who feels a personal obligation to help the poor? That's the government's job now.

Playboy: To return to the point you raised earlier, you think a negative income tax will change this?

Friedman: I hope it will. But before we really get into that, let me stress one thing. If we were starting with a clean slate— if we had no government welfare programs, no Social Security, etc.—I'm not sure I would be in favor of a negative income tax. But, unfortunately, we don't have a *tabula rasa*. Instead, we have this extraordinary mess of welfare arangements, and the problem is: how do you get out of them? You can't simply abolish them, because when we enacted these programs, we assumed an obligation to those who are now being helped by them. In fact, we have *induced* people to come under the protection of these programs.

Playboy: What do you mean?

Friedman: I mean that the law of supply and demand works

very generally. If there is a demand for poor people, the supply of poor people will rise to meet the demand. In setting up programs such as Aid to Dependent Children and all the other welfare programs, we have created a demand for poor people. Don't misunderstand me. I'm not blaming poor people. You can hardly blame them for acting in their own interest. Take a poor family in the South, working hard for a very low income. They learn that in New York City they can get $300 a month—or whatever it is—without working. Who can blame such a family for moving to New York to get that income? The blame falls on those of us who set up the incentives in the first place. The blame also falls on us for creating a system that not only induces people to seek its benefits but forces them to stay in the program once they're enrolled and demeans them terribly in the process of helping them.

I remember how impressed I was, six or eight years ago, when a young man who was writing a book on welfare programs in Harlem came to see me. He said, "You know, I've been reading *Capitalism and Freedom*, where you talk about the extent to which government bureaucracy interferes with the freedom of individuals. You really don't know the extent of this. *Your* freedom hasn't been much interfered with; *my* freedom hasn't been much interfered with. When do *we* meet a government bureaucrat? Maybe when we get a parking ticket or talk about our income taxes. The people you should have been talking about," he said to me, "are those poor suckers on welfare. They're the people whose freedom is really being interfered with by government officials. They can't move from one place to another without the permission of their welfare worker. They can't buy dishes for their kitchen without getting a purchase order. Their whole lives are controlled by the welfare workers." And he was absolutely right. The freedom of welfare recipients is terribly restricted. Whether we're doing this for good purposes or bad, it's not a wise thing to do. Not if we believe that individuals should be responsible for their own actions.

Playboy: For those who don't know how it works, would you explain how welfare forces people to stay on the dole once they're enrolled?

Friedman: If someone on welfare finds a job and gets off welfare, and then the job disappears—as so many marginal jobs do—it's going to take him some time to go through all the red tape to get back onto the program. This discourages job seeking. In the second place, if he gets a job that pays him, say, $50 or $75 a week, he's going to lose most of that extra money, because his welfare check will be reduced accordingly—assuming he's honest and reports it. Since he gets to keep only a small fraction of his additional earnings, there's small incentive for him to earn.

Also, the present setup has encouraged fathers, even responsible fathers, to leave their families. Again, it's a matter of incentives. If a man is working and has an income above the minimum, he's not entitled to welfare. But if he deserts his family, *they* can receive welfare. That way, he can continue to earn his income and contribute it to his family, in addition to the welfare they get. Many ADC families are actually created by fake desertions. Of course, you have real desertions, too. If a deserted woman is going to be immediately eligible for welfare, the incentive for the family to stick together is not increased, to put it mildly. So the problem is: how do you get out of all this? And this brings us back to the question you asked a moment ago. I see the negative income tax as the only device yet suggested, by anybody, that would bring us out of the current welfare mess and still meet our responsibilities to the people whom the program has got in trouble.

Playboy: How would the negative tax work?

Friedman: It would be tied in with the positive income tax. The two are similar. Ideally, I'd like to see a flat-rate tax above and below an exemption. I've already discussed the flat-rate tax above an exemption. The tax on income below the exemption would be a negative one. Instead of paying money, the low-income person would receive it. Consider the current tax system. If you're the head of a family of four, with an income of roughly $4,000, your personal exemptions, plus automatic deductions, plus low-income allowance, will mean that you pay no tax. Suppose you're the same family of four with an income of $6,000; you'd end up with a taxable income of $2,000—that is, $6,000 minus $4,000—and you'd pay a fraction of that $2,000 in taxes. Now suppose you had the same family of four with an income of $2,000, you'd have a taxable income of minus $2,000—that is, $2,000 minus $4,000. But under present law, with a taxable income of minus $2,000, you pay no tax and that ends the business.

With a negative income tax, an income of $2,000 would be subject to negative taxation. Instead of paying taxes, you'd *get* some money. Just how much would depend on the negative tax rate. If the negative tax rate were 20 percent, you'd get $400. If the rate were 50 percent, you'd get $1,000. The 50 percent negative tax rate is simplest, so it's the one I always like to use for illustration. If you have no income at all, for example, you would have a negative taxable income of $4,000—that is, zero minus $4,000. You would be entitled to receive 50 percent of that: $2,000.

Playboy: In other words, your system would amount to a guaranteed annual income of $2,000 for a family of four?

Friedman: Yes. But it's very important, in all systems like this, to keep in mind you're talking about two different numbers: the minimum income, which would be guaranteed to every family or taxpayer; and the break-even point, which is the point at which people would stop receiving money and start paying it. In the example I just gave, $2,000 is the base—the amount you'd receive from the government if you earned nothing at all. On the way between the base and the break-even point, which is $4,000 in this example, you would receive fifty cents less from the government for every extra dollar you earned, so you'd get to keep fifty cents. This provides a consistent incentive for additional earnings. Above $4,000, you'd be on your own. You'd receive nothing extra. In fact, you'd have to start *paying* taxes, partly to help those who are less fortunate than you.

Playboy: Do you think your negative tax program would be an adequate substitute for our present welfare programs—Aid to Dependent Children, food stamps and the rest?

Friedman: I believe it would be far superior to the present programs—superior from the point of view of the recipients and also of the taxpayers. But you asked whether it would be adequate. I really don't think you can discuss negative taxation in terms of adequacy or fairness. You have to ask a different question: how much are you and I willing to tax ourselves in order to benefit someone else? The great fallacy in these discussions is the assumption that somehow somebody else is going to pay the bill. Early in his campaign, Senator McGovern came out with a proposal to give a grant of $1,000 to every person in the country. That was really a form of negative income tax, but one on a very high level. Essentially, what McGovern proposed was a $4,000 guarantee for a family of four, with a $12,000 break-even point. The result would have been to sharply reduce the incentive to work for people in a very wide income range. It would have reduced the incentives for people making between $4,000 and $12,000 by enabling them to collect from the government rather than pay taxes; and it would have reduced incentives for people making more than $12,000 by requiring them to pay much higher taxes. And much of the extra money collected from people making above $12,000 would have gone not to the desperately poor but to people with middle-class incomes.

We have to ask not only how much the recipients get but also who pays for it. Can you really justify taxing people receiving $13,000 a year in order to raise the income of people receiving $11,000 a year? So while I'm in favor of a negative income tax, I don't favor *any* negative income tax. I want one that has both the guarantee and the break-even point low enough so that the public will be willing to pay the bill, and one where the marginal tax rate, between the guarantee and the break-even point, will be 50 percent or so, low enough to give people a substantial and consistent incentive to earn their way out of the program.

Playboy: Do you think any of these proposals you've been discussing—on taxes, welfare, and so on—has a chance of public acceptance?

Friedman: There have been some hopeful signs. Some things I've been saying for a number of years now are receiving a little more attention. Some of the proposals I've made concerning international financial arrangements, for instance. Also, the negative income tax has become a fairly respectable notion. But you see, the problem is twofold. First, you have to sell your ideas, to convince people that government programs generally do the opposite of what their well-meaning proponents intend—that they aren't getting their money's worth for taxes. But even if people are convinced by the arguments, there is the problem of getting them to give up what they see as in their special interest. Everyone wants to make sure that he is getting his. Nobody will let go until he's sure the other guy is, too. And that's the biggest problem.

Playboy: Is there a solution?

Friedman: If there is, it would be in bundling things together. That's how we keep government out of the censorship

48

business. It's not a matter of taking one case at a time and deciding each case on its merits. If we did that, we would have free speech for very few. Someone would be able to get a law passed prohibiting free speech for Seventh-day Adventists. Or vegetarians. Or Black Panthers.

We talked earlier about reducing the tax rates and closing the loopholes. The right wing would be more than willing to give up the loopholes in return for lower rates; and the left wing would probably be more than willing to give up the high rates in return for closing the loopholes. So it looks as if there's a deal to be made. But you can't make a deal through the usual legislative channels, because neither side trusts the other—and both are right. The only way I can see to make such a deal is by a constitutional amendment that says, for example, Congress can impose an income tax as long as the only deductions are for strict occupational expenses and a personal exemption, and as long as the highest tax rate is no more than twice the lowest. Personally, I would prefer a flat rate, but to achieve consensus, it would be better to limit the degree of graduation. That would give both sides some assurance that the deal wouldn't come unstuck.

Playboy: Even if a consensus of right and left could be achieved on a modified version of your flat-rate tax proposal, there are many critics—particularly among the young—of what they feel are your basic assumptions. How would you answer those who claim that capitalism cannot foster a just and orderly society, since it's based on the emotion of greed?

Friedman: What kind of society isn't structured on greed? As a friend of mine says, the one thing you can absolutely depend on every other person to do is to put his interests ahead of yours. Now, his interests may not be greedy in a narrow, selfish sense. Some people's self-interest is to save the world. Some people's self-interest is to do good for others. Florence Nightingale pursued her own self-interest through charitable activities. Rockefeller pursued his self-interest in setting up the Rockefeller Foundation. But for most people, most of the time, self-interest is greed.

So the problem of social organization is how to set up an arrangement under which greed will do the least harm. It seems to me that the great virtue of capitalism is that it's that kind of system. Because under capitalism, the power of any one individual over his fellow man is relatively small. You take the richest capitalist in the world; his power over you and me is trivial compared with the power that a Brezhnev or a Kosygin has in Russia. Or even compared in the United States with the power that an official of the Internal Revenue Service has over you. An official of the IRS can put you in jail. I doubt that there is a person in the United States who couldn't be convicted of technical violation of some aspect of the personal income tax.

One of the great dangers I see in the American situation is that there is a strong temptation in government to use the income tax for other purposes. It's been done. When gangsters couldn't be convicted under the laws they had really violated, they were gotten on income-tax evasion. When John F. Kennedy threatened steel executives in 1962 to get them to drive down their prices, there was the implicit threat that all their taxes would be looked at. Now, that is a much more serious threat—the power an official has in the pursuit of *his* self-interest—than anything Howard Hughes is capable of. We want the kind of world in which greedy people can do the least harm to their fellow men. That's the kind of world in which power is widely dispersed and each of us has as many alternatives as possible.

Playboy: Critics of capitalism feel that too many alternatives cause waste, that we don't need forty-seven models of Chevrolet when one would do.

Friedman: If consumers really preferred one model at a lower price than forty-seven models, GM would be foolish not to meet their desires. There are forty-seven models because that is what consumers want. That's what the critics really complain about—that under capitalism, consumers get what they want rather than what the critics think they should have. It's always amused me that the intellectuals who talk loudest about the waste of competition in business are the loudest defenders of the waste of competition in the intellectual world.

Isn't it absolutely wasteful that millions of writers should be deciding what to write on their own—a hundred writers may be writing on the same subject—with no social priorities being imposed on what subjects they write about? Isn't it deplorable that thousands of scientists should each be picking his own subjects for investigation? Shouldn't there be a central planning board that decides which subjects have the highest social priority and assigns those subjects to the researchers most suited to pursue them, to see that there is no duplication?

Suggest this to any of the intellectuals who whine about the waste of competition in the business world and almost all of them will be horrified. Most of them would recognize that it would be terrible. It would be terrible because the essence of the intellectual world is that it's a search for the unknown, an attempt to find new things by a process of trial and error in which you have a great deal of duplication. For every nine people who go off on a bum lead, one person's going to go on a right lead. The same thing is true in the business world.

Playboy: What about the criticism that capitalism leads to material extravagance and aesthetic starvation?

Friedman: The historical fact is precisely the reverse. The greatest opportunity for the expression of nonmaterial motives is in free-enterprise societies. The great triumphs of literature, art, architecture, and science have all been the products of individuals. Are the great examples of architecture the state buildings of Russia or some of the homes Frank Lloyd Wright designed for private people? Did Thomas Alva Edison produce his inventions for a central planning board under a Five-Year Plan or did he produce them under a system of individual incentives?

Only small minorities, whether in a communist society or in a capitalist society, are concerned with nonmaterial ends. Nonmaterial undertakings, therefore, will flourish most in the society where minorities have the greatest opportunities. A free-enterprise society is precisely the kind of society in which a minority can more or less do what it wants. It's free to pursue its own interests, but not in a collectivist society: if it's a perfect democracy, it will be dominated by the majority; if it's a dictatorship, it will be dominated by one minority, but other minorities will not be free to move.

Say I'm in a collectivist society and I want to save an endangered species; I want to save the heron. I have to persuade people in charge of the government to give me money to do it. I have only one place I can go; and with all the bureaucratic red tape that would envelop me, the heron would be dead long before I ever saw a dollar, if I ever did. In a free-enterprise capitalist society, all I have to do is find one crazy millionaire who's willing to put up some dough and, by God, I can save the heron. That's why the variety of minority views expressed in the Western world is enormously broader than in a Soviet society.

Playboy: Yet our minorities right now are criticizing capitalism for many injustices.

Friedman: Of course. Everybody always takes the good things in the world for granted and attributes all the evils of the world to the system. In addition, many of the difficulties they complain about are the result of government action, not of the market.

Playboy: Don't you think blacks have a legitimate complaint when they see that they can't be hired on an equal basis with whites in a job market that's controlled not by the government but by individuals who are freely making the choice to discriminate against them?

Friedman: Of course they have a complaint. But are they better or worse off than they would be in an alternative system? The fact is that blacks are far better off in the U.S. than they are under other systems. Let's get some facts straight. The average income of blacks here is far higher than the average income of *all* the people in the Soviet Union. The official government definition of the poverty line in the U.S. is higher than the average income in the Soviet Union; it's higher than the income received by 90 percent of the people on the world's surface. Now, that doesn't mean blacks aren't subject to injustice; of course they are. Of course there's discrimination. I'm opposed to it; I'd like to see it eliminated. But the point is that—even with discrimination—blacks are far better off under our present system than they would be under alternative kinds of systems, and changing the system isn't going to eliminate people's prejudices.

Let me give you a different example. The Jews—because they were a persecuted people who had the same attitudes toward capitalism in the nineteenth century as many blacks now have toward it in the U.S.—played a disproportionate role in the Communist party and in achieving the Soviet Revolution. They were represented out of all proportion. Has that been good for the Jews? What country in the world today engages in the most extreme anti-Semitic persecution? The Soviet Union. It's not an accident, because if you have a society with concentrated power, if you have a collectivist society, it's going to be in a position to exercise the preferences and prejudices of its rulers. Moreover, it's going to have an *incentive* to do so, because it's going to need a scapegoat and it will choose some group like the Jews or the blacks to be the scapegoat.

I personally have been very sensitive to this issue because I'm Jewish and I'm very much aware of the history of anti-Semitism. One of the paradoxes I puzzle over is that few people in the world have benefited as much as the Jews from free-enterprise capitalism and competition, yet few other groups have done so much to undermine it intellectually. Let me ask you a question. In what institution in the U.S. are blacks most discriminated against?

Playboy: Schools?

Friedman: Is there any doubt that they're more discriminated against in schooling? Is there any doubt, if you're a parent in a black ghetto, that the thing you will find hardest to acquire is decent schooling for your child? Is it an accident that the schooling is provided by the government? A black in a ghetto who has the money can buy any car he wants. But even if he has the money, he can't get the schooling he wants, or at least he'll have to pay an enormously higher price for it than a white person will. A white person with that income can move into a nice suburb and get the schooling he wants. A black person will have great difficulty doing it.

Let's suppose, on the other hand, that you didn't have government schooling. Let's suppose you had the kind of system that I'm in favor of, which is a system under which the government, instead of providing schooling, would give every parent a voucher for a sum of money equal to what it's now spending per child and the parent could spend that at any school he wanted to. Then you'd have private-enterprise schools developed and blacks could buy much better schooling for their children than they can get under the government.

Under free enterprise, a person who has a prejudice has to pay for that prejudice. Suppose I'm going to go into business producing widgets and that I'm a terrible racist and will hire only whites. You're going into business producing widgets, too, but you don't give a damn about race, so you're going to hire the person who's most productive for the lowest wage. Which of us is going to be able to win out in the competitive race?

Playboy: That depends on the unions.

Friedman: You're departing from competition. One of the major sources of black discrimination has been the unions, but the unions are an anticompetitive element; they're a private monopoly; they're against the rules of free enterprise.

Playboy: You blame the government for discrimination against blacks in the school system because the government controls the schools. But isn't this discrimination really based on residential real-estate patterns that are the result of individual choice?

Friedman: Yes, to some extent it is. But those residential patterns don't necessarily imply segregation of schooling. They don't imply segregation of the kinds of automobiles people have. They don't imply segregation of the kind of movies people go to. If you had a free-enterprise school system, you'd have a much wider variety of schools available to blacks— schools of a higher quality. Moreover, residential segregation itself is partly stimulated by the fact that government provides schooling.

Let me illustrate. You're a well-to-do fellow and you want to send your child to a good school. You don't send him to a private school, because you're already paying taxes for schools and additional money you'd pay for tuition wouldn't be deductible. So, instead, you get together with some of your friends and establish a nice high-income suburb and set up a so-called public school that's really a private school. Now you won't have to pay twice and the extra amount you pay will be in the form of taxes—not tuition—which will be permitted as a deduction in computing your personal income tax. The effect of this will be that your children's education will be partly subsidized by the poor taxpayers in the ghetto. The fact that schooling is generally provided by the state, paid for through taxes that are deductible in computing the federal income tax, promotes a great deal of residential segregation.

The crucial point is this: in a *political* system, 51 percent of the people can control it. That's an overstatement, of course, since no government that's supported by only 51 percent of the people will do the same things that one supported by 90 percent of the people will do. But in a political system, everything tends to be a yes-or-no decision; if 51 percent vote yes, it's yes. A political system finds it very difficult to satisfy the needs of minority groups. It's very hard to set up a political arrangement under which, if 51 percent of the people vote one way and 49 percent vote the other way, the 51 percent will get what they want and the 49 percent will get what they want. Rather, the 49 percent will also get what the 51 percent want.

In a *market* system, if 51 percent of the people vote, say, to buy American cars and 49 percent of the people vote to buy foreign cars and the government lets their votes be effective and doesn't impose tariffs, 51 percent will get American cars and 49 percent will get foreign cars. In a market system, if 40 percent of the people vote that they want to send their children to integrated schools and 60 percent vote that they want to send them to segregated schools, 40 percent will be able to do what they want and 60 percent will be able to do what *they* want. It's precisely because the market is a system of proportional representation that it protects the interests of minorities. It's for this reason that minorities like the blacks, like the Jews, like the Amish, like SDS, ought to be the strongest supporters of free-enterprise capitalism.

Playboy: It's clear by now that you agree with Thomas Jefferson that the government that governs least governs best, that you don't think the federal government should interfere with any private, free-market arrangements whatsoever. But what about such efforts on the municipal level? Some communities, for example, are trying to keep out subdivisions, industry, nuclear power plants, and so on, in order to reduce the impact of commercialism. Do you feel they have this right?

Friedman: Of course. What you want is a world in which individuals have a wide variety of alternatives. You want pluralism, multiplicity of choice. When you get down to small units of government, you have it. If you don't like what one town does and can't change it, you move to another town. You have competition among towns for the provision of services. No reason you shouldn't. On the whole, the formal restrictions on governmental activity should be most severe at the federal level, less so at the state level and least of all at the local level.

Playboy: Then you aren't an anarchist?

Friedman: No. Although I wish the anarchists luck, since that's the way we ought to be moving now. But I believe we need government to enforce the rules of the game. By prosecuting antitrust violations, for instance. We need a government to maintain a system of courts that will uphold contracts and rule on compensation for damages. We need a government to ensure the safety of its citizens—to provide police protection. But government is failing at a lot of these things that it ought to be doing because it's involved in so many things it shouldn't be doing.

What we've really been talking about all along is freedom. Although a number of my proposals would have the immediate effect of improving our economic well-being, that's really a secondary goal to preserving individual freedom. When we began to move toward the welfare state back in the thirties, the justification was that the defects inherent in capitalism jeopardized our economic well-being and therefore reduced freedom. In the ways I've shown, these programs have failed. But it's not enough to object to them simply because they didn't improve—or, in fact made worse—the situations they were designed to correct. We need to resist them on principle. Someone will always come along and say the programs failed because they were underfunded; or because the wrong people were running them. Wage and price controls, for example, are unpopular with a number of people not because they reduce freedom but because they aren't working.

Galbraith said a few years ago that there wasn't anything wrong with New York City that couldn't be fixed by a doubling of the budget. Of course, that's happened and things are worse now than when he made the remark. So one of the things that encourages me just a little is the proven inefficiency of government, regardless of how big it gets. I think people are catching on to it. They sensed that McGovern wanted to ride still further the wave that was started with FDR, and they were fed up enough with that trend to vote overwhelmingly against him.

Playboy: So you're hopeful?

Friedman: Not completely. You have to consider the ideological climate. The spirit of the times has gone against freedom and continues to go against it. There are still intellectuals who believe that concentrated power is a force for good as long as it's in the hands of men of good will. I'm waiting for the day when they reject socialism, communism, and all other varieties of collectivism; when they realize that a security blanket isn't worth the surrender of our individual freedom even if it *can* be provided by government. There are faint stirrings and hopeful signs. Even some of the intellectuals who were most strongly drawn to the New Deal in the thirties are rethinking their positions, dabbling just a little

58

with free-market principles. They're moving slowly and taking each step as though they were exploring a virgin continent. But it's not dangerous. Some of us have lived here quite comfortably all along.

welfare ... to ... recipients of the ... from the
programs as much. They end ... might even
work... this ... of the... have lied out
policy ... effects.

Economic Myths and Public Opinion

January 1976

This morning I'm going to deliver a sermon. My theme comes from Josh Billings, the famous American humorist of the nineteenth century, who said, "The trouble with people ain't ignorance, it's what they know that ain't so." I propose to discuss five myths about American society which are very widely accepted, which have a great deal of influence on public attitudes and public opinions, and yet which in my opinion are wholly false.

The Myth of the 19th Century Robber Baron

The first myth might be called the robber baron myth. In your courses in history—ordinary political history, to a lesser extent even in courses on economic history—you will have learned that the nineteenth century in the United States was an era of rugged, unrestrained individualism in which heartless monopoly capitalists exploited the poor unmercifully, ground the helpless under their heels, and profited at the expense of the rest of the community. The rich got richer

60

and the poor got poorer; Wall Street was set against the working man. You will have learned from the standard history book that the farmers in the Middle West were being ground between the millstones of falling prices for the products they sold and higher prices for the products they purchased. You will have learned that that was the reason for interest in the greenback political movement, the reason for the development of the populist sentiment in the Middle West and the South, the reason for that magnificent speech by William Jennings Bryan in 1896, when he asked whether mankind shall be crucified on a cross of gold.

That's the myth, and there is hardly any myth more deeply imbedded in people's attitudes. The myth was spread by the reformers, the muckrakers of the early twentieth century, by the intellectuals who contributed to the drastic change that has occurred in our attitude toward the market on the one hand and government on the other, which has in turn produced such a drastic change in the character of our society in the past forty or fifty years.

There is only one element of that myth that is correct. It was an era of rugged, unrestrained individualism. It was an era with the closest approximation to pure economic laissez-faire in American history. It was an era in which, except for the Civil War, spending by the federal government never exceeded about 3 percent of the national income, a sum which is derisory by today's standards when federal government spending is approaching 30 percent of the national income. It was an era in which there was, for most of it, no ICC, no FCC, no SEC, and you pick out any other three letters of the alphabet and it wasn't there either.

It was a period when about the only interference with what people could do, aside from the taxes that were being imposed to finance a small armed force, courts, legislatures, and the like, consisted of a protective tariff on imports. Laissez-faire economists objected then as now to such tariffs, but the level of the tariff was mild compared to the duties that were imposed later.

This situation did not develop, interestingly enough, out of any philosophical belief in laissez-faire. It developed much more simply. In the 1830s, state governments throughout the country proceeded to engage in what we would call socialist enterprises. They built canals, they set up commercial banks and extensive banking systems, they financed railroads, they put up industries. It was a great era of government enterprise. But in the recession, or panic, of 1837, many of these government enterprises went broke. They turned out to be inefficient in the same sense in which all government enterprises have been inefficient from that day to this. By contrast with the situation today, however, they were allowed to fail. It was this experience that set the United States on the road to laissez-faire.

While the nineteenth century was a period of rugged individualim, almost every other feature of the myth is false. Far from being a period in which the poor were being ground under the heels of the rich and exploited unmercifully, there is probably no other period in history, in this or any other country, in which the ordinary man had as large an increase in his standard of living as in the period between the Civil War and the First World War, when unrestrained individualism was most rugged. The evidence of this is to be found in the statistics that economists have constructed of what was happening to national income, but it is documented in a much more dramatic way by the numbers of people who came to the United States during that period. That was a time when we had completely unrestricted immigration, when anybody could come to these shores and the motto on the Statue of Liberty had some real meaning. This was a country of hope and of promise for immigrants and their children, and as many as a million immigrants a year came in 1906 and '07 and '08. By 1914, roughly a third of the population was foreign-born or the immediate descendants of foreign-born.

Did people come to this country to be ground under the heels of merciless capitalists? Did they come to make their own conditions worse? There is no more dramatic way in which people can vote than with their feet. The fact that East Germany had to build a wall to keep people from going to West Germany is striking evidence of which country had the better conditions of life. In the same way, the fact that year after year hundreds of thousands of people left the countries of Europe to come to this country was persuasive evidence that they were coming to improve their lot, not to worsen it. Far more effective evidence, I believe, than any statistics on per capita real income, which show that real income went up decade after decade at a rate of about 2, 2.5, 3 percent per year. They came with empty hands. They came from the most deprived groups in the old world, from Czechoslovakia, from Germany, from Italy. It was the poor and the miserable who flocked here, and they found a home and the opportunity to improve their lot. And they found it, not despite rugged individualism but because of rugged individualism. It was rugged individualism that induced the developments in industry, in trade, that offered opportunities for people.

Of course, our condition is far better than theirs. In an absolute sense, their level of living was low. But we must compare their level of living, not to ours but to the level they left in Europe. We stand on their shoulders. We are able to live as well as we do because of their achievements, because of what happened during that period of the nineteenth century. I must say, it seems to me disgraceful for so many people to denigrate the experience of their parents, when that experience has made it possible for them to live in a free society at their present high level.

So much for economic development. What about the charge that the agricultural community was being ground down, that it was being exploited by the Wall Street bankers? That we needed to have a Greenback movement and a populist movement and a William Jennings Bryan?

Again, the contrary evidence is very simple and very clear. In the first place, if agriculture was being especially exploited, you would expect the number of people on farms to go down, but the number rose by leaps and bounds during the period. If agriculture was in a bad state and being exploited, you would expect the price of farmland to go down, but the price went up rapidly. The prices of farm products did go down. But they went down because the great fertile areas of the Middle West were being opened up and brought into production. Output was growing rapidly, the cost of producing crops was going down thanks to great technological innovation in the form of reapers and other agricultural machinery, and the cost of transportation was falling. The result was a great outpouring of production which produced a decline in the prices of farm products at the same time that it produced a very rapid rise in the incomes of farmers and induced many people to enter farming.

On a different aspect of this experience, was it a period of heartless monopoly capitalism? Quite the contrary, it was the period of the greatest private eleemosynary activity in the history of the United States. The period of unrestrained, rugged individualism was a period when the modern type of nonprofit community hospital was first established and developed. It was the period of the Carnegie Libraries and their spread through the philanthropy of Andrew Carnegie. It was the period when so many colleges were founded throughout the country. It was the period of the founding of the Society for Prevention of Cruelty to Animals, and the spread of foreign missions. There was no income tax, no deductibility of contributions, so what people spent on charity came out of their pocket and not, as now, largely out of taxes they would otherwise pay. And yet, in every aspect of private charitable activity, it was a boom period.

So the generally accepted historical picture of the nineteenth century is an extraordinary myth. Years ago I wrote a book with a collaborator on the monetary history of the United States, and in the course of writing it I read many of the general histories of the nineteenth century. As an economist, I was appalled by the level of ignorance of economic matters that was displayed in those history books, by the extent to which the historians were willing to take the cries and the claims of reformers and political agitators for reality.

Everybody, of course, always wants to improve his lot. Everybody would like to see the price of the things he sells go up, and the price of things he buys go down. But since what one man sells another man buys, that's hardly a feasible situation. We find the same inconsistency when people talk about inflation. What people mean by inflation is not the rise in their own wages but the rise in the prices other people are charging them. And that was the case in the nineteenth century. The people who were in the Greenback and the Populist movements were saying, "We want to do still better," but the historians have tended to take their exaggerated complaints for reality.

That's Myth Number One, a myth which has done enormous harm, in my opinion, by leading people not to recognize the true sources of the strength of this country and the true origins of our greatness.

The Myth of the Great Depression

The second myth is the Great Depression myth, the myth that that decade-long catastrophe—at the worst of which, in 1932–33, 25 percent of the labor force was unemployed—

reflected the failure of private enterprise. Somehow, people believe that the Great Depression occurred because private enterprise could not organize society properly, that it was necessary for government to step in to save society, that the New Deal and all that followed was a necessary corrective to the mistakes and disasters produced by the deficiencies of private enterprise and unbridled competition.

The trouble with these beliefs is that they are completely wrong. The elementary truth is that the Great Depression was produced by government mismanagement. It was not produced by the failure of private enterprise, it was produced by the failure of government to perform a function which had been assigned to it. Since time immemorial, government has been granted the function, wisely or not, of controlling the monetary system. In our Constitution, government is given the power to coin money and determine the value thereof. We had the Great Depression because government failed in that task. In 1914, we had a supposedly great reform. But experience shows that not all reforms are improvements. In this case, the great "reform" was the establishment of the Federal Reserve System, a central banking system. It was established supposedly to prevent what were called banking panics.

The immediate occasion was the banking panic of 1907, when the Knickerbocker Trust Company went broke—like the Franklin National Bank, except that unlike the case of the Franklin National, tax money was not used to bail it out. It went broke, the public got worried about the stability of banks, there were runs on banks, and this led to what was called the banking panic in which the banks of the country suspended the convertibility of their deposits into currency. Banks continued to operate, but you could not walk into a bank, give it a check, and have it give you currency—at that time, gold or greenbacks or national bank notes. If you gave someone a check, it would be stamped, "payable only through the clearing house." That meant it could be deposited to his account at another bank but it would not be honored for currency unless he was a regular customer at the bank who had been accustomed to getting currency for payroll purposes. That was done to prevent banks from failing. After two or three months, confidence was restored in the banks, the suspension of convertibility was ended, and there were almost no bank failures. It was a very traumatic episode. In response to the panic of 1907, there was a Congressional investigation, and the Federal Reserve System went into operation in 1914 to prevent any such development in the future.

What was the actual course of events? From 1929 to 1933, far from preventing bank failures and bank collapse, the Federal Reserve System actually produced them.

On December 11, 1930, the Bank of United States failed. It was the biggest bank that had ever failed in the United States. Until then, the depression had been a more or less garden variety recession. But the failure of the Bank of United States set off runs on banks. According to its charter and its objective, the Federal Reserve System was supposed to step in and enable banks to meet demands of their customers by buying bonds on the open market or by providing currency through discounting assets of its member banks. It failed to perform this function. On the contrary, it allowed the runs to develop and banks to fail, until finally in March 1933 there was an absolutely unprecedented catastrophe in which all banks were closed for a week—including the Federal Reserve Banks, which had been set up to prevent such an outcome but instead ended up producing by far the worst and the most disastrous panic in American history.

From 1929 to 1933, the quantity of money in the United States fell by one-third. For every one hundred dollars of currency or deposits that people owned in 1929, there were

67 dollars available in 1933. One-third of all the banks were permitted to fail. This was easily preventable, and I can say that not merely from hindsight. There were many people at the time who were urging on the Federal Reserve System a policy which would have prevented this outcome, including some at the Federal Reserve Bank in New York. All this is documented in the book mentioned earlier, A *Monetary History of the United States*.

The reason for the Great Depression myth is very simple. Private enterprise has no press agent. Government does. Every government agency will inform you that anything bad that happens is the result of forces outside its control. But anything good that happens—who do you suppose produced that? If it weren't so tragic, it would be amusing to read the annual reports of the Federal Reserve System from its inception. Every year of prosperity, the Federal Reserve report says, "Thanks to the wise and farsighted policy of the Federal Reserve, the United States had a good year." Every year of recession or depression, the Federal Reserve report reads, "Despite the best efforts of the Federal Reserve System, events beyond our control . . . ." Even in 1932 and 1933, you have such statements in the Federal Reserve Board's annual report.

At any rate, far from being evidence of a defect in the private enterprise system, the Great Depression is evidence of the deficiency of governmental arrangements to manage the economy.

The Demand for Services Myth

Let me come to a third myth: the myth of a demand for government services. From the 1930s onward, there has been an enormous expansion in the scope of government. In 1929, just prior to the Great Depression, total government expenditures at all levels—federal, state, and local—were about 10 percent of national income. Today, the comparable figure is about 40 percent. Even that greatly understates government expenditures in a true economic sense, the control over expenditures by government.

To give a simple example: Anybody who buys a new automobile is required to spend something like $500 to $1,000 on items that he would not voluntarily choose, the safety and antipollution devices. Suppose that instead of government mandating that those be on every car, government had imposed a $1,000 tax on every new car and had used the proceeds to buy those attachments. We would then include that money as part of government spending, and it would raise the 40 percent figure. From an economic point of view, there is no difference between these two procedures. It might be good to have such devices on cars, or it might be bad, but that isn't the question. The question is what is the fraction of the national output whose use and allocation is determined through the political mechanism rather than through the decisions of individuals deciding separately how they want to spend their own money. And the answer is that it's well over 40 percent if we include these mandated expenditures.

In the process of going from 10 percent to well over 40 percent, the myth developed that these expansions in programs occurred in response to an overwhelming public demand, that the government has had to step in because the failure of private markets produced a grass roots demand that government do these things. This is a myth that could not be farther from the truth. Almost every expansion of governmental activity has had to be sold to the populace at large by misleading advertising that would make Madison Avenue blush. The community has had to be brought kicking and screaming to approve them.

Let me give you the greatest sacred cow of them all, Social Security. In the first place, it has nothing to do with social, and it has nothing to do with security. It's an utter misnomer; it's a program whereby you impose a very bad tax in order to provide very inequitable benefits. In the Orwellian language used to sell Social Security, what you and I would call taxes are called contributions. Is an involuntary payment a contribution? The tax you and your employer pay under Social Security is so labeled. If you buy an insurance policy or a retirement annuity or a pension, and you ultimately get your pension, that's a benefit, you paid for it. But if I get it from other taxpayers, ordinarily I would call it a subsidy. But under Social Security, subsidies are called benefits.

Much more fundamentally, the program was sold to the American people under essentially false pretenses, on the ground that the ordinary people were so shiftless, so little concerned with their own future that unless they were compelled by government to contribute to a fund and paid a pension afterward, they would all become charges of the state. The situation of the Great Depression, when people became charges of the state because of the state's mismanagement of money, was presented as typical. It was factually false that, the Great Depression aside, any significant number of people had become charges of the state because they had failed to provide for their own old age. Yet, that was the argument used to sell Social Security.

Again, maybe Social Security is a good thing. I'm not for the moment talking about that. I happen to think it is not. I think it's a terrible program, but maybe I'm wrong. I'm here concerned with the myth. Did Social Security reflect a grass roots demand for services? The answer is no. It was sold under false pretenses, and has since been expanded under similar false pretenses year after year by people who are in the business of selling government programs to the country.

Let me give a much simpler and more recent example, which I have already referred to: the safety and antipollution provisions for automobiles. Mr. Nader ran a crusade a few years ago that cars were unsafe and that we ought to have an all-wise government agency step in and protect us from ourselves, require us to have safety devices on the car, require us to fasten seat belts. Again, was there a grass roots demand for government to intrude into that area? Not a bit, it was a manufactured crusade which produced laws, the results of which most people don't like. Indeed, the absurd interlock system whereby you can't start your car unless you have first mastered the mechanics of the gremlins that the manufacturers built into your seat belts, led to such a national outrage that Congress repealed it. I doubt that people realize how extraordinary an episode that is. As a connoisseur of governmental intervention, I have tried to accumulate over the years the occasions on which an intervention has been eliminated. The list is very short. It includes postal savings, it includes Prohibition. It now includes the repeal of the provision for compulsory interlock. You will find it hard to add many to that list.

Consider another simple example. I was in Florida not long ago, just the week after Congress had passed a mass transit bill providing for billions of dollars to be spent in local communities on mass transit. There was a story in the local paper about a proposal to expand bus service, which had been put up to the local voters three years in a row in the form of approval of a bond issue. Three years in a row it had been turned down. Any student of democracy would say that that was pretty clear evidence that it was not something which the populace desired. But what happened? The newspaper story was, "Now that Washington has passed a mass transit bill, we'll be able to have that bus system," because the money will come from Washington. That surely was not a case where there was a grass roots demand.

The Free Lunch Myth

This leads to my next myth—the myth that government can spend money at nobody's expense. What was really involved in that last story was that somehow the local people do not pay out the money coming down from Washington, somebody else does. Of course, the truth is that the money makes a round trip between Florida and Washington, and there is a discount taken off for cash as it passes through Washington. Some of you may remember that wonderful description of government by the French economist, Frederic Bastiat, who said that government is that fiction whereby everybody believes that he can live at the expense of everybody else.

That is a widespread myth, that it is possible to spend money with nobody paying for it. You have everybody screaming that we ought to have new, bigger, more generous government programs. Where are we going to raise the money? Tax business. But business corporations can't pay any taxes. A corporate executive may sign the check, but where does he get the money? From his stockholders or from his customers or from his employees. Unlike the federal government, he doesn't have a printing press in his basement. So the only way he can pay money to the government is by imposing a burden on somebody. Government cannot spend money at nobody's expense, which in turn leads me to my final myth.

The Myth of Helping the Poor at the Expense of the Rich

Maybe government cannot spend money at nobody's expense, but, after all, we all know that government spends money to benefit the poor at the expense of the rich. Again, however, this is a myth. It is a myth which is promoted because everybody wants to do things for good purposes. We all

72

are in favor of helping the poor—provided you and I are defined as the poor.

I was at the recent summit conference President Ford called in Washington. I was amused by the parade of special-interest spokesmen who came to the platform, and one after another said, "It is absolutely essential that we cut the government budget to beat inflation. I will tell you how to cut the government budget: spend more on me."

The elementary fact is that almost all government programs are either a complete waste and help nobody, or they benefit the middle and upper-middle classes at the expense of both the very poor and the very rich. That proposition could be the subject of a longer talk, so here I can only illustrate it.

Consider the case mentioned earlier—Social Security. That is a program widely regarded as helping the poor at the expense of the middle and upper income classes. The facts are, first, that the tax which finances Social Security is the most regressive tax in our system. It's a payroll tax on wages up to a maximum, the reverse of what is regarded as a graduated tax. The benefits are related hardly at all to the amount of taxes anybody has paid, and in any event are to a large extent inequitable. A man who has a million dollars of income a year from securities will receive his full Social Security benefit after age 65. But if between ages 65 and 72 he works and gets income from labor, then not only does he get no benefits if he earns more than a modest amount, but he also has to pay additional taxes on the wages.

Much more fundamentally, youngsters from poorer families go to work and start paying Social Security taxes at age 16 or 17. People who are going to be in the upper classes go to college and graduate school; they don't start paying Social Security taxes until 24 or 25 or 26. On the other side of the picture, it is a demographic fact that richer people live longer than poorer people, so they will receive Social Security benefits for more years. The poor fellow at the bottom has been suckered into paying taxes for more years in order to provide better-off people with benefits for more years—and that is what is known as a program of helping the poor at the expense of the rich.

I have been making this statement for many years, so I am delighted to note that a recent study by the Brookings Institution, which can hardly be regarded as biased on my side, has documented the charge in great detail. It has demonstrated beyond a shadow of doubt that on average the effect of Social Security is to redistribute income from lower income groups to middle income groups.

Take any other program you name, and you will find a similar distributional effect. There is only one program I know which probably gives more money to people in lower income classes than to the people who pay taxes, and that is one of the worst programs we have, namely, direct welfare. It's a bad program, not because it gives money to the poor, but because it produces poor people, because it encourages people to be on welfare instead of being on wages. I don't blame them. If you and I are fools enough to make it to their advantage to subsist on welfare rather than work, they would be foolish not to take advantage of it. Nonetheless, I have a great deal more sympathy for that program than for almost any other, because it is about the only one that really contributes to people in lower income classes rather than to the people who pay the taxes.

The great scandal of our times, in my opinion, is government expenditure on higher schooling. There is no other program so perverse in its distributional effects. In the great state of California, which has one of the most extensive public higher education systems in the country, over 50 percent of the students at the colleges and universities come from the top 25 percent of the families by income. Five percent come from the bottom 25 percent. When I want to be demagogic, I say that's a system under which the people in Watts send to college the children from Beverly Hills.

One could go on and on along this line. But I conclude by urging you to be more skeptical of some of these myths, to be skeptical of the myth of the robber baron, the myth of the Great Depression, the myth that there is an underlying demand for government services, the myth that government can spend money at nobody's expense, and the myth that government has benefited the poor at the expense of the rich. We have been moving in a direction in which we have an increasingly limited control over our own lives, and that movement has been nourished by a series of arguments which, quite simply, are untrue.

II. Economic and Political Freedom

A. The Citizen and the State
B. Policy, Politics, and Principles

INTRODUCTION

If we are to live as an orderly society, communal ground rules must either impose or conduce order.

We can survive and work with one another in an arrangement of decree and coercion, with police power firmly exercised by a few and little independence and autonomy for the mass of the community. With variations on the theme, the bulk of history has been a story of centralized social direction, of edicts from on high, of suppression of individual view and initiative, of political tyranny accompanied by economic poverty.

Is there an alternative—other than anarchy—to imposing order by suppression? Adam Smith, the Scottish moral philosopher of the eighteenth century, envisioned a societal order based on an efficient economy which harnesses and utilizes, rather than represses, the ambition and initiative of people. Milton Friedman is one of the conspicuous contemporary economists in the Smithian tradition.

We cannot abolish scarcity; we cannot convince people to prefer less rather than more of desirable things. But we can establish institutions and evolve procedures which will permit people, within very broad and well-defined limits, to pursue their selfish interests in a manner which will contribute to the social wellbeing. These institutions and procedures are largely manifested in and specified by rights of people to use of property. Property rights inevitably must be limited—I cannot throw "my" brick through your window without your consent—but it is apparent, in looking around the world and its history, that some social mechanisms yield vastly greater freedom, wealth, and stability than do others.

The basic lessons of analysis and experience would seem evident. And yet, even in this Land of the Free, there are always many—including some in high places—who hunger to exercise authority over others. In effect, if typically not in intent, they seek to emulate our authoritarian adversaries, dragging us away from our splendid experiment with freedom and efficiency and forcing us back into the lamentable traditional stream of history.

Dr. Friedman emphasizes that individual responsibility is to be paired with individual opportunities—available choices to engage in legitimate activities in accordance with one's own purposes, criteria, and preferences. And such uncoerced but coordinated interactions of free people through open markets yield mutual benefits for all participants.

The role of government is critical in defining and making effective this arrangement in which individuals prosper by making themselves valuable to others in the community. But the state has not been content to limit itself to establishing the necessary ground rules and to providing a few critical, general services. Increasingly, it has become "paternal," causing both waste and divisiveness by its controls and directives, its intrusions and regulations, its "laws that do harm." "We are long past the stage of the entering wedge," warns Dr. Friedman. "Bit by bit, the principle that the government owns us has come to be taken for granted."

A. The Citizen and the State

A. The Citizen and the State

Is Capitalism Humane?

1978

I want to talk about an issue that is very much related to the whole problem of human freedom. It has to do with the question of whether capitalism is humane and what that means.

The arguments in the debate which has been going on for so long between the proponents of capitalism and of socialism have changed. The argument used to be strictly about the form of economic organization: Should we have government control of production and distribution, or should we have private market control? The argument of the proponents of government control used to be that centralized control was more efficient.

Nobody makes that argument anymore. Hardly a person in the world will claim today that nationalized industry, or socialism as a method of economic organization, is an efficient way to organize things. The example of Great Britain, the example of Russia, the examples of some of the other countries around the world that have adopted these measures, plus the domestic-grown examples of the post office and its fellows have put an end to that kind of talk.

The interesting thing is that, nonetheless, there is widespread opposition to capitalism as a system of organization. There is widespread support for some vague system labeled socialism. I believe that there is a simple explanation for this phenomenon. That explanation is an emphasis on moral values coupled with ignorance and misunderstanding about the relationship between moral values and economic systems.

The problem with this approach is that moral values are individual; they are not collective. Moral values have to do with what each of us separately believes and holds to be true—what our own individual values are.

Capitalism, socialism, central planning are means not ends. In and of themselves, they are neither moral nor immoral, humane nor inhumane. We have to ask what are their results. We have to look at what are the consequences of adopting one or another system of organization. From that point of view, the crucial thing is to look beneath the surface. Don't look at what the proponents of one system or another say are their intentions, but look at what the actual results are.

Socialism, which means government ownership and operation of means of production, has appealed to high-minded, fine people, to people of idealistic views, because of the supposed objectives of socialism, especially because of the supposed objectives of equality and social justice. These are fine objectives, and it is a tribute to people of good will that those objectives should appeal to them.

But you have to ask the question: Does the system—no matter what its proponents say—produce those results? Once you look at the results, it is crystal clear that the system does not. Where are social injustices greatest? Social injustices are clearly greatest where you have central control. The degree of social injustice, torture, and incarceration in a place like Russia is of a different order of magnitude than it is in those Western countries in which most of us have grown up and in which we have been accustomed to regarding freedom as our natural heritage.

Again, look at the question of equality. Where is there the greatest degree of inequality? In the socialist states of the world. I remember about fifteen years ago my wife and I were in Russia for a couple of weeks. We were in Moscow with our tourist guide and I happened to see some of the fancy Russian limousines, the Zivs, that were sort of a takeoff of the 1938 Packard. I asked our tourist guide out of amusement how much those sold for. "Oh," she said, "those aren't for sale. Those are only for the members of the Politburo."

In a country like the Soviet Union there is an enormous inequality in the immediate literal sense that a small select group has all of the services and amenities of life, and large masses have a very low standard of living. Indeed, more directly, the wage rate of foremen is much higher relative to the wage rate of ordinary workers in the Soviet Union than it is in the United States.

Capitalism, on the other hand, is a system of organization that relies on private property and voluntary exchange. It has repelled people, it has driven them away from supporting it, because they have thought it emphasized self-interest in a narrow way. They were repelled by the idea of people pursuing their own interests rather than some broader interests.

Yet it is clear that the results go the other way around. Only those countries in which capitalism has prevailed over long periods have experienced both freedom and prosperity. Of course, there is not perfect freedom—we all have our defects. Yet, in those mostly Western countries that have had capitalism there has been far more freedom, far more social justice, and less inequality than in the centrally controlled countries.

The question that you have to ask is, has socialism failed because its good qualities were perverted by evil men who were in charge? Was it simply because Stalin took over from Lenin that communism went the way it did? Has capitalism succeeded despite the immoral values that pervade it? I believe that the answers to both questions are in the negative. The results have occurred because each system has been true to the values it encourages, supports, and develops in the people who live under that system.

In discussing moral values here, we are concerned with those that have to do with the relations among people. In judging relations among people, I do not believe that the fundamental value is to do good to others whether they want you to or not. The fundamental value is not to do good to others as *you* see their good. Neither is it to force *them* to do good.

I believe that the fundamental value in relations among people is to respect the dignity and the individuality of fellowmen, to treat them not as objects to be manipulated for our purposes or in accordance with our values but as persons with their own rights and their own values—as persons to be persuaded, not coerced, not forced, not bulldozed, not brainwashed. That seems to me to be the fundamental value in social relations.

The essential notion of a capitalist society (which I'll come back to) is voluntary cooperation, voluntary exchange. The essential notion of a socialist society is force. If the government is the master, if society is to be run from the center, people ultimately have to be ordered what to do.

Whenever we depart from voluntary cooperation and try to do good by using force, the bad moral value of force triumphs over good intentions.

In the past few decades there has been a great decline in the moral climate. We see it in the rising crime statistics, in the lack of respect for property, in the kind of rioting that broke out in New York after the blackout, in the problems of maintaining discipline in elementary schools.

Why? Why have we had such a decline in moral climate? I submit to you that a major factor has been a change in the philosophy which has been dominant, a change from belief in individual responsibility to belief in social responsibility. If you adopt the view that a man is not responsible for his own behavior, that somehow or other society is responsible, why should he seek to make his behavior good?

Don't misunderstand me. On a scientific level it's true that what we are is affected a great deal by the society in which we live and grow up. Of course all of us are different than we would have been if we had grown up in a different society. So I'm not denying in the slightest the effect on all of us of the social institutions within which we operate, both on our values and on our opportunities.

I am saying only that a set of social institutions that stresses individual responsibility, that treats the individual—given the kind of person he is, the kind of society in which he operates—as responsible for and to himself, will lead to a higher and more desirable moral climate than a set of institutions that stresses the lack of responsibility of the individual for what happens to him and relieves him of blame or credit for what he does to his fellowmen.

I go back to the essence of capitalism and its relevance to the question of humanity. The essence of a capitalist system in its pure form is that it is a system of cooperation without compulsion, of voluntary exchange, of free enterprise.

I hasten to add that no actual system conforms fully to that notion. In the actual world we are always dealing with approximations, with more or less. In the actual world we always have impediments to voluntary exchange.

But the essential character of a capitalist system is that it relies on voluntary exchange, on your agreeing with me that you will sell something to me if I will pay you a certain amount for it. The essential notion is that both parties to the exchange must benefit. That was the great vision of Adam Smith in his *Wealth of Nations:* that individuals each separately pursuing his own self-interest could promote the social interest through exchange between people on the basis of mutual benefit.

This notion extends far beyond economic matters narrowly conceived. That's really the main point I want to get across, and I want to give you two very different kinds of example.

Consider the development of the English language. There was never any central government that dictated the English language and set up some rules for it. There was no planning board that determined what words should be nouns and what words adjectives. Language grew through the free market, through voluntary cooperation. I used a word, you used a word; if it was mutually advantageous to us to keep on using the word, we would keep on using it. Language grows, it develops, it expands, it contracts through the free market.

How did scientific knowledge and understanding arise? How do we get the development of science? Is there somehow or other a government agency that decides what are the most important problems to be studied, that prevents cooperation? Unfortunately, such agencies are developing, but in the history of science that isn't the way science developed. Science developed out of free-market exchange.

Capitalism is often reproached as being materialistic. It is often reproached as erecting money as a chief motive. Money is not a very noble motive, but it's cleaner than most. Look at the facts.

In any society, whatever may be its form of organization, the people who are not interested in material values are a small minority. There are no societies in the world today that are more materialistic than the collectivist societies. The Russian society, the Chinese society, the Yugoslav society— these are societies that put all their stress on materialism, on achieving economic goals and five-year plans, that destroy the non-materialistic achievements of mankind. Why? Because they are in a position to suppress minorities.

In order for a society to be at once humane and to give opportunity for great human achievements it is necessary that the small minority of people who do not have materialistic objectives have the greatest degree of freedom. And the only society that anybody has ever invented, that anybody has ever discovered, which comes close to doing that is a capitalist society.

When you hear people objecting to the market or to capitalism and you examine their objections, you will find that most of those objections are objections to freedom itself. What most people are objecting to is that the market gives people what the people want instead of what the person talking thinks the people ought to want. That is true whether you are talking of the objections of a Galbraith to the market, whether you are talking of the objections of a Nader to the market, whether you are talking of the objections of a Marx or an Engels or a Lenin to the market.

In a market society, in a society in which people are free to do their own thing, in which people make voluntary deals, it's hard to do good. You've got to persuade people, and there's nothing in this world that is harder. But the important thing is that in that kind of society it's also hard to do harm.

It's true that if you had concentrated power in the hands of an angel he might be able to do a lot of good, as he viewed it, but one man's good is another man's bad. The great virtue of a market capitalist society is that, by preventing a concentration of power, it prevents people from doing the kind of harm which concentrated power can do.

So I conclude that capitalism per se is not humane or inhumane; socialism is not humane or inhumane. But capitalism tends to give much freer rein to the more humane values of human beings. It tends to develop an atmosphere which is more favorable to the development on the one hand of a higher moral climate of responsibility and on the other to greater achievements in every realm of human activity.

Fair Versus Free

July 4, 1977

In presenting his energy program, President Carter stressed "fairness" as an essential ingredient of an acceptable program. The Federal Communications Commission seeks to enforce a "fairness doctrine" on radio and TV stations. We suffered numerous "fair trade" laws, until they were declared unenforceable. One businessman vies with another in proclaiming his faith in competition—provided that it is "fair."

Yet, scrutinize word for word the Declaration of Independence, the Constitution, and the Bill of Rights, and you will not find the word "fair." The First Amendment does not protect the "fair" exercise of religion, but the "free" exercise thereof; it does not restrain Congress from abridging the "fairness" of speech or of the press, but the "freedom" of speech or of the press.

From Umpire to Big Brother

The modern tendency to substitute "fair" for "free" reveals how far we have moved from the initial conception of the Founding Fathers. They viewed government as policeman and umpire. They sought to establish a framework within

91

which individuals could pursue their own objectives in their own way, separately or through voluntary cooperation, provided only that they did not interfere with the freedom of others to do likewise.

The modern conception is very different. Government has become Big Brother. Its function has become to protect the citizen, not merely from his fellows, but from himself, whether he wants to be protected or not. Government is not simply an umpire but an active participant, entering into every nook and cranny of social and economic activity. All this, in order to promote the high-minded goals of "fairness," "justice," "equality."

Does this not constitute progress? A move toward a more humane society? Quite the contrary. When "fairness" replaces "freedom," all our liberties are in danger. In *Walden*, Thoreau says: "If I knew for a certainty that a man was coming to my house with the conscious design of doing me good, I should run for my life." That is the way I feel when I hear my "servants" in Washington assuring me of the "fairness" of their edicts.

There is no objective standard of "fairness." "Fairness" is strictly in the eye of the beholder. If speech must be fair, then it cannot also be free; someone must decide what is fair. A radio station is not free to transmit unfair speech—as judged by the bureaucrats at the Federal Communications Commission. If the printed press were subject to a comparable "fairness doctrine," it too would have to be controlled by a government bureau and our vaunted free press would soon become a historical curiosity.

What is true for speech—where the conflict is perhaps clearest—is equally true for every other area. To a producer or seller, a "fair" price is a high price. To the buyer or consumer, a "fair" price is a low price. How is the conflict to be adjudicated? By competition in a free market? Or by government bureaucrats in a "fair" market?

Businessmen who sing the glories of free enterprise and then demand "fair" competition are enemies, not friends, of free markets. To them, "fair" competition is a euphemism for a price-fixing agreement. They are exemplifying Adam Smith's remark that "People of the same trade seldom meet together, even for merriment and diversion, but the conversation ends in a conspiracy against the public, or in some contrivance to raise prices." For consumers, the more "unfair" the competition, the better. That assures lowest prices and highest quality.

Rules or Actions

Is then the search for "fairness" all a mistake? Not at all. There is a real role for fairness, but that role is in constructing general rules and adjudicating disputes about the rules, not in determining the outcome of our separate activities. That is the sense in which we speak of a "fair" game and "fair" umpire. If we applied the present doctrine of "fairness" to a football game, the referee would be required after each play to move the ball backward or forward enough to make sure that the game ended in a draw!

Our Founding Fathers designed a fair Constitution to protect human freedom. In Thomas Jefferson's ringing phrases from the Declaration of Independence, "Governments are instituted among Men . . . to secure . . . certain alienable Rights, that among these are Life, Liberty, and the Pursuit of Happiness."

The Paternal State

January 22, 1979

The widespread public dissatisfaction with the performance of government that was demonstrated in last fall's election is generally attributed to the recent rapid growth in government spending—from 32 percent of the national income in 1957 to 35 percent in 1967 and 41 percent in 1977. No doubt that is one reason for dissatisfaction, but it is by no means the only one.

Another is inflation plus the growing recognition that inflation is produced primarily in Washington. Some people gain from inflation, others lose, but all recognize that inflation is a form of taxation that no one has voted for. The tax revolt is partly a modern version of the Boston Tea Party—a protest against taxation without representation.

A third reason is slow growth in productivity as a result of higher OPEC oil prices, an explosion in government regulation of industry, the distorting effects of inflation, and higher government spending. The average real spendable earnings of a family—allowing for both inflation and taxes—have shown little or no improvement in recent years. And the average conceals the sharply different effects of inflation on different groups. Many families are much better off and many are much worse off. It is one thing to accept rising government spending out of a growing income, another thing, out of a declining income.

Government's Changed Role

More important by far than any of these reasons, in my opinion, is the drastic change that has been occurring in the role of government: from providing traditional services—national defense, police and fire protection, elementary and secondary education, highways, the courts—to engaging in a wide range of new and expanded programs.

Expenditures on the traditional services can and do generate discontent about waste and inefficiency, but they do not set group against group. Expenditures for Social Security, welfare, Medicare, Medicaid, and other transfer programs, as well as for the host of new regulatory agencies, also generate discontent about waste and inefficiency, but in addition they involve taking from some to give to others, or imposing some people's values on other people. In the process, they inevitably set group against group.

Our government has been changing from a service state through which we jointly finance activities from which all or most of us benefit to a paternal state that increasingly decides for us what is good for us and increasingly redistributes income, taking from some and giving to others. Those who pay are understandably unhappy—but so are most of those who receive. They know that their cause is just and that they should get still more.

A simple calculation shows how drastic the shift has been. Not only has all of the increase in total government spending (Federal, state, and local) gone into nondefense spending, but in addition, spending on national defense declined from 12 percent of national income in 1957 to 11 percent in 1967 and 6 percent in 1977. As a result, nondefense spending rose from 20 percent of national income in 1957 to 26 percent in 1967 and 35 percent in 1977—an increase of roughly a third in each decade. And this calculation seriously understates the size of the shift. Spending not only on defense but also on other traditional services has decreased as a share of total government spending.

Threat to Security

The rapid growth of the paternal state threatens both national security and domestic harmony. It threatens national security by absorbing the taxable capacity of the nation, leaving little margin for a rapid expansion in military strength should international developments so require—a fact that other countries cannot fail to notice. It threatens domestic harmony by undermining a common sense of values, a feeling of community, of being members of the same society; by producing a Balkanization of the populace, as each special-interest group seeks to further its objectives at the expense of everyone else.

Fortunately, widespread public dissatisfaction with the performance of government may make it politically possible—and even profitable—to prune at least some of the lushest branches of the paternal state and return government to its traditional functions before the paternal state completely destroys our free society.

Will Freedom Prevail?

November 19, 1979

Inflation, unemployment, big government—these headline issues of the 1970s will remain headline issues of the 1980s. Important as they are, however, they are only the surface manifestations of a more fundamental issue—the values that will shape our society.

Individual responsibility, equality of opportunity, personal freedom, limited government—these were the values of our Founding Fathers. Their counterpart is an economy organized predominantly by free-market capitalism and a government that is small and decentralized.

These values have been giving way to a very different set: social responsibility, equality of outcome, personal welfare, paternalistic government. Their counterpart is an economy organized predominantly by central direction and a government that is large and highly centralized.

The conflict between the two sets of values was at first not evident, but is now plain. No one can fail to recognize how greatly the role of government has changed, how much of our lives it controls.

There is concern about the family. Defenders of the new

values blame capitalism. Its emphasis, they say, on rational calculation, material success, competition, exchange, undermines traditional nonrational institutions such as the family and church. But why should these effects show up only now, when capitalism is on the decline? The growth of government has done far more to undermine the family in the past fifty years than these amorphous effects did in the preceding millennium.

Consider Social Security. The young have always contributed to the support of the old. Earlier, the young helped their own parents out of a sense of love and duty. They now contribute to the support of someone else's parents out of compulsion and fear. The voluntary transfers strengthened the bonds of the family; the compulsory transfers weaken those bonds.

Consider education. The turmoil over what shall be taught, busing, neighborhood schools, mirrors a conflict over who shall control—parents or professional educators. Another basic function of the family is being taken over by the state.

The conflict affects every aspect of our life: family vs. government; private vs. communal property; freedom vs. fairness in speech, employment, trade; free choice as consumers vs. government protection of ourselves from ourselves.

The outcome is by no means certain: once government's grasp has extended as far as it has, it is not easily loosened.

The key issue of the 1980s is whether we shall be able to do so, and thereby reinvigorate the human freedom and economic freedom that together have made the U.S. a magnet for the poor and oppressed people of the world—or whether we shall succumb to creeping collectivism and become a totalitarian society.

What Belongs to Whom?

March 13, 1978

In defending continued regulation of oil prices, the authors of "The National Energy Plan," a White House document issued a year ago, wrote: "In 1973–74, the oil-producing countries raised the world oil prices fourfold. Deregulation of oil and gas prices would make U.S. producers the beneficiaries of those arbitrary price rises, and yield windfall profits from the increased value of oil and gas in existing fields. *The producers have no equitable claim to that enhanced value because it is unrelated to their activities or economic contributions.*" (My italics.)

In all the attention paid to energy and President Carter's proposals, there has been little discussion of the italicized sentence. Yet it expresses a philosophy that is fundamentally subversive of the basic principles on which this nation rests—the "unalienable" right of "all men" to "life, liberty, and the pursuit of happiness," in the words of the Declaration of Independence; the provision that "no person shall . . . be deprived of life, liberty, or property, without due process of law," in the words of the Fifth Amendment to the Constitution.

The Economic Basis . . .

The subversive nature of the italicized sentence has been little noticed because it was directed against oil and gas producers—stigmatized, justly or unjustly, in the public mind as big bad companies receiving "obscene" profits. But suppose we paraphrase the same argument for a different case: "Rising construction costs and a limited number of residential sites have raised sharply the prices of homes. Letting homeowners retain the proceeds they can derive from selling their homes would make them the beneficiaries of those arbitrary price rises, and yield windfall profits from the increased value of existing homes. The homeowners have no equitable claim to that enhanced value because it is unrelated to their activities or economic contributions."

And if you are not a homeowner, what about antiques? Or stamps? Or classic cars? Or, why not also the earnings of a rock star? Or a football player? Where can one stop?

Clearly, the subversive principle implicit in the sentence is that private property is not a right but a privilege that is conferred by an all-powerful state for the purpose of providing incentive.

Well, you may say, appeal to tradition aside, what's wrong with the argument that people are entitled to rewards only if the size of the reward is related to their "activities or economic contributions"? Isn't the presumption that increases (or decreases) in value will be related to the behavior of economic agents the basic justification for private property?

. . . of Liberty

Not at all. The preservation of liberty, not the promotion of efficiency, is the primary justification for private property.

Efficiency is a happy, though not accidental, by-product—and a most important by-product because liberty could not have survived if it had not also produced affluence. No doubt there is a large element of chance, of luck, in the rewards individuals receive in a free market from their property and their labor. No doubt there is also a large element related to economic contribution. But any attempt to separate the two in each individual case requires that someone decide which rewards are justified by economic contribution and which are not. And who can that be but the all-powerful state?

I am tempted to say about oil: "Beware the entering wedge. Accept the principle as applied to unpopular persons or groups, and you will be hoist on it yourself." But that is wrong. We are long past the stage of the entering wedge. Bit by bit, the principle that the government owns us has come to be taken for granted. Treasury Secretary Michael Blumenthal talks about how the Administration proposes "to give" so many billions of dollars in tax reductions to business or to individuals (i.e., anything not taken is "given" through the generosity of the government) and his interviewers raise not an eyebrow. The Treasury reports as "tax expenditures" sums not collected from citizens because of provisions of the tax laws—the ardent defenders of free speech raise no protest about the implied relation between the citizen and his government.

Is it not time that we rebelled against the doctrine that each of us has indelibly stamped on his back: "Property of the U.S. Government. Do not fold, spindle or mutilate"?

B. Policy, Politics, and Principles

Laws That Do Harm

October 25, 1982

There is a sure-fire way to predict the consequences of a government social program adopted to achieve worthy ends. Find out what the well-meaning, public-interested persons who advocated its adoption expected it to accomplish. Then reverse those expectations. You will have an accurate prediction of actual results.

To illustrate on the broadest level, idealists from Marx to Lenin and the subsequent fellow travelers claimed that communism would enhance both freedom and prosperity and lead to the "withering away of the state." We all know the results in the Soviet Union and the People's Republic of China: misery, slavery and a more powerful and all-encompassing government than the world had ever seen.

Idealists from Harold Laski to Jawaharlal Nehru promised the suffering Indian masses that "democratic economic planning" would abolish famines, bring material prosperity, resolve age-old conflicts between the castes and eliminate inequality. The result has been continued deprivation for the masses, continued violence between the castes and widened inequality.

105

Perverse Results: To come down to less sweeping cases, *rent control* has been promoted for millenniums as a way to hold down rents and ensure more housing for the disadvantaged. Wherever it has been adopted, the actual result has been precisely the opposite for all but a few favored tenants. Rent control has encouraged the wasteful use of housing space and has discouraged the building of more housing units. As a result, rents actually paid—whether legally or under the table—by all tenants except those who do not move have skyrocketed. And even the tenants who do not move complain about not being able to.

Over two years ago, when the San Francisco supervisors were contemplating a form of rent control, I republished in a local paper a *Newsweek* column of mine on rent control, prefacing it with the comment that only a "fool or a knave" could support rent control after examining the massive evidence on its effects. Needless to say, that did not prevent the majority of a board of supervisors, consisting of neither fools nor knaves, from enacting the ordinance I objected to. And the lessons of experience have not prevented the adoption of rent control in other cities—or the repetition of that same experience.

Urban renewal programs were urged to cure "urban blight" and improve the housing available to the poor. The result was a "Federal Bulldozer," as Martin Anderson titled his searching examination of urban renewal. More dwelling units were torn down than were constructed. The new units constructed were mostly for middle- and upper-income classes. Urban blight was simply shifted and made worse by the still higher density created elsewhere by removing the poor from the "renewed" area.

In *education*, professionalization, integration, bilingualism, massive doses of federal assistance—all have been promoted to improve the quality of schooling and reduce racial tension and discrimination. The result was predictable: a drastic lowering of educational performance and an increase in actual segregation of races, at least in the North.

President Nixon introduced *price controls* on August 15, 1971, to eliminate inflation, which at the time was running at about 4 to 5 percent per year. When controls ended in 1974, inflation soared into double digits.

The *Interstate Commerce Commission* was promoted in the 1880s and 1890s by the Ralph Naders of the day to discipline monopolistic railroads and benefit their customers. One group in today's Nader conglomerate has published a devastating study of the ICC demonstrating that it strengthened the monopoly power of the railroads, and later of trucking. The users of transportation have had the dubious privilege of paying higher prices for poorer service.

Name an Exception: Need I go on? I challenge my readers to name a government social program that has achieved the results promised by its well-meaning and public-interested proponents. I keep repeating "well-meaning and public-interested proponents" because they have generally been the dupes of others who had very clear self-interested motives and often did achieve the results that they intended—the railroads in the 1890s for example.

The amazing thing to me is the continued gullibility of intellectuals and the public. I wish someone would explain that to me. Is it simply because no one has given this widely documented generalization a catchy name—like . . . (suggestions welcome)?

The Politics of Economics

October 16, 1978

A newspaper story about President Carter's decision to propose a national health-insurance plan noted: "Carter's decision was contrary to advice of Treasury Secretary Blumenthal, Council of Economic Advisers chairman Charles Schultze and Budget Director James McIntyre." As happens time and again, politics overrode economics.

Is bad economics good politics? Unfortunately, the answer is not always NO. But fortunately, neither is the answer always YES. Consider three recent examples.

1. *Wage and Price Controls.* When President Nixon imposed controls on August 15, 1971, he was fully aware, as he has been ever since, that the controls were bad economics. In his memoirs, he writes that the "decision to impose [economic controls] was politically necessary and immensely popular in the short run. But in the long run I believe that it was wrong. The piper must always be paid, and there was an unquestionably high price for tampering with the orthodox economic mechanisms."

As Nixon says, the controls were good politics at the time. There was a run on U.S. gold that was certain to require an end to the U.S. commitment to tie the dollar to gold at a fixed price. Had Nixon simply closed the gold window— something he should have done long before—and done nothing else, the action would have been extremely unpopular. In the temper of the times, he would have been castigated as a do-nothing, negative President. By combining the closing of the gold window—a move to a free market abroad—with price and wage controls—a move in the opposite direction at home—as well as with other measures labeled as "stimulative," he was able to present a package that was hailed to the headlines as an activist, practical program.

There was wide backing for controls at the time—not only from the Galbraithians and liberal Democrats, but also from consumers and even a large part of the business community. Moreover, the controls did suppress inflation temporarily, and the economy did recover. The disastrous economic effects came *after* Nixon's landslide reelection in 1972, which the controls helped to bring about.

2. *The Energy Policy and Conservation Act.* When President Ford decided in December 1975 to sign this act, which extended for forty months controls on the price of domestically produced crude oil, he was well aware that it was bad economics. He had vetoed one earlier bill extending price controls. He signed this bill against his own convictions and against the advice of his top economists—Alan Greenspan, William Seidman, William Simon. He signed it because he was persuaded by his political advisers that it was good politics to do so.

In the event, his action was not only bad economics but also turned out to be very bad politics. His failure to veto the bill alienated potential supporters in Texas, Oklahoma, and other oil-producing states. It gave strong encouragement to

Ronald Reagan's entry into the race. The subsequent loss of Texas to Reagan in the primary and to Carter in the election can be traced pretty directly to this one action by President Ford.

Of course, in as close a contest as the 1976 presidential election, any one of a large number of factors might have reversed the result. But almost surely, one of those was Ford's signing of the bill extending price controls on oil. Had he vetoed it, he might well be president today.

3. *The Carter Economic Program.* President Carter's policies on energy, inflation, and taxes are all bad economics— as judged by economists of almost every variety of ideological opinion. The president's poll standing on economic issues suggests that they are bad politics as well.

The Crystal Ball

What conclusion can we draw from these and the many similar examples that could be adduced? The most important, I believe, is that the political crystal ball is even more clouded than the economic crystal ball. There is no reliable way to predict whether particular economic-policy actions will be good politics. In many cases, it is equally difficult to predict their short-run economic effects. It is generally far less difficult to know whether they will promote the long-run health of the economy. Consequently, it is not chimerical to hope that our leaders might let long-run economic considerations determine their policies. That might be good politics.

Rising above Principle

January 19, 1976

President Ford's recent straddle on the picketing and energy bills was a dazzling example of the political art of rising above principle.

Consider first the picketing bill. This bill provided that a labor union striking a subcontractor on a construction site could legally picket the whole project, with every likelihood of closing it down. The bill violated principles that the president had long held and strongly expressed in favor of greater freedom of individual workers from union control. Nonetheless, the president initially assured representatives of labor unions—and his own Secretary of Labor, John Dunlop—that he would sign such a bill. Before final passage, a storm of protest arose and the president vetoed the bill—keeping a promise being, of course, the principle politicians are most adept at rising above.

The energy story is the reverse. For more than a year, the president has stressed his opposition to government price controls in general and oil-price controls in particular. He has repeatedly asserted that he would veto any energy bill that did not provide for the rapid decontrol of the price of crude oil. Indeed, he vetoed one bill this summer on this ground—but then began his ascent above principle by agreeing to a temporary extension of controls while a "compromise" was worked out. Calling the bill that finally passed a "compromise" is an egregious case of misleading labeling. It not only continued earlier controls but expanded them, departing even further from free-market principles than the earlier bill. Yet this time the president signed it.

Public Interest

In my opinion, both bills were against the public interest. But of the two, the picketing bill would have done far less harm than the energy bill will do. By strengthening slightly the power of the construction unions, the picketing bill would have raised costs and reduced efficiency in an important industry. But the power of the construction unions derives from much more basic sources than their ability to picket—notably from the Davis-Bacon Act, which has the effect of imposing union wage rates on contractors performing any appreciable amount of work for the government. Even so, the unions have been losing power, by virtue of pricing themselves out of the market. The picketing bill would at most have slowed this process.

The energy bill is a different story. By keeping an unrealistic price ceiling on "old" oil and imposing one on "new" oil, it will discourage domestic production. We are already subsidizing the importation of oil. Continuation of the system of entitlements plus elimination of the tariff on imported oil will raise this subsidy substantially. Even the most persistent official defender of the energy bill, Frank Zarb, the federal energy administrator, claims only that it may temporarily reduce gasoline prices by no more than one cent a gallon. The White House estimates it will initially increase imports by 150,000 barrels a day, as against a hypothetical reduction of 200,000 barrels a day several years from now. The immediate effect will be to strengthen OPEC. The ultimate result will be higher prices for consumers, not lower prices—and a further extension of government intervention into a crucial industry. A double whammy—domestically and to our foreign policy.

Political Interest

The president presumably acted in what he regarded as his political interest. But I wonder whether his straddle will serve even that purpose. By signing the energy bill, he may have avoided a temporary rise in gasoline prices in response to the end of controls. If so, that is a definite political gain. But offsetting that gain are real costs. His ideological supporters like myself will be alienated more by his failure to stick to principle on energy than we will be pleased by his return to principle on picketing. His ideological opponents will not be appeased by his signing the energy bill—and the veto of the picketing bill has made it certain that construction unions that have often supported Republican candidates will not only oppose this one but campaign vigorously against him.

Beyond these specific effects, the president's behavior widens still further the gap between his rhetoric and his actions. His rhetoric is exemplary and courageous. His actions are weak and vacillating. Is politics always an exception to the rule that actions speak louder than words.

What Carter Should Do

June 18, 1979

As I was daydreaming the other day, I fancied that I heard President Carter give the following talk:

"For many years, your government has been trying to fine-tune monetary and fiscal policy in order to avoid both unemployment and inflation. A growing number of people—inside government and outside—have concluded that such fine-tuning has not worked. It has not prevented repeated recessions. It has not prevented worse and worse inflation.

"Our government's failure in this important area inevitably raises questions about its performance in other respects.

"That troublesome question has prompted me to reappraise what government can and should do. I speak to you to report my conclusions and to recommend a major change in government policy."

The New Deal: "The role of the Federal government has been expanding ever since the Inauguration of President Franklin D. Roosevelt. What have been the results?

"One of the first New Deal objectives was to cure the problems of agriculture. The tractors that crowded the streets of

Washington some months ago, as well as the explosive rise in food costs, are ample evidence that these problems remained. Government programs have not preserved the family farm. They certainly have not assured food to the public at reasonable cost. But they have cost the taxpayer many tens of billions of dollars.

"Another problem area attacked early in the New Deal was housing. Public housing was followed, after World War II, by urban renewal, and, in 1965, by a new Cabinet department, the Department of Housing and Urban Development. Has adequate housing been assured for all, and especially for the poor? Has urban blight been eliminated? Hardly. The urban-renewal program, according to one expert, Martin Anderson, destroyed 'four homes, most of them occupied by blacks, for every home it built—most of them to be occupied by middle- and upper-income whites.' Public-housing projects built at great expense—for example, the Pruitt-Igoe houses in St. Louis—have literally been blown up because they had become a hotbed of crime and a breeding ground of poverty.

"Other costly social programs—welfare, job creation, health, and so on in endless variety—were enacted for the noblest of motives. Yet, they have repeatedly failed to achieve their intended objectives.

"Regulation of industry has neither protected the consumer from high costs nor promoted healthy and innovative enterprise. Deregulation of airlines—the first real break in a ninety-year trend—has been a boon to both airline companies and their passengers.

"What of energy—our nation's No. 2 problem after inflation? The United States, I discovered, never had a problem of energy shortages and crises, except during World War II, until government interfered on a large scale—first, in 1954, when ceiling prices on natural gas encouraged excessive use and discouraged production; then in 1971, when President

Nixon imposed his ill-advised freeze on all prices and wages; then in 1973 and 1974, when price controls were removed from all products except petroleum products; then in 1975, when President Ford continued the Federal Energy Administration instead of letting it expire and signed a bill continuing controls on the prices of domestically produced crude oil.

"These government interventions in energy were consolidated during my Administration into a Department of Energy. We pay $16.50 a barrel under long-term contract for oil from OPEC and even more on the spot market, but force domestic producers to sell oil for as little as $5.90 a barrel. In the process, we tax domestic production of oil in order to subsidize oil imported from abroad. The Department of Energy spends $3.50 of the taxpayers' money per barrel of domestically produced oil, without producing a single drop of oil. These counterproductive governmental policies have increased our use of foreign oil—even though we recognize the danger of depending on a thin line of oil tankers stretching halfway around the world.

"OPEC is a convenient excuse for the energy crisis. But OPEC itself was created largely by our own foreign and economic policies—and it could never have reached its present level of influence and power without the unintended and unwitting support of our mistaken domestic policy.

"We must learn from experience. We must not repeat past mistakes. Accordingly, I am today initiating a major change in government policy.

"On economic policy, I have requested the Council of Economic Advisers and the Office of Management and Budget to prepare a series of budgets for coming years that will cut government spending as a fraction of national income, eliminate deficits, and reduce taxes. I shall recommend that Congress adopt such a budget policy. In addition, I am recommending to Congress that it limit the discretion of the Federal Reserve System, and instruct it to reduce the rate of monetary growth over the next few years to a level that is commensurate with the real growth of the economy.

"On energy, I recommend that the Department of Energy be abolished. Effective the earliest possible date, I am removing all controls on the prices of crude oil, natural gas, and other petroleum products, confident that the market will promptly bring the energy crisis to an end.

"These changes will start the process of replacing short-term improvisations by long-term planning and of reducing government intervention in your lives."

A Radical Program: "These recommendations represent a real change in direction. But I do not make them lightly. And I do not make them without sincere admiration and respect for the dedicated services of our public officials. The fault is not theirs; the fault is in the system, not in the people who have been administering it.

"These recommendations do not take us into uncharted seas. On the contrary, they return us to the basic principle that produced the miracle of America: reliance on individual initiative and voluntary cooperation. We must have compassion for the less fortunate among us. We must see to it that no resident of the United States is without assistance in time of real need. But that compassion must be joined with realism. It must be expressed in ways that take account of the experience of the past fifty years.

"If you, the citizens of the United States, will join with me in this task, we can, in Abraham Lincoln's words, 'have a new birth of freedom.' "

* * * *

This talk will never be given. Yet, is it only a daydream that the policy it outlines would not only be good for the country but might also prove a political triumph for President Carter? He might ask Margaret Thatcher.

Balanced on Paper

June 23, 1980

As I observe the hullabaloo about the Congressional budget resolution for fiscal 1981 (October 1, 1980, through September 30, 1981), I am moved as a citizen and taxpayer to shout at the president and most members of Congress: "Have you no shame?" Yet that is an irrational reaction.

The president has made a great to-do about his determination to achieve a balanced federal budget for 1981, and so have representatives and senators of both parties. They have been patting themselves on the back for their great efforts to assure that the resolution specified a balanced budget—boasting of long and arduous labors and difficult compromises and deploying all the other rhetoric that our elected officials are addicted to in the misleading advertisements they transmit to their constituents.

Yet suppose you were to poll the 435 representatives and 100 senators on the question: "Will the final 1981 budget be in balance?" How many would answer yes? I doubt that even a baker's dozen would do so—provided you could guarantee complete anonymity.

Accounting Tricks: Members of Congress know, as every informed observer knows, that the balance is strictly on paper—that the actual outcome is almost certain to be another large deficit. And even a paper balance—actually a paper-thin surplus of $200 million in a budget of over $600 billion—was achieved only after strenuous accounting sleight of hand. Spending was shifted from fiscal 1981 to fiscal 1980, and tax revenue the other way, in order to "balance" the 1981 budget by increasing the already large deficit for 1980. Projected spending and revenue for 1981 are calculated on favorable assumptions for budget balance—good economic conditions and high inflation during 1981. These assumptions are accepted by the same president and the same members of Congress who stress their determination to end inflation despite recession. The talk is of fiscal restraint, austerity, and the like, but the paper balance was achieved only by providing for a massive increase in taxes combined with a continued increase in government spending (in real terms, after allowing for inflation).

What are we to make of this contrast between the public show and the private beliefs of our elected representatives? Or of the cooperation by the media in foisting this Potemkin village on a suspecting public? Headlines proclaim the "adoption" of a "balanced budget" for the first time in twelve years. Six or seven paragraphs down, you will be told that knowledgeable observers doubt that the budget will in fact be balanced, citing the likely effect of the deepening recession on government spending and tax receipts, and citing also the past record of budget resolutions—a record of actual spending and actual deficits that have consistently exceeded the amounts specified by the resolution.

Some decades ago, John K. Galbraith used to bemoan an alleged contrast between private affluence and public squalor. I doubt that even he is brazen enough to do so today in the light of existing government budgets. However, there is a different contrast that deserves much fuller attention—between the moral standards that guide people as private citizens and as "representatives" of the public.

Double Standard: Most members of Congress are honest, decent people who you and I would be proud to have as personal friends and who we would trust implicitly to tell us the truth and to honor their obligations. Yet, as "public servants," they consistently behave very differently, making assertions that they know to be untrue, making promises that they know will not be kept, voting for legislation that they know to be undesirable.

It is tempting to berate politicians and government officials for hypocrisy. But that is a mistake. Such a double standard could not long continue if it were not a route to political success. Politicians who behave differently tend not to be reelected. (James Buckley is a dramatic example.) With some notable exceptions, only hypocrites survive. And we, the voters, are responsible for that outcome. Ultimately we, not those we elect, are to blame.

There is little point in looking to the moral regeneration of either politicians or ourselves for a solution to this basic weakness in our political system. We shall do far better to seek a change in our effective political constitution that will narrowly limit the power of those whom we elect and thereby alter the incentives of both politicians and voters.

III. Government
Regulation

A. The Nature of Regulation and Bureaucratic Behavior
B. Consequences of Regulation: Energy
C. Free Market Solutions and the Big Brother Alternative

INTRODUCTION

The student of open markets is a student of mechanism and process through which preferences are registered and costs are taken into account, with uncoerced individuals adapting to available options according to criteria of personal well-being. In such a societal arrangement, markets are cleared, and the economy is equilibrated.

This picture of freedom and efficiency is appreciably distorted by government regulatory intrusions. The intrusions are always for fine alleged purposes, generally involving "consumer protection" and the promotion of competition. But typically consumers are left with fewer and more expensive options as suppliers are favored or restricted, with windfall gains provided to some existing suppliers, costs increased for most, and would-be competitors frustrated.

The base of concentrated power is thus government, not business. Businesses, sometimes helped and often hurt by government, exert such power as they have, not by manipulating the public but by influencing government, which can dispense subsidies and provide protection against both domestic and foreign competition as well as tax and increase the costs and complexities of operations. Such antics of regulation—licensing of occupations, price controls and supply allocations, assigning of transportation routes and communication channels, environmental controls and safety requirements, conditions of hiring and firing and educating, tariffs and quotas—have reduced competition and aggregate wealth, created spe-

cial interest enclaves, and weakened the link between usefulness of economic performance and reward.

Some of such foolishness is found in energy policy over many years, culminating in the fiasco of gasoline lines in the 1970s. "Economists may not know much," concedes Milton Friedman. "But we know one thing very well: how to produce surpluses and shortages." All that is required is for Big Brother to decree a price too high (farm products, labor services) or too low (gas, apartments, credit). Government has perverted in various ways the normal workings of the price mechanism, which would have promoted efficient adaptation to changing technological and competitive circumstances. Through imposing price floors and ceilings, tax subsidies and penalties, supply allocations, and importation manipulations, both consumers and producers have been given wrong signals, wasting our scarce resources, creating confusion and promoting community divisiveness, and reducing our strength in an unfriendly world.

The community generally is best protected, not by prohibitions and directives, but by competitive processes of the market, which provide consumer options and supplier incentives to please consumers. Dr. Friedman provides a large sample of the market distortions, buyer and supplier distractions, and efficiency and equity dilutions when government decrees are substituted for free markets. The examples are fascinating—in a snake-house sort of way.

A. The Nature of Regulation and Bureaucratic Behavior

Regulatory Schizophrenia

June 29, 1981

The schizophrenic attitude of the Reagan Administration toward deregulation is well illustrated by some remarks attributed to Reese Taylor, President Reagan's nominee for chairman of the Interstate Commerce Commission. He is reported as having said that he'd like to slow the agency's pace in deregulating the trucking industry, and that he favored "keeping 'appropriate' controls on bus lines seeking to enter markets to prevent excessive expansion of bus authority."

By contrast, President Reagan is clearly on record as favoring the reduction of regulation in order to promote competition and to revitalize our free-enterprise system. Indeed, deregulation is one of the four pillars of President Reagan's economic program.

Moreover, the Reagan Administration has moved promptly and effectively to deregulate. Measures already taken include prompt oil decontrol, the rescinding of many regulations issued in the final months of the Carter Administration and a moratorium on the rest, assignment to the Office of Management and Budget of responsbility for reviewing all proposed regulations to ensure that benefits exceed costs and the establishment of a Cabinet committee headed by Vice-President Bush to survey existing and proposed regulations and to ride herd on their elimination or simplification.

Pro-free Enterprise . . . The apparent schizophrenia reflects, I believe, a confusion between two very different positions: being pro-free enterprise and being pro-business—which, in practice, always means pro-*existing* business. The contrast is clearest in foreign trade. Tariffs are anti-free enterprise, yet pro-existing business. "Voluntary" restrictions on auto exports by Japan are anti-free enterprise yet pro-Chrysler, -Ford, and -General Motors.

The contrast is less clear for regulation. Some regulations are both anti-free enterprise and anti-existing business. For example, oil price control restricted competition and the free market and also harmed many oil-producing and oil-refining businesses. Yet even in this case, "tin can" refineries set up to take advantage of subsidized foreign oil were harmed by the end of price control.

The regulations that have multiplied fastest in the past decade have been directed toward the environment, health, safety, and consumer protection. These have all tended to substitute the judgment of bureaucrats for the judgment of the market, and hence have been both anti-free enterprise and anti-existing business. They have all imposed heavy costs on industry, generally for questionable benefits. With respect to these regulations, no confusion arises.

The situation is very different for the more traditional areas of regulation, such as ICC regulation of railroads and trucking. Though such regulations were adopted in the name of promoting competition, in practice the agencies administering them have become captives of the industries they were supposed to regulate. As a result, their effect has been to suppress competition, preserve monopoly, and harm both consumers and potential competitors.

Trucking is a particularly egregious case. An ICC permit to operate is a valuable piece of property—to the person who has it. It is valuable because it restricts entry and thereby enables truckers to charge higher prices than they otherwise could. Private wealth, public nuisance.

. . . vs. pro-Business: The great virtue of free enterprise is that it forces existing businesses to meet the test of the market continuously, to produce products that meet consumer demands at lowest cost, or else be driven from the market. It is a profit-*and-loss* system. Naturally, existing businesses generally prefer to keep out competitors in other ways. That is why the business community, despite its rhetoric, has so often been a major enemy of truly free enterprise.

We cannot expect existing businesses to promote legislation that would harm them. It is up to the rest of us to promote the public interest by fostering competition across the board and to recognize that being pro-free enterprise may sometimes require that we be anti-existing business.

The failure to distinguish between being pro-free enterprise and pro-business is by no means special to the Reagan Administration. It has been endemic. It has led persons opposed to particular existing businesses to oppose free enterprise. It has led them to regard proponents of free enterprise as simply paid apologists for existing businesses. It has led them to support government measures that have achieved the very opposite of their intended purpose.

The Corporate Clout

May 5, 1980

> Corporations are those massive structures of orga-
> nized economic and political power that decide where
> Americans shall live, what they shall eat, where they
> will work, and how they will die . . . in this coun-
> try corporate power has had an unchallenged pre-
> eminence [over government].

> —Alan Wolfe in the *Saturday Review*

These words come from a criticism of my wife and me for
blaming, in our book "Free to Choose," big government instead of big business for our ills. They could equally well
serve as the manifesto of the "Big Business Day" recently
organized by Ralph Nader, when activists assembled to protest the evils of "big business" and were exhorted to do something about it. The favorite cure: bigger government.

Influential Americans: An interesting contrast is provided by
a survey of U.S. opinion leaders reported recently by *U.S.
News & World Report*. The opinion leaders were asked to
name the five people "you think exercise—through position,

132

power, ability, or wealth—the most influence in national decision making." Of the persons designated by this poll as the ten "most influential," seven are elected or appointed government officials, and one, Rosalynn Carter, is the wife of a government official. Only one, David Rockefeller, who ranked 5th, is from private enterprise. The final person in the top ten is Walter Cronkite, who ranked 8th, a representative of the fourth estate.

Of the twenty next "most influential Americans," ten are connected with government and four with the news media. Of the remaining six, one heads a trade union (13th), two head major corporations (25th and 29th), one heads a bank (30th), and two are private citizens who fall into none of these categories (22d and 28th).

Not much sign there of a country run by big business; rather, by big Washington—the home base of most of the top 30.

The anti-big-business group will dismiss this evidence as a facade, as window dressing. These are the puppets, they will say. The strings are really being pulled behind the scenes by "corporate power," especially by multinational corporations.

That contention has some merit, but it cannot explain a top corporate income-tax rate of 46 percent; or the still higher effective tax rate produced by the distortion of corporate profits by inflation. It cannot explain the enactment of a so-called "windall-profits tax" on petroleum products estimated to total $227 billion in the next decade, against the concerted opposition of the multinational oil companies. And this list can be extended indefinitely.

Corporations do exert power, and too much power. However, they typically exert that power by their ability to influence government rather than through the marketplace. The Chrysler Corporation could never, through the market, have forced workers who earn less than most Chrysler employees to pony up funds to bail it out of financial difficulties, and, incidentally, pay those high wages. Yet that is just what it has succeeded in doing through government. The U.S. Steel Corporation could never, through the market, have forced buyers of its steel to pay more than the price at which Japanese or other foreign steel was available. Yet that is just what it did through the now abandoned "trigger price" system enforced by the U.S. Treasury, and what it is trying to get the government to do on a still larger scale.

Influential Regulators: Airline fares were kept high and service limited, not through the market but through the Civil Aeronautics Board, as has been demonstrated since the partial deregulation of air travel. The trucking industry imposes billions of dollars of extra cost each year on all of us, not through the market but through the Interstate Commerce Commission. Opposition to the deregulation of trucking comes not from the trucking industry's customers, nor from potential competition, but from big business, big labor (the Teamsters), and the trucking firms themselves.

The Big Business Day protestors are barking up the wrong tree. With few exceptions, big business—or small business for that matter—can exercise arbitrary power over the rest of us only when it can form an alliance with government, whether Federal or local. The protestors would do far more to promote their ostensible objectives by urging complete free trade abroad, and a wider measure of free enterprise at home, rather than by asking for another dose of government intervention.

Good Wealth, Bad Wealth

August 10, 1981

Mr. Smith uses savings of $60,000 accumulated over many years to build a factory producing widgets much desired by consumers. Mr. Jones uses savings of $60,000 accumulated over many years to buy a medallion entitling him to operate a taxicab in New York City, rendering services much desired by consumers.

Both Smith and Jones have created private wealth—embodied in a factory in the one case, in a taxicab medallion in the other. Both use their private wealth to serve the public. From a private point of view, their cases are indistinguishable and equally deserving of commendation.

Private vs. Public: From the public point of view, the two cases are radically different. Smith's wealth adds to the total supply of physical capital available to serve the public; it adds to the productive capacity of the community. Jones's does not. It simply transfers wealth to Jones from whoever owned the medallion before. Moreover, the existence of such a category of wealth—a share, as it were, in a governmentally created cartel—harms the community as a whole.

The medallion has a market value only because the sum that customers are willing to pay for the services rendered by the cab exceeds the cost of owning and running the cab, including, of course, the value that Jones attributes to his own labor. In the absence of the cartel, the excess of returns over costs would lead more persons to enter the taxicab business. The fares fixed by local authorities for taxicab service would go down, or cabs would be more easily obtainable, until costs and returns came into balance. Consumers would be better off and so would the additional owners of cabs and all hired drivers of cabs.

I make this comparison not to attack the limitation of taxicab licenses—though that limitation deserves to be attacked—but to illuminate a major source of confusion about the role of government in regulating industry, and a major source of the difficulty in ending undesirable regulation.

To continue with my example, suppose that the numerical limitation on taxicabs were eliminated, and licenses were freely issued. The effect on Jones would be identical to the effect on Smith of government expropriation of his factory without compensation—something specifically prohibited by the Fifth Amendment to the Constitution ("Nor shall private property be taken for public use without just compensation"). It is entirely understandable that Jones would oppose the one measure with the same righteous wrath with which Smith would oppose the other.

Though privately identical, the two actions would have wholly different effects on the public interest: the one eliminates "artificial" wealth that was created by government edict and that harms the public; the other confiscates physical wealth that benefits the public.

Ethics vs. Politics: On an ethical level, Jones is as deserving of compensation for the taking of his wealth as Smith would be for the taking of his wealth—the only qualification being that Jones acquired the medallion in the knowledge that an exclusive privilege granted by government could be withdrawn by government. Yet acting in accordance with that ethical judgment would be disastrous. It would require government to compensate every vested interest in society, however created, for any harm done to it as a result of legislation (including the taxpayers providing the funds to pay compensation!). Aside from the impossibility of determining even the rough monetary effects of legislation, such a principle would enshrine the status quo and prevent the correction of past errors. Moreover, its logical counterpart is that government should receive the monetary equivalent of any gains to persons from the legislation—again not only a practical impossibility but a measure that in principle would drastically change the effect of legislation by eliminating any incentive for persons to take advantage of potential benefits—just as compensating for losses would eliminate any incentive to minimize losses.

My simple comparison has relevance to a wide range of problems—ICC restrictions on trucking and busing, CAB restrictions on airlines, FCC controls on television, radio, and telephones, price ceilings on crude oil and natural gas, licensing of occupations, rent controls, and on and on. All are cases of private wealth created by measures that harm the public. We have in the process created a Frankenstein monster that it will not be easy to subdue.

B. Consequences of Regulation: Energy

The Energy Crisis

1978

I want to start this discussion of energy by reading to you a quotation of something that was written some time ago by an eminent expert on energy.

"The question concerning the duration of our present cheap supplies of oil cannot but excite deep interest and anxiety wherever or whenever it is mentioned: for a little reflection will show that oil is almost the sole necessary basis of our material power. . . .

"The constant tendency of discovery is to render oil a more and more efficient agent, while there is no probability that when our oil is used up any more powerful substitute will be forthcoming. . . . We cannot make up for a future want of oil by importation from other countries. . . . Considering how greatly our manufactures and navigation depend upon oil and how vast is our consumption of it compared with that of other nations, it cannot be supposed that we shall do without oil more than a fraction of what we do with it. . . .

"It is then simply inferred that we cannot long continue our present rate of progress."

Now if I were to ask you who wrote that and when, I

suspect most of you would say, "Well, that must have been written about five or six years ago by a very, very prescient man, a man who really saw the future very well." Truth to tell, those words, with one exception, were written more than a century ago. The one exception is that everywhere I used the word "oil" the original had the word "coal," and it dealt with Great Britain and not with the United States. The excerpts are from a book called *The Coal Question* written by a great English economist, W. Stanley Jevons, and published in 1865. He at that time in writing about the coal question said exactly the same thing, as you can see, that our supposed experts have been saying about the oil question in these recent years.

What conclusion do we draw from that? Jevons was a very eminent and able man; he was no charlatan. He was one of the great economists of the nineteenth century, but he was dead wrong. Should we draw the conclusion that therefore no problem will arise? Not at all.

Should we draw the conclusion that what we have to do is try to pin it down and make sure how much future resources we have? That's not the right conclusion either.

The fact is that we cannot get out of the energy problem by being able to predict things that are not predictable. The right conclusion is that the crystal ball is inevitably cloudy and that is the nature of the world we live in; that all specific predictions about the precise amount of this, that, or the other deserve skepticism; and that what we need is not some kind of specific detailed blueprint for the future. What we need is an adjustment mechanism that will enable us to adapt to what happens as it develops.

And of course, as nearly everybody knows, there is such a system—namely, the price mechanism—which successfully steered us over several centuries from wood to coal to whale oil to petroleum to natural gas. That is a mechanism in which it is in the self-interest of millions of people to make their best guesses about the future, in which it's unnecessary to have a single blueprint, in which you have an automatic adjustable process as things develop.

If we have a problem today in the energy area—as we do—it is solely, in my opinion, because that system has not been allowed to work. The price mechanism has not been allowed to work by the U.S. at home, and it has not been allowed to work by the OPEC cartel abroad, which has created a monopoly and has raised the price drastically by keeping the amount of oil available to the market down to the amount demanded at that price.

The problem in energy and in the approach to energy is part of a much broader problem. It is what you might call the difference between the economic way of thinking and the engineering way of thinking.

The broader problem is epitomized by the famous Club of Rome report, *Limits of Growth,* which got so much attention a few years ago. That was a report in which engineers said we have finite resources, and we are faced with a terrible future in which sooner or later we are going to run out of steel or coal or whatever you want to name. They said we have to adjust our sights; we must recognize that there are limits to growth and reconcile ourselves to that prospect.

This approach is completely wrong. It confuses physical limits with limits to economically available resources. Today the total world volume of known oil reserves is higher than it has ever been, not only in absolute barrels but relative to a year's consumption, relative to the population.

Evidence from prices is even more decisive than the evidence from these calculated figures on reserves—for they are engineering figures. Prices really tell you something about what has been happening to the availability of energy. The basic fact here is that the real cost of energy, adjusting for inflation—the amount you have to pay for a unit of energy expressed in terms of other goods or expressed in terms of the number of minutes you have to work to pay for it—has been going down for at least a hundred years. The real cost of energy relative to prices in general in the U.S. went down by 28 percent from 1950 to 1970.

It may surprise you to know that a gallon of gas that you buy at the service station, including taxes, costs less today in real terms relative to other goods and services than it did twenty years ago. In the interim, the cost went down sharply. In the past three years it has come back up sharply, but it is still below the level at which it was twenty years ago.

Why is it relevant to the energy crisis that the real cost has been going down? This goes back to the way in which the market operates with respect to exhaustible resources. In economics we have a very simple test of whether anything is an exhaustible (or economically finite) resource, namely: Is its price rising over time relative to other goods and services? But if we look at the price of energy and of oil, its real price has been going down for a century—and without any artificial government-imposed controls.

How can that be? There are only two possible explanations. Perhaps the oil companies who have been selling this oil are extremely stupid and shortsighted and have been throwing away billions of dollars out of their ignorance or incompetence, which seems to me a rather extreme assumption. At any rate, if that were the case it would have been possible to make a great deal of money by buying a few of them up and setting them on a sensible course. The only other explanation is that from an economic point of view oil is not an exhaustible resource.

In any economic sense, oil—or, more generally, energy—far from being an exhaustible resource, is a producible resource at more or less constant or indeed declining cost because of the improvements in the technology of drilling and exploring and so on. You can find more oil, and therefore if the future price tended to rise above the present prices, that would give somebody an incentive to go out and find more and add to the supply. Of course, that situation may change.

But is it sensible to talk the way so many people talk about the oil industry? I interpret them as saying that the whole history of oil is divided into two periods: from 1859 when oil was first discovered in Titusville, Pennsylvania, to 1973 and from 1973 to 1978. Conceivably that could be true, but it seems to show a very shortsighted point of view and a lack of perspective to divide all of 120 years of history into two parts, one 115 years long and one five years long, and say, "We know that there has been a fundamental change." Maybe, but if we allowed the market to work and if there were such a fundamental change, it would show up in the form of a change in the price pattern and in the incentives to people to find, exploit, and use oil.

Well, then, you will say, "Why is it that we have an energy crisis? Why does President Carter propose a major far-reaching program that would restructure the whole energy industry? Why does he say that this is the first priority item, that fighting the energy fight is 'the moral equivalent of war'?"

The answer, I believe, is that three forces have coalesced to produce a real energy problem. The first and the most immediate was the establishment of an effective OPEC cartel, of an effective monopoly, which, beginning in 1973, was able to raise the price of oil substantially. The second factor has been the cumulative effect over time of government controls and regulations beginning, to go to the most important of them, with the fixing of the price of natural gas from the fifties and of oil from 1971. And the third has been a change in the philosophical attitudes of the public toward the role of government in these affairs. Consider these three things in turn: the cartel, the cumulative effect of regulations, and the change in philosophical attitudes.

There is a very simple interpretation of what's happening in oil and in the cartel: a group of nations got together and formed a monopoly. Again, just as with the theory of exhaustible resources, there is a well-developed economic theory of how a cartel will tend to behave.

Let's suppose you were able to form a cartel. What should you do? The thing that is most obvious is that your monopoly power is very much greater at the time you form the cartel than it will be later on. Therefore the sensible thing for you to do, the way to exploit a cartel, is first to push up the price very high and then over time, as people start to restrict their consumption and other sources of supply come in, you gradually let the price come down. That is what has been happening. The real price of oil today is decidedly lower than it was in 1973 when the cartel was first formed, because price rises elsewhere have been greater than any rise in the dollar price of oil.

The price has not been coming down as fast as I thought it would, or as it would have if it weren't that we and the rest of the world have been helping the cartel. We have been helping the cartel by doing everything we can to prevent people from having an incentive to discover and produce more oil. Not only the United States has been guilty; every country, whether it be Great Britain or other countries, has seen this as a great opportunity to make a killing, and so they have tried to impose heavy taxes or to offer exploration on terms which would bring back to the government a large fraction of the gross receipts. The result is that there has been less exploration and a less intensive research for new sources than would otherwise have occurred.

But the United States has been the worst sinner. It's fascinating to note that energy consumption has dropped in every major country in the world except the United States since 1973. The reason it has not dropped in the United States is because we in the United States have been trying to prevent the price of energy from reflecting fully the higher OPEC cartel price. We, in fact, have been subsidizing the import of oil. As I'm sure all of you know, the effect of the entitlement program in oil is that we are paying a subsidy of roughly three dollars a barrel on every barrel of oil imported from OPEC, or from anybody else outside this country. An incredible policy but a fact.

Let me turn to the second main factor, which has been the cumulative effect of government contols and regulations, and here the oil industry must bear much of the blame. I would not want for a moment to suggest the idea that we have a wicked government on one side and a pure snow-white oil industry on the other—very far from it. No industry in this country speaks more loudly about the virtues of free enterprise, yet few have done more to undermine it than the oil industry.

Until the 1970s, government controls and regulations were very strongly pro-Texas and Oklahoma oil industry. Beginning in the 1920s, the oil industry induced the Federal government to introduce a specially favorable treatment of taxes, the infamous percentage depletion arrangements. Beginning in the 1930s, you had prorationing of oil by state boards— the Texas Railroad Commission, the Oklahoma Commission, and so on—essentially a state-administered cartel allocating production quotas to various outfits.

In 1959, President Eisenhower—so you can see I'm strictly bipartisan—introduced oil import quotas. That's an absolutely marvelous example of the perversity of government, of how government has an absolute genius for doing precisely the opposite of what needs to be done. In 1959 the situation was that foreign oil was cheap and plentiful; domestic oil was, relatively speaking, expensive and scarce. So what did we do? We kept out the cheap plentiful oil and we encouraged domestic oil by imposing a quota on the amount of oil that could be imported from abroad. The result was to make the price of oil in the United States about $1.50 a barrel higher than the price of oil in the world market.

Now comes 1973 and what happens? Foreign oil becomes scarce and expensive; domestic oil becomes, relatively speaking, cheap and available. So what do we do in the full wisdom of the government? We impose a tax on the production of domestic oil and give a subsidy to importing the expensive, scarce foreign oil. If you could think of more perverse policies, you have a better imagination than I have.

You had two other sets of controls that entered in: the controls on the price of natural gas starting in the 1950s and on the price of oil starting in 1971. As with any price control which holds the price below the market price, control of the price of natural gas encouraged consumption and discouraged production. It was inevitable that you were then going to have shortages and disruptions of supply for natural gas.

The harm done was greatly exacerbated by the imposition of general price and wage controls on August 15, 1971, by President Nixon, which included control on the price of oil. We tend to forget that the price and wage control measures of 1971 bear a great deal of responsibility for our present oil problem. They have been eliminated on every other product but not on oil. The retention of price controls on oil has discouraged production, encouraged consumption, increased the fraction of our energy that comes from abroad, and established new vested interests in the maintenance of controls.

The third factor that entered in, as I mentioned earlier, was a change in philosophical attitudes. One thing is clear if we come back to our earlier distinction between economics and engineering: there is no economic argument for the regulation of oil. There is no argument on economic grounds for having a Department of Energy, for having a Federal Energy Administration, for having price controls, and there is almost no professional economist who will argue otherwise.

As Professor Edward Mitchell said in a piece he wrote on the ideology of oil: "The last five chairmen of the President's Council of Economic Advisers, spanning the Johnson to Carter Administrations, have supported the decontrol of both oil and gas." Those five chairmen run the gamut of professional opinion from what would be called left to right, yet every single one of them was in favor of the deregulation of oil and gas.

The bulk of informed professional opinion believes that the energy industry is effectively competitive, or would be if the government got its cotton-picking hands out of it. So there is no economic argument along these lines.

You have had a great deal of talk about obscene profits. There again there is no argument. A number of careful studies of profits in the oil industry demonstrate that, on the average of good years and bad, profit is not out of line; indeed, if anything, it is somewhat low relative to invested capital by comparison with other industrial groups. So there is no economic argument on any level for the regulation of oil.

Why then do we have it? Again I quote Edward Mitchell, who said about Carter's energy program:

"The preference of houses over cars, nonenergy over energy, solar energy over oil, indeed almost any other source of energy over oil, is what leaps out at you when you read the national energy plan. You will not find these preferences explained in any economics book. The answer is to be found in political philosophy."

An even more striking example of philosophy is the attitude that has been expressed toward so-called windfall profits. Let me quote to you a sentence from President Carter's national energy plan: "The producers have no equitable claim to that enhanced value from deregulation because it is unrelated to their activities or economic contribution."

To see how radical a doctrine that is, how fundamentally subversive of our system, let me apply the same principle in another context: the owners of homes "have no equitable claim to" any rise in their value "because it is unrelated to their activities or economic contribution."

Is there anybody who would say that was an expression of the philosophy that should guide America? Who is going to decide what change in value is related to "activities or economic contribution"? If people are going to be entitled to keep a rise in value only insofar as it flows from their own "activities or economic contribution," then somebody has to decide.

That sentence in the national energy plan is a sentence declaring the alleged case for a government that owns everything. If it has the right over the supposed owners to the rise in the value of oil, it has the right to the rise in the value of houses; it has the right to the rise in the value of your services. It has, indeed, complete ownership rights to you and me as well as to our property.

That's, as I say, a thoroughly subversive doctrine, and yet there is no doubt that it is the direction in which philosophical attitudes have been moving.

So our present energy problem, like our present problem in many other areas, derives from the cumulative effects of the cartel, of government controls and regulations, and of the change in philosophical attitudes.

What are the present status and prospects then for U.S. regulation? You have many predictions that President Carter will not get his way, that there will come out of Congress an energy plan that will be very different from what he put in. I think that's wrong; I think President Carter has already gotten his way in what really counts. He has already gotten the major element of the whole program, namely, a Department of Energy, a Department of Energy which has 20,000 employees and a budget of $10 billion—a budget roughly equivalent to the profits of all of the American oil companies combined. He is going to spend—what is it?—three dollars a barrel for oil in order to keep the price of oil from rising.

But more important, you therefore have 20,000 full-time employees who have a strong motivation to propagandize for and to work for the government takeover of the oil industry. Is there any doubt that that is what they will be doing? Let every other element of that program be defeated in Congress, and it's only a question of time until they are enacted because what really matters is having the position of power from which to move.

The final question is, why have we moved in this direction? Why have we adopted these counterproductive controls on the prices of gas and oil? Why have we enacted this enormously expensive boondoggle of a Department of Energy? The answer is straightforward. The enactment of such intervention has been and remains politically profitable.

This is only a particular manifestation of the general sentiment in society at large toward more and more government control. After all, this isn't the first industry that's being nationalized. Passenger traffic has been nationalized through Amtrak; freight traffic is on the way to being nationalized through Conrail. It's a continuation of that same trend that the energy industry is on the way to being nationalized.

What is the bottom line? What will be the effect on the price and the availability of energy? Obviously the situation is not very favorable, but I think it's a mistake to go to the other extreme and become a purveyor of doom and gloom. Just as you should never underestimate the ability of people to adjust their beliefs to their interests, you should also never underestimate the ability of people to get around controls that interfere with their interests.

There is a strong incentive for people all around the world to find ways of getting around artificially expensive energy, to find ways to produce and benefit from alternate forms of energy. As a result, the price of crude oil will come down in real terms as it has been coming down since 1973. Sooner or later the cartel will break down.

We are not going to head for doom and gloom. The price of energy will come down. We are not going to have a worldwide shortage of energy, but we are going to pay a heavy price. We shall have a lower standard of living than we could have had, we shall have a lower rate of growth than we could have had, and we shall end up stuck with another major government parasite sucking our life blood and making it more difficult to overcome the adverse effects of government controls on our lives.

Blaming the Obstetrician

June 4, 1979

The explanations of the energy crisis and gasoline shortage that gush forth from government officials, newspaper reporters, and TV commentators are tantamount to blaming the obstetrician for the baby.

A rapacious oil industry did not produce the gasoline shortage. Wasteful consumers did not produce the gasoline shortage. Hard winters did not produce the gasoline shortage. Not even Arab sheiks produced the gasoline shortage.

After all, the oil industry has been around for a long time— and has always been rapacious. Consumers have not suddenly become wasteful. We have had hard winters before. Arab sheiks have desired wealth as far back as human memory runs.

Why Now? The subtle and sophisticated people who fill the newspaper columns and the airwaves with such silly explanations of the gasoline shortage seem never to have asked themselves the obvious question: why is it that for a century and more before 1971, there were no energy crises, no gasoline shortages, no problems about fuel oil—except during World War II?

There is an energy crisis, there are gasoline lines, for one reason and one reason only. Because government has decreed that there shall be. Of course, government has not done so openly. The president never sent a message to Congress asking it to legislate an energy crisis and long gasoline lines. But he who says A must say B. The government, beginning with President Nixon on August 15, 1971, imposed maximum prices on crude oil, gasoline at retail, and other petroleum products. And, unfortunately, the quadrupling of crude-oil prices by the OPEC cartel in 1973 prevented those maximum prices from being absolished when all others were. Maximum legal prices for petroleum products—that is the key element common to both World War II and the period since 1971.

Economists may not know much. But we know one thing very well: how to produce surpluses and shortages.

Do you want a surplus? Have the government legislate a *minimum* price that is *above* the price that would otherwise prevail. That is what we have done at one time or another to produce surpluses of wheat, of sugar, of butter, of many other commodities, and, most tragically, of teenage labor. The minimum wage is a legislated price above the price that would otherwise prevail for the labor of many teenagers. Like every minimum price, it enhances the amount supplied and reduces the amount demanded, and so produces a surplus, in this case of unemployed teenagers.

Do you want a shortage? Have the government legislate a *maximum* price that is *below* the price that would otherwise prevail. That is what New York City and, more recently, other cities have done for rental dwellings, and that is why they all suffer or will soon suffer from housing shortages. That is why there were so many shortages during World War II. That is why there is an energy crisis and a gasoline shortage.

There is one simple way to end the energy crisis and the gasoline shortage tomorrow—and I mean tomorrow and not six months from now, not six years from now. Eliminate all controls on the prices of crude oil and other petroleum products. The gasoline lines would melt faster than the snows of winter.

Other misguided policies of government and the monopolistic behavior of the OPEC cartel might keep petroleum products expensive, but they would not produce the disorganization, chaos, and confusion that we now confront.

Gas Would Cost Less: And, perhaps surprisingly, this solution would reduce the cost of gasoline to the consumer—the *true* cost. Prices at the pump might go up a few cents a gallon, but the cost of gasoline today includes the time and gasoline wasted standing in line, and hunting for a gas station with gas, *plus* the $10.8 billion annual budget of the Department of Energy, which amounts to around nine cents per gallon of gasoline.

Why has this simple and foolproof solution not been adopted? So far as I can see, for two basic reasons—one, general, the other, specific. First, to the despair of every economist, it seems almost impossible for most people other than trained economists to comprehend how a price system works. Reporters and TV commentators seem especially resistant to the elementary principles they supposedly imbibed in freshman economics. Second, removing price controls would reveal that the emperor is naked—it would show how useless, indeed harmful, are the activities of James Schlesinger and his 20,000 employees. It might even occur to someone how much better off we were before we had a Department of Energy.

Projecting Energy Futures

September 15, 1980

There is currently a glut of crude oil in the world. Its price, which doubled in the past year, is now declining, as are the retail prices of petroleum products in the United States.

The "experts" are nearly unanimous in predicting that these developments are temporary; that the current glut will soon disappear and be replaced by renewed scarcity; that the price of oil, even after adjustment for inflation, will climb steadily and gradually for most of the 1980s.

Feast or Famine: One thing seems to me certain: this consensus forecast is wrong. The future will either be much better or much worse. One possible outcome is that the price, adjusted for inflation, will decline sharply during the next four or five years, and supplies of crude oil will be ample. The other possible outcome is that another crisis will occur—like the activation of the OPEC cartel in 1973 and the turmoil in Iran in 1978. In that case, the price of oil will again shoot up sharply as it did on those two occasions, and crude-oil supplies will be scarce.

Political rather than economic developments will determine which outcome is realized. If political instability in the Persian Gulf is restricted to Iran, the real price of oil will continue to decline. On the other hand, internal disturbances in Saudi Arabia, Iraq or any other major oil-producing country, comparable with the Iranian revolution, would precipitate another oil crisis.

I have been much criticized—indeed, awarded a booby prize by the Association for the Promotion of Humor in International Affairs—for my prediction in this space in 1974 that OPEC could not long maintain the quadrupled price of oil, that the cartel would go the way of earlier cartels and break down. I was wrong. But my mistake was in timing, not direction. In addition, I did not foresee the occurrence of the Iranian revolution—there my crystal ball was indeed opaque.

From 1974 to the fall of the Shah in 1978, the price of oil, corrected for inflation, did decline—by about 25 percent—as a result of both economies in consumption and an increase in non-OPEC production, two reactions to be expected from the sharply higher price of oil. In the five years before the OPEC price hike, world oil consumption rose by no less than 43 percent; in the five years after the price hike, consumption rose only 12 percent. On the supply side, OPEC production went *down* by 4 percent from 1973 to 1978; non-OPEC production went *up* by 22 percent. And developments in both demand and supply would have been decidedly more favorable had it not been for the perverse energy policies followed by many countries, most especially the United States. Those policies sought to shelter retail prices of energy from the full effect of the OPEC price hike, inhibiting conservation; they taxed domestic production of energy and subsidized the cost of imported oil, inhibiting the production of energy. Even I underestimated the capacity of government to do the wrong thing!

Nonetheless, by 1978 the OPEC cartel was in trouble. It was saved by the ayatollah. Iran accounted for nearly one-tenth of world oil production during the first nine months of 1978. The threat to this major source of supply produced panic among the users of oil and unleashed a major increase in demand. The resulting bonanza for producers of oil other than Iran inevitably forced a sharp jump in price.

The higher price of oil, in turn, is reinforcing the incentives for conservation and additional production. Moreover, though government policy continues to interfere with market adjustment, for the most part it has shot its bolt and can do little additional harm. The current glut and the weakening price of oil are evidence that the market adjustment is occurring and is proceeding more rapidly this time than earlier. This process will continue and oil prices will continue downward—*provided that there is not another Iran.*

Illusory Surplus: There is widespread fear that ever-growing Arab financial surpluses will disrupt the world's financial system. If my analysis is correct, this fear is illusory. If the price of oil declines, the surpluses will evaporate. If one or more additional Irans occur, the surpluses will also vanish, at least for the countries involved—as Iran's is vanishing. That outcome would raise major problems—but how to "recycle" Arab surpluses will be the least of them.

C. Free Market Solutions and the Big Brother Alternative

Who Protects the Consumer?

1978

In recent years consumer advocacy has been something of a real growth industry. It has been sparked in this country, of course, by Ralph Nader, who played the same role in developing the consumer advocacy industry that Henry Ford played at a much earlier date—and with much greater benefit to the consumer, I may say—in developing the automobile industry. But since Ralph Nader has developed into a multinational conglomerate, he has had many imitators and many successors; and there has been a whole host of organizations and agencies that have developed supposedly to represent the consumer.

The old agencies—the ICC, FDA, SEC, CAB, FCC, FTC, FPC—have been supplemented by a host of new ones: the NHTSA, the OSHA, the OPA, the EEOC, the CPSC, the CFTC, the NTSP, and so on. Note that one of the effects of the increasing crowding of the spectrum has been that they have had to go from three alphabetical letters to four.

In 1975 there were at least twenty-seven major federal govemment regulatory agencies. They issued 60,000 pages of rules or proposed rules in the *Federal Register*. Their regulations occupied no less than 72,200 pages in the Code of Federal Regulations. I went to my bookshelf and measured what that would mean, and that turns out to be not a five-foot shelf of great books, but a literal twenty-four-foot shelf of not-so-great books.

The expenditures of these agencies on your behalf have literally tripled from $1.6 billion in 1970 to $4.7 billion in 1975 and, unless I am greatly mistaken, we ain't seen nothing yet.

Those are only the direct expenditures; those are what the government spends through the budget. They do not include the costs which those agencies have imposed on the rest of us in the form of the standards mandated on us. If you take the simplest example that is most familiar to all of us, the so-called antipollution and safety requirements on automobiles, those amount to about $500 to $1,000 worth on any automobile. If the government imposed a tax on each automobile of $500 and used the proceeds to pay directly for those items, that would appear in the Federal budget. But there is no economic difference whatsoever between that and the present situation in which you and I pay for them directly, but are forced to pay for them whether we want them or not. So the Federal budget figures are a gross underestimate.

Well, we have had this enormous growth, and we are continuing to have it, in these agencies in expenditures, in rules, in regulations. Is the consumer better protected as a result? Can he now settle back and say, "Well, now, I'm all taken care of, I can forget about that"? My thesis, and one I am going to try to persuade you of, is that the answer is a resounding no! That on the contrary these agencies, these regulations, these bureaucrats have not only picked our pocket but they have left us less well protected than we were before.

When we as consumers really need help, we will find the self-styled consumer advocates conspicuous by their absence.

The banning of cyclamates and the proposed ban on saccharin, some of these people would claim, is pro-consumer. But then if you ask them whom are you protecting the consumer against, the answer is clear: himself. They are, they believe, pro-consumer by which they mean that they are forcing you to do what you would do of your own free will if you were as sensible and as smart as they are.

After all, the argument about saccharin and cyclamates is that they carry the risk of producing cancer. I have no competence whatsoever to question the scientific evidence on that; I wouldn't try to. But obviously the right way to handle it from the point of view of a believer in freedom is to let people know and let them make their own choice. Let everyone know what the risks are, saying they are one in ten million or one in a thousand—whatever may be the best evidence—have a free press. But then the question is: Ought you not be able to make your own choice?

I am saying that I don't believe that some people sitting in Washington ought to be able to make that judgment for me. That's my business. I belong to me, not to them. It's my life at stake.

And let me point out to you how utterly inconsistent and contradictory are the people involved in this. There's not a person in one of these consumer agencies who would deny for a moment that the smoking of cigarettes is a far greater source of death from cancer and from other diseases than even the most extreme figures you could put on cyclamates and saccharin. If it is right, if it is correct, if it is proper public policy to protect the consumer against himself with respect to saccharin or with respect to cyclamates, the same logic says it is proper policy to prohibit smoking of cigarettes.

I refer to cigarettes, but of course you realize that the same thing is true of booze. Again, there is overwhelming evidence that the consumption of alcohol causes far more human deaths both directly and indirectly through accidents on the highways than any conceivable effect from saccharin or from cyclamates. Indeed, there is no doubt whatsoever that if you could effectively prohibit drinking you would save more lives on the highways than by all of the so-called safety equipment on cars. The seat belts and air bags don't even hold a candle, in terms of the number of lives that would be saved, to the cessation of alcohol.

Needless to say, I am not in favor of prohibition. I'm not in favor of prohibition of alcohol; I'm not in favor of the prohibition of smoking; I'm not in favor of the prohibition of cyclamates or saccharin. I am simply in favor of letting everybody know what the risks are and letting everybody do what he, in the fullness of his own wisdom and judgment, wishes to do.

Let me emphasize that I'm not questioning the motives of the people involved. There's an old saying that you all know, about what it is that the road to hell is paved with. Intentions are one thing; it's results we want to look at. Let me give you an even better quote and this is one from Justice Brandeis going back, I think, to the year 1928 or 1929 in one of the Supreme Court cases: "Experience should teach us to be most on our guard to protect liberty when the government's purposes are beneficial. Men born to freedom are naturally alert to repel invasion of their liberty by evil-minded rulers. The greater dangers to liberty lurk in insidious encroachment by men of zeal, well-meaning but without understanding."

How can the consumer be protected? How is he protected? The clear answer, the answer that in my opinon cannot be denied, is that the most effective protection of the consumer is free competition, free competition at home and free trade throughout the world. It is the free market, the free private market, with free competition everywhere that is his best protector. The great danger to the consumer is from monopoly whether it be private or public. The great protection to the consumer is having alternative sources of supply. The thing that keeps the consumer from being exploited by Mr. X is that if Mr. X tries to charge him too much he can turn to Mr. Y.

People often say to me, why do you make such a big difference between private enterprise and government enterprise? What difference does it make whether you have a great big General Motors Corporation, it's a bureaucracy of the most extraordinary size, or whether you have a great big government corporation producing automobiles? Well it makes a big difference, and the difference is that there is no way in which General Motors can get a dollar from you unless you agree to hand it over. General Motors cannot send a policeman to pick your pocket, but the U.S. government can, and as a result General Motors must serve your interests in a way which the U.S. government as a whole, or a government agency, does not have to. It's the possibility of other competition. It's because if General Motors doesn't serve your interest, you can buy a Ford product or a Chrysler product, or you can buy a Volkswagen, or you can buy a Toyota. That's what prevents General Motors from exploiting you.

Let me emphasize: competition does not protect the consumer because businessmen are more softhearted than bureaucrats or because they are more altruistic or because they are more generous, but only because it is in the self-interest of the entrepreneur to protect the consumer. And on this subject let me quote to you from what the father of modern economics, Adam Smith, wrote 200 years ago in *The Wealth of Nations*.

"It is not from the benevolence of the butcher, the brewer, or the baker that we expect our dinner, but from their regard to their own self-interst. We address ourselves not to their humanity but to their self-love and never talk to them of our own necessities but of their advantages. Nobody but a beggar chooses to depend chiefly upon the benevolence of his fellow citizens." So it's not from benevolence but from self-interest.

To return to the FDA, suppose it weren't there. What would prevent business from distributing adulterated products? It would be a very expensive thing to do. Consider the story that many of you have heard of a New Jersey firm which had been producing and marketing a high-quality soup product for fifty years very profitably. After fifty years of apparently safe operation, one case of adulterated or contaminated soup cans got out. That company very shortly went bankrupt. That's not a very sensible business practice.

What about the claim that the consumer cannot judge the quality of complex products, that he therefore requires the government's support and help? The market provides a very excellent answer. When it comes to complicated products, the consumer doesn't really trust his own judgment; he trusts the judgment of middlemen. Let me illustrate. No ordinary consumer is an expert about the quality of shirts, ties, shoes, goodness knows what. If one of them goes bad, if you find it's defective, do you go back to the shirt manufacturer? No, you go to the department store from which you bought it. The department store is acting as your middleman. Indeed, the reason the department store can exist and make money is because it can get the consumer to have confidence that the department store will sell him a good product for the price. In the same way you rely on a Sears Roebuck or a Montgomery Ward or a General Electric or a General Motors, not because they are altruistic but because it is in their self-interest to get the reputation and the standing which would be destroyed if they consistently turned out bad products.

What about the claim that consumers can be led by the

nose by false advertising, the claim that people like John Kenneth Galbraith have done the most to promote? The simplest answer is that the consumer can't be. And if you don't believe it, ask Mr. Ford what happened to the Edsel, promoted by an enormously expensive advertising campaign—one of the great duds of all times. The fact is that the consumer ultimately is going to decide on the quality of the product he buys and not on the claims. On the contrary he is going to be put off by the claims.

Finally, and most important, does it pay enterprises to engage in false advertising? It's like the question of whether it pays them to produce shoddy products. Of course occasionally a fly-by-night outfit can make some money by fooling people. But you know, Abraham Lincoln was absolutely right when he said many, many years ago, "You can fool some of the people all the time, you can fool all of the people some of the time, but you can't fool all of the people all of the time."

The profits of most enterprises depend on continuing customers; they don't depend on a one-time sale. And it is therefore in the long-run self-interest of the company to be sure that its advertising corresponds to the product it is selling. As I say, of course, there will always be some shoddy products, there will always be some quacks, there will always be some con artists. We've got to wait until the next world before we get rid of them. But we have to look at the real world.

I think that as consumers we are pretty good, if you leave us alone. But I think in our role as citizens we're terrible. And for good reason. If you're going to buy something every day it pays you to look into whether that's good or bad. If you are going to deal with the grocer daily, you'd better be pretty sure that he is a reasonably reliable grocer and that you'll get what you order and that he won't shortweight you or shortchange you.

But you may get to vote once a year—on what? On a long, long list of propositions, with very little relationship between your vote and what ultimately happens. How much time does it pay you to inform yourself about that? It's just a waste of time and energy; you're not going to influence anything.

So it's understandable, in my opinion, why the individual is far better as a consumer in his private capacity than he is as a citizen in his public capacity. And what we have to do from that point of view is to drive home that lesson and make individuals recognize the enormous importance of setting a limit to the powers that we grant to the government.

Whose Intolerance?

October 6, 1975

Can anyone watch the TV pictures of armed guards escorting little children to school, of serried ranks of police, National Guardsmen, and federal marshals "protecting" schoolchildren and schools, without recognizing that something is badly wrong with the methods that we have adopted to achieve a desirable objective? Can enforced confrontation of race with race produce racial harmony? Can forcing parents to equate better schooling for their children with either segregated schools or compulsorily integrated schools have any other result than to intensify racial division—undermining both racial tolerance on the part of whites and self-confidence on the part of blacks?

Needed: Freedom of Choice

What is wrong? I submit that the answer is intolerance—not intolerance of whites for blacks, which surely exists, but intolerance of liberal reformers who "know" what is good for other people and are prepared to force it on them, intolerance of liberal reformers who can and mostly do exercise choice among schools for their own children—by living in affluent suburbs or sending them to private schools—but refuse to grant a similar freedom of choice to the less fortunate parents who at present have no alternative to the public school.

No doubt, the violent reaction of whites to compulsory integration via forced busing partly reflects racial intolerance. However, true tolerance requires tolerance of what we regard as intolerance. It requires us to persuade, not force, to set an example, not retire to our cozy segregated (by income) existence while sending out the police, the National Guard and federal marshals to force on others not the values we actually live by but values we believe others should live by.

Moreover, much opposition to busing does not reflect racial intolerance at all. It reflects simply the natural and commendable desire of parents to protect their children and to enable them to get as good an education as possible. I suspect that it reflects also increasing outrage at the continued reduction in the area of free choice—not only in choosing schools but in the many other respects in which government controls our lives. Schools are important and offer a dramatic outlet for cumulative frustration.

There is a far better way to promote racial tolerance and at the same time to reverse the tragic decline that has been occurring in the quality of our schools. That way is to extend, not restrict, free choice of schools by parents. Instead of the present system under which school boards allocate pupils to schools, let every parent be given a governmental education "voucher" for each child that can be used in total or partial payment for school tuition at any "approved" public or private school, freely chosen by the parents. Let absence of racial discrimination be one requirement for approval of a school. The financial cost to the community can be kept to its present level by making the maximum dollar value of the voucher equal to current government spending on schooling per child of school age, whether now attending public or private school. Require public schools to compete openly for students and to close down if they cannot do so successfully.

Answer: School Vouchers

This voucher plan would give all parents the opportunity to chose schooling for their children that the more affluent among us now have. It might well lead to more busing than now, but it would be voluntary, not forced. It would promote racial tolerance by leading to the choice of schools on the relevant ground of the interests and aptitudes of the students, not the irrelevant ground of the color of their skin. It would simultaneously ease the other major problems of public education. It would promote a rapid improvement in the quality and diversity of education as competition worked its magic in schooling, as it has in every other area. It would counter the increasing militance and power of teachers' unions by diversifying the employers of teachers, and by replacing government as employer by private enterprise. It would remove the threat to personal security of teachers and students because schools that did not provide such security would rapidly lose custom.

An admirable reform. But, I fear, it is also a forlorn hope—stifled at its conception by an alliance between intolerant liberal reformers and an intransigent educational bureaucracy.

The Draft Isn't the Issue

September 29, 1980

The controversy about whether to reintroduce a draft is the wrong battle about the right question—how to raise the quality of the U.S. military forces.

Whether you approve of the draft on moral, ethical, or political grounds, or disapprove of it, as I do, the draft is simply irrelevant to that basic question. Grant it every virtue proponents attribute to it, and major personnel problems would remain. Solve those problems, and the military arguments for conscription evaporate.

The Big Hitch: The draft affects first-term recruits. Yet the key personnel problem of the military is the retention and recruitment of skilled persons, from mechanics to airline pilots.

A draft—*with no other change*— would not solve this problem. It could provide more young men and women for the military to train. But neither general reasoning nor past experience gives any reason to expect that the draft would lead to more reenlistments, especially among the abler first-termers. Beyond the first term, how would a draft persuade skilled

172

personnel to remain in the military despite higher wages in the civilian economy?

True, a draft might fill the Reserves. It has done so in the past by persuading those who are anxious to avoid being drafted to sign up as Reserve members. But that sabotages the main argument advanced for the draft—that it would provide the military with higher-quality recruits. The Reserves would also gain from the trained ex-draftees who would sign on after completing active duty. But that undermines the secondary argument that the draft would encourage retention of able first-termers in the military.

If the draft will not solve the personnel problem, what will? In my opinion, two related measures are necessary: first, higher pay and improved conditions of service for military personnel, particularly at junior and intermediate levels (the number of generals per thousand military personnel is at an all-time high); second, horizontal recruitment of skilled personnel.

The first measure is self-evident; the second less so. The military has long insisted on getting skilled personnel primarily by recruiting 18- and 20-year olds, training them, and promoting them through the ranks. This costly and inefficient practice may have been justified at one time when almost every person in the military had to be prepared to engage in direct personal armed combat. It makes no sense today when many, perhaps most, persons in the military will never be anywhere within sight of an enemy, even in case of major war. No business enterprise could afford to adopt such a personnel policy.

The alternative is the kind of horizontal recruitment that has been practiced in every major war. Does the military need skilled plumbers and mechanics to keep its aircraft carriers in operation? Computer and electronic specialists? Let us recruit them from civilian occupations, regardless of age. No reason the terms offered cannot include the requirement that recruits submit to military discipline and wear uniforms. It is simply absurd and counterproductive to restrict the pool of potential recruits to 18-, 19- and 20-year-olds—or any other narrow class. Is a 30- or 40-year-old man or woman unable to operate radar or repair delicate electronic equipment? Why pay for the training of persons when there is no guarantee, and no possibility of one, that the training will be useful and used only in the military service?

Higher Pay: These changes would eliminate the major problems that are said to bedevil the all-volunteer force. Improved pay would increase voluntary enlistments. When the pay of first-termers was comparable to civilian pay—as it was immediately after the draft was ended in 1973—there was no shortage of recruits. But today the pay level of first-termers has been eroded by inflation and inadequate raises so that it is decidedly less than civilian pay.

Horizontal recruitment would broaden the pool of potential enlistees and reduce the demand for 18-, 19- and 20-year-old recruits. It would also reduce manpower needs for training programs. It would therefore improve both demand and supply.

The obstacle to these solutions is dual: on the side of the military, bureaucratic inertia; on the side of Congress, the unwillingness to face up to the immediate financial cost (despite the long-run financial saving) of paying skilled people wages comparable to those that they can command in civilian life.

Chrysler: Are Jobs the Issue?

September 10, 1979

In its high-powered campaign to induce Washington to bail it out, Chrysler Corporation has stressed jobs. Let Chrysler go bankrupt, the logic goes, and 500,000 jobs will be at stake—the jobs of the 130,000 people employed directly by Chrysler and the jobs of the numerous others employed by parts suppliers, Chrysler dealers, and so on in remoter and remoter circles.

To put it plainly, this is hogwash. Bankruptcy is one thing. Idling Chrysler factories and assembly lines is a very different thing. A concern that goes bankrupt generally continues to operate under administrators appointed by the court, with instructions to recover as much as they can to meet the obligations that are in default. Many a company emerges from bankruptcy after an interim period to resume full operation as a private enterprise under new management and with a clean financial slate.

Useful Facilities: Similarly, parts suppliers and the other enterprises now related to Chrysler will not stop operating. They will go on serving whatever Chrysler operations continue, as well as any automobile manufacturers that inherit the business Chrysler loses. No doubt many of the related enterprises will suffer losses, along with Chrysler stockholders, but that is a risk they knowingly run in order to be able to enjoy profits.

Even if Chrysler did not continue to operate as a single enterprise, its facilities would not go up in smoke or go to wrack and ruin or even stand idle. If its facilities are worth using to produce automobiles, it will pay other automobile companies to buy and operate them, or new companies will be set up to acquire them. If Chrysler facilities are not worth using to produce automobiles, but have value for other activities, they will be purchased for those purposes.

If Chrysler is not bailed out, the facilities worth using would be taken over by people who would be risking their money in the belief that they can make more effective and productive use of them than Chrysler's present management. In the process, they would create new jobs.

If Chrysler is bailed out, it will cost the taxpayer money. The cost may be hidden in the form of loan guarantees, but it is real nonetheless. It includes the possible loss if Chrysler cannot repay the loan. It includes also the slightly higher interest rate that the government will have to pay because it has increased its liabilities. Bailing out Chrysler will not change the total amount of capital available to the economy. But it will divert capital to Chrysler from other more productive uses.

Bailing out Chrysler would simply preserve unproductive jobs at the expense of productive jobs. However, the people who would be denied jobs by a Chrysler bailout do not even know who they are, so they cannot speak out to counter the self-serving claims of the firm's present management.

The private-enterprise economic system is often described as a profit system. That is a misnomer. It is a profit and *loss* system. If anything, the loss part is even more vital than the profit part. That is where it differs most from a government-controlled system. A private enterprise that fails to use its resources effectively loses money and is forced to change its ways. A government enterprise that fails to use its resources effectively is in a very different position. If Amtrak loses money, it is more likely to get a larger appropriation from Congress than to be forced to change its ways. Indeed, Congress may even instruct it to expand.

Bad Management: An enterprise may lose money for reasons beyond its control that are not likely to be repeated; or it may lose money because it is mismanaged. If it is possible to tell which, the market will distinguish. In the first instance, people who risk their own money will bail the enterprise out of its temporary difficulties; in the second, they will replace the management or force the enterprise to close down. Often it is not possible to tell whether bad luck or bad management is to blame. In that case, the market is likely to act as if it were due to mismanagement. That undoubtedly is harsh on some individuals and some companies. But it is highly beneficial for the community as a whole. It assures that resources are directed toward those enterprises that can use them most effectively.

This system produced the remarkable growth in the productivity of the U.S. economy during the past two centuries. Our increasing rejection of this system in favor of a government-controlled economy is a major reason why productivity in recent years has gone into reverse.

New York City

November 17, 1975

New York City's financial crisis is more important for the
rest of us as a cautionary tale than for its direct effect on our
well-being. How we—and New York City—deal with the immediate crisis matters less than whether we draw the right
lesson from the experience.

New York City is a special case. For the latest year for
which comparable figures are available (1972–73), local government spending *per person* (including federal and state aid)
in the New York metropolitan area was more than $1,100.
This was one-third more than was spent by San Francisco–
Oakland, New York's West Coast competitor for the title of
big spender, and more than twice as much as was spent by
my own city of Chicago. New York's spending is higher in
almost every separate category—education, welfare, health,
police, fire, you name it. Yet in my experience, the average
citizen of New York gets if anything less in return for his
money than the average citizen of Chicago. In addition, New
York is the only major city that has maintained rent control
ever since World War II. The result has been wholesale

abandonment of dwelling units and a drastic erosion in the tax base.

The Disease

New York's lavish spending reflects the most welfare-state-oriented electorate in the U.S. In this sense, New York's problems are a foretaste of what other cities, other states, and the country as a whole can expect if their electorates continue to imitate New York's left surge. Trying to do good by spending someone else's money is a sure-fire recipe for financial disaster. If New York City does not persuade you of that, simply cast your eyes across the Atlantic to Great Britain.

The unlimited growth of welfare-state spending spells not only financial crisis but also the loss of self-government: already New York City is being governed by caretakers appointed by the State of New York rather than by its own elected officials.

This effect of welfare-state policies on democracy is obscured for New York City because control has passed from its citizens to another democratic government, the State of New York. It is much more sharply etched in the destruction of personal freedom in Chile, Argentina, and now India. These may seem farfetched comparisons, yet they illustrate the same fundamental tendency for an overgrown government sector to destroy freedom—even if the governmental growth is for good purposes.

Default by New York City would have no major adverse consequences for the rest of us. New York City's instinct for self-destruction is matched only by its exaggerated sense of self-importance. Its total liabilities are large for a single city, but trivial compared with the total financial assets in the country—a small fraction of 1 percent. Some individuals and institutions would of course be seriously hurt by New York's default, as they were by Penn Central's and Equity Funding's and the like. But the overall effect would be small, and there is no chance that it could cause a serious financial panic.

New York's troubles have already made it more difficult for New York State and some other cities and states to borrow—but is it a bad thing for cities and states to be under greater pressure to limit their spending to their tax receipts? In any event, the other side of that coin is that more funds have been available for the federal government and for business, lowering their borrowing costs.

The Therapy

Default would be hard on the city's elected officials and public employees in the short run, but would be therapeutic for the other denizens of the city both in the short and long runs. It would be still better for New York City to tighten its belt and create a large enough current-account surplus to pay off its debt without default. But that is a pipe dream.

The rest of us are not responsible for New York City's plight. Nevertheless, if there were some way in which we could aid the city without doing more harm than good, we should do so. Unhappily, there is not. Every proposal founders on the very fallacy that has brought New York to its present condition—the belief that it is desirable to do good with someone else's money—in this case, that of taxpayers outside New York. The rest of us deserve the same fate if we do not learn this lesson from New York's experience.

Gammon's 'Black Holes'

November 7, 1977

Dr. Max Gammon, a British physician, recently completed a five-year study of the British health system. In reporting his findings, Gammon was led to formulate a brilliant extension of one of C. Northcote Parkinson's famous laws.

Parkinson's law was "work expands so as to fill the time available for its completion." Gammon, without referring to Parkinson, adds what he calls the "theory of bureaucratic displacement." In his words, in "a bureaucratic system . . . *increase in expenditure* will be matched by *fall in production.* . . . Such systems will act rather like 'black holes,' in the economic universe, simultaneously sucking in resources, and shrinking in terms of 'emitted' production."

Useless Work . . .

In words that are more in Parkinson's style: in a bureaucratic system, useless work drives out useful work.

Gammon illustrates his theory from the British National

Health Service (NHS). He points out that in the eight years "between 1965 and 1973, the total number of staff employed in NHS hospitals in Great Britain increased" by 28 percent (and administrative and clerical staff by 51 percent). On the other hand, "the average number of beds occupied daily" declined by just over 11 percent. He goes on to note that the long waiting lists for beds throughout the period ensure that the number of beds occupied is a valid measure of output. Input up, output down.

The U.S. is still, fortunately, some way from a national health service. However, the rising costs of medical care—as government has expanded its role and bureaucracy has multiplied—presumably reflect an early stage of the process documented by Gammon.

A clearer example for the U.S. is schooling, which is predominantly governmental, as health care is in Britain, and where the law of bureaucratic displacement has been proceeding apace. In the five years from the school year 1971–72 to 1976–77, total professional staff in all U.S. public schools went up 8 percent, cost per pupil went up 68 percent in dollars, and 21 percent after correction for inflation: *input clearly up.*

Number of students went down 4 percent, number of schools went down 4 percent. And I suspect there will be few demurrers from the proposition that quality of schooling went down even more drastically than the quantity. *Output clearly down.*

Is this due to bureaucratic organization? As some evidence, the number of school districts went down by 10 percent, continuing a trend toward greater centralization and bureaucratization of education that has been going on now for decades. For a somewhat earlier five-year period for which the data are available (1968–69 to 1973–74), when total professional staff went up 10 percent, and teachers 14 percent, supervisors went up 44 percent.

Moreover, the increasing expenditures on schooling have been accompanied by the long decline in SAT scores of high-school graduates to which so much attention has recently been drawn by the Willard Wirtz report for the College Board. Need we look beyond Gammon's brilliant theory to explain why?

. . . Drives Out Useful Work

As a final example of the law of bureaucratic displacement operating in reverse, I quote from a *New York Times* story of August 21, 1977: "The New York City government provided about the same level of services in 1976–77 as in the previous fiscal year but, thanks to improved productivity, did it with 12,000 fewer employees. . . ." That is, reduced input (government employees) resulted in higher output (level of services).

Gammon's theory is more than a smart-aleck curiosity. It is a direct consequence of the pursuit by all of us of our self-interest. In a market, we can pursue our self-interest only by persuading people to buy what we have to sell, hence we are driven to serve our customers' interests. In a government bureaucracy that is exempt from competition, the customers have nowhere else to go. Their interests are largely irrelevant. Hence, the bureaucrat can serve his self-interest at their expense by expanding his empire and reducing his workload.

The fault is not with the people who run the system, but with the system itself. More fundmentally, the fault is with those of us who are responsible for replacing the economic market with the political market.

Bureaucracy Scorned

December 29, 1975

In this day and age, we need to revise the old saying to read, "Hell hath no fury like a bureaucrat scorned."

The most recent and flagrant example is the attempt by bureaucrats at HEW to impose an "affirmative action" program on Hillsdale College—a small, independent college in southern Michigan.

The affirmative-action program is one of those bureaucratic monstrosities that have become all too familiar: noble objectives, ignoble results. The objective is to eliminate discrimination on the basis of sex or race; the results are mountains of paper, hiring criteria that are irrelevant to the mission of institutions of higher learning and, frequently, the substitution of reverse discrimination for no discrimination. Par for the course.

Most colleges and universities have accepted—and lobbied extensively for—federal funds, and their receipt of federal funds is the legal justification for HEW jurisdiction over their hiring and other practices. They are hoist on their own petard when they now complain that he who pays the piper is calling the tune.

No Refuge . . .

But Hillsdale and a few other institutions (for example, Rockford and Wabash colleges) are in a different position. In order to retain their complete independence, these colleges have refused to accept federal funds for any purpose. In consequence, they have with clear conscience regarded themselves as not subject to HEW control. George Roche, Hillsdale's president, even had the audaciy to write a book attacking the whole affirmative-action program as a threat to the quality and standards of higher education (*The Balancing Act*, Open Court: La Salle, Ill., 1974). And to add insult to injury, it is an excellent book.

The scorned bureaucrats have now struck back. Some students at Hillsdale receive federal grants or loans under veterans and similar programs. HEW claims that this makes Hillsdale a "recipient institution" subject to HEW control.

By this line of reasoning, the corner grocer and the A&P are "recipient institutions" because some of their customers receive social-security checks. The *New York Times* and the *Chicago Tribune* are federal contractors because welfare recipients buy papers. How silly can you get?

Yet no argument is too silly to serve as a pretext for extending still further the widening control over all of our lives that is being exercised by government bureaucrats. The HEW grab is in the same class as the widening judicial interpretation of "interstate commerce," as the imposition of forced busing despite widespread disapproval by both blacks and whites, as the growing paperwork we are all called on to do at the behest of the Internal Revenue Service, as the detailed regulation of business practices in the name of clean air, safety, protecting pensions, and so on and on without end. I doubt that there is a single adult resident of the United States—certainly none who has ever had the legal obligation to file an income-tax return—who could not be subjected at the very least to a costly legal battle to avoid being convicted of violating some law or regulation.

In one sense, it is poetic justice that my colleagues and I at colleges and universities should now be suffering under the bureaucratic lash. For we have done more than any other group to produce a climate of opinion favorable to big government. So long as affirmative-action programs were directed at greedy businesses and grasping trade unions, academia for the most part cheered. And even now that its own ox is being gored, the typical reaction is that the academic world is "different."

. . . for Freedom

But perhaps the recognition will come, even if only slowly, for freedom is for everyone or no one, and not a special privilege of the intellectual, that government controls destroy freedom for everyone and not only the intellectuals, that they typically fail to accomplish their noble objectives no matter on whom imposed.

If that happens, the heavy-handed bureaucratic assault on colleges and universities may prove a blessing in disguise. Just as intellectuals bear major responsibility for instilling the view that big government is Santa Claus, so they can do more than any others to drive home the lesson that big government is really Frankenstein.

IV. Money and Monetary Policy

A. Inflation
B. The Federal Reserve
C. Interest Rates

INTRODUCTION

Money matters much. It is the key variable in the "equation of exchange": MV = PQ. M is the number of dollars; V is the average number of times per year a dollar is spent on current, final output; P is the price index; and Q is the real output on which the spending is done. Total monetary expenditure (MV) equals total money value of output (PQ). And the sum of the proportionate changes in money and velocity about equals the changes in the price level and output.

	M	V	P	Q
1965–70	27.8%	12.4%	23.0%	16.8%
1970–75	34.6%	15.9%	37.3%	13.7%
1975–80	42.4%	19.0%	41.3%	20.0%
[Annual rate: 1975–80]	[7.3%]	[3.5%]	[7.2%]	[3.7%]
1965–80	145.0%	55.1%	138.5%	59.3%
[Annual rate: 1965–80]	[6.2%]	[3.0%]	[6.1%]	[3.2%]

Why the accelerating inflationary binge? Expenditure rose at an increasing rate, averaging over 9 percent per year from 1965 to 1980, mainly because of money increase. Output did well to go up at more than 3 percent. So prices surged at an average rate of 6.1 percent. When spending swamps output, of course the price level inflates. Milton Friedman has long taught that "inflation is a monetary phenomenon—nothing else. If you control growth of the money supply, you control inflation; if you don't, inflation cannot be limited."

Inflation, in turn, pulled up interest rates. Ironically, the Fed's major concern traditionally has been interest rates, not money. But pumping out more money will dampen interest rates only momentarily. In a setting of persistent inflation and resulting expectations of inflation, continued rapid money expansion results in both higher prices and higher interest rates. Further, wild short-run gyrations in the rate of money growth—bouncing between −15 percent and +25 percent over two or three months—contribute to low rates of expansion of production and employment.

Such considerations long ago led Dr. Friedman to advocate a "monetary rule": year after year, with no attempt at fine-tuning the economy, increase the amount of money at a rate which is both small and steady. Implementation of the rule would not eliminate all jiggles in the level of economic activity, but it would yield results vastly better than those we have been inflicting on ourselves.

A. Inflation

Prosperity Without Inflation

December 15, 1980

It's perfectly possible to have both sustained economic growth and low inflation. The only thing needed is a dose of good government—monetary policy on the one hand and fiscal and regulatory policy on the other.

In monetary policy, the Federal Reserve must terminate its tendency to swing widely from one extreme of monetary growth to the other. In the last year, this has caused wild swings in interest rates and dramatic downs and ups in the economy. If this erratic policy were to continue, it would be impossible to achieve steady growth with low inflation.

Controlling the growth of money is important because, ultimately, inflation is a monetary phenomenon—nothing else.

If you control growth of the money supply, you control inflation; if you do not, inflation cannot be limited. Secondly, this control is important because money is pervasive and affects the entire economy.

The recent instability in monetary growth produced the economy's instability. The economy requires a background of a stable monetary policy so that people can make their plans.

Government "Has Been a Bull in the China Shop"

Curing inflation is a necessary condition for making progress on our second problem: slow and erratic growth. But two other areas also need to be attacked if we are to speed growth:

First, the government is absorbing an ever larger fraction of the economy's resources, leaving less for the private sector to grow on. There has been no period in peacetime history when government spending has been as high a fraction of national income as it is currently.

Second, government is reducing incentives for people to save, to invest, to innovate. High marginal tax rates cause people to seek out tax shelters rather than productive investments. In addition, government regulation and extensive control over the details of economic activity mean that a large fraction of the investment that is undertaken is done to meet specific regulations rather than to add to the nation's productive capacity.

For instance, a major source of slow growth has been our incredible energy legislation. First it required enterprises to burn one kind of fuel, then another. It led to scarcities, then ample supplies of natural gas. The federal government has been a bull in the china shop, rushing one way and another and making it very difficult for the shop owners to keep things in order.

Don't Balance the Budget: Cut Federal Spending Instead

To get out of this situation, the steps that must be taken are clear: They are ones that President-elect Reagan committed himself to during the campaign.

First, the Kemp-Roth tax recommendations. These include an annual 10 percent across-the-board reduction in individual income-tax rates for the next three years, and then indexing the tax system against inflation as well as accelerated depreciation for business in order to encourage productive investment. Second, an immediate revision of the U.S. budget, with a lower ceiling on total expenditures. Third, a reduction of the regulatory burden on industry by executive order, such as lifting the ceiling on crude oil and gasoline prices. Fourth, presidential support for a policy of stable and steady monetary growth.

On the budget, it is not essential to balance it. It's much more important that government spending be lowered as a share of national income. Total government spending—federal, state and local—now takes well over 40 percent of national income, the federal government two-thirds of that. I would much rather have a 300-billion-dollar federal budget that is 200 billion dollars in deficit than a balanced budget of 600 billion dollars.

A Timetable for Steady Growth, Low Inflation

If all these recommendations were followed, we would achieve the goals of steady growth and low inflation in four to five years, based on the experience in other nations.

It would work something like this, assuming we start immediately: After a brief initial period, inflation would be dropping. In the first year or two, unemployment would remain relatively high, and growth would be relatively slow. In the final three years, you would have rapid growth along with declining inflation. Thus you'd move into a healthy economy in the second or third year.

In this timetable, I assume that federal spending is reduced gradually and that monetary policy produces a steady decline in the rate of growth of the money supply—not a sudden shock, but a reduction of about 1 percentage point a year for the next five years.

"There Is No Perfect Alternative—Only Bad Options"

It wouldn't take a depression to get us back on track. Our problems are not that extreme. But individuals must realize that, in the short run, there is no policy that will do the job and have a good effect on them.

There is no perfect, painless alternative—only bad options.

There are two choices: You let inflation continue or speed up, in which case everybody gets socked. In this case, all you're doing is postponing the evil day of dealing with the situation. By then, inflation will be even worse. Alternatively, you go through a period of difficulty as a side effect of an effective cure for inflation. For individuals, this means a year or so of low economic growth, relatively high unemployment, and slow growth in incomes.

"Inflation Is Entirely Made in Washington"

As for the government's role in the economy, inflation is entirely made in Washington—and nowhere else. Events such as crop shortages and oil-price increases send the price of those goods up relative to other things, but they don't produce inflation.

There has been a persistent policy on the part of governmental officials of blowing a smoke screen. They say: "Don't blame us for inflation. It's due to bad Arab sheiks or greedy businessmen or grasping trade unionists or spendthrift consumers." They're trying to find alibis.

"Government Cannot Fine-tune the Economy"

Real economic growth can be interfered with by the government, but it cannot be produced by the government. Washington can provide a favorable background, but real growth fundamentally is produced in the private sector by individuals saving money, investing money, taking risks, innovating.

196

The government cannot fine-tune the economy to eliminate every up and down. Its attempts to do so have made the ups and downs worse, not better. There are severe limits to the good that the government can do for the economy, but there are almost no limits to the harm it can do.

"Election Produced a Clear Mandate for Change"

Despite the inevitable difficult period at first, I'm quite optimistic these recommendations for stable, low-inflation growth will be carried out. The results of the election said that the people of America are fed up with the inflation we've experienced, the uncertainties we've experienced, the burdens we've experienced. The election produced a clear mandate for change.

On the other hand, if we were simply to continue along the path of the previous twenty years, we would get more of the same, but in a more extreme way. We're now on a roller coaster of inflation, with each peak higher than the previous one. So we could have inflation in the 15 to 20 percent range.

We would have worse stagflation, higher unemployment. But sooner or later, public opinion would be sufficiently strong that the kinds of policies I've described would be put into effect. I'm quite hopeful there will be a change.

Money and Inflation

September 20, 1976

In 1863, a famous British economist, W. Stanley Jevons, published a pamphlet analyzing the effect of the California and Australian gold discoveries. One conclusion was that "An expansion of currency occurs one or two years prior to a rise of prices."

Prices Lag . . .

On July 13, 1976, the *Times* of London published an article by its editor, William Rees-Mogg, with the provocative heading HOW A 9.4% EXCESS MONEY SUPPLY GAVE BRITAIN 9.4% INFLATION. In his article, Rees-Mogg erroneously attributes to me rather than to Jevons the demonstration that "there was a time lag, normally of about two years, between changes in the money supply and consequential changes in prices." Accordingly, he compares the increase in money supply each year in excess of the increase in output with the increase in prices two years later. For individual years, there is wide variation. But for 1964 to 1973 as a whole, the excess money supply rose at the average rate of

9.4 percent per year; and for 1966 to 1975, prices rose at the average rate of 9.4 percent.

Of course, the identity of these two numbers is a coincidence. Many factors other than changes in money supply affect the precise rate of inflation. But rough agreement between the two numbers—and even more important, their tendency to rise and fall together—is no coincidence. For example, the corresponding numbers for the U.S. are 4.2 percent for money and 5.8 percent for prices For the prior decade, 1954 to 1964, they are 0.6 percent for money and 1.8 percent for prices, so both went up together by roughly the same amount.*

For the U.S., as for Britain, this relationship is of long standing. Our own money-supply estimates go back to 1867. Throughout that period, changes in prices have tended to follow changes in money supply by roughly two years.

More recently, Congressman Stephen Neal, chairman of a House subcommittee on domestic monetary policy, reported that staff studies indicate that "the rate of inflation rises and falls in the wake of increases and decreases in the supply of money," with the peak effect taking place after a lag of twenty-three months.

A lag of two years is *not* a natural constant that will prevail under all circumstances. It has characterized countries that, like the U.S. and Britain, have generally experienced only moderate rates of inflation during peacetime. In countries like Israel, Brazil, Chile, or Argentina that have experienced much higher and more variable rates of inflation, the lag is only a few months.

---

* For the U.S., these figures are for money supply defined by M_2 (currency plus all commercial bank deposits), and for output defined by GNP at constant prices. The corresponding money figures for M_1 (currency plus demand deposits) are 1.7 for 1964 to 1973 and −1.5 for 1954 to 1964.

The close relation between money and prices has persisted despite major changes in the determinants of the supply of money. When Jevons wrote, and for the next half-century, changes in the supply of money were produced mainly by gold discoveries or improvements in the methods of extracting gold from ore or developments in private banking. Today, gold no longer plays any monetary role and banking developments only a minor one. The money supply is controlled by the government—through the Federal Reserve in the U.S., the Bank of England in the U.K.

. . . so Does Understanding

Rees-Mogg's article aroused a storm of controversy. In the ten days after it was published, the *Times* printed some twenty-five letters denouncing, praising, or amplifying the article. The controversy is understandable. As Rees-Mogg wrote, "These figures have changed further my own attitude to incomes policy [i.e., wage and price control]. If the Excess Money Supply determines the rate of inflation equally closely in years subject to incomes policy and in years without, there seems to be no evidence left that incomes policy has any significant influence on inflation." Yet the current British Labor government is pinning most of its hopes for curbing inflation on a form of incomes policy—the so-called "social contract" with the unions whereby they agree to accept a low limit on wage increases.

The old chestnut goes: "What is a share of Penn Central worth?" Answer: "Together with a quarter, it will get you a cup of coffee." Similarly, the social contract, together with low monetary growth, will curb inflation. With rapid monetary growth, it will be another unsuccessful experiment.

Inflation and Jobs

November 12, 1979

Orthodox wisdom has it that unemployment is a cure for inflation. A minority has it that unemployment causes inflation. Both views are half-truths.

Unemployment is neither a cure nor a cause of inflation. It is a side effect both of a successful cure and of the acceleration of inflation.

A medical example will clarify the difference between a side effect and a cure or cause. You have acute appendicitis. Your physician recommends an appendectomy, but warns that, after the operation, you will be confined to bed for some days. You refuse the operation, but take to your bed for the indicated number of days as a less painful cure. Silly, yes, but faithful in every detail to the confusion between unemployment as a side effect of a cure for inflation and as a cure.

Your physician neglected to say, because it was so obvious, that if you refused the operation, you would also have to go to bed—with little likelihood of ever getting up well. That is faithful in every detail to the confusion between unemployment as a side effect of inflation and as a cure.

Unemployment . . . Unemployment seems to be an unavoidable side effect of curing inflation, just as going to bed is of an operation, and there are many policies that simultaneously add to unemployment and inflation, just as staying in bed may produce illness (though not appendicitis). I know of no example of a country that has cured substantial inflation without going through a transitional period of slow growth and unemployment. I know of no example of a country that has experienced accelerating inflation without running into serious economic difficulties. Japan, Great Britain, Chile, Brazil illustrate both propositions. All got into serious economic difficulties as a side effect of accelerating inflation. All went through a transitional period of slow growth and unemployment in curing—or at least reducing—inflation.

Why is unemployment a side effect of curing inflation? Because a cure changes the economic environment in ways that were not widely anticipated by the economic actors and that they misinterpret.

The only cure for inflation is to reduce the rate at which total spending is growing. (For our present purpose, it does not matter how spending is slowed, so the important difference between monetarists and fiscalists about how to slow spending is not relevant to this column.) Suppose total spending is slowed. Sellers of goods and services find that the demand for their products is less than they had anticipated. That fact hits them hard. But they have no way of knowing why demand is less, whether because something has happened that is specific to them or because spending has slowed down all over. The reduction in demand will not be even because it will be superimposed on the continuous ebbs and flows of demand in a dynamic economy, which will always blur and often swamp the effects of a slowdown in spending.

If the demand for men's hats, for example, is less than anticipated because fashion dictates that men go bareheaded, the correct response would be lower output and employment in the hat industry, and also a lower price of hats (or a smaller increase in price). If the demand for hats is less than anticipated because total spending slows, the correct response would be a lower price of hats and a lower wage for hatmakers (or lesser increases) with no change in either output or employment. But how is the poor hatmaker to know?

Not knowing, his initial response will be a mixture, the proportions depending on the background that has shaped anticipation. If the hatmaker's prospects have generally changed because of circumstances special to hats, he will respond primarily by reducing output and employment. If his prospects have generally changed because of lower total spending, he will respond primarily by lowering prices.

That is why prices respond sooner and by a larger amount, and output and employment respond less, to swings in total spending in many South American countries than in the United States. Those countries have had much experience over a long period with wide swings in total spending and in the rate of inflation. Everybody has come to expect them, and has devised ways of adapting to them. The United States has not had the same experience. We have had major depressions from time to time, but not major inflations—except in wartime.

However, circumstances are changing. Thanks to our recent experience, sellers in the U.S. are more likely now than they were earlier to respond to increases in demand by raising prices rather than output and to reductions in demand by lowering output rather than prices. Experience has persuaded them that an acceleration of total spending is more likely than the reverse. They therefore regard a rise in demand as less likely to reflect something special to them than a decline in demand.

The tendency of sellers to lower output and employment

when demand falls is reinforced by contractual arrangements that fix prices and wages in advance for some time. Even when prices and wages are not fixed explicitly, it is often undesirable to change them frequently. As a result, output and employment are generally more flexible over short periods than prices and wages, though less flexible over long periods.

Unemployment produced by a slowdown in spending will be temporary even if the slowdown persists. The reason is that as sellers react to the initial slowdown, they discover their mistake. They discover that the slowdown is not peculiar to them. More reductions (or smaller increases) in prices and wages occur and a favorable price-wage-price spiral sets in. As it does, output and employment increase and prices settle down to a level or a rate of change consistent with the new level or rate of change of total spending.

. . . or Unemployment: Unemployment is a side effect of the acceleration of inflation for the same reason that it is a side effect of the cure for inflation. The only difference—and it is a vital one—is in timing. The initial mistaken response to an unanticipated acceleration of total spending will be an increase in output and employment. When the mistake is discovered, the reaction will produce lower output and employment.

This is an oversimplified exposition of an extremely complex subject—but I hope that it suggests why we do not have a choice between lower unemployment and higher inflation. Like the person with appendicitis, we have only bad choices: unemployment as a side effect of curing inflation, or unemployment as a side effect of acceleration of inflation. If we make the first choice, we shall have the unemployment sooner. However, if we then adopt stable policies, we need not repeat the cure. If we make the second choice, we shall have the unemployment later. However, we shall have it all to do again. That is why continued inflation means more not less unemployment.

Why Inflation Persists

October 3, 1977

Nearly three years ago, I wrote: "Four times in the past
fifteen years we have started on a cure for inflation. Three
times we have abandoned the cure before it had time to complete its task—in 1963, 1967, 1971. Each time, the result
has been a higher plateau of inflation, producing a new attempt at a cure. Will we make the same mistake the fourth
time in 1975? Or this time, will we have the courage and the
wisdom and the patience to see the cure through?" (*Newsweek*, November 4, 1974.)

Abandoning the Cure

As of today, the answer is that we have made the same
mistake a fourth time. Once again, we have paid the cost of
a recession to stem inflation, and, once again, we are in the
process of throwing away the prize. From a high of more
than 12 percent in 1974 (from December 1973 to December
1974) inflation fell to less than 5 percent (December 1975 to
December 1976). It has now risen sharply, may temporarily
recede as we work through the bulge produced by the special
problem of the hard winter, but then, I fear, will resume its

206

upward march, not to the "modest" 6 percent the administration is forecasting, but to at least several percentage points higher and possibly to double digits again by 1978 or 1979.

There is one and only one basic cause of inflation: too high a rate of growth in the quantity of money—too much money chasing the available supply of goods and services. These days, that cause is produced in Washington, proximately, by the Federal Reserve System, which determines what happens to the quantity of money; ultimately, by the political and other pressures impinging on the System, of which the most important are the pressures to create money in order to pay off exploding federal spending and in order to promote the goal of "full employment." All other alleged causes of inflation—trade union intransigence, greedy business corporations, spendthrift customers, bad crops, harsh winters, OPEC cartels, and so on—are either consequences of inflation, or excuses by Washington, or sources of temporary blips of inflation.

There is one and only one basic cure for inflation: slowing monetary growth. But that cure is easier to state than to put into effect: witness our repeated abandonment of the cure. The Fed is supposedly independent. But, as Dooley said of the Supreme Court, "It follows the election returns." Its behavior reminds me of nothing so much as the remark attributed to a U.S. Army officer in Vietnam, "We destroyed the village in order to save it." Similarly, the Fed refrains from using its independence because it is afraid of losing it.

Listen to Chairman Arthur F. Burns in testimony to the House of Representatives (July 29, 1977):

"The trend of growth in monetary aggregates, I regret to say, is still too rapid. Even though the Federal Reserve has steadily sought during the past two years to achieve lower ranges for monetary expansion, the evolution of its projections has been extremely gradual; indeed, at the pace we have been moving (*note: with respect to projections, not behavior*) it would require perhaps a decade to reach rates of growth consistent with price stability. I must report, moreover, that despite the gradual reduction of projected growth ranges for the aggregates during the past two years, no meaningful reduction has as yet occurred in actual growth rates."

Meaning: promises have been in the right direction but too modest; performance has been in the wrong direction.

The Performance of the Fed

The following table documents Chairman Burns's description of performance: the high rates of monetary growth from 1971 to early 1973 fostered the inflation that peaked in 1974. The sharply lower monetary-growth rates from 1973 to 1975 produced the serious recession of 1974 and 1975 and the subsequent tapering off of inflation. The sharp rise in early 1975 sparked the recovery; the slowdown in late 1975 produced the economic pause in the second half of 1976 that played such a prominent role in the Ford-Carter election battle. Since

	Recent Rates of Monetary Growth (percent per year)	
	M_1	M_2
December 1971 to January 1973	9.3	11.4
January 1973 to February 1975	4.5	7.7
February 1975 to June 1975	9.5	12.0
June 1975 to December 1975	2.8	7.0
December 1975 to June 1976	5.8	10.5
June 1976 to August 1977	7.1	10.9

M_1 = currency plus adjusted demand deposits; M_2 = M_1 plus commercial-bank time deposits other than large CDs.

then, monetary growth has been rising, not falling, and is now about where it was in 1972.

Inflation will not be stopped by words, only by actions. At the moment, we have the worst of two worlds. Nominal independence of the Federal Reserve without its effective exercise permits Congress and the president to evade responsibility for the creation of money to finance large government deficits. The power of Congress to legislate and of the president to approve such deficits without explicit responsibility for the resulting monetary growth gives the Federal Reserve an excuse for its inflationary behavior.

Again, let me quote Chairman Burns, this time from a speech on August 13, 1977, proclaiming "The Importance of an Independent Central Bank":

"Theoretically, the Federal Reserve could thwart the nonmonetary pressures that are tending to drive costs and prices higher by providing substantially less monetary growth than would be needed to accommodate these pressures fully. In practice, such a course would be fraught with major difficulty and considerable risk. Every time our government acts to enlarge the flow of benefits to one group or another the assumption is implicit that the means of financing will be available. A similar tacit assumption is embodied in every pricing decision, wage bargain, or escalator arrangement that is made by private parties or government. That fact that such actions may in combination be wholly incompatible with moderate monetary expansion is seldom considered by those who initiate them."

Fish or Cut Bait

It matters little whether the Federal Reserve is unable or unwilling to exercise its independence in deeds as well as words. In either case, let us be done with the fiction that "independence" is somehow or other a bastion against inflation. Let us put the responsibility for the rate of monetary growth—and therewith for the subsequent rate of inflation—squarely and openly on the Administration and Congress. Instead of simply requiring the Federal Reserve to *report* its "projections" or "targets" for monetary growth, let the Congress require the Fed to *achieve* specified rates of monetary growth (or specified levels of the quantity of money) within specified ranges of tolerance. That would combine responsibility and power. It would also enable the ordinary citizen to know whom to hold accountable for inflation.

Inflationary Recession

April 24, 1978

Nearly a dozen years ago, I warned of an inflationary recession (*Newsweek*, October 17, 1966). We have since then had three inflationary recessions and a fourth is almost surely on the way.

During the first, the brief minirecession of 1967, consumer prices rose 2.4 percent per year; during the longer and more severe recession from December 1969 to November 1970, prices rose 5.3 percent per year; during the still longer and even more severe recession from November 1973 to March 1975, prices rose 10.8 percent per year; during the coming recession, prices are likely to rise at least 7 percent per year.

Each scenario has been the same: rapid growth in the quantity of money followed by economic expansion and then, much later, by rising inflation; a public outcry against inflation, leading the authorities to reduce monetary growth sharply; some months later, the beginning of expansion, along with a decline in inflation. Back to the starting point.

A Wrong Interpretation

The simultaneous decline in unemployment and inflation produced orgies of self-congratulation by the powers that be. However, this happy state proved short-lived as inflation once again started to accelerate. Needless to say, the political Establishment tried to prolong the happy glow by attributing the acceleration of inflation to special events—bad weather, food shortages, labor-union intransigence, corporate greed, the OPEC cartel, or any straw at which they could grasp. Never any sign of *mea culpa*.

We have now almost completed a fourth repetition of the same scenario, as the accompanying table makes clear.

HOW MONEY MATTERS

MONETARY GROWTH			INFLATION	
Period	Percent per year		Period	Percent per year
	M_1	M_2		CPI
Dec. 1971 to Jan. 1973	9.3	11.4	Dec. 1973 to Jan. 1975	11.7
Jan. 1973 to Feb. 1975	4.6	7.7	Jan. 1975 to Feb. 1977	6.2
Feb. 1975 to Oct. 1977	6.5	10.1	Feb. 1977 to Oct. 1979	7 to 10*
Oct. 1977 to Mar. 1978	3.9	6.1		

M_1 = Currency plus adjusted demand deposits; M_2 = M_1 plus commercial-bank time deposits other than large CDs; CPI = Consumer Price Index.
*Projections

Consider the rates of monetary growth. The first entry shows the high growth after the 1969–70 recession; the next, the sharply lower growth that responded to galloping inflation and produced the 1973–75 recession; the third, the swing back to high growth, and the final entry, the recent slowdown in response to accelerating inflation. This slowdown has already lasted long enough to assure at least a minirecession of the 1967 variety.

Consider now the consequences for inflation. Although a change in monetary growth initially affects output and employment, its ultimate effects are primarily on inflation. More than a century ago, a famous English economist, W. Stanley Jevons, examined the relation between monetary growth and inflation. In 1863, he wrote: "An expansion of currency occurs one or two years prior to a rise of prices." His finding has held ever since for both the U.K. and the U.S.—of course not precisely, but on the average.

Accordingly, the second half of the table gives the rate of inflation, as measured by consumer prices, for a period two years later than the period of monetary growth in the first half of the table. The correspondence between the rates of growth of M_2 and CPI is striking. Similar comparisons for a much longer period yield the same results. In general, the rate of inflation tends to run something like 0 to 3 percentage points lower than the rate of M_2 growth two years earlier. On this basis, we can predict that inflation from February 1977 to October 1979 will average something like 7 to 10 percent (it has averaged 6.6 percent from February 1976 to February 1977 and is still rising). We can also predict that no sustained reduction in inflation can be expected before mid- or late 1979. If my analysis is correct, what role is played by the many factors other than money that politicians, economists, and journalists write about? Three roles: first, they may affect monetary growth—pressures from Congress and the administration to finance rising government spending and to keep interest rates low are a major reason for high monetary growth; second, they account for the 0 to 3 percentage-point variation in the margin between monetary growth and inflation; third, they affect the shorter-run ups and downs in the inflation rate.

Monetary growth is determined by the Federal Reserve System. The able and public-spirited men who run the system did not permit or produce the wild swings in monetary growth out of malice aforethought. Why then have these swings occurred through the whole of the more than sixty years of the Fed's existence? In my opinion, for two basic reasons: first, because of pressures on the Fed from the president, Congress, and the public, and second, because of the unwillingness of the Fed to reform obsolete operating procedures, developed when it conceived its mission to be to control credit conditions rather than monetary growth.

The Right Perspective

What is the right policy now? That is easy to say, hard to do. We need a long-term program dedicated to eliminating inflation. The Fed should announce that it proposes to increase M_2 at the annual rate of, say 8 percent during 1978, 7 percent during 1979, 6 percent during 1980, 5 percent during 1981, and 4 percent during 1982 and all subsequent years. To relieve the fiscal pressures on the Fed, such a monetary policy should be accompanied by a budget policy of reducing federal spending as a fraction of national income—also gradually but steadily.

Such a monetary and fiscal program would eliminate inflation by 1983—for good. Such a gradual program would avoid economic disruption. Indeed, the confidence it engendered might well foster a vigorous and healthy expansion in investment and economic activity—and even a stock-market boom.

The difficulty with this prescription is to make it credible. Promises are one thing. Performance, as we have learned, is something else. The program is technically feasible. But is it politically feasible not only to announce it but to stick to it? I doubt that it currently is. I hope I am wrong. But, just in case I am not, hold on to your hats as the inflation roller coaster goes on its not-so-merry way.

Monetary Instability

June 15, 1981

The chart on page 216 is an updated version of one published nearly two years ago (*Newsweek*, August 20, 1979) in a column in which I discussed the task facing Paul Volcker as he assumed the chairmanship of the Federal Reserve Board.

The chart shows that monetary growth has been highly unstable over the past two decades—even when growth is measured over a full year so that shorter-term instability is averaged out. Moreover, the fluctuations in monetary growth have become wider over time and have occurred around a rising trend.

The Indictment: This pattern of monetary growth has had extremely adverse effects on our economy. Monetary growth is *a*—or *the*—major factor determining the rate of inflation over the longer term. As the chart shows, ups and downs in monetary growth have been followed by corresponding ups and downs in inflation. The interval between changes in money and subsequent changes in inflation has been long and variable, averaging roughly two years. The wider fluctuations in money in the 1970s than in the 1960s produced wider

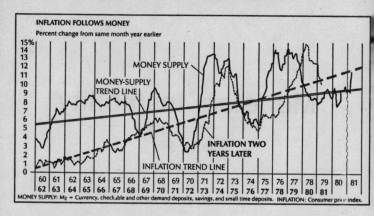

INFLATION FOLLOWS MONEY

Percent change from same month year earlier

MONEY SUPPLY

MONEY-SUPPLY
TREND LINE

INFLATION TWO
YEARS LATER

INFLATION TREND LINE

60 61 62 63 64 65 66 67 68 69 70 71 72 73 74 75 76 77 78 79 80 81
62 63 64 65 66 67 68 69 70 71 72 73 74 75 76 77 78 79 80 81

MONEY SUPPLY: M₂ = Currency, checkable and other demand deposits, savings, and small time deposits.   INFLATION: Consumer price index.

fluctuations in inflation as well. And the upward trend in monetary growth produced an even steeper upward trend in inflation.

As I wrote in the earlier column, "There is no mystery about the steeper trend in inflation than in money. It reflects the widening recognition that inflation is the way of the future. Those inflationary expectations make it prudent for all of us to reduce the fraction of our assets that we hold in the form of money. The problem is not . . . a lack of confidence. The problem is rather that the public is very confident that the government will produce inflation and will mismanage the economy. We do not need more confidence in bad policies. We need better policies."

The updated chart provides some basis for judging policy since 1979.

The Verdict: In commenting on the chart in mid-1979, I wrote: "Although the inflation rate has not yet peaked, it is very probably headed for a downturn. But that downturn will be temporary if the recent monetary explosion continues."

The inflation rate did peak in early 1980—after a rather longer time delay than usual—and has been coming down ever since. However, monetary growth has continued to be highly unstable. The decline in monetary growth that started at the end of 1977 and produced a decline in inflation beginning in early 1980 apparently ended in early 1979 or early 1980. Since then, the chart gives every indication that another major upward swing is under way.

Equally important, the recent fluctuations in monetary growth have continued to move around an upward trend.

Unless the recent upward swing and the longer upward trend are promptly reversed, the current decline in inflation will end within a year or so and will be followed by a new burst of inflation—one that will carry us to even higher levels of inflation than the nearly 15 percent peak in early 1980. Monetary policy will have torpedoed President Reagan's whole economic strategy—an essential element of which is a gradual reduction in monetary growth.

In my 1979 column, I suggested as a "long-term goal . . . gradually reducing the growth rate of a selected monetary aggregate: for example to 8 percent for M_2 in 1979, 7 percent in 1980, 6 percent in 1981, 5 percent in 1982, 4 percent in 1983 and all future years." The actual outcome has been very different. M_2 has increased by 8.8 percent in 1979, 9.7 percent in 1980 and at an annual rate of more than 12 percent in the first four months of 1981.* We are back to square one.

The failure in monetary policy does not reflect a difference between the Federal Reserve's goals and President Reagan's.

---

* For 1979 and 1980 the percentages cited are the changes from December of the prior year to December of the indicated year. Since the chart was published in 1979, the Fed has changed the definition of M_2. However, the old and new definitions show very similar growth rates. The earlier chart used the old definitions, the present chart, the new one.

It does not reflect a difference between the Fed and myself about the appropriate rates of monetary growth. The Fed has repeatedly set similar targets. Neither does the failure of monetary policy reflect a lack of power to achieve those target rates of growth. The Fed has adequate power to do so. The failure reflects rather the Fed's unwillingness to change its operating procedures to enable it to control monetary growth more promptly and more reliably—and this, despite a near-consensus among specialists both inside and outside the system about the changes that are needed. The Fed has given lip service to changing its procedures, but it has repeatedly failed to put its money where its mouth is.

Deficits and Inflation

February 23, 1981

Government deficits can and sometimes do contribute to inflation. However, the relation between deficits and inflation is far looser than is widely believed. Moreover, the major harm that deficits do is to foster irresponsible government spending.

A few facts will illustrate the uneasy connection of deficits with inflation. The current federal deficit is running between 2 and 3 percent of our national income. Japan's current deficit is running about 6 percent of its national income, or two or three times ours; Germany's, about 2 percent, or roughly the same as ours. Yet both Japan and Germany now have, and for some years have had, lower inflation rates than we.

Economics: Large federal deficits in the United States accompanied inflation in both world wars. However, for the first full fiscal year after World War I, the government had a surplus and consumer prices rose nearly 25 percent. In 1932 and 1933 federal deficits ran about 5 percent of national income, yet prices fell drastically. More recently, inflation was 7 percent in 1975, when the deficit was 5.6 percent of the

219

national income, and 6.1 percent in 1969, when there was an actual surplus of 1 percent of the national income. The years of highest inflation, 1974 (12.2 percent) and 1979 (13.3 percent), had deficits in the neighborhood of 1 percent of the national income.

This patchy record is accounted for, I believe, by two major factors: First, surpluses or deficits can be a result of inflation and deflation as well as a possible cause. That is the main reason inflation after World War I coincided with a budget surplus and deflation in 1932 and 1933 coincided with budget deficits. Second, deficits have a direct effect on inflation when they are financed by creating money (as they were in the two world wars). But, wartime periods aside, many other factors typically affect the rate of monetary growth, so that there is only the loosest relation in practice between monetary growth and deficits.

Deficits are bad primarily because they foster excessive government spending—the chief culprit, in my opinion, in producing both inflation and slow economic growth. If spending is financed by creating money to meet deficits, the link between spending and inflation is direct. If spending is financed by borrowing or taxes, the link is indirect but nonetheless real. Both borrowing and taxes crowd out private spending, absorbing resources that might otherwise be used for private consumption or productive capital investment. One effect is upward pressure on interest rates, and hence, given the Federal Reserve's unfortunate propensity to operate through interest rates, higher monetary growth. In addition, by reducing private incentives to work, save, and engage in productive ventures, and by crowding out private investment, high government spending inhibits economic growth so that any given rate of monetary growth produces a higher rate of inflation.

Scenario: The political appeal of a "balanced budget" has often been counterproductive. Big spenders have pushed through government programs leading to higher deficits. Fiscal conservatives, having lost that battle, have responded by supporting an increase in taxes to narrow the deficit. The fiscal conservatives have been turned out of office, partly for having the courage to raise taxes. The big spenders have been reelected, partly for their irresponsibility in raising spending. They have then set off on another spending spree and launched yet another cycle of higher spending, bigger deficits, higher taxes.

That scenario persuaded me, years ago, to be in favor of tax reductions under almost any circumstances. Cutting taxes reverses the cycle. If the tax cut threatens bigger deficits, the political appeal of balancing the budget is harnessed to reducing government spending rather than to raising taxes. That is the right way to achieve a balanced budget. It is the way that President Reagan proposes to follow. Much hinges on his success.

Some supporters of current tax rates have claimed that the lower rates will yield higher revenue. Certainly, a rate cut will encourage the reporting of higher taxable income. But the aim should be not higher revenue but lower revenue and lower spending. If a legislated rate cut did mean higher revenue, that would simply demonstrate that the rates had not been cut enough.

B. The Federal Reserve

5. The Federal Reserve

The Case for a Monetary Rule

February 7, 1972

I and most other monetarists have long favored a policy of a steady and moderate rate of growth of the quantity of money. We have strongly opposed the Fed's trying to fine-tune the economy.

Recent policy conformed to our prescription only in 1970.

Critics ask why we are so modest. Why not use the powerful instrument of monetary policy to offset other forces pushing the economy toward inflation or recession? Why tie the hands of the Fed? Why not trust their discretion in adapting to changing circumstances?

We favor the rule of steady monetary growth for several reasons.

1. *The Past Performance of the Fed.* Throughout its history, the Fed has proclaimed that it was using its powers to promote economic stability. But the record does not support the claim. On the contrary, the Fed has been a major source of instability.

The Fed was responsible for converting what would have

been a serious recession after 1929 into a major catastrophe by permitting the quantity of money to decline by one-third from 1929 to 1933, even though it had ample power to prevent the decline.

In recent years, the Fed set off the accelerating inflation that President Nixon inherited by expanding the money supply too rapidly in 1967 and 1968, then stepped too hard on the brake in 1969, and too hard on the accelerator in the first seven months of 1971. Federal Reserve officials have often admitted their errors after the fact—as Chairman Burns did in July 1971, in testimony before the Joint Economic Committee—and have promised better performance in the future. But then the same forces have produced a repetition of the same errors.

We conclude that the urgent need is to prevent the Fed from being a source of economic disturbance.

2. *The Limitations of our Knowledge.* Economic research has established two propositions: (1) there is a close, regular, and predictable relation between the quantity of money, national income, and prices over any considerable period of years; (2) the same relation is much looser from month to month, quarter to quarter, or even year to year. In particular, monetary changes take time to affect the economy, and the time delay is itself highly variable.

The first proposition means that a steady price level over the long pull requires that the quantity of money grow at a fairly steady rate roughly equal to the average rate of growth of output.

The second proposition means that any attempt to use monetary policy for fine-tuning is likely simply to introduce additional instability. And this is indeed what has happened.

3. *The Promotion of Confidence.* An announced, and adhered to, policy of steady monetary growth would provide the business community with a firm basis for confidence in mon-

etary stability that no discretionary policy could provide even if it happened to produce roughly steady monetary growth.

4. *Neutralization of the Fed.* An independent Fed may at times be too insulated from political pressures—as it was in the early 1930s—and yet at other times unduly affected by political pressures. If we really knew enough to use monetary policy for fine-tuning, we would probably experience a four-year cycle, with unemployment reaching its trough in years divisible by four and inflation reaching its peak in the succeeding year.

A monetary rule would insulate monetary policy both from the arbitrary power of a small group of men not subject to control by the electorate and from the short-run pressures of partisan politics.

Is the rule that we have proposed technically feasible? Can the Fed control the quantity of money? No serious student of money—whatever his policy views—denies that the Fed can, if it wishes, control the quantity of money. It cannot, of course, achieve a precise rate of growth from day to day or week to week. But it can come very close from month to month and quarter to quarter.

As I wrote some five years ago, if the monetary rule were followed, "other forces would still affect the economy, require change and adjustment, and distort the even tenor of our ways. But steady monetary growth would provide a monetary climate favorable to the effective operation of those basic forces of enterprise, ingenuity, invention, hard work, and thrift, that are the true springs of economic growth. That is the most that we can ask from monetary policy at our present stage of knowledge. But that much—and it is a great deal— is clearly within our reach."

What Is the Federal Reserve Doing?

March 10, 1975

The Federal Reserve System clearly did not want to exacerbate inflation from 1971 to 1974. It clearly does not now want to convert a serious recession into a major contraction. Yet it did exacerbate the inflation, and its current policy has already deepened the recession. It would be hard to find a more distressing example of the inability of a bureaucracy to learn from its own past mistakes. Its inflationary policy in 1971–74 was a replay of its inflationary policy in 1963–66, and in 1967–68; its current contractionary policy is a replay of its contractionary policy in 1966–67, and in 1969.

From January 1971 to June 1974, the Federal Reserve permitted the quantity of money to grow at the average rate of 7 percent a year for money defined to include currency and demand deposits (M_1) and at the average rate of 10 percent a year for money defined to include also commercial-bank time deposits other than large CDs (M_2). These are the highest rates since the end of World War II. They are higher than the rates that Federal Reserve officials, the Joint Economic

228

Committee of Congress, and outside economists regarded at the time as noninflationary. The majority of the Joint Economic Committee repeatedly recommended that the Fed keep M_1 growth between 2 and 6 percent a year, and the minority that it keep it between 2 and 4 percent. High rates of monetary growth unquestionably fostered inflation.

In the middle of 1974, the Fed shifted to a restrictive monetary policy. As has occurred repeatedly during its sixty-year history, when it shifted it did so too late and too far. Since June 1974, M_1 has grown at 1 percent a year, M_2 at 5 percent a year. These are rates that Federal Reserve officials, Congressional experts, and outside economists have all regarded as undesirably low.

The table on page 231 shows the actual rates of monetary growth from month to month and the "range of tolerance" that the Federal Open Market Committee specified each month as its target. In five out of seven months for M_1, and four out of seven months for M_2, the actual rate of growth has fallen short of the desired rate, and in the past two months, drastically short. These shortfalls partly account for the recent deepening of the recession.

Right End, Wrong Means

What explains the failure of the Fed to achieve its own objectives? In its public apologia for its distressing performance, the Fed has been pulling out every ancient and discredited cliché: "You can't push on a string," "You can lead a horse to water, but you can't make him drink," and so on ad nauseam. In short, "Don't blame us. We're innocent victims of forces beyond our control." As a longtime Fed watcher, I can assure you that this is par for the course. Whenever things go well, the Fed is delighted to claim credit. Whenever they go badly, forces outside its control are responsible.

I believe that the correct explanation for the Fed's failure is its insistence on following an anachronistic method of operation. In times past, the Fed mistakenly regarded interest rates as the appropriate criterion of policy. After literally decades of criticism, it finally recognized that it could not control interest rates except for brief periods and that its target should be the quantity of money. In 1970, it began to state its objectives in these terms. But—with the inertia that characterizes every large bureaucracy—it continued to use the operating techniques that it had developed earlier. It tries to control monetary growth by the highly indirect method of controlling a particular interest rate—the federal-funds rate. As the final columns of the table show, it does achieve its federal-fund target, but at the cost of not achieving its monetary-growth targets.

So long as the Fed tries to control monetary growth through the federal-funds rate, it will fail. When, as has been happening recently, the credit market weakens, market rates will fall below the target rate, and the Fed will have to drain reserves to achieve its target. When the credit market stabilizes, the target rate will be set too low, and the Fed will have to flood the market to achieve its target. We shall then have a monetary explosion. The Fed will again become an architect of inflation. Indeed, I regard the inflationary policy to which the Fed will be driven as the major danger from its present over-restrictive policy.

A Viable Alternative

The alternative is for the Fed to adapt its operating technique to its monetary growth targets. It should forget interest rates, leaving them to the highly efficient credit market. It should instead calculate each week how large an addition to reserves (or to base or high-powered money) is required to produce the desired monetary growth, and then provide that addition. This technique would not yield precisely the desired rate of growth on a week-to-week or even month-to-month basis. But it is literally inconceivable that over a period of seven months it could depart from its objective as widely as it has in the past seven months.

Numerous scholars have explored this alternative operating mechanism, have demonstrated its feasibility and have urged its adoption. Perhaps recent Congressional pressure will prove more successful in breaking down bureaucratic inertia than reason and evidence have so far been.

MISSING THE MONEY TARGETS*

| Month | Rate of Growth from Preceding Month (percent per year) | | | | Level of Federal-Funds Rate (percent) | |
| | M_1 | | M_2 | | | |
	Actual	Range of Tolerance	Actual	Range of Tolerance	Actual	Range of Tolerance
1974: July	2.1	3½–7½	5.2	5½–8½	13.0	11¼–12¼
Aug.	0.9	2–6	5.0	4½–7½	12.2	11½–13
Sept.	1.7	4¾–6¾	3.2	5½–7½	11.7	11½–12½
Oct.	4.7	3–6	8.5	5–7½	10.7	10½–12
Nov.	6.8	4¾–7¼	9.7	5¾–8¼	9.6	9–10½
Dec.	2.1	6½–9½	2.5	8–10½	9.0	8½–10
1975: Jan.	−8.9	5–7	3.1	7½–10	7.7	7½–9

*Computed from Federal Reserve publications.

How to Hit the Money Target

December 8, 1975

Last spring, the Congress adopted House Concurrent Resolution 133 requiring the Federal Reserve to report periodically its "objectives and plans with respect to the ranges of growth or diminution of monetary and credit aggregates in the upcoming twelve months."

The Fed has now reported three times: in May, July, and November. One result has been to demonstrate the wide divergence between the Fed's stated objectives and its actual performance.

The Fed's objectives have been essentially constant: an annual rate of growth of 5.5 percent to 7.5 percent in M_1 (currency plus demand deposits); of 7.5 or 8.5 percent to 10.5 percent in M_2 (M_1 plus time and savings deposits at commercial banks other than large CDs). But actual monetary growth has been highly erratic. When the Fed reported to the House Banking Committee in July, M_1 and M_2 were *above* the upper limits for that date it had specified in May. When it reported to the Senate Banking Committee in November, M_1 and M_2 were *below* the lower limits for that date it had specified in May and July.

Erratic swings in monetary growth are not a new phenomenon. They have been the major defect in Federal Reserve performance over the whole of its sixty-two-year history. Unduly rapid growth fueled the great inflations of World Wars I and II and the more recent double-digit inflation of 1974. Unduly slow growth or actual decline produced or deepened the sharp contractions of 1920–21, 1929–33 and 1937–38, as well as the milder recessions of the whole period.

The new phenomenon is that, for the first time, we know that at least the recent erratic swings were the result not of mistaken objectives but rather of a failure to achieve those objectives.

Consequences

The consequences of this failure have been extremely serious. The sharp reduction in monetary growth that occurred in mid-1974 (see table) helped convert the mild recession then under way into the steep slide that began in late 1974. The reversal in January 1975 was overdue. It helped to induce the recovery that began a few months later and that is still con-

---

RATES OF MONETARY GROWTH

Annual Rate of Growth (percent per year)

	M_1	M_2
June 1970 to June 1973	7.3	10.9
June 1973 to June 1974	5.6	8.7
June 1974 to Jan. 1975	0.9	5.1
Jan. 1975 to June 1975	10.0	12.7
June 1975 to Oct. 1975	1.0	5.9

---

tinuing. But it was overdone. Continued monetary growth at anything like the rate that prevailed from January to June 1975 would have produced, after some time, a new burst of double-digit inflation.

A slowdown was therefore needed in June, but it too was overdone. Monetary growth fell even more than in mid-1974. However, the 1974 slowdown lasted seven months and came during a recession, when nonmonetary forces were reinforcing the monetary slowdown. This time, the slowdown has come during a vigorous recovery, when nonmonetary forces are working to offset it, and so far has lasted only four months.

Nonetheless, considerable damage may already have been done. Extremely restrictive monetary growth since June may well account for the clear faltering in the pace of expansion in October, a smaller increase in industrial production and in personal income, and a higher level of unemployment. If the slow rate of monetary growth from June to October were to continue for several additional months, the expansion would almost surely be aborted and converted into a new recession.

I do not, however, expect that to happen. The far greater danger, I believe, is another swing from one extreme to the other—another monetary explosion. There are some signs that such an explosion is already beginning. If so, it will probably keep the interruption of the expansion from being more than a stutter but once again it will threaten double-digit inflation.

Causes

Some observers have interpreted the failure of the Fed to achieve its stated objectives as evidence that it cannot do so, that in this area it is a helpless giant. There is a sense in which that conclusion is correct, but a more fundamental sense in which it is wrong.

The conclusion is correct in the sense that the operating

procedures that the Fed now uses to implement its stated objectives tend to produce major discrepancies between objectives and performance. So long as it continues to use those procedures, it will continue to subject the economy to erratic swings in monetary growth.

The conclusion is wrong in the sense that there are alternative procedures that have been extensively discussed and explored by experts outside as well as inside the Federal Reserve System that are entirely feasible and that would enable the Fed to reduce sharply the discrepancies between actual and intended monetary growth.

The Fed currently attempts to control the money supply indirectly, by controlling a particular interest rate (the federal-funds rate). That procedure is an anachronistic survival of an earlier day when the Fed regarded the control of interest rates, rather than of the money supply, as its primary objective. Its persistence is a tribute to bureaucratic inertia.

The Fed can control the federal-funds rate—there have been only minor discrepancies between the target rate and the actual rate. The trouble is that any error tends to cumulate and be self-reinforcing.

Solution

The alternative procedure is to let all interest rates be determined by the market—as they already mostly are—and instead control the money supply by controlling the amount of reserves available to the banking system. The Fed can control the amount of reserves, and the growth in reserves is more predictably related to the growth in the money supply than is the federal-funds rate.

The alternative procedure would not enable the Fed to hit its target on the nose. There would still be sizable errors from week to week or even month to month. But the errors would tend to cancel over time, rather than be self-reinforcing, as they now are. It is literally inconceivable that if the Fed had followed this procedure it would have departed as far from its own objectives as it did during 1974 and 1975.

The Congress has already made a signal contribution to improved monetary performance by requiring the Fed to specify its objectives publicly in advance, for a year ahead, in terms of monetary-growth rates. It may make a further contribution if its hearings lead the Fed, however belatedly, to streamline its operating procedure so that it can put its money where its mouth is.

Are These Monetary Swings Necessary?

June 14, 1976

We are currently in the midst of a monetary explosion. The quantity of money, defined to include currency and demand deposits (M_1), grew at an annual rate of more than 9 percent from January to April; defined to include also commercial-bank time deposits other than large CD's (M_2), it grew at an annual rate of more than 13 percent. Both totals have since continued to rise rapidly.

If these growth rates were to continue, they would inevitably lead to a sharp resurgence of inflation—not immediately but by early or late 1977. However, to judge from past Federal Reserve behavior, they will not continue. After perhaps another month or two, they will be followed by a swing back to the other extreme—to growth rates well below the level that the Fed has specified as its target. Such swings have characterized Fed performance.

The Recent Record

Here is the record for the past two years:

| | Rate of Growth (percent per year) | |
	M_1	M_2
Apr. 1974 to Feb. 1975	2.8	6.2
Feb. 1975 to June 1975	10.0	12.2
June 1975 to Jan. 1976	2.4	7.5
Jan. 1976 to Apr. 1976	9.3	13.6
Average, Apr. 1974 to Apr. 1976	4.6	8.5

These average rates of growth are too high for the long run, because they would lead to inflation of about 5 percent per year. However, for these two years, which came after even higher rates of rates of inflation, the averages were about right, and roughly corresponded to the Fed's targets.

But look at the wild swings: from 2.4 to 10 percent for M_1, from 6.2 to 13.6 percent for M_2. These were no part of the Fed's intention.

The Fed has claimed that the swings have no great effect on the economy, that the economy smooths such brief fluctuations in monetary growth and is affected only by average growth. This contention has merit for sufficiently short periods. Clearly, day-to-day or week-to-week fluctuations will not leave any significant imprint. But what about fluctuations lasting six or eight months?

The chart on page 239 makes it clear that these swings have proceeded long enough to have a significant impact on the economy. The two solid and dotted curves show the rates of growth of M_1 and M_2; the dashed curve, the rate of growth

of personal income as a measure of the general economy.*
The first two curves show the four swings in money recorded in the table. Each of the first three swings in money
was clearly followed by a swing in income. Presumably the
recent monetary explosion will also be followed by a corresponding swing in income, but it is too soon to know whether
it has yet begun.

Had the Fed avoided the swings in money, there might
still have been swings in income, but they surely would have
been much milder.

HOW MONEY MATTERS

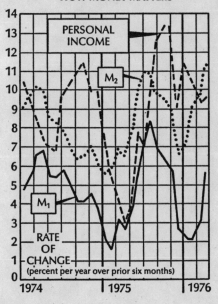

---

*To smooth out erratic movements, all rates of growth are averaged over
six-month periods.

Rationalization vs. Reasons

The Fed claims that the swings in money have served to reduce swings in interest rates and to counteract shifts in the demand for money. The chart contradicts the second claim—because if it were correct, the swings in money would have stabilized, not destabilized, income. I believe that the first claim is equally fallacious.

The swings in money continue not because they serve a useful function, but primarily because bureaucratic inertia keeps the Fed from streamlining its obsolete procedures.

A Memorandum to the Fed

January 30, 1981

On Oct. 6, 1979, the Federal Reserve announced "a change in the method used to conduct monetary policy to support the objective of containing growth in the monetary aggregates."

Despite vigorous efforts by the Fed to implement the policy, monetary growth has varied over a wider range since Oct. 6, 1979, than in any period of comparable length for at least the last two decades. The fact is recognized by the Fed itself, by its defenders, and by its critics.

There is, however, much disagreement about, first, why monetary growth has varied so widely and, second, whether the Fed has the ability to achieve steady monetary growth in line with its targets over periods measured in weeks or months rather than quarters or years.

Chairman Paul Volker, in testimony to Congress, blamed last year's "abnormal" fluctuations in money supply and interest rates on a sharp second-quarter recession followed by a stronger-than-anticipated recovery, the temporary imposition of credit controls last spring, market uncertainty over the Fed's decision to let interest rates fluctuate more widely, and irresponsible inflationary expectations.

This explanation reminds me of the man on trial for murdering his parents who asked for mercy on the ground that he was an orphan.

The sharp second-quarter recession very likely was produced, and certainly was intensified, by the Fed's own actions: first, a *decline* in M_{1-B} at the annual rate of 5.1 percent from February to May—the sharpest decline during any three-month period in at least the last two decades; second, the imposition of credit controls in March—at the request, it is true, of President Carter, but under the authority of the "independent" Fed.

The "stronger-than-anticipated recovery" was sparked by a *rise* in M_{1-B} at the annual rate of 15.9 percent from May to October—the most rapid rise during any five-month period in at least the last two decades—reinforced by the removal of credit controls. These were entirely the Fed's doing.

Intensifying the Recession

By sharply intensifying the recession, the initial decline in money supply led the Fed to overreact in the opposite direction—a pattern that has frequently occurred in the past.

As to "irresponsible inflationary expectations," what is "irresponsible" about such expectations in view of (1) the past record of inflation—a roller coaster about a rising trend; (2) the past record of government monetary policy—a similar roller coaster about a rising trend?

The wide swings in interest rates also were not, in my opinion, a result of the Fed's decision to let interest rates fluctuate more widely, but rather of the Fed's failure to match the change in its announced objectives with a comparable change in its operating procedures. Of this, more later.

Over the years, two major excuses have repeatedly been offered by the Fed and its defenders for erratic and inflationary monetary policies; first, large federal government deficits; second, unpredictable changes in the "demand for money."

The first excuse has merit on a political level, none whatsoever on a technical level. The same political forces that have fostered rising deficits—pressures to increase government spending without legislating additional taxes and to react promptly to offset any increases in unemployment—have also affected the Federal Reserve and induced it to become an erratic engine of inflation.

Deficits and Monetary Growth

On the technical level, however, there is no necessary connection between deficits and monetary growth. To illustrate: As a percentage of GNP, deficits in the U.S. have varied from a low of 0.4 percent for the fiscal year ended June 30, 1974, to a high of 4.6 percent for the year to June 30, 1976. But growth in M_{1-B} was almost the same in the two years: 4.3 percent from July 1973 to July 1974; 4.7 percent from July 1975 to July 1976. For the year ended September 30, 1979, the deficit was 1.8 percent of GNP, yet M_{1-B} grew 7.8 percent from October 1978 to October 1979.

To illustrate in a different way: Deficits have been running about 6 percent of gross national product in Japan, or roughly three times ours, and about 2 percent in Germany, or the same as ours. Yet both countries have a better recent record than we do of achieving monetary growth targets and holding down inflation.

In short, there is no technical reason why the Fed must monetize deficits. Insofar as it does so, it is because of political pressures to hold down interest rates or to stimulate the economy.

The second excuse, alleged instability in the demand for

money, involves a serious intellectual confusion between "money" and "credit." Most credit is not money, by any definition of money; much money is not credit (as is clearest with a commodity standard such as gold). Federal Reserve notes used to be described as "promises to pay." They are clearly not that today. They are simply fiat, not in any meaningful sense a credit instrument, and that is equally true of deposits at Federal Reserve Banks.

Interest rates are the price of credit, not the price of money. The price of money is the quantity of goods and services that will "buy" a piece of money (the reciprocal of the price level). Fluctuations in interest rates reflect instability in the demand for credit rather than for money properly defined, though interest rate changes may indirectly affect the quantity of money demanded. The so-called money market is really a credit market.

Yet the excuse in terms of instability in the demand for credit does have some validity because—and only because—the Fed continues to try to control the money supply through interest rates, in particular the federal-funds rate. That is neither the only nor the best way to control the money supply. The key defect in trying to control the money supply by pegging the federal-funds rate is that mistakes are cumulative and self-reinforcing, and so lead to the kind of wide swings in monetary aggregates that we have increasingly experienced in recent years.

If the Fed picks too low a federal-funds rate, it has to add excessively to the supply of federal funds, that is, the monetary base (currency plus Federal Reserve deposits), in order to maintain that rate. As the money supply responds, monetary expansion tends to stimulate spending and the demand for loans and to increase inflationary expectations. The result, after an interval, is upward pressure on market interest rates. To peg the federal-funds rate at the initial level, the Fed must add more and more to the base, increasing still further the upward pressure on interest rates. Similarly, if the Fed picks too high a funds rate, it must drain an excessive amount from the base, discouraging spending, decreasing demand for loans, and ultimately adding to downward pressure on interest rates.

The short-term effect of higher monetary growth is to lower interest rates, and the short-term effect of lower monetary growth is to raise interest rates. But the longer-term effects are in the opposite direction. These opposite effects mean that in using the federal-funds rate as its operating target, the Fed is always balancing on a knife-edge. That is why this policy has produced such wide swings in both interest rates and monetary growth.

The Fed unquestionably has the power to peg the federal-funds rate within very narrow limits over short periods but only by surrendering control of the base in the short run, and of the interest rate itself in the longer run. It can regain control only by changing the pegged rate—which it sooner or later does. But it takes time to recognize a mistake and further time to overcome bureaucratic inertia, so the ultimate changes in the pegged rate have to be sizable and are typically overdone.

Last year provides an almost textbook example. The money supply peaked in mid-February 1980, when the funds rate was about 15 percent. But the Fed did not recognize promptly what was happening and kept pushing the funds rate up—to over 19 percent by early April, which is just when the money supply started collapsing.

The money supply reached its trough at the end of April, at which point the federal-funds rate was again about 15 percent. Again, the Fed was late and kept pushing the funds rate down for two more months, to less than 9 percent by late July. By that time the money supply had exploded, rising at an annual rate of over 13 percent from the end of April to the end of July. The Fed then belatedly started pushing the federal-funds rate up.

The money supply peaked in mid-November when the funds rate was again about 15 percent. Again, the Fed was late in recognizing the change and kept pushing the funds rate up to nearly 20 percent in mid-December and again in January. It looks as if the springtime pattern is being repeated. The money supply declined from mid-November to the end of December at an annual rate of 15 percent. If history continues to repeat, we shall again have a precipitous drop in money and the economy followed by an inflationary overreaction.

Unnecessary Wide Swings

Had money supply growth been steadier during the year, interest rates would have been steadier as well—and conversely. Note that a 15 percent interest rate in 1980 corresponded to a "real" interest rate, corrected for inflation, of about 3 percent, in line with long-run experience.

These wide swings are unnecessary. An alternative procedure of controlling the base directly and letting the market determine interest rates could produce steady and predictable monetary growth and at the same time avoid wide swings in interest rates.

The base consists of the Fed's own liabilities, on which it has accurate day-to-day figures. The Fed can add to its liabilities by purchasing government securities or making loans to banks; it can subtract from its liabilities by selling securities or reducing lending. The only limitations to its ability to determine how much to add or subtract from the base are self-imposed: first, its policy of pegging the federal-funds rate; second, its decision in 1968 to base reserve requirements on deposits two weeks earlier—which means that the total reserves for the current week are predetermined, so that the

246

only practical option the Fed has is whether to supply them through open-market operations or through the discount window.

Eliminate these obstacles and the Fed can exercise highly precise and prompt control over the size of the base. Control of the monetary base will not produce rigid and precise control of a monetary aggregate such as M_{1-B}. The link between the base and M_{1-B} has elements of looseness deriving from changes in the public's desired ratio of currency to deposits, the banks' management of their liabilities, which affects required reserves, and the banks' desired ratio of excess reserves to deposits. Nevertheless, controlling the supply of money through the monetary base avoids the chief technical defect of trying to control the demand for money through the federal-funds rate. Mistakes in controlling the base are not cumulative and self-reinforcing.

If the Fed increases the base by, say 6 percent, when 7 percent would have been the amount required to achieve its target growth rate in M_{1-B}, the error does not cumulate. The growth in M_{1-B} simply falls short of its target by one percentage point, nothing more. Moreover, such errors are likely to be random from month to month and hence to average out, even if not corrected, whereas errors in the federal-funds rate tend to get larger until corrected, and the correction itself is generally too little at first and then too much.

Just as the Fed can control the federal-funds rate only by surrendering control over the base, so it can control the base only by surrendering control over the federal-funds rate or any other interest rate. If it did so, and thereby produced steadier growth in the monetary aggregates, interest rates might be more volatile over intervals of days or weeks. Almost certainly, however, interest rates would be far less volatile over periods of months and years, and possibly even weeks. The belief that the Fed can or does control interest rates is a myth that dies hard. But surely if it could, the prime rate would never have hit 21.5 percent.

A Specific Proposal

These are the specific steps that I believe the Fed should take to improve its control of the money supply and to become a major source of stability in economic policy instead of the unguided missile it has so often been:

Announce that it will no longer specify a target range for the federal-funds rate (or any other interest rate).

Specify in advance the amount it proposes to add to, or subtract from, the monetary base week by week over a substantial future period. It should determine these target amounts by estimating as best it can the additions or subtractions necessary to achieve a desired target for a *single* selected monetary aggregate. (It matters far less whether that aggregate is M_{1-A} or M_{1-B} or M_2 or M_n than that a single aggregate be chosen.) Numerous studies have demonstrated that the necessary additions or subtractions to the base can be calculated fairly accurately.

Improving the Monetary Link

To improve the link between the monetary base and the selected monetary aggregate, the Fed should specify that required reserves are to be calculated from contemporaneous deposits, not from deposits two weeks earlier as at present. There is essential unanimity among experts, including most of those employed by the Fed, that the introduction of lagged reserve accounting in 1968 has made monetary control more difficult with little if any compensating advantage. Only bureaucratic "operating problems" have prevented a correction of this mistake. The Fed announced its intention to make this change some months ago, but has repeatedly postponed the effective date.

Create a Penalty Rate

To avoid indirectly pegging the federal-funds rate, the Fed should convert the discount rate (the rate at which it lends to banks) to a penalty rate and link it to a market rate so that it moves automatically and gradually, not as now at discrete intervals, generally too late. For example, it might set the discount rate each week at two percentage points above the average rate on three-month Treasury bills during the prior week.

In cooperation with other responsible agencies, the Fed should seek to accelerate the elimination of Regulation Q controls on interest rates, as already provided for by current law.

I have said nothing about the precise monetary growth targets the Fed should specify because that is not where the problem is. The Fed has known what monetary growth it should aim for. But it has been reluctant to adopt procedures that would enable it to achieve those goals.

Improvement in Federal Reserve performance would not by itself enable the Reagan administration to achieve its goals of reduced inflation and healthier economic growth. But failure of the Fed to improve its performance could frustrate achievement of those goals. And, fortunately or unfortunately, moral suasion is the only instrument the new president has to induce the Fed to make changes in its procedures that are so badly needed and so long overdue.

The Yo-Yo Economy

February 15, 1982

The present recession is notable not for its severity, but for its timing. Its onset cut short an expansion that had lasted only twelve months (from July 1980 to July 1981)—the second shortest expansion in the more than one hundred years of U.S. history for which economists have dated business cycles. Moreover, that expansion followed the shortest recession on record—the six-month recession that lasted from January to July 1980. If the current recession also proves to be brief—as most economic forecasters anticipate—we shall have experienced by far the shortest triplet of recession-expansion-recession.

Gyrating Interest Rates: What accounts for this unprecedentedly erratic behavior of the U.S. economy? The answer that leaps to mind is the correspondingly erratic behavior of interest rates. Short-term interest rates had already hit historic highs in 1979. In the next two years, the rate on three-month Treasury bills bounced up and down between a high of nearly 17 percent and a low of a trifle over 6 percent—gyrations

without precedent during the more than a century for which
we have data.

What produced the unprecedented volatility in interest
rates? The accompanying table suggests the answer: unprecedented volatility in monetary growth. The first part of the
table updates one that I recently published in *Newsweek* (December 21) and records the volatility in monetary growth.
The second part shows what happened to short-term interest
rates some weeks after each up and down of the monetary yo-
yo. The evidence is dramatic. Four out of five surges in the
quantity of money were followed by a rise in the Treasury-
bill rate; all five declines in the quantity of money were followed by a decline in the bill rate. It is notable also that the
one exception—after the September 16, 1981 peak in monetary growth—followed the smallest rise in monetary growth.

INTEREST RATES FOLLOW MONEY

Money Turning Point	Date	Interval in Weeks	Annual Rate of Change in M_{1-B}	Three-Month Treasury Bills		
				Three	Four	Five
					Weeks Later	
Peak	Oct. 3, 1979			12.6%	12.1%	12.3%
Trough	Nov. 28, 1979	8	−1.4%	12.1	12.0	12.1
Peak	Feb. 20, 1980	12	+12.1	15.3	14.8	15.6
Trough	Apr. 30, 1980	10	−12.4	8.2	7.7	7.5
Peak	Nov. 26, 1980	30	+15.0	16.2	14.6	14.3
Trough*	Feb. 4, 1981	10	−13.1	14.2	14.4	13.8
Peak	Apr. 22, 1981	11	+23.8	16.8	16.6	15.6
Trough	July 1, 1981	10	−10.6	15.5	15.1	15.4
Peak	Sept. 16, 1981	11	+7.2	13.8	13.4	13.4
Trough	Oct. 28, 1981	6	−5.1	10.3	10.2	10.4
Peak	Jan. 13, 1982	11	+24.6	13.2†		

*Corrected roughly for NOW accounts.   †Preliminary

The yo-yo swings in monetary growth affected the economy directly, as well as through interest rates. Each surge in monetary growth was followed after some months by an acceleration in spendable income, output, and employment; and each decline in monetary growth, by a retardation. Consider the following pattern, which averages out some of the gyrations:

1. From October 3, 1979, to April 30, 1980, M_{1-B} (currency plus checkable deposits, now relabeled M_1) declined at an average annual rate of 0.2 percent. A cyclical recession came three months later, from January 1980 to July 1980.

2. From April 30, 1980 to April 22, 1981, M_{1-B} grew at the annual rate of 9.9 percent. A cyclical expansion came three months later, from July 1980 to July 1981.

3. From April 22, 1981, to October 28, 1981, M_{1-B} declined at the annual rate of 1.3 percent. A cyclical recession started three months later, in July 1981.

If this pattern continues, and the monetary explosion from October 28, 1981, to January 13, 1982, is not followed promptly by a decline of comparable size, this recession too will be a short one. Indeed, it may already have passed what will subsequently be recognized as a trough.

As in a good mystery story, we now know what happened but not yet who—or, in this case, what—triggered these developments. The crucial clue is given by the dating. The unprecedented volatility of the money supply followed the Federal Reserve's October 6, 1979, announcement of a major change in its operating procedures. The objective of the change—to move from operating through an interest rate to operating through bank reserves—was welcomed by many of us. Unfortunately, however, the actual changes in procedures, though far-reaching, did not go far enough to enable the new procedures to produce the desired results. As I noted in my earlier column, it was one step forward, two steps backward.

The technical steps needed to end yo-yo monetary growth are well known and the Fed has the authority to take them. They have the support of most monetary economists inside and outside the Federal Reserve System. They include: replacement of lagged reserve accounting by contemporary reserve accounting; selection of a single monetary target to replace the Fed's juggling between targets, depending on which one gives the most favorable picture of Fed policy; imposition of equal percentage reserve requirements on all deposit components of the selected target; linking the discount rate to a market rate; and reduction in the churning that the Fed engages in (so-called "defensive open-market operations").

Lip Service: The Fed knows how to produce more stable monetary growth. The problem is that, despite the lip service they pay to that objective, the key policymakers of the Fed do not regard the achievement of stable monetary growth as sufficiently important to justify the bureaucratic disruptions required.

Most discussions of monetary policy center on whether policy is "too tight" or "too easy." That is not my complaint. Average monetary growth over the past two years has been fairly good—decidedly lower than earlier. That is why inflation has been declining. However, the average conceals the erratic alternation of "too tight" and "too easy." That alternation has put the economy through a dismaying roller coaster. It must be replaced by steady monetary growth in order for the Fed to regain the confidence of the financial community and for President Reagan's economic program to succeed in both ending inflation and providing a stable basis for healthy, non-inflationary economic growth.

An Aborted Recovery?

August 23, 1982

The government influences the general course of the economy through fiscal policy—taxing, spending, and deficit—and through monetary policy—controlling the quantity of money. Fiscal policy is determined by Congress and the president; monetary policy by the independent Federal Reserve system. The news media consistently give fiscal policy top billing. Daily headlines chronicle epic battles in Congress and between the legislative and executive branches over the budget. There is occasional recognition of the Fed's role in producing past inflation and recent disinflation, but the big story is about the irresponsible fiscal policy that is frustrating the attempts by the Federal Reserve to curb the ups and downs of the economy while continuing to restrain inflation.

Irresponsible fiscal policy—excessive spending, burdensome and inequitable taxes, and massive deficits—does account for the sharp slowdown in economic growth in the past decade. It has also produced steady pressure on the Federal Reserve to monetize deficits and thereby has contributed to inflation. But I believe that monetary policy, not fiscal policy, is primarily responsible for the recent sharp ups and downs in the economy and for our present serious economic difficulties.

Monetary Gyrations: The accompanying table summarizes some of the evidence supporting that view. In October 1979, the Federal Reserve, faced with the failure of its earlier policies to stem a flight from the dollar, changed its operational goal from controlling interest rates to controlling the money supply. It did succeed in bringing down the *average* rate of growth in the quantity of money. That is why inflation has come down so sharply. But, paradoxically, as the first two columns in the table show, monetary growth over short pe-

MONEY SUPPLY'S UNEVEN COURSE

PERIOD	Monetary Growth (M$_1$) at an Annualized Rate	CHANGE IN	
		Interest Rate* One Month Later**	Industrial Production Three Months Later
Oct. 1979 to Apr. 1980	+1.8%	−3.2	−15.9
Apr. 1980 to Apr. 1981	+11.1	+7.7	+9.7
Apr. 1981 to Oct. 1981	−0.2	−5.4	−16.4
Oct. 1981 to Jan. 1982	+15.3	+2.6	−0.3
Jan. 1982 to June 1982	+1.3	−2.1	−6.9†

*90-day Treasury-bill rate.   **Percentage-point change.   †To July 1982.

riods has become much more erratic: annual rates of less than
2 percent for six months, over 11 percent for a year, negative
growth for six months, over 15 percent for three months, and
finally, only 1.3 percent for the past five months.

The next two columns of the table show what happened to
the interest rate on ninety-day Treasury bills one month later
and to industrial production three months later—roughly the
time it takes for a change in monetary growth to have its
impact. Contrary to what passes for conventional wisdom,
but very much in line with a more sophisticated view, the
interest rate went *down* after each period of slow monetary
growth and went *up* after each period of rapid monetary
growth.

The changes in industrial production are equally consistent. As it happens, the cyclical peaks and troughs dated by
the National Bureau of Economic Research come precisely
three months after the turning points in monetary growth and
so coincide precisely with the periods to which the entries in
the first column of the table refer. Industrial production went
down at nearly a 16 percent rate during the recession from
January 1980 to July 1980; up at a 9.7 percent rate during
the expansion from July 1980 to July 1981; down at a more
than 16 percent rate from July 1981 to January 1982, and at
a much lower rate since January.

The three-month monetary explosion from October 1981
to January 1982 was responsible for slowing the decline in
industrial production and led me to conclude that a recovery
had begun. I believe now that a putative recovery did get
under way, but was aborted by a drastic cut in monetary
growth. Monetary growth of 1.3 percent per year cannot sus-
tain a recovery in an economy in which the basic rate of
inflation is still something like 6 to 9 percent.

During the 32 months from October 1979 to June 1982

the money supply grew at the average rate of 6 percent. Suppose that the money supply had grown steadily at about that rate instead of gyrating from one extreme to the other. To be specific, suppose it had grown at rates between 3 and 9 percent for periods as long as three months, which would have meant a narrower range for longer periods. The economic picture would have been completely transformed—entirely for the better.

1. Inflation would have come down as much as it has, since that depends on longer-term monetary growth.

2. The recession that terminated in July 1980 would have lasted longer but would have been milder. More important, the subsequent economic recovery would have been healthier and longer lasting. It would almost surely still be going strong.

3. Unemployment would be decidedly lower and going down, not up.

4. Interest rates would have been stabler and a good deal lower—probably by something like 3 to 5 percentage points.

5. Lower interest rates and lower unemployment would have meant lower government spending. Higher levels of economic activity would have meant higher revenues. On both scores, the deficit would have been lower. The much-needed cuts in tax rates would have been able to exert their full supply-side effect. And there would have been less resistance to the further reductions in spending and tax rates that are so urgently needed.

6. In particular, the occasion would never have arisen for the introduction of the bill to raise taxes $98.9 billion—a monstrosity that should not be passed. Bad monetary policy does not alter the need to lower tax rates rather than to raise them.

We shall not have a healthy and lasting recovery along with steadily declining inflation until the powers that be recognize the importance of curbing the erratic ups and downs in monetary growth and take effective steps to ensure reasonably steady growth in the quantity of money along a gently declining path.

C. Interest Rates

Interest Rates and Inflation

August 23, 1976

Is an interest rate of 10 percent high? Or low? That depends. If prices are constant, an interest rate of 10 percent is high. But if prices of goods and services are rising at 10 percent per year, an interest rate of 10 percent is low. If, for the moment, we neglect tax effects, the "real" interest rate is then zero. If you borrow $1,000 at 10 percent and invest the money in goods that rise in price at the rate of 10 percent, a year later they will be worth enough to repay both the $1,000 principal and the $100 interest. If those goods rendered services to you, or enabled you to produce more, you received that benefit at no cost.

Nominal vs. Real

In these recent years of inflation, almost every homeowner has been happily aware of the difference between the "nominal" interest rate and the "real" interest rate. He has seen the market value of his house go up, and his mortgage—even neglecting payments on principal—decline as a fraction of the value of the house. Inflation has been paying off his debt and increasing his equity.

Almost every purchaser of government savings bonds has been unhappily aware of this difference. He has been receiving 3 or 4 or 5 percent per year interest—but prices have been rising faster, so that, when he cashes in his bond, the proceeds will buy decidedly less than he could have bought with the sum that he originally invested in the bond. He has been paying for the privilege of lending to the government. To add insult to injury, he must pay income tax on the so-called interest!

The financial markets too have been aware of the difference between nominal and real interest rates, as the accompanying chart makes clear. Over the period it covers (1972 to date), inflation has clearly dominated the movement of the interest rate. Throughout the period, higher inflation has meant higher interest rates, lower inflation lower interest rates.

Adjusted for inflation, interest rates have been abnormally low. Over the past century, the U.S. commercial-paper rate has averaged 4 percent, but inflation has averaged only 1.7 percent, so the "real" yield was 2.3 percent. In the past four and a half years, the commercial-paper rate has averaged 7 percent, but inflation has averaged 7.5 percent, so the "real" yield has been *minus* 0.5 percent.

The Effect of Taxes

This comparison understates the difference between recent years and the past century because it neglects taxes. Unfortunately, these are levied on the nominal rather than the real yield. Consider an individual whose marginal tax rate is 33.33 percent. If he had received an interest payment of 7 percent, he would have had less than 5 percent left after taxes; subtract the 7.5 percent average rate of inflation, and his "real" yield would have been *minus* 2.5 percent!

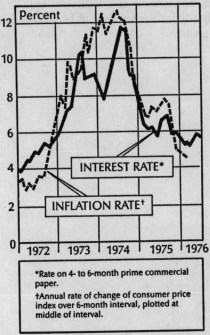

THE PRICE OF MONEY

*Rate on 4- to 6-month prime commercial paper.
†Annual rate of change of consumer price index over 6-month interval, plotted at middle of interval.

Sources: Federal Reserve, Commerce Department.

To put it differently, inflation is currently running at about 6 percent a year. An individual whose marginal tax rate is 33.33 percent must receive 9 percent just to break even with inflation—his real return would be zero. To get a real after-tax return of 2.3 percent, he would have to receive 12.5 percent interest.

At current rates of inflation, interest rates today are low, not high. The market is acting as if it expected inflation to decline still further over the coming years. If that expectation is disappointed, interest rates will rise. Individuals will not indefinitely pay for the privilege of lending to the goverment or to one another.

The Fed and Inflation

December 29, 1980

"Interest rates are expected to increase further as Fed escalates its inflation fight." (*Wall Street Journal*, November 24, 1980.)

It would be hard to pack more errors into a single sentence. Yet the sentence reflects what appears to be received wisdom among financial commentators.

Error No. 1. Escalates what Fed inflation fight? The Fed controls the quantity of money. Yet as the accompanying chart shows, the rate of monetary growth has exploded since May 1980. Indeed, M_{1-B} has grown more rapidly in the six months from May to November than in any other six months in at least the past two decades. Far from fighting inflation, the Fed has been pouring gasoline on the inflation fire.

Error No. 2. Why are interest rates high? As a weapon to fight inflation, or as a result of the inflationary monetary growth?

Over any long period of time the answer is clear. High monetary growth means high inflation, and high inflation produces high interest rates. Low monetary growth means low inflation, and low inflation produces low interest rates.

TRACKING TRENDS

Monetary growth has exploded since May,
fueling inflation and forcing up interest rates.

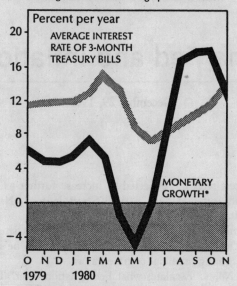

Percent per year

AVERAGE INTEREST
RATE OF 3-MONTH
TREASURY BILLS

MONETARY
GROWTH*

O N D J F M A M J J A S O N
1979   1980

*Rate of change in M$_{1\text{-}B}$ (currency and all checking
accounts) over prior three months, annual rate.

Over shorter periods, the situation is more complex. The
initial impact of slower monetary growth is to raise interest
rates; of faster monetary growth, to lower interest rates. However, as the markets have learned the longer-term relationships, the duration of the short-term effect has become shorter
and shorter. It used to last about six months. The accompanying chart suggests that it now lasts only about one or two
months. The sharp rise in monetary growth from December
to February was followed by a rise in short-term interest rates
from December to March. The downturn in monetary growth

266

from February to May was followed by a decline in interest rates from March to June. The explosion in monetary growth beginning in May was followed a month later by an explosion in interest rates.

Error No. 3. Would interest rates come down if the quantity of money grew even faster? Perhaps for a month or two, but then interest rates would again shoot up, as they did after monetary growth turned up in May.

The rapid response of interest rates reflects market anticipations of the future effects of monetary growth. The economy itself does not respond as rapidly. The typical pattern is that higher monetary growth is followed some three to nine months later by higher growth in total spending. The higher spending, in turn, first takes the form of higher growth in output and employment, and only later still of higher inflation. Similarly, lower monetary growth is followed after roughly the same time intervals by lower growth in spending, output, and employment, and lower inflation. The total delay between monetary change and inflation is on the order of eighteen to twenty-four months. The inflation we are now experiencing reflects monetary growth in late 1978 and early 1979.

If the prompt response of interest rates to monetary growth continues, and if the mild decline in monetary growth from October to November proves the start of a sustained decline, interest rates should start heading down by the turn of the year or shortly thereafter. If monetary growth were then kept steady at a modest level, the decline in interest rates would last and the stage would be set for prosperity without inflation.

Given the recent monetary explosion, a sharp and sustained reduction in monetary growth is likely also to produce renewed recession in early 1981. However, the alternative is far worse. If the Fed were to continue, let alone accelerate, the rapid monetary growth of the past six months, we would be heading for inflation in the neighborhood of 20 percent by the end of 1981 or early 1982—and even higher interest rates. When we finally did bite the bullet, we would face a far more severe recession at even higher interest rates and higher inflation.

Interest Rates and the Budget

June 28, 1982

During the current controversy over the budget, it has been taken for granted on all sides that large projected deficits explain current high interest rates—both long and short. That proposition has some validity for long-term interest rates. It has none whatsoever for short-term interest rates.

Long-Term Rates: The current level of long-term rates—around 14 to 15 percent for high-grade corporate bonds—is the sum of two items: a "real" interest rate and the anticipated inflation rate. The real interest rate—the difference between the nominal rate and the rate of inflation—has averaged about 3 to 4 percent over long periods. That leaves about 11 percentage points as the allowance for anticipated inflation. And that is not an unreasonable expectation.

If President Reagan succeeds in cutting government spending and if the Federal Reserve maintains moderate monetary growth on the average, inflation three to five years from now will be less than 5 percent and will stay there. On the other hand, if we revert to past policies of explosive government spending and high monetary growth, inflation three to five years from now will be more than 20 percent. There is little chance that inflation will be between 5 and 20 percent. As of now, the two extreme outcomes appear about equally likely. Average 5 and 20 and the resulting 12.5 percent is not far from the 11 percent imbedded in the curent rate. The budget battle can bring down long-term interest rates only by bringing down this average inflation expectation.

Wide uncertainty about long-term prospects renders both borrowing and lending at long-term unattractive—making the long-term market very thin. Since both borrowers and lenders have shifted to the short-term market, the uncertainty does not explain the high rates in the short-term market.

Short-Term Rates: The rate at which people are willing to lend or borrow for a short period, say ninety days, depends on the inflation they expect over that ninety-day period. That inflation rate does not depend on budget deficits projected for fiscal 1983, 1984, and 1985. No hypothetical, unachieved reductions in those deficits will have any significant effect on the rate of interest at which the Treasury or anyone else can borrow for ninety days in 1982.

The empirical evidence confirms what theory suggests. Chart A (p. 271) plots the interest rate on three-month Treasury bills and the three-month rate of inflation in consumer prices monthly from 1978 to the present. In early 1980 both series became more volatile. In mid-1980 the interest rate, which had consistently been lower than the inflation rate, became higher than the inflation rate and has remained so ever since. The "real" short-term rate shifted from being negative to being positive and attained levels rarely reached in the past.

The dramatic change in the behavior of the two series preceded Mr. Reagan's election as president, let alone his inau-

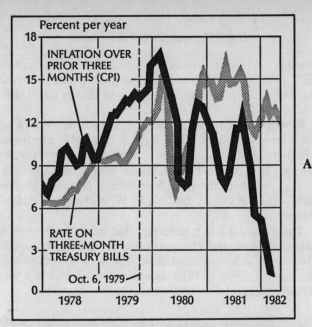

Percent per year

18

INFLATION OVER
PRIOR THREE
MONTHS (CPI)

15

12

9

A

6

RATE ON
THREE-MONTH
TREASURY BILLS

3

Oct. 6, 1979

0

1978   1979   1980   1981   1982

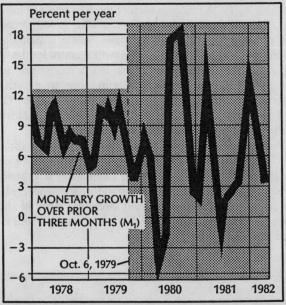

Percent per year

18

15

12

9

B

6

3

MONETARY GROWTH
OVER PRIOR
THREE MONTHS (M₁)

0

-3

Oct. 6, 1979

-6

1978   1979   1980   1981   1982

guration. Whatever may be the explanation of the "abnormal" behavior of short-term interest rates, it can hardly be the emergence more than a year later of fears of future deficits.

If budget fears do not explain the changed behavior of interest rates, what does? Chart B (p. 271) is highly suggestive. Monetary growth over successive three-month periods shows precisely the same shift in volatility as interest rates and inflation at just about the same time. The explanation for that shift is clear; it follows the Oct. 6, 1979, change in Federal Reserve procedure.

The Federal Reserve complains that excessive attention is paid to week-to-week changes in the reported money supply. However, the bottom chart shows not week-to-week volatility, but volatility over three-month periods—which is a very different thing.

Money and Rates: Each of the four peaks in monetary growth after Oct. 6, 1979, precedes each of the four peaks in interest rates. Each of the three troughs in monetary growth precedes each of three troughs in interest rates. There is little doubt that the fluctuations in monetary growth account for the fluctuations in short-term interest rates. It is a more open question whether the abnormal volatility in monetary growth explains the abnormally high level of short-term interest rates. Yet I have been able to find no other explanation that is not clearly contradicted by the empirical evidence.

The one mildly optimistic feature of the charts is that interest rates have been tending to become less volatile even though monetary growth has not. The market is apparently learning to live with the Fed's erratic performance, which also offers hope that the generally declining trend of short-term rates since the first half of 1981 may continue and even speed up.

Sending Mixed Signals

October 19, 1981

President Reagan has taken the elimination of inflation as one of his major objectives. His fourfold economic policy of lower marginal tax rates, lower government spending, deregulation, and monetary restraint is well designed to achieve that objective and to revitalize the economy. He has repeatedly warned the financial community that it will make a mistake if it counts on continued high inflation.

Actions vs. Words: The U.S. Treasury Department is telling the financial community the precise opposite—not in words, but in actions. For example, on Sept. 30, 1981, it sold twenty-year Treasury bonds—that is, borrowed from the public—on terms that would yield a lender 15.78 percent a year for the next twenty years. That will prove to be a good deal for the Treasury—which is to say, for the U.S. taxpayer—if, and only if, inflation averages decidedly more than 10 percent a year for the next twenty years. If inflation averages decidedly less, the lender will have gotten a good deal, the taxpayer, a raw deal. The Treasury will be paying 15.78 percent on those bonds when it could be borrowing at around 5 percent, which

273

was the average interest on long-term bonds in the United States from 1875 to 1975, when inflation averaged less than 2 percent a year.

What is the market to believe? What the President says? Or what the Treasury does?

It is inexcusable for the administration to talk one way and act another. In my view, the best way to make words and actions match would be for the Treasury to borrow long-term only on a purchasing-power basis. Instead of promising to pay $1,000 twenty years from date, say, plus $157.80 a year in interest each year, let it promise to pay twenty years from date $1,000 times the ratio of the price level then to the price level at time of issue. If prices at the end of the period were the same as at the beginning, it would pay $1,000. If prices had doubled, it would pay $2,000, and so on. In addition, let it promise to pay interest at, say, 3 percent a year in real terms—that is, $30 for the first year and that amount adjusted for inflation in each future year.

Such a purchasing-power security would be in great demand and fill a real need. For the first time, it would provide persons of modest wealth a safe and effective way to hedge against whatever the future might bring—whether inflation or deflation. Indeed, I suspect that, if offered at auction, it would sell at a decided premium. The net real cost to the taxpayer might even end up zero or negative.

Whether or not that turns out to be so, such a policy would eliminate the mixed signals. In effect, the Treasury would say to the market, "This administration is determined to end inflation. As agents of future taxpayers, we are not willing to burden them with interest payments that will be unconscionable when inflation comes down."

And, I may add, if the administration fails to end inflation, at least those persons who loaned money to the government would not suffer—as have all those who bought long-term government bonds in the past decade.

Purchasing-power securities are not a new idea. Some of us have favored their issue—primarily on the ground of equity—for decades. Many governments around the world issue such securities currently or have done so in the past. But the urgency for the United States to do so is far greater today than it was during earlier administrations that were less firmly dedicated to ending inflation.

Second Best: An alternative that is less desirable but also less radical is for the Treasury simply to refrain from issuing any long-term securities at current interest rates, and to announce publicly that it is doing so. Let the Treasury limit all borrowing to terms of less than, say, two years, until the market recognizes that the president's program will reduce inflation and values Treasury long-term securities accordingly. Current and future taxpayers will be better off paying high interest rates temporarily than being stuck with them for decades.

An additional helpful measure would be for the Treasury to announce a definite and firm schedule of proposed borrowing for the next six months or so. Every week, it seems, the financial pages trumpet a fresh Treasury borrowing—as if it were a completely unexpected event. Far better to have a single announcement in advance for a considerable period—and stick to it.

These two measures would both remove a major source of uncertainty that now plagues the financial markets and strengthen the administration's credibility.

V. Fiscal Policy and Taxation

A. Planning and Fiscal Stimulation
B. Taxation: Analytic Confusion, Political
Hypocrisy, and Reform
C. Welfare

INTRODUCTION

Every person plans. He thinks ahead, considers options, and acts in determined ways to attain desired consequences. Those individual, uncoerced actions become efficiently melded interactions as people respond to opportunities and constraints of the price-directed market.

But those of collectivist bent do not trust or find appealing the coordination of a free people through the institutions and processes of the market. They insist that we pronounce grand community goals—but are not prepared to stipulate adequate means for attaining those goals. They favor constraining, channeling, and stimulating selected market activities through detailed regulations. They would manipulate the price-level and redistribute the national-income. And all this even though both meditation and experience inform us that the resulting diversions and waste will make a poor world still poorer—and less free.

Efficient central planning requires, as Milton Friedman points out, that we know much which is unknowable, predict much which is unpredictable, and enforce much which is unenforceable. Government has a legitimate—indeed, essential—role. But it tries to do many things it should not do, and ends by doing almost nothing well.

Fiscal policy—taxation and government spending—supposedly is to assure full employment, stable prices, and equitable sharing of both the social output and the burden of the public budget. But "expansionary" fiscal policy actually is not very stimulative, the price level is determined primarily by monetary policy (which can be complicated by irresponsible fiscalism), and no diddling with incessantly rising government taxing and spending—rising both absolutely and relative to national output—will create more resources for the community or yield better use of those we have.

We have had several decades of ballooning deficit budgets. (During the 1970s, federal spending surged at 12 percent and transfer payments at 15 percent per year—which was much larger than the substantial rate of inflation and implies doubling within five or six years.) That ridiculous performance has led Dr. Friedman to support Constitutional constraints on the growth of federal spending and directives to balance the federal budget. The essential objective is to reduce government spending as a proportion of national income. In addition, he has long favored a "flat" income tax, with everyone receiving the same income paying the same amount of tax and with everyone paying the same proportion of income in excess of a bare minimum as tax.

A. Planning and Fiscal Stimulation

National Economic Planning

July 14, 1975

We are suffering from inflation and recession produced by government attempts to promote full employment. Though it is now twenty-one months since the OPEC countries turned off the oil spigot, government still has no coherent plan to solve the resulting energy crisis. Postal service gets poorer and more expensive. The Interstate Commerce Commission has destroyed private railroad passenger travel and is well on its way to destroying private freight carriage. The Civil Aeronautics Board is performing a similar service for airlines. You can complete the litany.

The conclusion drawn by Senators Jacob Javits and Hubert Humphrey, encouraged by a recently formed Initiative Committee for National Economic Planning, is that the *private* economy has failed and must be reformed by establishing a new federal agency for economic planning—designed to operate without compulsion, relying instead solely on that infinite wisdom that government bureaucrats bring to every problem!

Old Fallacies

Apparently, old fallacies never die. Thirty years ago, "national economic planning" threatened to be the wave of the future. In Britain, the Labor Party's postwar victory over Winston Churchill spelled a commitment to central planning. In France, one proposed form of planning followed another through revolving governments. In the U.S., the Employment Act of 1946 rode the same wave. In British colonies heading toward independence, graduates of the London School of Economics spread the Fabian message of democratic socialism through central planning.

Friedrich Hayek's great polemic, *The Road to Serfdom*, was aimed at this wave. Dedicated to "socialists of all parties," its brilliant analysis of the defects of central planning and its demonstration of the tendency for such planning to destroy political freedom is as relevant today as then.

In the event, Hayek's fears proved fully justified. Wherever it was tried, central control of the economy was a failure. In Britain, sucessive versions of central planning have produced today's stagnation, raging inflation, and bitter internal divisions that threaten the maintenance of British democracy. In the former colonies, central planning has stifled economic growth, produced widely shared misery, and undermined democratic institutions. India is the most tragic example.

France's "indicative planning" was mostly talk—and France prospered. Germany, under Ludwig Erhard's guidance, rejected economic planning. The dramatic success of Germany's free-market economy reinforced the lesson of British failure.

What explains the failure of central planning? Can no planning be better than planning? That semantic trap confuses the real issue The real issue is not planning vs. no planning, but what kind of planning, by whom, for what purpose.

For Us or by Us?

The central planners want planning by them for us. They want the government—by which they really mean themselves—to decide "social priorities" (i.e., tell us what is good for us); "rationalize production" (i.e., tell us where and how we should work); assure "equitable distribution" (i.e., take from some of us to give to others of us). Of course, all this can be voluntary—if we are willing to turn our lives over to them. Otherwise, "antisocial behavior" must be restrained—who can gainsay that? The iron fist must be there—just in case.

Such planning, from the top down, is inefficient because it makes it impossible to use the detailed knowledge shared among millions of individuals. It undermines freedom because it requires people to obey orders rather than pursue their own interests.

I am for planning, too, but planning by each of us separately in light of our individual, though shared, values, coordinated by voluntary exchange in free markets. Such planning, from the bottom up, enlists the interests of each in promoting the well-being of all. Government has its role—to provide a stable legal and monetary framework, enforce contracts and adjudicate disputes, and protect us from coercion by our fellow citizens. If we could limit government to these, its proper functions, perhaps it could perform them successfully.

This is a plan too—a far better plan than establishing yet another federal agency to control our daily lives.

Humphrey-Hawkins

August 2, 1976

A centerpiece of the Democratic fall campaign is the "Humphrey-Hawkins Full Employment and Balanced Growth Act of 1976." Support of that bill has become the litmus test of the true-blue Democratic faith of every candidate from Jimmy Carter to the aspirant for dogcatcher.

The present expanded version of the Humphrey-Hawkins bill embraces the earlier Humphrey-Javits bill. It proposes to establish a process of long-range economic planning to achieve "a full-employment goal . . . consistent with a rate of unemployment not in excess of 3 per centum of the adult Americans in the civilian labor force, to be attained . . . within not more than four years after the enactment" of the act, as well as a long list of other goodies.

Adam Smith's Critique

The best critique of this bill that I have come across was published 200 years ago in that great book, *The Wealth of Nations*, by Adam Smith—the original Adam Smith, not the current imposter who has had the effrontery to adopt that pseudonym.

Wrote Smith: "The statesman, who should attempt to direct private people in what manner they ought to employ their capitals, would not only load himself with a most unnecessary attention, but assume an authority which could safely be trusted, not only to no single person, but to no council or senate whatever, and which would nowhere be so dangerous as in the hands of a man who had folly and presumption enough to fancy himself fit to exercise it."

Has any contemporary political writer described Hubert Humphrey more concisely?

Not to put too fine a point on it, the Humphrey-Hawkins bill is as close to a fraud as has ever served as a campaign document. It is full of pious promises but contains no measures capable of fulfilling those promises. It would not reduce unemployment but simply add to government employment and reduce private employment, in the process making us all poorer and very likely igniting a new inflationary binge.

How can such a bill do otherwise? Easy enough to say that the government will be the employer of last resort. But where does the government get the money? Ultimately, from you and me, by hook or by crook. If it spends, we don't. If it employs people, we don't.

Of course, people on welfare could be relabeled "civil servants assigned to home duty," thereby reducing recorded unemployment without additional spending. But to do more—and Humphrey-Hawkins promises to do far more—requires more government spending. The extra spending could be financed by higher explicit taxes. In that case, taxpayers would have less to spend and would hire fewer people. The extra spending could be financed by higher borrowing. In that case, the lenders, or the borrowers outbid by government, would have less to spend. Government employment would replace employment in building homes or factories. Finally, the government could print the money, which would tax us indirectly via inflation. We would have more pieces of paper to spend but could buy less. For a time, that could mean more government spending without less private spending, but surely by now we have learned that that is a fool's paradise that would not last.

Is anyone so naive as to suppose that the government jobs created will be more productive than the private jobs destroyed?

Visible Good, Invisible Harm

Why do Democrats believe that Humphrey-Hawkins is such potent political soothing syrup? Do they have such a low opinion of the intelligence of the American people? I do not think so. It is for a very different reason—one that is the source of so many harmful government policies: the visible vs. the invisible effects of government measures.

People hired by government know who is their benefactor. People who lose their jobs or fail to get them because of the government program do not know that that is the source of their problem. The good effects are visible. The bad effects are invisible. The good effects generate votes. The bad effects generate discontent, which is as likely to be directed at private business as at the government.

The great political challenge is to overcome this bias, which has been taking us down the slippery slope to ever bigger government and to the destruction of a free society.